Red Plenty

947.085 WORLD'

11 APR 2012

– 5 NOV 2022

– 9 APR 2014

– 4 DEC 2017

'It is part detective story – who or what is killing the Soviet economy? – and part a brilliant explanation of some very intricate history and economics.' *Economist*

'At the time of Khrushchev's fall from power, the Soviet Union still pursues the dream of a planned economy, and still goes on proving that a planned economy produces an abundance of nothing except plans. Francis Spufford evokes the chaos with boundless comic sympathy and a piercing eye for historic detail. Here is a writer who knows the exact texture and voltage of a sweater made from viscose and polyester.' Clive James

'With rarely a dull page, Spufford imparts a wealth of information on such unlikely subjects as Soviet chemical fibre-production, machine-tool specifics and Volga car design. The punctilious descriptions of life in a planned economy are surprisingly fascinating to read, as they combine with the heroics of people both real and invented.' Ian Thomson, *Financial Times*

RED PLENTY

Francis Spufford

faber and faber

First published in 2010
by Faber and Faber Limited
Bloomsbury House,
74–77 Great Russell Street,
London WCIB 3DA
This paperback edition first published in 2011

Typeset by RefineCatch Limited, Bungay, Suffolk
Printed in England by CPI Bookmarque, Croydon

A CIP record for this book
is available from the British Library

ISBN 978-0-571-22524-8

10 9 8 7 6 5 4 3 2 1

For my mother

Contents

The Cast

in order of first appearance

CAPITALS indicate the part of a name most often used in the
  book
* indicates a real person
(I.2, IV.1, etc) indicates the part and chapter numbers of
  further scenes in which the person appears

On the tram in Leningrad

* LEONID VITALEVICH Kantorovich, a genius (I.1, II.1,
  III.1, VI.2, VI.3)

Visiting the United States

* Nikita Sergeyevich KHRUSHCHEV, First Secretary of the
  Communist Party of the Soviet Union and Chairman of the
  Council of Ministers (I.2, III.2, V.1, VI.3)
* NINA PETROVNA Khrushcheva, his wife (I.2, VI.3)
* Andrei GROMYKO, Soviet Foreign Minister (I.2)
* Oleg TROYANOVSKY, Khrushchev's interpreter (I.2)
* Dwight D. EISENHOWER, President of the United
  States (I.2)
* Henry Cabot LODGE, US Ambassador to the United
  Nations (I.2)
* Averell HARRIMAN, a millionaire acting as East–West
  liaison (I.2)

At the American Exhibition in Sokolniki Park

GALINA, a student at Moscow State University and
  Komsomol member (I.3, V.3)

VOLODYA, ditto, her fiancé (I.3, III.2)

KHRISTOLYUBOV, a minor apparatchik (I.3)

FYODOR, a Komsomol member from an electrical factory (I.3, V.2)

ROGER TAYLOR, an African-American guide at the exhibition (I.3)

Walking to the Village

EMIL Arslanovich Shaidullin, a well-connected young economist (I.4, II.1, III.1, V.2, VI.2)

MAGDA, his fiancée (I.4)

Her FATHER (I.4)

Her MOTHER (I.4)

Her GRANDFATHER (I.4)

SASHA, her brother (I.4)

PLETKIN, the collective farm manager (I.4)

At the conference in the Academy of Sciences

* Vasily Sergeyevich NEMCHINOV, a reforming economist and academic politician (II.1)

* BOYARSKII, a political economist of the old school (II.1)

In the basement of the Institute of Precise Mechanics

* Sergei Alexeievich LEBEDEV, a pioneering Soviet computer designer (II.2, VI.1)

In Moscow on the day of the Party Congress

* Sasha/Alexander GALICH, a writer of stage comedies, screenplays and ideologically acceptable song lyrics (II.3, VI.2)

MORIN, a Thaw-minded newspaper editor (II.3)

MARFA TIMOFEYEVNA, a newspaper censor (II.3)

GRIGORIY, a doorman at the Writers' Union (II.3)

At Akademgorodok in 1963

ZOYA Vaynshteyn, a biologist (III.1, VI.2)

VALENTIN, a graduate student in mathematics (III.1, VI.2)

KOSTYA, a graduate student in economics (III.1, VI.2)

HAIRBAND GIRL, Valentin's would-be girlfriend (III.1)

* Andrei Petrovich ERSHOV, a computer programmer (III.1)

MO, a sardonic intellectual (III.1, VI.2)

SOBCHAK, an exasperated intellectual (III.1)

In Novocherkassk

BASOV, regional Party Secretary (III.2)

* KUROCHKIN, director of the Budenny Electric
  Locomotive Works (III.2)

* Anastas MIKOYAN, long-serving Presidium (Politburo)
  member (III.2)

* Frol KOZLOV, Presidium member and heir apparent to
  Khrushchev (III.2)

The MONK-FACED MAN, a veteran operative of the
organs of security (III.2)

At Gosplan

Maksim Maksimovich MOKHOV, Deputy Director of the
Sector of Chemical and Rubber Goods (IV.1)

On the train from Solovets

ARKHIPOV, KOSOY and MITRENKO, the management of
the Solkemfib viscose works (IV.2)

PONOMAREV, an engineer and former political prisoner
(IV.2)

In Sverdlovsk

CHEKUSKIN, a tolkach or 'pusher'; a buying agent (IV.3)

SEÑORA LOPEZ, a Spanish dancing teacher (IV.3)

RYSZARD, a junior manager in the chemical equipment
  division of Uralmash (IV.3)

STEPOVOI, an inexperienced executive (IV.3)

KOLYA, a king thief (IV.3)

The LIEUTENANT, a policeman (IV.3)

VASSILY, a truck driver and Spartak fan (IV.3)

At the leadership compound in Moscow

Khrushchev's CHAUFFEUR (V.1)

* MELNIKOV, commandant of Khrushchev's first security
  detail in his retirement (V.1)

Khrushchev's COOK (V.1)

* Khrushchev's SON, Sergei Khrushchev, a rocket designer (V.1)

At the government dacha

* Alexei Nikolaevich KOSYGIN, Chairman of the State
  Planning Committee (Gosplan) (V.2)

In Galina's flat, and the labour ward

FYODOR'S MOTHER, an annoyingly slim woman in her
  forties (V.3)

IVANOV, her lover (V.3)

A tired DOCTOR (V.3)

INNA OLEGOVNA, a midwife (V.3)

In the Kremlin corridor

FRENCHIE, a secretary (VI.1)

At Akademgorodok in 1968

MAX, Zoya's ten-year-old son (VI.2)

TYOMA (short for Artemy), a doorkeeper in the Institute of
  Cytology and Genetics (VI.2)

The DIRECTOR of the Institute of Cytology and Genetics
   (VI.2)

A note on the characters

Although the list above divides the people in this book into two categories, real and imaginary, there are a couple of characters who, while fictional, exist in a relationship to real historical individuals: they occupy similar historical positions, they play similar professional roles, they share to a limited degree in the life-histories and life-events of the real people who prompted their invention. Yet they *are* inventions. They are fictional people standing roughly where real people stood: Zoya Vaynshteyn displacing the real fruit-fly biologist Raissa Berg, and Emil Shaidullin rudely elbowing aside the eminent economist Abel Aganbegyan. It is important to understand that Zoya and Emil, as represented here, came straight out of my head. Their characterisations were not the result of any process of interview or research or investigation on my part, and are not intended to reflect any judgement of mine on the character of the real scientists whose places they have taken. No characteristic, trait, action, thought, intention, utterance or opinion of these characters should be taken as an indication of any corresponding characteristic, trait, action, thought, intention, utterance or opinion belonging to the real individuals.

PART I

This is not a novel. It has too much to explain, to be one of those. But it is not a history either, for it does its explaining in the form of a story; only the story is the story of an idea, first of all, and only afterwards, glimpsed through the chinks of the idea's fate, the story of the people involved. The idea is the hero. It is the idea that sets forth, into a world of hazards and illusions, monsters and transformations, helped by some of those it meets along the way and hindered by others. Best to call this a fairytale, then – though it really happened, or something like it. And not just any fairytale, but specifically a Russian fairytale, to go alongside the stories of Baba Yaga and the Glass Mountain that Afanaseyev the folklorist collected when he rode out over the black earth of Russia, under its wide sky, in the nineteenth century.

Where Western tales begin by shifting us to another time – 'Once upon a time' they say, meaning elsewhen, meaning then *rather than* now *– Russian* skazki *make an adjustment of place. 'In a certain land', they start; or, 'In the three-times-ninth kingdom . . .' Meaning elsewhere, meaning* there *rather than* here. *Yet these elsewheres are always recognisable as home. In the distance will always be a wood-walled town where the churches have onion domes. The ruler will always be a Tsar, Ivan or Vladimir. The earth is always black. The sky is always wide. It's Russia, always Russia, the dear dreadful enormous territory at the edge of Europe which is as large as all Europe put together. And, also, it isn't. It is story Russia, not real Russia; a place never quite in perfect overlap with the daylight country of the same name. It is as near to it as a wish is to reality, and as far away too. For the tales supplied what the real country lacked, when villagers were telling them, and Afanaseyev was writing them down.*

Real Russia's fields grew scraggy crops of buckwheat and rye. Story Russia had magic tablecloths serving feasts without end. Real Russia's roads were mud and ruts. Story Russia abounded in tools of joyful velocity: flying carpets, genies of the rushing air, horses that scarcely bent the grass they galloped on. Real Russia fixed its people in sluggish social immobility. Story Russia sent its lively boys to seek the Firebird or to woo the Swan Maiden. The stories dreamed away reality's defects. They made promises good enough to last for one evening of firelight; promises which the teller and the hearers knew could only be delivered in some Russian otherwhere. They could come true only in the version of home where the broke-backed trestle over the stream at the village's end became 'a bridge of white hazelwood with oaken planks, spread with purple cloths and nailed with copper nails'. Only in the wish country, the dream country. Only in the twenty-seventh kingdom.

In the twentieth century, Russians stopped telling skazki. *And at the same time, they were told that the* skazki *were coming true. The stories' name for a magic carpet,* samolet, *'self-flyer', had already become the ordinary Russian word for an aeroplane. Now voices from the radio and the movie screen and television began to promise that the magic tablecloth* samobranka, *'self-victualler', would soon follow after. 'In our day,' Nikita Khrushchev told a crowd in the Lenin Stadium of Moscow on 28 September 1959, 'the dreams mankind cherished for ages, dreams expressed in fairytales which seemed sheer fantasy, are being translated into reality by man's own hands.' He meant, above all, the* skazki's *dreams of abundance. Humanity's ancient condition of scarcity was going to end, imminently. Everyone was going to climb the cabbage stalk, scramble through the hole in the sky, and arrive in the land where millstones revolved all by themselves. 'Whenever they gave a turn, a cake and a slice of bread with butter and sour cream appeared, and on top of them, a pot of gruel.' Now, instead of being the imagined compensation for an empty belly, the sour cream and the butter were truly going to flow.*

And of course, Khrushchev was right. That is exactly what did happen in the twentieth century, for hundreds of millions of people. There is indeed more food, and more kinds of food, in one ordinary supermarket of the present day, than in any of the old hungry dreams, dreamed in Russia or elsewhere. But Khrushchev believed that the plenty of the stories was coming in Soviet Russia, and coming because of something that the Soviet Union possessed and the hungry lands of capitalism lacked: the planned economy. Because the whole system of production and distribution in the USSR was owned by the state, because all Russia was (in Lenin's words) 'one office, one factory', it could be directed, as capitalism could not, to the fastest, most lavish fulfilment of human needs. Therefore it would easily out-produce the wasteful chaos of the marketplace. Planning would be the USSR's own self-turning millstone, its own self-victualling tablecloth.

This Russian fairytale began to be told in the decade of famine before the Second World War, and it lasted officially until Communism fell. Hardly anyone believed it, by the end. In practice, from the late 1960s on all that the Soviet regime aspired to do was to provide a pacifying minimum of consumer goods to the inhabitants of the vast shoddy apartment buildings ringing every Soviet city. But once upon a time the story of red plenty had been serious: an attempt to beat capitalism on its own terms, and to make Soviet citizens the richest people in the world. For a short while, it even looked – and not just to Nikita Khrushchev – as if the story might be coming true. Intelligence was invested in it, as well as foolishness: a generation's hopes, and a generation's intellectual gifts, and a tyranny's guilty wish for a happy ending. This book is about that moment. It is about the cleverest version of the idea, the most subtle of the Soviet attempts to pull a working samobranka out of the dream country. It is about the adventures of the idea of red plenty as it came hopefully along the high road.

But it is not a history. It is not a novel. It is itself a fairytale; and like a fairytale it is wishful, irresponsible, not to be relied on. The notes at the back indicate where the story it tells depends on invention, where the explanation it gives depends on lies. Remember, as you read, that this story does not take place in the literal, historical Union of Soviet Socialist Republics, but only in some nearby kingdom; as near to it as wishes are to reality, and also as far away.

In a certain kingdom, in a certain land, namely, the very land in which we live . . .

I.

The Prodigy, 1938

A tram was coming, squealing metal against metal, throwing blue-white sparks into the winter dark. Without thinking about it, Leonid Vitalevich lent his increment of shove to the jostling crowd, and was lifted with the rest of the collectivity over the rear step and into the cram of human flesh behind the concertina door. 'C'mon citizens, push up!' said a short woman next to him, as if they had a choice about it, as if they could decide to move or not, when everyone inside a Leningrad tram was locked in the struggle to get from the entry door at the back to the exit at the front by the time their stop came around. Yet the social miracle took place: somewhere at the far end a small mob of passengers burped out onto the roadway, and a squeezing ripple travelled down the car, a tram-peristalsis propelled by shoulders and elbows, creating just enough space to press into before the door closed. The yellow bulbs overhead flickered, and the tram rocked away with a rising hum. Leonid Vitalevich was wedged against a metal post on one side, on the other against the short woman. She was wedged against a tall fellow with a big chin and blond hair standing on end. Beyond him was a clerk with a glazed eye, like a herring on ice, and three young soldiers who had already started their evening spree judging by their breath. But the smell of vodka merged with the sweaty sourness of the workers a little further forward, whose factory had plainly lodged them in a barracks without a bathroom, and the fierce rosewater scent the short woman had on, into one, hot, composite human smell, just as all the corners and pieces of sleeve and collar he could see fused into one tight kaleidoscope of darned hand-me-downs, and worn leather, and too-big khaki.

He was wearing what he thought of as his 'professor outfit', the old suit cobbled together by his mother and sister which had been supposed to make him look like a plausible Professor L. V. Kantorovich when he first started teaching at the university six years ago, aged twenty. He'd been standing at the blackboard in the lecture theatre, taking a deep breath, chalk in hand, about to launch into the basics of set theory, when a helpful voice from the front row said, 'I'd stop messing about if I was you. They take things seriously here. You'll only get in trouble when the professor arrives.' He'd had to learn to be sharp, to make his presence felt. Even now, when the world was filling up with surprisingly young scientists and army officers and plant managers – the older ones having taken to disappearing by night, leaving silence behind them, and gaps in every hierarchy to be plugged by anxious twentysomethings working all hours to learn their new jobs – even now, pinched and tired as he was, dull-skinned like everyone else on the tram, he still had the occasional difficulty with someone misled by his big adam's apple, and his big eyes, and his sticking-out ears. This was the problem with being what people called a prodigy. You always had to be saying something or doing something to persuade people that you weren't what they thought they saw. He couldn't remember it ever being any different, though he presumed that before he learned to talk, and then almost immediately to count, and to do algebra, and to play chess, there'd been a milky time when he was only Dr and Mrs Kantorovich's ordinary baby. But at seven, when he worked out from his big brother's radiology textbook that you ought to be able to tell how old a rock was from the amount of undecayed carbon in it, he'd had to get past Nikolai's indulgent medical-student smile before he would pay attention, and start talking about the idea seriously, the way he needed. 'You must have read this somewhere. You *must* have done. Or been talking to someone . . .' At fourteen, he had to persuade the other students at the Physico-Mathematical Institute that he wasn't just an annoying shrimp who'd wandered in by mistake; that he *belonged* in their company, even though he was a head shorter than any of them, and had to bounce as he walked along the corridor with them to keep his face in the general domain of the conversation. At eighteen, presenting original work at the All-Union Mathematical Congress, he measured his success by his ability to get the yellow-fingered, chainsmoking geniuses to stop being kind. When they gave up being encouraging, when they made their first sarcastic remark, when they started to sneer and to try to shred his theorems, he knew they had ceased seeing a kid and started to see a mathematician.

Automatically, Leonid Vitalevich gripped his wallet tight in his trouser pocket, against pickpockets. Gangs worked the trams, and you couldn't tell which of these faces, these polite faces, aggressive faces, drunken faces, was really a pokerface, a front for a hand down below extracting surplus value. He couldn't see anything beneath chest level, so it was best to be careful; couldn't see his feet, though he could certainly feel them, now that the fuggy warmth of the tram had thawed the crust over the annoying hole that'd appeared today on the sole of his left shoe. He had a small wad of newspaper in there, and it was turning soggy. This was the third time this winter the shoes had sprung a leak. He would have to go back to the retired cobbler Denisov this Sunday, take him another present, listen to more self-contradictory reminiscences about the old man's adventures with women. Of course it would be much better to get a new pair of shoes altogether, or maybe boots. Who could he ask? Who would know somebody who knew somebody? He would have to think about it. He gazed through the sliver of window visible between heads, and fragments of city slid by: a patrol car parked on a corner, grand facades streaked with damage from leaking gutters, red neon flashing FIVE – IN – FOUR, FIVE – IN – FOUR, the word *more* on the bottom corner of a poster, which he knew at once would read in full *Life has become better, more cheerful!* Those posters were all over the place. The slogan advertised Soviet Champagne. Or the existence of Soviet Champagne advertised the slogan, he wasn't sure which. But now he was looking without seeing. His thoughts had dived into his satchel, clutched tight with his other hand. Halfway down a lefthand page in his notebook, the blue ink scribble of equations broke off, and now his mind was racing on from that point, seeing a possible next move, seeing the thread of an idea elongate. Today, something had happened.

He had been doing a bit of consultancy. It went with being attached to the Institute of Industrial Construction; you had to sing for your supper every so often. And he didn't really mind. It was a pleasure to put the lucid order in his head to use. More than a pleasure, a relief almost, because every time the pure pattern of mathematics turned out to have a purchase on the way the world worked, turned out to provide the secret thread controlling something loud and various and apparently arbitrary, it provided one more quantum of confirmation for what Leonid Vitalevich wanted to believe, needed to believe, did believe when he was happy: that all of this, this swirl of phenomena lurching on through time, this mess of interlocked systems, some filigree-fine, some huge and simple, this tram full of strangers and smoky air, this city of Peter built on human bones, all ultimately made sense, were all intricately generated by some intelligible principle or set of principles working themselves out on many levels at once, even if the expressions didn't exist yet which could capture much of the process.

No, he didn't mind. Besides, there was a duty involved. If he could solve the problems people brought to the institute, it made the world a fraction better. The world was lifting itself up out of darkness and beginning to shine, and mathematics was how he could help. It was his contribution. It was what he could give, according to his abilities. He was lucky enough to live in the only country on the planet where human beings had seized the power to shape events according to reason, instead of letting things happen as they happened to happen, or allowing the old forces of superstition and greed to push people around. Here, and nowhere else, reason was in charge. He might have been born in Germany, and then this tram ride tonight would have been full of fear. On his professor suit would have been a cotton star, and dark things would have looked out of people's faces at him, just because his grandfather had worn earlocks, had subscribed to a slightly different unverifiable fairytale about the world. He would have been hated there, for no reason at all. Or he might have been born in America, and then who could say if he would even have had the two kopecks for the tram at all? Would a twenty-six-year-old Jew be a professor there? He might be a beggar, he might be playing a violin on the street in the rain, the thoughts in his head of no concern to anyone because nobody could make money out of them. Cruelty, waste, fictions allowed to buffet real men and women to and fro: only here had people escaped this black nonsense, and made themselves reality's deliberate designers rather than its playthings. True, reason was a difficult tool. You laboured with it to see a little more, and at best you got glimpses, partial truths; but the glimpses were always worth having. True, the new consciously-chosen world still had rough edges and very obvious imperfections, but those things would change. This was only the beginning, the day after reason's reign began.

Anyway. Today he had had a request from the Plywood Trust of Leningrad. 'Would the comrade professor, etc. etc., grateful for any insight, etc. etc., assurance of cordial greetings, etc. etc.' It was a work-assignment problem. The Plywood Trust produced umpteen different types of plywood using umpteen different machines, and they wanted to know how to direct their limited stock of raw materials to the different machines so as to get the best use out of it. Leonid Vitalevich had never been to the plywood factory, but he could picture it. It would be like all the other enterprises which had sprung up around the city over the last few years, multiplying like mushrooms after rain, putting chimneys at the end of streets, filling the air with smuts and the river with eddies of chemical dye. All the investment that hadn't gone into new clothes and everyday comforts had gone into the factories: they were what the tired people on the tram had got instead. At the plywood factory, he supposed, there would be a raw brick barn, cold enough inside at this time of year to turn the workers' breaths to puffs of steam. He guessed that the machinery would be the usual wild mixture. Aged pre-revolutionary presses and stampers would be running alongside homegrown products of the Soviet machine-tool industry, with here and there a silky import, efficient but hard to maintain. Together, under the exposed girders of the roof, this mismatched orchestra of devices would be pouring out a discordant symphony of hisses, treadlings, clunks and saw-edged whines. The management wanted help tuning the orchestra up. To be honest, he couldn't quite see what the machines were doing. He had only a vague idea of how plywood was actually manufactured. It somehow involved glue and sawdust, that was all he knew. It didn't matter: for his purposes, he only needed to think of the machines as abstract propositions, each one effectively an equation in solid form, and immediately he read the letter he understood that the Plywood Trust, in its mathematical innocence, had sent him a classic example of a system of equations that was impossible to solve. There was a reason why factories around the world, capitalist or socialist, didn't have a handy formula for these situations. It wasn't just an oversight, something people hadn't got around to yet. The quick way to deal with the Plywood Trust's enquiry would have been to write a polite note explaining that the management had just requested the mathematical equivalent of a flying carpet or a genie in a bottle.

But he hadn't written that note. Instead, casually at first, and then with sudden excitement, with the certainty that the hard light of genesis was shining in his head, brief, inexplicable, not to be resisted or questioned while it lasted, he had started to think. He had thought about ways to distinguish between better answers and worse answers to questions which had no right answer. He had seen a method which could do what the detective work of conventional algebra could not, in situations like the one the Plywood Trust described, and would trick impossibility into disclosing useful knowledge. The method depended on measuring each machine's output of one plywood in terms of all the other plywoods it could have made. But again, he had no sense of plywood as a scratchy concrete stuff. That had faded into nothing, leaving only the pure pattern of the situation, of all situations in which you had to choose one action over another action. Time passed. The genesis light blinked off. It seemed to be night outside his office window. The grey blur of the winter daylight had vanished. The family would be worrying about him, starting to wonder if he had vanished too. He should go home. But he groped for his pen and began to write, fixing in extended, patient form – as patient as he could manage – what'd come to him first unseparated into stages, still fused into one intricate understanding, as if all its necessary component pieces were faces and angles of one complex polyhedron he'd been permitted to gaze at, while the light lasted; the amazing, ungentle light. He got down the basics, surprised to find as he drove the blue ink onward how rough and incomplete they seemed to be, spelt out, and what a lot of work remained.

And now, on the tram, he was following his thought into implications, into what he was suspecting might be a world of implications. Clearly, the world had got by quite well until now without this idea. In the era before half past two this afternoon, the people arranging the flow of work in factories had been able to do so with a fair degree of efficiency by using rules of thumb and educated intuition, or else the modern age would not be as industrialised as it was: would not have trams and neon, would not have airships and autogyros thronging the sky, would not have skyscrapers in Manhattan and the promise of more in Moscow. But a fair degree of efficiency was very far removed from a maximum degree of efficiency. If he was right – and he was sure he was, in essentials – then anyone applying the new method to any production situation in the huge family of situations resembling the one at the Plywood Trust should be able to count on a measurable percentage improvement in the quantity of product they got from a given amount of raw materials. Or you could put that the other way around: they would make a measurable percentage saving on the raw materials they needed to make a given amount of product.

He didn't know yet what sort of percentage he was talking about, but just suppose it was 3%. It might not sound like much, only a marginal gain, an abstemious eking out of a little bit more from the production process, at a time when all the newspapers showed miners ripping into fat mountains of solid metal, and the output of plants booming 50%, 75%, 150%. But it was predictable. You could count on the extra 3% year after year. Above all it was free. It would come merely by organising a little differently the tasks people were doing already. It was 3% of extra order snatched out of the grasp of entropy. In the face of the patched and mended cosmos, always crumbling of its own accord, always trying to fall down, it built; it gained 3% more of what humanity wanted, free and clear, just as a reward for thought. Moreover, he thought, its applications did not stop with individual factories, with getting 3% more plywood, or 3% more gun barrels, or 3% more wardrobes. If you could maximise, minimise, optimise the collection of machines at the Plywood Trust, why couldn't you optimise a collection of factories, treating each of them, one level further up, as an equation? You could tune a factory, then tune a group of factories, till they hummed, till they purred. And that meant –

'Watch what you're doing!' cried the short woman. 'Take your head out of your arse and watch what you're doing, why don't you?' The big man had seized the chance, the last time they all shuffled up the tram, to free his hand and light a cigarette. But as it hung at the corner of his mouth, cardboard holder pinched in two dimensions to act as a filter, a jolt from the track had knocked the whole burning load of tobacco out of the paper tube at the end, and it had fallen, smouldering, onto her shoulder. Her arms were pinned.

'Sorry, sister,' said Big Chin, trying to flap the embers off her and down.

'What good is sorry, you big lummox? Get it off me. Oh, look at my coat. There's a hole right through –'

– and that meant that you could surely apply the method to the entire Soviet economy, he thought. He could see that this would not be possible under capitalism, where all the factories had separate owners, locked in wasteful competition with one another. There, nobody was in a position to think systematically. The capitalists would not be willing to share information about their operations; what would be in it for them? That was why capitalism was blind, why it groped and blundered. It was like an organism without a brain. But here it was possible to plan for the whole system at once. The economy was a clean sheet of paper on which reason was writing. So why not optimise it? All he would have to do was to persuade the appropriate authorities to listen.

Suppose that the Soviet economy could be made to grow by an extra 3% a year – an extra 3% year after year, compounded. It would mount up fast. After only a decade, the country would be half as rich again as it would have been otherwise. Quicker than anyone imagined yet could come the golden age whose promise was implicit in the rhythm of every production line, but which had still to free the world from scarcity; the golden age the Party promised, but said it could not deliver till the heavy work of construction was done, except in the symbolic form of Soviet Champagne. Seen from that future time, when every commodity the human mind could imagine would flow from the industrial horn of plenty in dizzy abundance, this would seem a scanty, shoddy, cramped moment indeed, choked with shadows, redeemed only by what it caused to be created. Seen from plenty, now would be hard to imagine. It would seem not quite real, an absurd time when, for no apparent reason, human beings went without things easily within the power of humanity to supply, and lives did not flower as it was obvious they could. Now would look like only a faint, dirty, unconvincing edition of the real world, which had not yet been born. And he could hasten the hour, he thought, intoxicated. He gazed up the tram, and saw everything and everybody in it touched by the transformation to come, rippling into new and more generous forms, the number 34 rattlebox to Krestovsky Island becoming a sleek silent ellipse filled with golden light, the women's clothes all turning to quilted silk, the military uniforms melting into tailored grey and silver: and faces, faces the length of the car, relaxing, losing the worry lines and the hungry looks and all the assorted toothmarks of necessity. He could help to do that. He could help to make it happen, three extra percent at a time, though he already understood that it would take a huge quantity of work to compose the necessary dynamic models. It might be a lifetime's work. But he could do it. He could tune up the whole Soviet orchestra, if they'd let him.

His left foot dripped. He really must find a way to get new shoes.

2.

Mr Chairman, 1959

Such a long journey. It was hard to sleep in the cutting roar of the turboprops, hard to sleep too with a headful of anticipations and anxieties, but he dozed in the end, the noise following him somehow into the kingdom on the far side of oblivion, still pulsing and beating in his ears as he hurried from room to room of a half-finished palace, constructed (he was glad to see) using the large-panel method he had recommended in his speech on architecture; and when he woke, the bright light of a morning high above the Atlantic was pouring in through the window of the airliner, making his eyeballs ache. He blinked, and tugged at his waistband. The vinyl seat had grown sticky. Around him, the entourage stirred into life as well, shifting to attention when they noticed that his eyes were open. But he did not need anything. The preparations were all done. Nina Petrovna, beside him, did not move, yet he knew that if he turned his head he would find her ready to hear whatever was on his mind, as she had been gravely ready their entire married life, knowing the importance of his work: at every midnight, at every dawn, in the middle of any family situation. He bent towards the window, and flattened his cheek against the cold glass to get a downward view. A few whitecaps were shrugging in and out of existence on a wide grey sea. A little black dot was tossing among them, and another was visible in the distance up ahead, along the line of the plane's flight: the trawlers, he supposed, strung out across the sea by security when he told them he didn't want the navy deployed.

'How much longer?' he asked.

'Still about an hour to the Canadian coast, Nikita Sergeyevich, and then two more after that to Washington,' said young

Troyanovsky the interpreter, eagerly. He was a good boy, almost American-looking himself in his buttoned-down shirt collar, and you could tell he wanted the work to start, so he could show what he was made of. That was a good attitude, he thought. Not much different from me, he thought. He rubbed his eyes and gazed up the plane. The engines sang out the same obliterating music. Along the aisle the lads from the Tupolev bureau were still intently listening to it through their headphones, crouched over an electrical box that had been explained to him as a kind of stethoscope for aeroplanes. They did not seem to be worried by what they were hearing in the twining streams of noise. But then he did not really see what they would be able to do if the remote chance they were guarding against came true, if the plane did suddenly crack at the seams in mid-air. The sky would be full of falling generals and diplomats, and him in the midst of them, plummeting to the waves in his summer suit, like a lead-weighted Easter egg. 'We're sure of the TU-114, as sure as we can be,' Tupolev himself had told him. 'It's just that it's a new design, we're still shaking it down, and we've had some readings from the airframe we weren't expecting. That's why I'd like to send my son along, with your permission, to keep an eye on things.' 'That isn't necessary,' he'd replied. 'People will think he's some sort of hostage!' 'Oh, no question of that, Nikita Sergeyevich. I just want to show you that we have confidence in the plane.' The plane was bigger than any passenger jet the Americans had. The plane was irresistible. And so Tupolev junior had come along for the ride – and there he was with the other technicians now, feeling the drowsy gaze resting on him; and looking up; and clearly not knowing what expression he should hoist hastily onto his face. He didn't blame him. What was the right demeanour for someone who was not-a-hostage? Especially since, to tell the truth, the boy *would* have been a hostage in this situation, or at least a surety, just a few years ago. He frowned. Tupolev's son instantly dropped his eyes.

Such a long journey. Such a long way travelled, he thought, since he had been a quick kid himself, the kid on the coalfield with the home-made motorbike and three gold roubles in his pocket on a Friday, and the fluffy white duckdown hair. (*That* hadn't lasted long.) Such a long journey to this point in time for the whole country; and none of it easy, none of it achieved without cost. No one gave us this beautiful plane. We built it ourselves, we pulled it out of nothing by our determination and our strength. They tried to crush us over and over again, but we wouldn't be crushed. We drove off the Whites. We winkled out the priests, out of the churches and more important out of people's minds. We got rid of the shopkeepers, thieving bastards, getting their dirty fingers in every deal, making every straight thing crooked. We dragged the farmers into the twentieth century, and that was hard, that was a cruel business and there were some hungry years there, but it had to be done, we had to get the muck off our boots. We realised there were saboteurs and enemies among us, and we caught them, but it drove us mad for a while, and for a while we were seeing enemies and saboteurs everywhere, and hurting people who were brothers, sisters, good friends, honest comrades. Then the Fascists came, and stamping on them was bloody, nobody could call what we did then sweetness and light, wreckage everywhere, but what are you going to do when a gang of murderers breaks into the house? And the Boss didn't help much. Wonderful clear mind, but by that time he was frankly screwy, moving whole nations round the map like chess pieces, making us sit up all night with him and drink that filthy vodka till we couldn't see straight, and always watching us: no, I don't deny we went wrong, in fact if you recall it was me that said so. But all the while we were building. All the while we were building factories and mines, railroads and roads, towns and cities, and all without any help, all without getting the say-so from any millionaire or bigshot. We did that. We taught people to read, we taught them to love culture. We sent tens of millions of them to school and millions of them to college, so they could have the advantages we never had. We *created* the boys and girls who're young now. We did the dirty work so they could inherit a clean world.

And now was the time when it all paid off, he thought. The wars were over, the enemies were gone, the mistakes were rectified. Forty-two years since the revolution, and at last the pattern of the new society was established. All the young people had known no other way of living. They had never seen a rich man going past in his carriage; they had never seen a private shop. And so at last it was becoming possible to make good on all the promises which they'd fed to people during the hungry years. All well and good, he thought, because we really meant them, we weren't trying to hoodwink anyone, but there's a limit to how long you can keep going on that kind of diet. You can't make soup out of promises. Some comrades seemed to think that fine words and fine ideas were all the world would ever require, that pure enthusiasm would carry humanity forward to happiness: well excuse me, comrades, but aren't we supposed to be materialists? Aren't we supposed to be the ones who get along without fairytales? If communism couldn't give people a better life than capitalism, he personally couldn't see the point. A better life, in a straightforward, practical way: better food, better clothes, better houses, better cars, better planes (like this one), better football games to watch and cards to play and beaches to sit on, in the summertime, with the children splashing about in the surf and a nice bottle of something cold to sip. More money to spend – or else more of a world in which money was no longer necessary to ration out the good things, because there were so many good things, all gushing out of the whatchamacallit, the thing like a cone spilling over with fruit. The horn of plenty. Fortunately, the hard part of the task was nearly done. They had almost completed the heavy lifting, they had heaved and shoved and (yes) driven people on with kicks and curses, and they had built the basis for the good life, their very own horn of plenty pouring forth the necessary steel and coal and electricity. They had done the big stuff. All that remained was to get the small stuff right. It was time to use what they had built to make life a pleasure instead of a struggle. They could do it. If they could produce a million tons of steel, they could produce a million tons of anything. They just had to concentrate on directing their horn of plenty so that, as well as spitting out girders, it now also overflowed with musical boxes. Now the sacrifices ended. Now came the age of cream and dumplings: the old dream of a feast that never had to end, but truly delivered, delivered in sober daylight, by science.

It had already begun to happen, in his opinion. If you looked at people on the street, all the old clothes had vanished, in the last few years. No more patches, no more darns. Everyone was wearing fine new outfits. The children had winter coats no one had worn before them. People had wristwatches on their arms, like his own good steel watch from the Kuibyshev plant. They were moving in their droves out of the horrible old communal flats, where four families shared a toilet and there were knife-fights over who used the stove, into pristine concrete apartment buildings. Of course, there was still a long way to go. No one knew that better than him. He saw the figures the economists prepared. A Russian worker still only earned around 25% of the average American income, even if you threw in the most generous allowance for all the things that cost money in America and came free in the Soviet Union. But he saw the other figures too, the ones showing that year after year this last decade the Soviet economy had grown at 6%, 7%, 8% every year, while the American one only grew 3% or so at best. He was not a man who was naturally excited by graphs, but he was excited by this one, when he understood that if the Soviet Union just kept growing at the same rate, propelled onward by the greater natural efficiency of central planning, the line of Soviet prosperity on the graph was due to cross the line representing American prosperity, and then to soar above it, in just under twenty years from now. He had seen victory on a sheet of cardboard. It was proven. It was going to happen. And this was the reason, deep down, why he had accepted President Eisenhower's invitation, when some might have asked whether they were ready for the test that was waiting for them in America: not just the test of negotiating with the richest, strongest capitalist state on the planet, but the deeper test, the test of comparison. Were they ready to measure up the Soviet way against the American way? Were they ready to let the people see a little bit of the scale of the task that still lay ahead? In his opinion, if you believed that the good times were coming, if you trusted that graph, it was necessary now to behave like it. It was necessary to make an act of faith. The people had earned the right to a bit of trust. He had said yes to the American exhibition in Sokolniki Park, this year, because he trusted the Soviet citizens who were going to visit it. Let them see the best the Americans can do. Let them see what they're competing with. Let them see what they're going to get themselves, in not too long, and more besides. Let the dog see the rabbit. Let them feel a bit hungry for the future. Maybe they'd pick up some ideas. It was always good to learn from the Americans.

So, yes, he believed they were ready. *Overtake and surpass*, the Boss used to say, again and again. *Overtake and surpass*. The strategy was still the same. The difference was that now it was more than a goal. Now it was happening. Accordingly, he had a deal he was going to offer the Americans. He thought the Americans would take it. He didn't see why they wouldn't. The deal was this. Since the great quarrel between capitalism and socialism was really an economic one, why not conduct it that way, instead of as a war? Why not handle it as a race to see who could do the best job at supplying the ordinary fellow on the beach with his cold drink? The two sides could co-exist while they competed. Everyone could step back from the guns (and the generals wouldn't eat up so much of the state budget, which would be handy). History could move forward peacefully. Naturally, the capitalists believed their system was the best. Naturally – here was the beauty of it – they would expect to win the contest. So why wouldn't they agree? All the capitalists had to do was to settle down and accept that the world was divided now, into two halves, one of which was not theirs any more. They just had to get used to the idea that Poland and China and Hungary and the rest had chosen in favour of a different way of life, and weren't coming back. Sometimes the Americans seemed to take the point; sometimes, mysteriously, they didn't. Take Nixon's visit to Moscow two months back when the exhibition opened, for example. 'Let's compete on the merits of our washing machines, not the strength of our rockets,' he'd said – the Vice President of the United States, Eisenhower's own right-hand man! Perfect! Yet that very same week, when the right hand of the United States was held out in friendship, the left hand was making gestures which, forgive me, you couldn't describe in polite company. That very same instant the United States Congress declared a 'Captive Nations Week', and started calling the Soviet Union a tyranny and its allies slaves. Well, that kind of insult would have to stop, if the Americans wanted peace. He was coming to America to offer peace, but it was up to the Americans whether they accepted it. It was up to them if they lifted their trade embargo. They were making a mistake if they expected him to bend the knee. He was not going to beg; no, never to beg.

Of course, the Boss would have hated the whole idea of this trip. The Boss had let them all know he thought he was the only one tough enough, clever enough, to go up against the owners of the world. 'Without me, the capitalists will make mincemeat of you,' he'd said. 'Without me, they'll drown you like kittens.' 'Oh, Nikita Sergeyevich,' he'd said. 'You try your best, but is your best good enough?' He remembered the time the Boss had reached out his stumpy nicotine-stained finger in a meeting, in front of all the others, and tapped him three times hard between the eyes, like a woodpecker irritably sounding a tree. And the time the Boss had emptied the coals from his pipe on the top of his bald head, stinging hot; hotter still than that, the flush of his shame remembering it, remembering that, when it happened, he had believed the Boss had the right to do it, and had admired him no less. *You're over, you bastard*, he told the remembered smile. *Goodbye*.

'Mr Chairman?'

'What? Are we nearly there?'

'Very nearly, sir, we're on the approach, but it seems there's a complication. You know that they're routing us into their military field at Washington because the runway isn't long enough at the airport. Well, it seems that now they don't have a set of steps tall enough to reach our doors, and they're telling us over the radio that you may have to climb down a ladder. We haven't replied yet.'

'What is this, a piss-take? Are they trying to make us look stupid the second we arrive?'

'We don't think so, sir. Apparently the Tupolev just stands further off the ground than the standard American plane does. It's a genuine size problem.'

'Oh, I see. Oh I *see*,' he said in instant good humour. 'Well, you tell them from me it isn't the size, it's what you do with it. No, no, seriously: tell them that if they can't keep up with Soviet technology we're happy to scramble into America down their ladder. Make it diplomatic but, you know, let them know. Don't wince like that, Gromyko, I can see you. I'll be as diplomatic as your heart desires. I'll point my little finger if they bring out the best china. Right, everybody. Where's that copy of the flag from the moon probe? I want it handy to give Eisenhower. Are we all ready?'

*

America was a hot green field glittering with the gold of braid and the silver of musical instruments, where he stood ramrod-straight next to the President, eyes prickling, while a capitalist band played the Soviet anthem. America was a fleet of low black cars, purring down wide avenues between lines of spectators, some clapping and smiling, some not. America was a long banquet table at the White House, covered in more kinds of spoon than you'd see in a spoon museum, surrrounded by faces all turned politely towards him, and towards Troyanovsky his faithful echo, all attentively straining, as if they were struggling to hear a voice from a very long way off, or a sound too high in pitch for their ears. 'For the time being you are richer than us,' he said. 'But tomorrow we will be as rich as you. The day after? Even richer! But what's wrong with that?' The listeners did not seem as charmed as he had expected by this frank, capitalist-style sentiment. Some musicians in the corner played a song named 'Zip-a-Dee-Doo-Dah'. No one could explain the words. America was a ride in the President's helicopter, out over Washington. Miles and miles of houses went by, like dachas but each standing on a separate green square in a grid of green squares. All of the paint and the tiles on the houses seemed neat and new: they gleamed in the September sun as if they had all this minute been taken out of their wrapping paper. 'Decent, fine, comfortable homes,' said Eisenhower. Then the helicopter swooped down low over a highway and hung there in mid-air just above a jostling flood of cars all trying to drive along at the same time, and pushing at each other nose to tail, and giving off a choking vapour. 'It's the rush-hour!' bellowed the President. 'He says they are all going to work,' Troyanovsky translated. Some of the cars had open tops, and you could see the drivers inside, all alone, sitting on plump benches as wide as beds. One of the cars was pink. Show the dog the rabbit, he reminded himself. Show the dog the rabbit.

*

America was a train to New York, specially reserved for the Soviet party. He had read about New York in Ilf and Petrov's famous travel book *One-Storey America*, and he was looking forward to seeing whether it had changed since the two Soviet humorists had visited it, just before the Great Patriotic War. As the train rumbled along through a strange alternation of city and wilderness, his aides laid out the texts for today's speeches on the table in front of him, and they went over them, making alterations, adding new remarks; also, they had clippings from American newspapers describing yesterday's events, both constructive in tone and at other times obviously provocative, designed to injure him in the eyes of the American public. The photographers seemed to specialise in catching people off guard, snapping them with their mouths open or an undignified expression on their faces. Nina Petrovna saw a photograph she found very unflattering, it so exaggerated how fat she was. 'If I'd known there would be pictures like these,' she said, 'I wouldn't have come.' 'Excuse me,' said one of the aides, 'I don't believe that's you.' They inspected the photo. It wasn't. 'Oh,' she said.

Eisenhower had sent along as his representative a man named Henry Cabot Lodge, the American Ambassador to the United Nations. He would be with them on the entire trip. 'Were you in the war, Mr Lodge?' he asked. 'Yes sir, I was.' 'May I ask your rank?' 'I was a one-star general, sir – what I guess you would call a "lieutenant general" in your army.' 'Aha! I was in the war too, and I was a major general. Therefore I outrank you,' he joked, 'and you should follow my orders!' The American smiled and saluted. 'Lieutenant General Lodge, reporting for duty,' he said. Lodge was a known anti-communist and ideologue, but it was important to have good relations with him.

The train passed through Baltimore, Philadelphia and Jersey City, America turning its back view to him as the carriages slid athwart streets and behind rows of red-brick buildings. He gazed and speculated. It was like looking at a man facing away from you, and trying to guess what was in his pockets. He saw rusted fire-escapes clamped to the back of buildings and bundles of electrical wires in fat festoons looping from wall to wall. He saw oil storage tanks, he saw rubber tyres burning on a wasteland in a black smeech of smoke, he saw billboards advertising trinkets and cigarettes. The Americans seemed keen on neon signs, not just for important or official purposes, but everywhere they could be fitted in, violet and green and red, in humming sputtering anarchy. Troyanovsky translated some for him: MOTEL, CRAZY GOLF, JACK'S VALUE AUTO. Sometimes the view turned disconcertingly to blank virgin forest, as if America had tendrils of Siberia reaching right up into its metropolises. Sometimes there were toy landscapes where all the trees were manicured and the grass was smoothed to a striped velvet, emerald and cream. Here, explained Mr Lodge, Americans of the privileged class met to play golf of the un-crazy variety. But on the whole an amazing amount of the space along the railroad line was taken up by the geometrical dachas arranged amid greenery. The Americans seemed to want to take the order of the city into the country with them: having dreamed of the forest, they woke, and tidily organised their dream. Everywhere, the famous wide roads ran, not quite as crowded as the Washington Beltway, but still busy everywhere with traffic. The train crossed a bridge: there was a 'gas station', and around the car waiting at the pumps young men in red-and-white caps really were scurrying to check the engine and wipe the windows, just as Ilf and Petrov had described.

Then the view thickened and grew industrial again, and on the horizon ahead arose the legendary skyline of Manhattan. The train dived into a long tunnel, slowed, and without emerging again into daylight drew to a stop at a platform as thick with dignitaries and policemen as a field of standing wheat. This was

New York, then. He knew from reading Ilf and Petrov that the city was not typical of America, that the rest of the country was more likely, as they'd said, to sprawl out one storey high rather than to tower up fifty storeys. But here he was, where the sky was scraped; in the enemy's headquarters, in the nerve-centre of capital, in the place where all its splendour and misery were concentrated to their very highest degree. Looking for splendour, looking for misery, he walked through the Pennyslvania Station with Lodge, the entourage, the Soviet press corps, a phalanx of American journalists and the Mayor of New York. The station was nothing special, he was glad to see; he had himself built better, far better, when he was running the construction of the Moscow metro. But the canyons between towers through which the motorcade rolled were amazing, truly amazing, and he glanced around with determined nonchalance so as not to crane his head like a bumpkin. Again, the streets were lined with citizens. Again some waved and others behaved otherwise. 'What is that *ooo-ooo* sound?' he muttered to Gromyko. 'It is . . . a noise of disapproval, Nikita Sergeyevich.' 'Really? How rude! Why did they invite me if they didn't want to see me?'

Among the onlookers, on the way to the Waldorf Astoria, he spotted a small white cart and a man in a white apron working at it.

'What is that?' he asked Troyanovsky.

'He is selling lunch to the people, sir. He is cooking an American dish –'

'I know this! This is a kiosk for *gamburgers*, isn't it? You are too young to remember, probably, but we had this in Moscow and Leningrad before the war. Mikoyan went on a fact-finding mission about food technology, mainly to France to pick their brains about champagne, but also here, and he brought us back ketchup, ice cream and *gamburgers*. Look at this! Gromyko, look at this! It is such a good idea. He takes a flat cake of minced beef – it is already cut to the right size – and he fries it quickly on the hotplate in front of him. In a few seconds it is done. He slips it between two round pieces of bread, also cut to the right size, then he adds ketchup or mustard, from those bottles, which are just to his right, where he can easily reach them. And the meal is cooked. With no waiting around. It's like a production line. It's an efficient, modern, healthy way of feeding people. That's why we liked it, that's why we set it up in some of the parks. Perhaps we should do it again. I wonder how much they are charging for a *gamburger*?'

'I can ask Mr Lodge.'

'Oh, he won't know! This is worker's food!'

'I believe, sir, about fifteen cents,' said Lodge, when the question had been relayed to him.

'At that price it must be subsidised quite heavily,' offered Gromyko.

'No!' said the Chairman in triumph. "No subsidy! This is America! Don't you see that the very fact that the *gamburger* kiosk is there means that somebody has worked out how to make a profit by selling the meal at fifteen cents. If the capitalist who owns the kiosk couldn't make a profit at that price, he wouldn't be doing it. That is the secret of everything we see here.'

'Not quite everything, surely,' said Lodge, after the inevitable pause. 'The profit motive isn't everything. We do have such a thing as public service. We do have a welfare state!'

'Oh, pfft,' he said, waving a hand in front of his face like somebody getting rid of an insect.

'You almost sounded as if you admired us,' said Lodge, curiously.

No reply.

Of course he admired the Americans. If you went to England, it was all hand-made trousers. If you went to France, it was cheese from cows who munched away on one particular hillside. How could you possibly arrange plenty for everyone on that sort of small-scale, old-fashioned footing? You couldn't.

But the Americans got it. Of all the capitalist countries, it was America that was most nearly trying to do the same thing as the Soviet Union. They shared the Soviet insight. They understood that whittling and hand-stitching belonged to the past. They understood that if ordinary people were to live the way the kings and merchants of old had lived, what would be required was a new kind of luxury, an ordinary luxury built up from goods turned out by the million so that everybody could have one. And they were so good at it! The bulk fertility of their industry was only the start. They had a kind of genius for lining up the fruitfulness of mass production with people's desires, so that the factories delivered desire to people in little everyday packages. They were magnificently good at producing things you wanted – either things you knew you wanted, or things you discovered you wanted the moment you knew that they existed. Somehow their managers and designers thought ahead of people's wants. Take the *gamburger*: so neat, so easy. It had been created by someone who had made it their serious mission in life to imagine a food you could hold in your fist while you rushed through the busy city. And this was not exceptional for America, it was characteristic. If you looked into the windows of their shops, if you looked at the advertisements in their magazines, you saw the same practical passion at work everywhere. Coca-Cola bottles exactly fitted the average person's hand. Bandages came as a packet of pink patches with a glue just strong enough for the human skin already applied to each one. America was a torrent of clever anticipations. Soviet industries would have to learn to anticipate as cleverly, *more* cleverly, if they were to overtake America in satisfying wants as well as needs. They too would have to become experts in everyday desire. Some comrades chose to be snotty about American cleverness in this direction: they called it trivial, they called it the sign of a self-indulgent society. In his opinion, this was just posturing. Intellectuals with their noses in the air might not care if they sat on hard stools or comfy chairs, but everyone else preferred a bit of padding under their arse. It was true, on the other hand, that there was no need to compete with American ingenuity when it turned ridiculous. In the American kitchen in Moscow, Nixon had showed him a gleaming steel device as elaborately sculpted as an aeroplane part, for squeezing lemons with. 'Do you have a gadget that puts the food in your mouth and presses it down?' he'd answered. It was also true that American workers paid a high price in exploitation and misery for their bottles of Coke. The marvellous techniques needed to be shaken free from the wrongs of American society. Yet America was still a mirror in which he could see a version of his own face. That was why it was frightening, that was why it was inspiring.

Lodge must have been thinking, during the car ride, of what he planned to say later, because in his speech at the lunch hosted by Mayor Wagner, he talked again about America's 'welfare state', even insisting that the American economic system could no longer be described simply as 'capitalism'. It made the Chairman impatient, this transparently unconvincing attempt to fiddle with the basic labels of things. What did they think he was, a simpleton? He opened his reply with a few jokes to ease the mood, then put Lodge firmly straight. 'Every snipe praises his own bog,' he said. 'You extol the capitalist bog.' The nature of the world was not altered just because, it seemed, capitalism's defenders had grown embarrassed about what they were defending. 'God knows,' he said, 'I see no difference between the capitalism that Marx wrote about and the capitalism Mr Lodge spoke of today.' 'If you like capitalism,' he said, 'and I know that you like it – carry on and God bless you! But remember that a new social system, the socialist system, is already treading on your heels.' There.

He had hopes of plainer speaking at the cocktail party he went to next, at the city house of Averell Harriman, a friendly millionaire who'd been acting recently as an unofficial channel between Moscow and Washington. Knowing that he was curious to see capitalism's true lions at close quarters, Harriman had invited over about thirty of the richest men in all America. Each guest had to possess or control at least $100 million in assets. These, then, would be the country's real masters, as opposed to the politicians like Nixon and Eisenhower who merely handled the bourgeoisie's public business. Now it might be possible to make some real progress. By 5.30 he was sitting on a couch in Harriman's library, under a large painting by Picasso. Light gleamed on the wood panelling from lampshades made of little pieces of multicoloured glass, like the glass in church windows. He eyed the picture covertly. Picasso might be one of ours, he thought, a friend of world peace etc. etc., but for himself he preferred art where you could tell what was going on. This thing looked, speaking personally, as if it had been painted by a donkey with a brush tied to its tail. But probably it was expensive. Everything else clearly was. It was not difficult to believe that he was in a sanctum of power; that he, a worker, had been admitted into the company of the princes of this world. Whether or not they wanted him there, the force and capacity of the Soviet state had obliged them to let him in. Think of it! Miners had gouged at the stubborn earth, railroadmen had blown on their hands at dawns colder than rigor mortis, machinists had skinned off bright curls of swarf, soldiers had died in the shit and the mud, so that one of their own could demand to be received in this quiet, rich room as an equal. Here he was. They *had* to deal with him.

He gazed greedily at faces. The capitalists looked surprisingly ordinary, for people who in their own individual persons were used to devouring stolen labour in phenomenal quantities. Their cheeks were not notably bloated, and for the most part they were wearing modest, modern clothes, rather than the uniform of striped trousers and shiny black top hat in which they had always been represented in the cartoons of his youth. Nor did they have the pigs' snouts the artists had given them, of course. But what mines of technique they must be, all the same. What secrets of ingenuity they must possess, as the owners, managers and contrivers of American abundance. He knew how it was to handle a workforce, from his time driving the metro through – the best school in the world, learning how to give your crews the kind hand when possible, the iron hand when necessary, learning how to read a man's possibilities and his limits, learning when to listen to the specialists and when to override them, learning shortcuts and tricks and traps. Knowledge had mounted up in him like floodwater. It must be the same here. These men here, at the very top of American capitalism, must contain whole reservoirs of distilled knowledge. Behind these faces must lie the deft, skilful organisation of industry after industry, service after service. Here were the arts, or some of them, of making factories satisfy desire.

'Mr Khrushchev,' said Harriman, 'welcome! I'm sure I speak for all of us, Republicans and Democrats alike, when I say how firmly united we are in support of President Eisenhower's foreign policy, and in consequence how strongly we support his initiative in inviting you to the United States. Now – we know that you have been answering questions from journalists and US senators almost continuously for the last forty-eight hours. You will probably be doing the same thing for most of the rest of your visit. We wondered if, this evening, you would like to rest your tired vocal chords, and perhaps ask us some questions instead?'

The chief of world socialism taking instruction from American moneymen? No.

'Bring on your questions,' he said shortly. 'I'm not tired yet.'

It was not questions, though, so much as little orations that the millionaires took turns to launch at him, one by one, glancing at each other as they did so. A Mr McCloy, chairman of the Chase Manhattan Bank, tried to tell him that American finance had no influence on American politics.

'You must understand,' he said, 'if Wall Street is seen as supporting a piece of legislation, it's the kiss of death in Washington.'

The chairman narrowed his eyes. It was the same bizarre tactic Lodge had used, the same bizarre effort, apparently, to persuade him that the earth was flat, the sky was green, the moon was made of cheese. Better to take it lightly.

'Very well,' he answered. 'From now on we will remember to pity you.'

The director of General Dynamics explained that, although his company manufactured atomic bombs, it had no stake in tension between the superpowers. Mr Sarnoff, the tycoon of the RCA radio empire, explained that he had left Minsk for the United States as a boy, and never regretted it, because of the virtues of American broadcasting, which he described for a long time.

He left a pause before he replied. 'Things have changed in Minsk,' he said.

No one seemed interested in putting pressure on the government to lift the trade embargo. 'What do you have that you want to sell us?' he was asked.

'This is a detail,' he said. 'If the principle is agreed, then junior officials can talk about specific products.'

'What do we have that you want to buy?'

'We have everything we need,' he said. 'We are not asking for favours.'

Outside, the late summer day had become one of those evenings where the sky has the pure, clear colour of darkening water, moving to black through deeper and deeper blues. Up the avenue, he saw, a dust of tiny golden lights was appearing, just as Ilf and Petrov had promised. A solitary strand of cloud crossed the blue between the buildings, thinning and tightening like a pulled string. Disappointment tightened in the Chairman too, as security men hustled him from Harriman's doorstep into the waiting car. Unfamiliar cooking smells came to his nose, mixed with pungent exhaust. Journalists surged forward: the streets were still very loud.

He was not quite sure what conversation he had imagined himself having, but that had not been it. In the guarded to-and-fro in there, the essential things had not been said. Nobody had seemed to regard economic competition as an alternative to the military variety, at least not in the sense that he had meant. *Relax*, he instructed himself. He was going to say it all himself anyway, in tonight's speech, without any idiot interruptions.

Back at the Waldorf Astoria the ballroom was now crammed with two thousand other businessmen, of slightly less ultimate lustre. These were the mere captains of industry, rather than the captains of the captains; capital's ordinary executives, instead of its innermost cabal. Perhaps they would be more receptive. In his experience, more junior apparatchiks often responded better to new initiatives. Indeed, there were times when the only way to get an organisation to change course was to behead it, and promote new leadership out of the middle ranks. If he were in charge of American capitalism, he thought, that would be the tactic he would adopt. It had been a favourite of the Boss's, and it worked; it had just been a mistake to think that the beheading had to be literal. Retiring people worked just as well.

Faces in front of him. Faces to each side of him, and above him too, because on all sides this ballroom had tiers of balconies like boxes at the theatre. He put on his reading glasses and exchanged a look with young Troyanovsky. They had rehearsed this speech carefully, revised it carefully too in order to incorporate Ambassador Menshikov's advice about which Soviet achievements had caused most soul-searching in the American press. But as always, now he no longer had to watch his tongue, he liked to think on his feet a little, he liked to feel that in front of an audience he was setting off on a journey not completely mapped out in advance.

Now then.

You've probably never seen a communist, he said. I must look to you like the first camel that arrives in a town where nobody's ever seen a camel before: everyone wants to pull its tail, and check it's real. Well, I am real; and in fact I'm just a human being like everybody else. The only difference is my opinion about how the social system should be run. And the only problem we all face today is agreeing that round the world each people should make their own choice about which system to have. Aren't there cases in your system, he said, where competing corporations agree not to attack each other? Why shouldn't we, representing the communist corporation, agree on peaceful co-existence with you, the representatives of the capitalist corporation?

It surprised him, he said, when Mr Lodge defended capitalism with such ardour earlier in the day. Why did he do it? Did he think he might convert Khrushchev? Or did he think, just maybe, that he had to stop Khrushchev converting the audience . . . No, don't worry; I have no such intention. I know who I'm dealing with – although, by the way, if anyone here *would* like to join in with building communism, we could certainly find them a job. We know how to value people, and the greater the benefit of their work, the more we pay them. That's the principle of socialism.

Seriously, though, he was delighted to be in the United States, and delighted to be meeting American businessmen. He was sure that there was much he could learn. In the same spirit, he said, there was something they might learn from him, which would do them good, even if maybe they didn't want to hear it. He was sure they wouldn't mind him speaking without diplomatic niceties, since businessmen are used to being utterly frank with each other.

They could learn, he said, that Russia wasn't going to fail. Look at the historical record, he said. Since 1913, we have raised our output thirty-six-fold, while yours has only risen four-fold. Maybe they would disagree that the reason for this more rapid development was the socialist revolution; he didn't want to impose his ideology on anyone. But in that case, what miracles had it been that brought about these amazing results? Why was it – he asked – that Soviet schools of higher learning trained three times as many engineers as US colleges did? It might interest them to know that, in the new Seven-Year Plan which had just commenced, the Soviet Union was proposing capital investments alone of more than $750 billion. Where did the funds for this come from? It could only be explained by the advantages of the socialist system, since miracles, as we all know, don't happen. When the plan was completed, the Soviet economy would be almost level with the American economy. And the plan was already ahead of schedule. The plan for 1959 had called for a 7.7% rise in industrial output, but before he left Moscow, Comrade Kosygin, Chairman of the State Planning Committee, had reported to him that in the first eight months of the year alone, there had already been a 12% increase. Let no one be in any doubt, he said, let no one hide their head in the sand like an ostrich: more rapidly even than we projected in our plans, we shall soon be able to overtake the United States.

Gentlemen, he said, these were only a few words about the potential of the Soviet Union. We have everything we need. Some people may have thought that I came to the United States to press for Soviet–American trade because without it the Seven-Year Plan cannot be fulfilled. They were making a big mistake. They would be making another if they believed that the trade embargo weakened the defensive might of the Soviet Union. Remember the Sputniks and the rockets, he said. Remember that we were ahead of you in developing intercontinental missiles, which you still do not have to this day – and an ICBM is a true, creative innovation, if you think about it. No, the embargo was simply obstinacy.

The US and the USSR had to choose between living in peace as good neighbours, or drifting into another war. There was no third alternative. They couldn't move to the moon. According to the information from the recent Soviet lunar probe, it was not very cosy there at the moment. So he reminded his audience that gigantic possibilities for good and evil were concentrated in their hands. They were influential people, and he urged them to use their influence in the right direction, and to come out for peaceful co-existence and peaceful competition.

That was supposed to be the speech's last line. It was where his typescript ran out. The listeners had laughed in some of the right places, looked grave in some of the intended places as well; but as he looked round the ballroom now, he thought he saw smiles of an offensive kind, cynical smiles.

'Some of you are smiling,' he said. 'It'll be a bitter pill to swallow when you realise you're wrong. Still, never mind, you'll have new opportunities to apply your knowledge and abilities, when the American people go over to socialism.'

Immediately catcalls and hooting burst out from troublemakers in the balcony.

'I am an old sparrow and you cannot confuse me with your cries,' cried the Chairman. 'I did not come here to beg! I represent the great Soviet state!'

3.

Little Plastic Beakers, 1959

If there was a joke, she was usually last to get it. If there was a catchphrase running around her group of friends, she would stumble over it or say it wrong somehow. She was popular with the boys, because when she decided to do something, she plunged in and definitely did it. She decided that it was foolish to be nervous about sex, so she slept in quick succession with Evgeniy, Pavel and Oskar. Then she had to have an abortion, and Oskar's girlfriend Marina made a horrible scene, which died down, but left behind a kind of nasty imprint in her dealings with her friends. From then on, there was something a little bit mean in the way the girls looked at her, something a little bit speculative in the glances of the boys. It was a relief when she met Volodya, who was not on the nutrition course with her but studied engineering. Volodya took things seriously too. She was sitting in a Komsomol meeting when she noticed him. It was an averagely boring meeting, but he was not tilting his head back and gazing at the ceiling, or making those little dismissive flicks here and there with his gaze which stood in, at meetings, for full-scale eyerolling. He was taking notes on a pad in small, neat, round handwriting. 'It's important for the future,' he said, when she asked him about it afterward. 'If you want to get to where you're going, it's important to show you're not just a passenger.' Being with Volodya was restfully like being with herself. He didn't tease. He didn't do flights of fancy, though he did play silly tunes on the trumpet when he was drunk. He too had plans, and like her, he wasn't embarrassed by the idea of carefully thinking through what would be necessary to achieve them. You made a picture of the life you wanted to have, and then you worked back from there to the present. Volodya even came from a family that resembled hers more than a little, though his hometown was down in the south, not in the Urals. Her father was deputy Party secretary in a small town, her mother was a biology teacher; his father was second acccountant at a manganese mill, his mother a chemistry teacher. 'Snap,' said Volodya. 'Snap,' she agreed. Lying nose to nose in his dormitory bed she felt part of an alliance. He was quite scrawny but his hands were warm and dry. They decided to merge their plans. Both had one more year to run before they graduated. They would marry next summer, they decided, with their degrees safely in their pockets. They talked with comfortable, unironic thoroughness about flats and jobs. Both agreed on the absolute importance of securing Moscow residency. They had come from the edges to the centre; they were not going back again, not returning to any more of those small-town evenings of reading the newspaper and trying to imagine the city. 'We'll have to make ourselves useful,' Volodya said. 'Make sure that our names get noticed.'

They volunteered for things. At first the things were tiny, clapping when a monument was unveiled or handing out towels when students from fraternal Poland came to the university. A period of probation was normal. They expected as much: the Komsomol would need time to sort out solid types from fly-by-nights. But reassuringly quickly, it seemed to be understood by those who made such matters their business that the two of them were indeed electing themselves (which was the only way it happened) into the ranks of the energetic and reliable, and then the activities they were called on for got more important; more interesting, even. Volodya was asked to join the university's Komsomol delegation to the conference on youth and sport which the Moscow City Soviet was holding, and she, she found herself one August morning sitting in a bus drawn up on a side road by Sokolniki Park.

It was a hot, overcast day with a sky of grey haze creased with brightness here and there. Pollen was blowing about.

'Everyone dressed smartly, I see. Good,' said a district official called Khristolyubov, whom it was hard not to stare at because he had lost one of his ears in the war, and moreover wore glasses, which he'd had to tie on behind his head with a cord. Still, presumably the war injury helped make up for the difficulty of running a Party career with a name that meant 'Christ-lover'. She wondered why he hadn't changed it. 'We've divided you into twos –' and he started to read a list from his clipboard. 'Galina with Fyodor,' he said eventually. She looked around, and saw that a few rows back a boy in a leather jacket was raising his eyebrows and a finger. Her heart sank slightly – he had the type of face which looks as if it is permanently kinked towards amusement even when it is at rest – but she nodded and gave him a comradely smile. 'Now remember,' Khristolyubov went on, 'don't miss *any* of the opportunities to put our point of view. Don't be rude to the guides, but use all of the openings that we've discussed, and don't forget to write in the visitors' book on the way out. The Americans are asking for comments? Give them comments.'

They got out, and scattered into the press of people waiting at the main gate of the exhibit, Fyodor-in-the-leather-jacket falling into step beside her.

'Off we go to America,' he said. She didn't know how to reply.

'Where are you at college?' she asked politely.

'No college,' he said. 'Factory. Electrical circuits.'

With their allotted tickets they didn't have to stand in line, and the next time the gate opened, in they went, up the avenue of poplars towards the golden dome where the tour began. American girls in polkadotted knee-length dresses led the way. They all had little round hats on, and white gloves, and identical black high-heeled shoes: it was a uniform. She smoothed at the white cotton dress she had chosen. It was simple, but she had added a green leather belt bought at the flea market and a green purse, nearly matching, which her mother had found in a department store. Simple was all right, if you had black hair and grey eyes. You needed plain colours and not too much fuss. Fyodor caught the gesture and glanced down. She frowned. The American girls' faces were ordinarily mixed between pretty and less pretty, except that all of them seemed to be flushed with the same pink good health, and, studying them more carefully, some of them turned out to be much older than she had first imagined. Some might be as old as thirty, yet these ones were as thin as the twenty-year-olds. Thinness seemed to be a kind of uniform too. They spoke good Russian, but you would have been able to tell they weren't Russian girls even without the clothes or the narrow waists, because they smiled all the time, so much it must make their faces ache, she thought.

As they got closer, she could see that the big curve of the dome was actually made of thousands of straight struts, arranged in a complicated pattern of triangles. It didn't look like a building at all; it seemed hard but flimsy, like the hollow shell of a marine animal that you might find on a beach, sucked thin by tides. Everybody looked up as they stepped in through the door of the dome, and murmured with surprise. Inside, the dome was all one huge room, with no ceiling, just the same crisply flimsy skin, which you could see from here was organised into six-pointed stars or flowers, repeating over and over. Now the result seemed halfway between an organism and a mechanism. It puzzled her a bit that the Americans would pick such a thing as the centrepiece of their exhibition. It was certainly impressive, in its way, but you could tell that it sat lightly on the earth, and would soon be gone. It looked strangely casual.

'Mm-hmm,' said Fyodor.

'. . . designed by a famous American architect, Buckminster Fuller,' one of the girls was saying. Right across the big floor of the dome, the same speech was being made to close-packed circles of listeners as more and more people poured in. White-gloved hands pointed to exhibits around the base of the walls, and to the cluster of seven giant white screens overhead, which filled most of the span of the golden wall in front of them. She tried to see the computer they had been told about with the answers to four thousand supposedly comprehensive questions about the United States. The suggested tactic there was a loud, increasingly indignant search for a question about unemployment. There, that was probably it, the panel of black glass glowing with columns of white text – but the lights in the dome had started to dim, and the crowd of Muscovites in their summer clothes were falling silent, and gazing upward at the screens.

On all seven screens, the night sky bloomed. It took a minute to realise that the constellations varied from screen to screen: instead of showing the same image seven times, as she had expected, the screens were showing seven different images. Quiet orchestral music started to flow from loudspeakers, music with the easy swoosh of a film score, yet what followed were not moving pictures but still frames that only moved by changing, all in time together sometimes but also in unpredictable independent rhythms as pairs, as threes, as fours. The stars faded out. Other lights faded in: aerial shots of big cities by night, twinkling. Then came seven dawns, and a burst on all seven screens of landscapes, empty early-morning landscapes with no people in them. Mountains, deserts, wooded hills, plains covered in crops. The photographs had a glassy, exact distinctness. Everything in them had sharp edges, and the colours were soaked with richness, so that lakes reflected the sky as a deep turquoise and all the browns of the land verged on red, a particular almost edible red pitched somewhere between the shades of chocolate and of blood. The pace slowed again. One farmhouse appeared, prosperous in the new morning light; then many; then screen after screen of houses, and streets from the air, flick flick flick, photographed from just far enough up so you could see the patterns of the streets repeating over and over, in grids and curves and spirals like snails' shells. Doorsteps, and painted front doors in a rainbow of colours as shiny as lacquer. Doorsteps with bottles of milk, doorsteps with newspapers left on them. The doors flew open! Out came men in hats, men in overalls, men kissing their wives, men wiping their mouths and handing their wives coffee-cups, and children, children holding boxes like miniature suitcases. The little boys had short haircuts, like soldiers, or convicts. The children went off to school in square yellow buses, and the men went to work, in a pelt of images of trains and cars. Some of these, suddenly, did move; all of a sudden, seven shining cars stretched out long and low were speeding on highways reduced by speed to blurs of that same rich red-brown. Still you couldn't watch them the way you'd watch a film in the cinema. You had to look around the seven screens, not at any one of them, and more was always going on than you could quite grasp, more was always going in at the corners of your eyes. More roads, more bridges, more tunnels. More highway intersections seen from the sky, gigantic, twisted like concrete knots and dotted with mad numbers of vehicles. One would have been a marvel: this many were a bombardment. More more more.

The American day proceeded. The men worked, in offices and factories. The children studied. The women, apart from the ones who were teaching the children in the schools, stayed at home, polishing and vacuuming huge rooms as uncluttered as stage sets. The camera lovingly kissed every surface. It was as enthusiastic over the grey metal of a filing cabinet as it was over faces. Everything shone, as if it had been new-minted that moment. She kept expecting that the screens would soon show technical or artistic achievements the Americans were specially proud of, and there were some industrial pieces of footage which made the audience in the dome stir, and squint to get a better view, but they were very short. She had never really had to think about the Americans before. They were the villains in the story. She would have supposed that they would seize this chance to tell a rival story, a counter-story, in which they were the heroes. Instead they seemed to have come with no story; no story beyond this untiring, universal brightness, this glow spreading from every object. Now evening had come, and families sat down to eat in front of plastic curtains printed with merry cartoon animals. Children joked and fathers sawed at roasted beef, luminously red-brown, red-brown, red-brown. She felt . . . taunted. She reached in her mind for the familiar comfort of her future, but the picture of the trim, comfortable life she had planned with Volodya, always so near and easy to lay hands on till now, didn't seem to be where she had left it. It had been displaced somehow by the picture show. She hunted quickly through her memory, expecting to find it shoved to one side by the press of this American stuff, yet still intact, still as tightly filled out as ever with reassurance. She hunted and hunted, but there it wasn't. She couldn't find it, couldn't frame it in her head as a solid thing. It had gone, as if the scouring wind of images had blown upon it, and it had abraded away. But she needed it. As she went on searching, a sensation she didn't recognise began to take hold of her. A kind of bubble was rising in her chest, rising and growing and wanting to break out. If it did she would shake or shout out, she could tell.

On the seven screens, the day ended seven ways, in tranquil black and white. Lovers embraced, a little girl kissed her sleeping father, a baby settled to stillness in a crib, a couple reached to switch off matching lamps screwed to the headboard of their bed. The screens all went dark. Then the one in the centre faded up again with one last, long image, of blue flowers in a jug. The crowd in the dome murmured the name of the flowers as people identified them. 'Forget-me-nots . . .'

'Hey. Hey. *Hey.*'

Fyodor was shaking her shoulder, and she was still staring up at the screens with her mouth open. There was work to do: already the crowd was being gathered up for the rest of the tour by new guides fanning out through the dome, men this time. She swallowed hard, and pushed the bubble of panic back down towards the place it came from. She would not permit it. She was a sensible person.

'Hello, hello,' said their new guide, making a gesture with both arms which expertly claimed for his own a group of fifteen people or so. 'Welcome once again to the American National Exhibition, would you like to follow me. My name is Roger Taylor, and I'm a student of the Russian language at Howard University in Virginia, just outside Washington, DC. Please, if I make any mistakes speaking your beautiful language, you should just sing out straight away and tell me. I'm sure I have an accent. Now, the theme of our exhibition here is the American Way of Life . . .'

She was trying urgently to catch Fyodor's eye, but he had already turned and was trailing out of the dome with the rest of the group, leaving her to digest by herself the fact that Roger Taylor, unexpectedly, was a Negro. The hand he was holding above his head like a sail or a shark's fin was – not black, she thought, more a kind of golden caramel. The debating points they had been given had not been devised with him in mind. Though the Komsomol, she thought angrily, had been sending activists into the exhibition for nearly two months now; they must have known that some of the guides were Negroes; they might have *said*. She hurried to catch up.

The group were walking across the turf towards the main pavilion, a long curved arc of a building so thoroughly constructed of glass that you could see right into it, to where many flights of metal steps went up and down between blocks of colour apparently floating in mid-air.

'. . . a fully-featured beauty salon,' Roger Taylor was saying, 'where you ladies are welcome to try out one of the facial treatments invented by Madame Helena Rubinstein, and to hear about the cosmetics which are in fashion in the USA right now. And we have a complete colour-TV studio, and a demonstration of packaged and convenience foods, and also –'

'Is this,' she interrupted, and was amazed at how harsh and loud her voice sounded. 'Is this the national exhibition of a powerful and important country, or is it the branch of a department store?'

Roger Taylor looked at her unsurprised, as if to say: ah-ha, so you're my designated opponent this time round, are you? And where's your friend? The rest of the group registered her presence too. She could feel it, a faint intensifying of reserve in the presence of authority, or in the presence of somebody connected to authority, however long the string. She had done it herself, this slight withdrawal with no actual movement, but never been on the receiving end.

'Well,' he said, 'I certainly hope you won't be disappointed, once you've had a chance to see some of the exhibits. But as I was saying before, the theme is the life people are leading in America today, so the exhibits are chosen to give you information about how ordinary Americans spend their time; how we work, how we dress, what we do for entertainment. The things you'll see today are chosen because they're typical, not because they're exceptional. Take this display for example –'

By now they had entered the pavilion and climbed up one of the flights of steps. The blocks of colour turned out to be panels of fine, translucent plastic fitted into a framework of thin rods to make cubic display cabinets. In them were gleaming aluminium saucepans and little stacks of plastic utensils. There were blue plastic bowls big enough to hold three or four broken eggs, there were little ivory plates ridged up and down and left to right as if the plastic surface had swallowed up a piece of chequered fabric, there were beakers standing in groups. The beakers had handles just big enough for a child's fingers, and smooth rims. In the flush of colour from the panels, they shone with their own colours as if they were lit from within. Spotlights were aimed up through them from below, and made the little plastic beakers into goblets of cheap emerald, cheap ruby, cheap sapphire. Everything about them said *ease*. She had seen Fabergé eggs in an art gallery, and they implied a world when you looked at them, a tiny world of tsars and tsarinas, a jewelled world in which jewels were at home. These implied a world too: a world which had been rid of friction, because its surfaces were easy to wipe, its draining-boards didn't crack and buckle, its paintwork didn't bubble with mineral salts. Roger Taylor's tour group stood on the metal landing and gazed into the cubbyholes of light floating before them. The beakers were out of reach, and this was good, because she wanted to put out a fingertip and stroke them.

'All of these pieces of cookware that you see here are well within the budget of the average American family,' he continued. 'This was a guiding principle of the exhibition. You don't have to be rich to buy any of these.'

'Nothing for millionaires, then?' asked an elderly worker. 'No diamond-studded toilet seats or gold plates?'

'I'm afraid not,' said Roger Taylor.

The old man gave a comical sigh of disappointment.

'What is this one for?' asked a woman in her forties.

'It's a salad spinner,' he said. 'You put your lettuce leaves in here after you've washed them, and wind the little handle, and the water flies off. But you should really ask my mother. I'm not a good cook.'

The group laughed. They liked him.

'Through here we have our supermarket,' he said, leading them to a balcony from which they could see a hall full of Russians pressing up against a counter manned by more of the guides. 'As you can see, it's quite crowded, so let's wait a moment before we go down.'

'Are the goods really for sale?' said a man in a check shirt with a face from the Far East, Chukchi or Mongolian or something like that.

'Unfortunately not,' said Roger Taylor. 'I'm afraid all we can do is show them to you. But I can promise you a free cup of Pepsi once we're done in here. (It's a kind of soft drink, ma'am.) In the meantime, why don't we have a look at this chart. As you can see, the average wage for an industrial worker in the USA is round about a hundred dollars a week – which comes to, say, a thousand roubles at the tourist exchange rate. What can you buy for that? Well, you could get yourself two men's suits. Or seventy-six of those saucepans we just saw. Or 417 packs of cigarettes. Or –'

'Hang on,' said Fyodor. 'Excuse me for interrupting, but how much of this hundred dollars does this "average worker" get to keep? Isn't it the case that he must pay nearly thirty dollars of it in taxes? I mention this because in the Soviet Union, as a matter of fact, we hardly pay taxes at all. And then what about rent? What about transportation? What about healthcare, which of course is not free in the United States? How much would you say is really left over for buying suits or saucepans?'

He said all this smiling, and he spoke quickly, rattling off his sentences. The group, which had murmured sympathetically at the mention of the American taxes, all turned their heads to see what Roger Taylor would say, with the spectatorial interest of a crowd at a soccer match who've just seen the ball kicked deep into the other side's half of the pitch.

The guide gave an acknowledging nod to Fyodor. He was smiling too. 'I suspect you can tell me,' he said. 'I suspect you're thinking of the figures published in this April's issue of the *Congressional Record*, am I right?'

'As a matter of fact I am. According to this newspaper – which is an official newspaper of the US government, I think – the "average" American worker can only afford to spend about

$7.50 of his wages on clothing. You can't buy a suit for that, can you?'

'But who wants to buy a suit every week?' countered Roger Taylor. 'What I can tell you is that, in the United States, the ordinary working guy takes it for granted that he'll own a suit to go out dancing in on a Friday night with his wife, and often he owns a car too, as we'll see when we get to the automobile exhibit outside. Maybe it takes a bit of organising to get the life he wants, a bit of care with the money, but isn't that true everywhere in the world? The important thing is that the standard of living for ordinary Americans has risen to the level you see here, and goes on rising, year by year.'

'Ah yes,' said Fyodor, 'the "ordinary" American with the "average" wage again. But how many people really earn these average wages? Isn't it true that millions of American families survive on incomes much smaller than these – that three million families must somehow get by on only a thousand dollars a year, which is only twenty dollars per week? These are workers too, living in dreadful misery. So how can we trust your average? How can you expect us to believe that all these fine products are really familiar to ordinary American workers? If life is so good, Mr Taylor, why do American steel-workers go on strike every single year?'

'Because they want their lives to be even better. Because they want to earn more.'

'Maybe they get the average', said the old man who'd wanted to see decadent toilet seats, 'by adding together the capitalist's wage and the worker's, and then splitting them!' He snickered.

'Actually,' said a bald man in square spectacles who had not said anything before, 'it would depend on whether you were talking about the mean or the median.' At this teacherly remark, no one spoke. 'I have a question, if you will permit me. Mr Taylor, I wonder if you could say a little more about the way that prices are *decided* in the American economy?'

'I'm not quite sure what you mean, sir.'

'I mean, how is it that the pack of cigarettes costs' – you could see him doing the sum in his head – 'twenty-four cents? Why twenty-four cents and not twenty-three cents or twenty-five cents? How is this arrived at?'

Roger Taylor shook his head. 'I'm sorry,' he said, 'but that's a question for an economist, not for a student of literature. I can't help you there.'

'Ah,' said the bald man.

The guide looked at Galina. *Any more?* said his expression, clear as daylight. She pressed her lips together.

'OK,' he said. 'I think there's enough space for us in the supermarket now,' and he led off down the stairs. 'Do you read Pushkin?' Galina could hear the salad-spinner lady asking him as they descended.

The trouble was that she did believe it. Oh, not that all Americans were rich and happy, or that they could necessarily afford all the products that Roger Taylor said they could; but that somehow, for at least some people in America, a life was going on whose existence she had not suspected till now, in which it was possible to obtain things, things as covetably pretty and convenient as the little plastic beakers, without having to do anything to deserve them. Without having to make a plan. Without having to part with anything except banknotes. Just by going shopping. Roger Taylor talked about the money things cost as if that were the only consideration. She wrestled with the idea. She felt the way you do when you reach the bottom of a staircase one step before you're expecting it, and jar your bones by trying to step into the solid floor with all the unbraked hurry of your descent. It seemed that life could be easier than she had imagined. But not, of course, for her. She was still living where it was necessary to pay for the life you wanted in boredom and embarrassment. *Unfair, unfair,* she thought.

They passed through the supermarket, Roger Taylor showing

off packages of fruit jelly, frozen maize kernels, tinned soup, and dry grey nodules that turned into mashed potato if you added boiling water. Then they emerged onto the grass again and drank black lemonade from cups made of waxed paper. The sweet liquid made the old man burp. American cars were parked behind a circular fence, waist high. They looked just like the ones on screen in the dome had done, with a shark-like length to them and chrome ornaments at the front for teeth. All the men in the group including Fyodor went and leaned on the fence. 'Ooh, baby,' crooned Fyodor, and was immediately enfolded in a male conversation about the desirability of the different models on display, and the Soviet car make which came closest in terms of lip-licking appeal. (The Gaz factory's Chaika, was the consensus.) He made a nominal effort to get Roger Taylor to agree that the vehicles represented bourgeois waste, but his heart wasn't in it, you could tell. He had speeded up his talking one notch further still, and this time the effect was that he seemed to hold each sentence at arm's length as he said it. 'Surely-these-are-just-an-indulgence-in-a-country-where-thousands-of-children-go-to-bed-hungry.' You-know-I-have-to-say-this. But the words were being said, and Fyodor could truthfully claim he had said them. She, on the other hand, was still silent. From time to time Roger Taylor looked at her in faint puzzlement.

'Where can we buy these?' asked the Mongol, without very much hope. 'Will they be imported?'

'So far as I know, there aren't any plans to,' said Roger Taylor. 'You'd have to take that up with your own authorities.'

She knew that if she didn't say something soon, she wouldn't be able to at all. Her tongue was thickening up, or something. She didn't feel even slightly eloquent.

Ahead of them, a kind of arcade jutted out, or perhaps more of a stretched-out bandstand, with another roof that looked as if it had grown. Pillars rose up and spread to join, like overlapping mushrooms. Inside, a low stage ran from left to right. Many tour groups were flowing in and coagulating into a crowd. Roger Taylor led his in, and they stood together at the back, half shaded by the roof, half by a big pine tree.

'Now we come to the fashion show,' he said. 'A parade of modern American formal wear and casual wear, modelled for you by my colleagues.'

Loud music started up which made Fyodor smile, and a line of male and female guides danced out onto the stage, the men dressed in stripey sweaters, the women in check dresses with skirts which flew out into wide circles. The crowd applauded; but she scarcely looked. She was gazing at Roger Taylor, and scrabbling through the list of things she could say. It felt almost companionable to be standing there next to him. He spoke, the group asked questions, and everything went along smoothly, even Fyodor's interventions. She found it hard to believe she could reach the quarrel she was supposed to be having with him. Unless she made it happen, the tour would soon end without her having done her job. Somehow she had to crack the surface of the situation. The bubble in her chest was back.

'You don't dance?' Madam Salad-Spinner asked him.

'I don't dance?' said Roger Taylor, pretending to be indignant. He clicked his tongue. 'Ma'am, what an insult. I'm a fine dancer. It just isn't my turn today.'

'I'm sure you dance *beautifully*,' said the woman, with a kind of motherly daring.

'You make everything in America sound so good,' Galina broke in, with a rush. 'You make it sound as if the country is nothing but a garden full of roses. But this is not true, at all, is it? Because, because, in America there are terrible social problems. What, what about, the great, terrible evil of racial discrimination, which you must know very well yourself?'

Roger Taylor looked exhausted for an instant, and she guessed suddenly that he was used to taking a rest for a little time while his tour groups watched the fashion show. But he hid the weary expression behind a new smile, and replied:

'If I gave anyone the impression that life in America was perfect, I apologise. Because, of course, it isn't. We have our problems, like any country, we've inherited our fair share of tough problems from the past; and, like you say, one of our biggest problems has been the way that our coloured citizens and our white citizens get along together. We fought a whole civil war to end slavery, you know, at the same time your Tsar Alexander was ending serfdom here. But we make progress, you know. We've come a long way as a society, and we go on getting better . . .'

So smooth, still so smooth. What could she say that would make more of an impression?

'Most important of all,' he was saying, 'we feel confident that our American system of values holds the key to defeating prejudice and injustice wherever it may be found. We believe –'

'Why do you keep saying *we*?' she interrupted. 'Why do you keep talking as if you are included?'

'I'm sorry?' he said, giving her, for the first time, a look of real dislike. It was also an accusing look, as if to say, *this game had rules, didn't you know that, didn't you notice that?*

She couldn't stop now. The words sounded horribly personal as they came out of her mouth, but this was the only way she could think of to combine the standard argument they'd been given against American racism with the awkward truth of Roger Taylor's colour.

'I mean,' she ploughed on, 'you keep saying "We Americans", "we do this", "we do that". But white Americans don't treat you as an equal, do they? You are from Virginia and Virginia is in the South of the United States, I think. So they won't even let you drink the same water as them.'

His expression was now unreadable. He had set his jaw, and a line had appeared on each side of his mouth. He moved his head from side to side very slightly, like someone trying to find a clear path forward. The others in the group had started to turn and pay attention. They were looking at her. You could tell by the way they had hitched their shoulders that they were annoyed: maybe because she was being unpleasant to nice Mr Taylor, maybe because she was insisting on pouring politics in their ears in the middle of their one chance to watch the fashion parade.

'I raise this point', she offered, 'because in the Soviet Union all nationalities –'

'It's true,' he said, overriding her. 'What you say. That's true. At present. But that is a local law; it can change, and if you ask me, it will change. But the Declaration of Independence won't change, and you know what that says? It says, "All men are created equal".'

Part of her was pleased that he had lost his lightfooted poise, that he was now picking his words slowly and painfully, that she was managing to kick back at the world that had teased her with the little plastic beakers. *I'm sorry, I'm sorry*, another part wanted to say, aware that the public humiliation she was involving them both in meant something different to him, something she only sensed dimly. But it was too late for courtesies.

'I don't see what good it does that those words are on a piece of paper. In fact,' she said, 'in fact, those words are a lie, aren't they, if they are contradicted by what really happens? Look,' she said, pointing at the stage, 'there's another lie.' The guides on the stage had stopped dancing, and were now acting out a wedding scene, to the sound of slow organ music. Two of the guides acting as wedding guests, a man and a woman, were also Negroes. 'You show us black and white behaving like friends, yet in your own newspapers, this has been denounced as something disgusting, that Negroes and white people would be together at a wedding.'

'A few Senators objected. As you see, they lost the argument, and the wedding scene is still in the show.'

'In the show, yes, but what about in reality? Would this really happen? I don't think so.'

'Maybe not this year,' said Roger Taylor, strain in his voice. 'But ask again next year. Ask again in five years.'

'And that's good enough, for you, is it,' she said, her own voice rising, 'that in five years things may be a little bit better. Do you think that's good enough? Do you think it's all right to wait, and wait, and wait?' She seemed to herself to be winning the argument, yet the bubble of panic was slipping free.

He breathed in and out through his nose, and stared at her. 'No,' he said. 'I don't think that's good enough. Tell me, what don't you think is good enough in Russia?'

'This is interesting music –' began Fyodor loudly.

Galina ignored him. 'We were talking about America,' she said. 'America, not Russia. Where your people are treated without any dignity! My question, Mr Taylor, my question is, why have you betrayed your people by coming to Moscow to represent a country like that?'

Roger Taylor's lips mouthed air, then dropped open, slack with shock, and nothing came out. *Rules?* said his disbelieving eyes. *Weren't there? Some? Any?* She had blown a hole in his charm, all right; he couldn't speak. She understood only in the barest theory why the question had done that to him, but seeing him speechless, voiceless, she was able to glimpse for a second how important charm might have been to him, as a covering, as a defence. She saw, hazily, how much it might have weighed with him to feel that he could count on possessing a thick skin of pleasing words, when he had judged it right to come and speak for a country which wasn't certain, this year, that it would share a drinking glass with him. There was dreadful silence.

Then an angry muttering hum arose from the circle gathered around them, apparently generated by all of the group at once without any of them being singly responsible for it. She had taken part in this type of mass ventriloquism, in her time, attacking unpopular teachers back in high school. But she had never had it aimed at her. It was her they were all angry with now.

Roger Taylor blinked, and abruptly seemed to calm, as if there were some substantial comfort in finding it was just her he had to deal with, not the whole ring of pale Muscovite faces. He took a half-step back from her outstretched finger, and deliberately exhaled his caught breath. 'I'm very glad', he said, with a dot of careful acid on every word, 'that my dignity means so much to you. In my opinion,' he said, 'I haven't betrayed anyone. And I think my opinion is the one that counts, don't you? Because the only way of telling that kind of thing is to look inside yourself, at your own conscience. And everybody has to do that. Everybody has to decide where to place their hopes, and what compromises are all right to make, and what compromises aren't OK. After all,' he said, 'we all do make our compromises – don't we?'

She was not a person who blushed. Now, she blushed.

'But –' she began.

'Why don't you leave the poor boy alone?' hissed Madam Salad-Spinner.

'Shhh!' agreed several of the group, emboldened. Unfriendly eyes regarded her.

Roger Taylor left a beat of silence; his silence, now. 'Why don't we go on,' he said, and he led the rest of the party away.

Fyodor left with them. A couple of minutes later, he darted back. She was still standing on the same spot. She had her hands over her face.

'That didn't go too well,' Fyodor observed. 'You shouldn't take things so seriously. Look, stay here; you're upset. I'll do the rest.'

'What will you tell them?' she asked.

'Don't worry so much,' he said. There was an expression she hadn't seen before on his face. 'We'll work something out,' he said.

4.

White Dust, 1953

Perhaps any great change demands a beginning in the imagination, a remembered moment about which you can say: for me at least, it began there. In the fervent early sixties, when the alliance for reform in economics was just dislodging the dogmatic monopoly that insisted all questions were already answered, and new criss-cross terrains for argument were opening up in department after department of thought where there had only been the catechism before, and there were constantly new people's ears to bend, and stealthy new academic turf wars to fight – when all that was going on, Emil Shaidullin would tell himself that for him the beginning was the day he walked to the village. 'Stalin was dead and the birds were singing,' he would think. Yet right there, already, hindsight had contaminated the data. He would be far more glad later that Stalin was dead than he had been that summer, as a student freshly graduated from the economics faculty of Moscow University. Then, the death of the General Secretary scarcely felt like an event you could be glad, or sorry, about. Like a shift in the earth's crust or a change in the climate, there it just was, huge, undeniable, but completely obscure in its significance as yet. If you were young in 1953, and lucky enough to come from a family that had not experienced the sharp end of his rule, you had no clear idea of what you had escaped, because an old Georgian had twitched his last on a government carpet; and you didn't know, either, what there was to escape into. No other world for the inhabiting suggested itself as an alternative to the armour-plated reality you had always been told was the inevitable, the only possible, version of existence. At the very most, that summer, a sort of loosening in the fabric of things was discernible. The newspapers had become just a little bit more unpredictable. But the birds *were* singing.

It had sounded simple enough, city boy that he was. He was working in Sobinka, a mill town a hundred kilometres or so out of Moscow on the Vladimir line. The book-keeping job he'd taken till his appointment to the Committee for Labour began didn't use much of his brain. He spent a lot of time gazing out of the window at a spray of dusty willowherb nodding up-down, up-down, up-down in the hot green torpor of August. When he could he cadged phone calls to his fiancée back in the city. 'I'm going to go and visit my parents after the exams,' she said. 'Why don't you come and collect me from the village this weekend? It's time you met them. They're getting curious about their future son-in-law. I'll boast about you some more before you come . . .' On Saturday morning he packed a satchel, and put on his best suit, a black broadcloth item with a rather English stripe, which he believed gave him a successful air, particularly when partnered with a dark shirt. For sure, it made him look like someone making their way in life. His fair hair curled as thick as ram's wool at his temples, and he would have had the face of a young boxer if it wasn't for his narrow chin. And his nose. He carefully spread open the shirt collar on his lapels. He put his grandfather's gold ring on his finger. Then he took the scrap of paper he'd scribbled the village's name on, and went to the railroad station.

The clerk behind the grille had to look the name up in a directory. No, he said, there wasn't a train that went there. He unfolded a tattered map of the region: 'The place you want, it's in here somewhere,' he said, and his finger sketched out a surprisingly large blank space between two of the train lines raying out from Moscow. 'You'd better get a ticket to Alexandrovsk and do the rest by bus.' At Alexandrovsk he found the bus depot at the end of a street of little painted plaster houses sagging in the sun. 'Where?' said the girl in the kiosk. She called over the driver of a bus parked in the shade. When he heard the name of the village he laughed, showing gappy teeth. 'You want to go *there*? Mister, you could wait a long time for a bus. On account of there being no road.' 'What do you mean, no road?' said Emil. 'I'm sorry,' said the driver, grinning. 'There just isn't. It's pretty marshy over there, and the only way in is a track along the top of the dyke. You can get a tractor in there, but not much else.' 'This is ridiculous,' said Emil. 'Moscow is only half an hour up the line. We're practically in the suburbs.' 'Nevertheless,' said the driver. He dropped Emil off at a corner out in the country where the metalled road turned a right angle and the track began. 'You see?' he said, pointing at a pair of wheel ruts that wavered away into green distance. 'Just follow them. It's nine, ten kilometres.' The bus left, gears grinding.

Emil hoisted his satchel and set off. The ruts must be deep sumps of mud when it rained. Now they were filled with dry white dust, which stirred up in little clouds as he stepped along, and settled, powdery, on the tall grasses. It was very quiet. He heard the grass swish against his legs as he walked, and not a human-made sound besides. Not a thread of speech in the air, not an engine in the distance, not a plane in the sky. For all the signs of it that there were here, Moscow might as well have been hundreds of kilometres away, thousands, instead of just over the horizon. Suddenly it was hard to believe it even existed. As his ears adjusted, new sounds declared themselves. Chirr, chirr went unseen insects in the grass. Every time he put a foot down, it muted the insects in a circle round about it, as if he had a disc of silence attached to each leg, but the moment he'd passed they started up again. In the air, dopplered strands of song flittered by. He had no idea what the darting birds were called, but he presumed that these would be the birds that poetry named, the larks, the thrushes. And it was hot. My, it was hot. The air baked. The sky was a dome of blue, so dark, so metallic-looking, you'd think you could have beaten it like a gong. The sun blazed straight overhead, apparently fixed in place. It shone down so whitely that the occasional clumps of trees along the path stood in puddles of shadow which seemed blue-green in contrast. Sweat trickled from Emil's hairline to his collar. From somewhere, a couple of flies presented themselves, and kept him company in zizzing orbits.

The only countryside he knew was the view from a train window. It was different being amidst it. The path ran along the top of a low causeway, only a metre or so high, and to left and right there spread out a wide floor for the big sky overhead. The ground rose a bit, off to the left, and a stand of trees darkened the horizon over there, but you couldn't call it a hill, it was just a wrinkle on the face of earth. Grain was standing in the fields the causeway crossed, giving off a hot straw smell. In some places, the wheat stood all to attention, in burly masses. In others it fell about as if it had been trampled, or as if small local whirlwinds had blown upon it. Ahead, though, it was getting steadily thinner and sicklier-looking, the ripe yellow blended more and more with a green like the green of the grass along the causeway, only brighter. Too bright, in fact; getting toward the unhealthy brightness of the green slime on top of a stagnant pool. And after a pair of dykes crossed the route of the causeway at right angles, with a ragged drainage ditch between, the crops stopped altogether, and the bright, sick green took over, glistening on ground that was evidently as unstable as jelly. Puddles appeared, spread, joined into shallow sheets of water reflecting the sky. A rotten, composty vapour rose round him. The birdsong dwindled. He lost a fly and gained some mosquitoes.

The sun hammered down. If anything it was hotter, now the air was damp. His hair stuck to his head like a helmet. Time for a rest. Fortunately he'd had the presence of mind to buy a drink at the kiosk. He pulled out the bottle and dropped to the grass. Instantly a mosquito bit him. Kvass was not his favourite drink, and the yeasty liquid was lukewarm, but he chugged it all gratefully, his adam's apple pumping up and down. Then he leant back on his hands and breathed. Moisture trickled through his system. He was so glad of it, it took him a while to process what he was seeing, as he gazed down the length of his body. Then he groaned out loud: a long, miserable, animal noise, like a dog in pain. Walking through the knee-high grass had coated his suit trousers almost to the knee with the dust, in a thick clinging layer. He scrubbed at the material, but his damp hands only turned the dust to muddy smears. He stood up: the dust had covered his backside too, and the back of his thighs. It was everywhere. It was everywhere, and he was in the middle of a marsh, in the middle of a fucking swamp, with a dusty path behind and a dusty path in front. With kilometres more of the fucking stuff to come.

He twisted his head round. As far as the eye could see, the world was vacant of human life.

'Shit!' he shouted at the top of his voice. 'Shit! Shit! Shit! *Shit!*'

A hundred metres away, a waterbird suddenly took off, disturbed by the noise.

'Oh shit,' he said to himself.

He walked on. What else was there to do? At every step a little more of the Moscow Region lovingly transferred itself onto him, and the mixture of dust and sweat made him dirtier and dirtier. By the time he arrived he would look like a scarecrow. After a while, he felt better. He had outwalked his lost temper, walked it away in the endlessly repeating hiss of the grass against his legs. Ahead the air squiggled and wavered with heat. It really was peaceful out here, in a hot, annoying, bug-clouded, swamp-scented kind of way. The rhythm of walking gave everything a calm regularity. He slapped at the mosquitoes without malice. He could feel his thoughts settling into place, with a wide margin of quiet around them. So the impression he'd wanted to make was ruined: oh well. Under the big sky it didn't seem like the end of the world. Here he was, plodding along in the heat, and all his education and all his good prospects didn't make him any less a human speck, inching across the wide, flat floor of Russia. After another while, he started to laugh. Let this be a lesson to you, Mr Economist, he told himself. Any time you get imperious, any time you start to mistake the big enclosing terms you use for the actions and things they represent, just you remember this. Just you remember that the world is really sweat and dirt.

But the descriptions of the world in economics *were* powerful. At least potentially they were. That was what had made him stick stubbornly to the subject, chance-found in the compulsory course on Marxist basics, when on the face of things it was such an intellectual poor relation, such a neglected little annex of politics. Politics gave the orders, in the economy of the USSR, and economists were allowed to find reasons why the orders already given were admirable. But that was going to change, he suspected. He believed that the Soviet Union was soon going to need more from its economists, because there was more to life – there was more to running an economy – than giving orders. It might do for the brute-force first stage of building an industrial base, but what came next surely had to be subtler, surely had to be adjusted to the richer and more complicated relationships in the economy, here on the threshold of plenty. At college, of course, everything had had to revolve around Stalin's little book *Economic Problems of Socialism*. They studied it as if it were holy writ, although you could search in vain in there for any 'problems' at all, in the sense of specific, unresolved issues looking for solutions. The World's Greatest Marxist was not enthusiastic about the unknown. Indeed, he mocked the idea that planning an economy required any intellectual engagement with it; maybe any intellectual effort in itself, at all. Get the chain of command right, Stalin seemed to be saying, build it on the right ideological principles, and all that was left was a few technical details, a little bit of drudgery to be carried out by the comrades at Gosplan with the adding machines. But Emil, pursuing the elusive whatever-it-was that had excited him in the first place, had also been and read some Marx. No one could stop you. The dull-red volumes of the *Collected Works* were all over the place. And while Marx didn't say much about economics after the revolution, he did insistently name the state he promised was coming, at history's happy end. He called it 'consciously arranged society'. Acting together, human beings were going to construct for the world a wealth-producing apparatus that far exceeded in efficiency the apparatus that formed ad hoc, by default, when everyone chaotically scrabbled for survival. If this were true, if this were truly the goal, Emil could not for the life of him see how the design of the economy could be an unimportant afterthought. He couldn't see how the transformation Marx predicted could be anything but a task that required every scrap of a society's deliberate intelligence, every reserve it had of analytical subtlety, every resource it possessed of creativity. This was the task of the ages they were talking about: history's highest, hardest achievement. 'Consciously arranged society' demanded conscious arranging, and conscious arrangers to do it.

He looked at economics, and he saw the source which would soon have to supply them. True, the tools economists should use for the task weren't clear yet. He had the sense, at the moment, of groping for intellectual support, of casting about and dimly receiving a hint here, a hint there. Like a radio technician delicately picking signals out of background static, he'd learned to recognise voices worth listening to, voices that meant something distinct even when they used the same compulsory words as everyone else. Here and there, people were speaking with secret passion. Here and there, economists were starting to talk to biologists and mathematicians, and to the scholars building electronic calculating machines. If you knew where to look, several different lines of new thought were stirring, seemingly all pointed in contrary directions, but (he believed) really due to fuse, soon, into the knowledge they were going to need. For economics, after all, was a theory of everything. It wanted to explain the whole of human activity. The world was sweaty, the world was dusty, but it all made sense, because beneath the thousand thousand physical differences of things, economics saw one substance which mattered, perpetually being created and destroyed, being distributed, being poured from vessel to vessel, and in the process keeping the whole of human society in motion. It wasn't money, this one common element shining through all its temporary disguises; money only expressed it. It wasn't labour either, though labour created it. It was value. Value shone in material things once labour had made them useful, and then they could indeed be used or, since value gave the world a common denominator, exchanged for other useful things; which might look as dissimilar from one another as a trained elephant did from a cut diamond, and consequently as hard to compare, yet which, just then, contained equal value for their possessors, the proof being that they were willing to make the exchange.

This was true the world over, in every kind of economy. But Marx had drawn a nightmare picture of what happened to human life under capitalism, when everything was produced only in order to be exchanged; when true qualities and uses dropped away, and the human power of making and doing itself became only an object to be traded. Then the makers and the things made turned alike into commodities, and the motion of society turned into a kind of zombie dance, a grim cavorting whirl in which objects and people blurred together till the objects were half alive and the people were half dead. Stock-market prices acted back upon the world as if they were independent powers, requiring factories to be opened or closed, real human beings to work or rest, hurry or dawdle; and they, having given the transfusion that made the stock prices come alive, felt their flesh go cold and impersonal on them, mere mechanisms for chunking out the man-hours. Living money and dying humans, metal as tender as skin and skin as hard as metal, taking hands, and dancing round, and round, and round, with no way ever of stopping; the quickened and the deadened, whirling on. That was Marx's description, anyway. And what would be the alternative? The consciously arranged alternative? A dance of another nature, Emil presumed. A dance to the music of use, where every step fulfilled some real need, did some tangible good, and no matter how fast the dancers spun, they moved easily, because they moved to a human measure, intelligible to all, chosen by all. Emil gave a hop and shuffle in the dust.

Was that something in the distance? A little dark blob had appeared on the causeway up ahead, and a new tendril of sound was curling its way from it to his ear: the sound of a motor. Emil waved his hand high over his head, and picked up the pace. *Shk-shk-shk* said the grasses briskly against his legs. The blob fattened in the pulsing air, got louder, was a tractor. A long-faced middle-aged man in overalls was driving it. His fiancée was sitting on the metal arch over the back wheel.

'We were starting to wonder where you'd got to,' she said, hopping down, 'so Poppa borrowed – good grief, why on earth did you wear a suit?'

'Well, somebody didn't mention that they lived on the other side of a hippopotamus wallow. So this is your dad?'

The driver grunted. He was squinting against the sun, and his weather-reddened brows were clenched together, so it was hard to tell if he was actively frowning at Emil or not, but he was certainly not smiling.

'Hello,' said Emil, and held up his hand to be shaken. He had to squeeze past the tractor's front wheel to reach. Magda's father took it for an instant and released it. 'I'm afraid I'm all dusty,' Emil said. 'Should I climb up, or follow you back? Are you turning round?'

'Where?' said the driver. 'No room. Got to go back in reverse.'

'Come round the side and step up on that,' said Magda, pointing. 'Come on – it's not like getting dirt on a car seat.'

The tractor only grated along, driven backwards, but it was twice as fast as he'd been walking, and after twenty minutes of engine noise too loud for easy speech, the ground lost its gelatinous shine, and the causeway merged with the slow rise of another modest hill. There were trees on its brow, and the corrugated iron shed of a Machine-Tractor Station, where his father-in-law-to-be parked their ride, slipping a couple of cigarettes to the technician on duty. The other side of the hill was in shade, now that the sun had crossed the zenith. Here the track descended again, to the curve of a creek which seemed to drain the marsh in this direction. It flowed slow and brown. There was a water-meadow beyond it, and a line of tall birches. Wooden houses were scattered higgledy-piggledy down to the water's edge.

The only houses in the country Emil had ever really looked at had been dachas; these appeared to be constructed on the same general plan, only the wood was old, not new, and the walls were thick, not thin, and where the lines of a dacha made a trim summery sketch in the air the lines of these houses sagged heavily, as if they left the earth with reluctance. Traces of ancient colour clung to the shutters, like the last streaks of dried skin and gristle stuck in the creases of old bones. They were lairs, burrows. Sunflowers leaned over the crooked palisades of garden plots. Broken tools and pieces of rusty metal lay in the long grass.

'Well, this is home,' said his fiancée. 'Or it was home.' Her father had gone ahead, shouting that they'd arrived. They strolled downhill together in the blissful shadow. A granny at a doorstep gazed at them as they passed. A boy of about eight belted round the corner of a house and stopped dead, a jack-rabbit arrested by the sight of something terrifying.

'Hey there,' said Emil. He scrubbed again at his jacket, then gave up.

'Feels a little strange to come back?' he asked.

'Stranger every time.'

Emil could imagine that. Even seeing her with the low shingle roofs of the village houses around her, he still instinctively believed that her natural environment must be urban, so deftly at home in the city she had seemed to be, so confidently embedded in its possibilities, when he first ran into her on the campus, grey scarf matching her grey eyes, under the giant spire of the new university tower. Knowing her had played a large part in his own pleasurable sense that he was turning into a Muscovite. Now she had invited him to see what had come before the poise. She was nervous, he could see, but there was also a kind of appeal in her look. She would like it, he thought, if he were able to show somehow that in his eyes this new part of her wasn't a total mystery, wasn't a complete surprise. But the truth was that he had no idea what life could have been like for her, growing up here. He didn't quite believe the place was real. It looked like the set for some Chekhov story of country life. He kept expecting a hospitable squire or a melancholy doctor to pop up and start talking about his gooseberry patch.

'I don't think your father likes me much,' he said.

'Give him a chance,' said Magda. 'Men in suits always mean trouble, in his experience. Nothing good comes from the city.'

'Well,' Emil said, nettled, 'apart from manufactured goods, you mean. And, you know, progress, and culture, and civilisation.'

'Oh yes?' she said. 'This is the village store. Look in here.'

To the left of the track, a shed had three steps up to a side door with a tin sign nailed over the lintel. Obediently, Emil pressed his nose against the glass pane in the bolted door. Through dingy glass, he could make out a counter, and a shelf behind it. The shelf was a graveyard for flies. That was its main function;

but at one end, as an afterthought, some rusty cans of kerosene had been stacked, and blocks of sugar wrapped in blue paper.

'There's a supply problem,' he said uncertainly.

'No,' she said, 'there isn't.'

'But –'

'There isn't,' she said. 'This is the back of the queue, that's all. Always the back of the queue. Come on, I can see my mother.'

Twisting her hands, a thin grey-haired woman like a beaten-down version of his fiancée was waiting in a doorway with a cluster of other people around her, and more people drifting into place between the houses to gawp, all silent, all unashamedly fixed on the spectacle Emil was providing. At the front of the group a sallow man in shirt and braces was standing with his arms crossed, an expression of bafflement on a face like a sweating cheese.

'Welcome, Mister, welcome –' began Magda's mother, but the sallow man interrupted.

'You're the student, right?' he said.

'Pletkin the manager,' murmured Magda.

'More or less,' said Emil. 'Yes.'

'You could have phoned the kolkhoz office. No need to've walked, someone like you, day like this. I'd've picked you up.'

'That's kind of you,' said Emil.

'No problem,' said Pletkin. 'After all, not every day, meet the young man's going to marry our clever girl here.' The words were friendly but the tone was on the edge of surly. Pletkin, Emil saw, was in a state of cognitive dissonance. He was set up to receive some well-connected stripling from the city, and instead he was having to make his obliging little speech, in front of all his people, to someone who looked like a tramp.

'He'm covered in shit!' said an old man who came up no further than the middle of Emil's chest. 'Magda's boy from the city, he'm covered in shit!' He began to wheeze with laughter. His next neighbour – beard, rags of a Red Army jacket – reached out and slapped him round the head with the mild exasperation of someone clouting a malfunctioning radio. Emil blinked, but Pletkin brightened, as if he had been provided with an axiom he could trust: *no one important is covered in shit*.

'Don't mind grandad there,' he said. 'But I've got to say, son, you are a hell of a mess. Come on down to the office and have a wash. All the home comforts. You won't find any of that in there, you know' – jerking his thumb at the dark door of the hut.

'Thanks,' said Emil, 'but I'm expected.'

'Suit yourself,' said Pletkin. 'Change your mind, want some hot water, come on over. Right, everyone who's not in this happy gathering, clear off. There's work to do.' And he ambled away, scratching his armpit. Emil saw that he had a rolled-up newspaper tucked into the straining equator of his pants, like a holstered weapon. Judging by the headline, it was the day before yesterday's. Prick, thought Emil; but he also felt a pang of anxiety as Pletkin left him to the closed faces of the villagers. For a moment even Magda's seemed to be sealed away from him into unfriendly strangeness. It was the reverse of what he had felt only a few minutes before. He was suddenly afraid he wouldn't be able to find the city girl in a village girl's face.

'Mister, welcome, you're most welcome,' said Magda's mother, who had evidently rehearsed her line and needed to say it. 'Welcome to the house and welcome to the family. Won't you come in and take a little drink.'

'It's a pleasure to meet to you. Please, call me Emil,' said Emil, and they stood aside and let him in. Inside, the house was a clutter of shadows, slowly resolving into wooden furniture and objects dangling from low rafters. Also, he couldn't help noticing, the house smelled, with the strong odours of humans living close together, laid down in layers over time and engrained in the woodwork, he guessed, to the point that you'd probably have to burn the place down altogether to dislodge the laminated fug of sweat and smoke and human waste. That blur of painted glass and tin plate over there must be an icon, the first Emil had ever seen that wasn't in a museum. Other figures crowded through the door, blocking off the light: Magda, her father, the old man, the fellow who'd slapped him. His eyes were still adjusting. Magda's mother seated him at the table and in front of him put a jamjar two-thirds filled with something clear. The men sat down opposite, a grimly nervous tribunal.

'My father you've met,' said Magda. 'My grandfather; my big brother Sasha.'

They got jars too. Emil sniffed his, trying not to be noticed. It wasn't water.

'Homebrew,' Magda muttered in his ear. 'A social necessity. Drink up.'

Emil tipped a mouthful into himself, cautiously. The caution was pointless: a tide of alcoholic fire flowed in across his tongue, hit his uvula with a splash and burned its way down his throat. After the burn came a fiercely warm afterglow, in which it became possible to taste what he'd just swallowed. It was faintly soapy, faintly stale. However they made it, the homebrew must be getting on for pure alcohol, much stronger than bottled vodka.

'Good stuff,' he said, and was pleased to find his voice was steady, not comically scorched. 'A toast,' he said, and held up the jamjar. 'To journey's end and new beginnings.' To himself, he sounded plainly fake; as theatrical as some perfect-vowelled stage actor hamming the part of the son-in-law from the metropolis. But they seemed to like it. They nodded, and gulped gravely at their jars. He gulped again too, and while he was recovering from the tide of fire, Magda's mother deftly topped him up from an ancient jerrycan, which was not what he'd had in mind. A tin plate of sunflower seeds appeared. Magda was hovering behind him somewhere. He could feel her ironic gaze on his neck.

'To marriage, then,' said Magda's father. Swig.

'Yeah, to the bride and groom,' said Sasha. Swig. Come on, this is better, thought Emil, this is going to be OK.

'To Christ and his saints,' said her grandfather. Silence.

'Grandad here is getting a bit confused,' offered Magda's mother.

'Soft in the head,' agreed Sasha, grinning with fury behind his teeth, and lifted a hand.

'I don't mind drinking to that,' Emil said hastily. 'It's what my grandfather says,' he said, though it wasn't, his grandfather having been brought up, long ago, as a good Kazan Muslim. Swig. Wary eyes everywhere.

'I told you,' said Magda from the shadows. 'Emil is all right.'

'I hope I am,' he said, a little approximately. He was feeling the firewater. Various things inside him seemed to be coming unscrewed, desocketed. 'I hope I'll be able to do you some good, you know, now that I'm in the family.'

'How's that?' said Magda's father.

'Tell them where your job's going to be,' said Magda.

'Well . . .' he said. It had seemed much less certain a thing to boast about, since he arrived in the village; but she was insistent.

'Go on, tell them.'

'Well, come September, I'll be working for, for' – no need to get into the detail of the bureaucracy – 'the Central Committee.'

'What,' said her father slowly, 'like, at the district office?'

'Er, no –' began Emil, but Magda interrupted.

'He means *the* Central Committee. Of the Soviet Union.'

Silence. Magda's dad looked at him as if he had just lost whatever comprehensibility he might ever have had; as if he had just been transformed into some dangerous mythological creature, right there at the table. But Sasha gave a long, low whistle.

'Don't you get it?' he said to his father. 'We're going to have a friend up top. *Right* up top.'

'Family,' corrected Magda.

Sasha grinned, properly this time, teeth gleaming in his beard. 'Oh,' he said, 'Pletkin is going to shit himself.' Caressingly: 'He is going. To. *Shit* himself. Why didn't you tell him, just now? You could have wiped the floor with him, the fat fucker.'

'I don't know,' said Emil. 'I suppose I didn't want to embarrass him. I thought he might, you know, take it out on you all somehow.'

'Nah,' said Sasha, thinking about it, 'too cowardly. Don't worry about him. Oh, this is going to be so sweet. C'mon, ma, give him a refill.'

Swig. Swig.

'I was thinking,' said Emil, 'that I could get you stuff from the shops. In Moscow. And later, you know, that maybe I could do something to fix the shop here. I don't quite get why it's like that.' He didn't. The shop should have been the village's connection to the general movement of the Soviet economy, the point at which the value they created – since they were independent producers, albeit collectivised ones – flowed back to them in the form of goods.

'Like what?' said Magda's father.

'Emil has never been anywhere off the road before,' explained Magda.

'For instance,' said Emil, 'I'm sorry, I don't mean to be rude, but I don't see how it can possibly absorb your incomes. Would you mind telling me what you earn?'

'How much do you want us to be earning?' asked Magda's father suspiciously.

'Dad, it's all right. It's really all right. You can talk to him.'

And they did, in dribs and drabs, with many swigs of homebrew to moisten them, as if he were a prince in disguise, travelling with a chest of gold to reward the virtuous and put-upon. They talked to him, and he was appalled. The answer to his question was, literally, kopecks. At the price the state paid for the wheat they laboured six days a week to grow, nothing was left in Pletkin's account-books, effectively, to pay them a wage. Cash came, if it came, from selling the vegetables from the private plots behind the huts, at the kolkhoznik market in Alexandrovsk. Their relationship to the state was not an economic relationship at all; it was primitive extraction. It was very nearly robbery. Something must be done. Fortunately, he was the man to do it. This was a task for conscious arrangers if ever there was one.

'Don't worry,' he said. Swig. 'I'll sort it out.'

'Yes, brother,' said Sasha.

It seemed to be evening now. Magda's mother was lighting oil lamps. A number of people came and went, but Emil found it safest to concentrate on the lamplit wooden tabletop just in front of him.

'Go on, Grandad, give us a story,' someone said. 'How's your memory tonight? Got a whole one in there?'

'Well, I'll try,' said the old man doubtfully. 'In the thrice-ninth kingdom of the thrice-tenth land, there lived a poor man who had, uh, a miraculous horse. No, he bought the miraculous horse, he bought it with . . . Or was it a miraculous wife he had? Dammit, I used to know all of 'em. No, it's gone. I'll tell you what, though,' he said, 'I can sing you a song from that fillum the fellow with the van showed us.' And he launched quaveringly into a tune Emil just about recognised as the title song from the old musical, 'The Happy-Go-Lucky Guys'.

'Did something bad happen here?' asked Emil, muzzily. Sasha laughed. Magda leaned towards him, her face a pink whirl at the far end of a tunnel.

'Are you all right?' she asked. He was all right, he was very all right. Hadn't they covered that earlier? In fact he was having a new idea. He was thinking to himself that an economy told a kind of story, though not the sort you would find in a novel. In this story, many of the major characters would never even meet, yet they would act on each other's lives just as surely as if they jostled for space inside a single house, through the long chains by which value moved about. Tiny decisions in one place could

75

have cascading, giant effects elsewhere; conversely, what most absorbed the conscious attention of the characters – what broke their hearts, what they thought ordered or justified their lives – might have no effect whatsoever, dying away as if it had never happened at all. Yet impersonal forces could have drastically personal consequences, in this story, altering the whole basis on which people hoped and loved and worked. It would be a strange story to hear. At first it would seem to be a buzzing confusion, extending arbitrarily in directions that seemed to have nothing to do with each other. But little by little, if you were patient, its peculiar laws would become plain. In the end it would all make sense. Yes, thought Emil, it would all make sense in the end.

That was the flourish, just for fun –
The real tale has now begun!

PART II

The problem was that Marx had predicted the wrong revolution. He had said that socialism would come, not in backward agricultural Russia, but in the most developed and advanced industrial countries: in England, or Germany, or the United States. Capitalism (he'd argued) created misery, but it also created progress, and the revolution that was going to liberate mankind from misery would only happen once capitalism had contributed all the progress that it could, and all the misery too. At that point, there would be so much money invested by capitalists desperate to keep their profits up, that the infrastructure for producing things would have attained a state of near-perfection. At the same time, the search for higher profits would have driven the wages of the working class down to the point of near-destitution. It would be a world of wonderful machines and ragged humans. When the contradiction became unbearable, the workers would act. They would abolish a social system that was absurdly more savage and unsophisticated than the production lines in the factories. And paradise would very quickly lie within their grasp, because Marx expected that the victorious socialists of the future would be able to pick up the whole completed apparatus of capitalism – all its beautiful machinery – and carry it forward into the new society, still humming, still prodigally producing, only doing so now for the benefit of everybody, not for a tiny class of owners. There might be a need for a brief period of decisive government during the transition to the new world of plenty, but the 'dictatorship of the proletariat' Marx imagined was modelled on the 'dictatorships' of ancient Rome, when the republic would now and again draft some respected citizen to give orders in an emergency. The dictatorship of Cincinnatus lasted one day; then, having extracted the Roman army from the mess it was in, he went back to his plough. The dictatorship of the proletariat would presumably last a little longer, perhaps a few years. And of course there would also be an opportunity to improve on the sleek technology inherited from capitalism, now that society as a whole was pulling the levers of the engines of plenty. But it wouldn't take long. There'd be no need to build up productive capacity for the new world. Capitalism had already done that. Very soon, it would no longer be necessary even to share out the rewards of work in proportion to how much work people did. All the 'springs of co-operative wealth' would flow abundantly, and anyone could have anything, or be anything. No wonder that Marx's pictures of the society to come were so rare and so vague: it was going to be an idyll, a rather soft-focus gentlemanly idyll, in which the inherited production lines whirring away in the background allowed the humans in the foreground to play, 'to hunt in the morning, fish in the afternoon, rear cattle in the evening, criticise after dinner, just as I have a mind . . .'

None of this was of the slightest use to the Marxists trying to run the economy of Russia after 1917. The Soviet Union inherited very few whirring production lines. Marxists elsewhere, in the countries where the revolution was supposed to have happened, had settled down over the years since Marx's death as 'Social Democrats', running parliamentary political parties which used the votes of industrial workers to get exactly the kind of social improvements that Marx had said were impossible under capitalism. Social Democrats still dreamed of the socialist future; but here and now they were in the business of securing old-age pensions, unemployment insurance, free medical clinics, and kindergartens equipped with miniature pinewood chairs. Except in Russia, obscure despotic Russia, which had the oddest Social Democrats in the world. With almost no industrial workers to represent, the Bolshevik ('majority') faction of the Russian Social Democratic Party was a tiny, freakish cult, under the thumb of a charismatic minor aristocrat, V. I. Lenin, who had developed a doctrine of the party's, and by extension his own, infallibility. The Bolsheviks had no chance of influencing events, and certainly no chance at getting anywhere near political power, until the First World War turned Russian society upside down. In the chaos and economic collapse following the overthrow of the Tsar by disorganised liberals, they were able to use the discipline of the cult's membership to mount a coup d'état – and then to finesse themselves into the leadership of all those in Russia who were resisting the armed return of the old regime. Suddenly, a small collection of fanatics and opportunists found themselves running the country that least resembled Marx's description of a place ready for socialist revolution. Not only had capitalist development not reached its climax of perfection and desperation in Russia; it had barely even begun. Russia had fewer railroads, fewer roads and less electricity than any other European power. Its towns were stunted little venues for the gentry to buy riding boots. Most people were illiterate. Within living memory, the large majority of the population had been slaves. Despite this absence of all Marx's preconditions, the Bolsheviks tried anyway to get to paradise by the quick route, abolishing money and seizing food for the cities directly at gunpoint. The only results were to erase the little bit of industrial development that had taken place in Russia just before the First World War, and to create the first of many bouts of mass starvation. It became inescapably clear that, in Russia, socialism was going to have to do what Marx had never expected, and to carry out the task of development he'd seen as belonging strictly to capitalism. Socialism would have to mimic capitalism's ability to run an industrial revolution, to marshal investment, to build modern life. Socialism would have to compete with capitalism at doing the same things as capitalism.

But how?

There was in fact an international debate in the 1920s, partly prompted by the Bolsheviks' strange situation, over whether a state-run economy could really find substitutes for all of capitalism's working parts. No, said the Austrian economist Ludwig von Mises, it could not: in particular, it couldn't replace markets, and the market prices that made it possible to tell whether it was advantageous to produce any particular thing. Yes, it could, replied a gradually expanding group of socialist economists. A market was only a mathematical device for allocating goods to the highest bidder, and so a socialist state could easily equip itself with a replica marketplace, reduced entirely to maths. For a long time, the 'market socialists' were judged to have won the argument. The Bolsheviks, however, paid very little attention. Marx had not thought markets were very important – as far as he was concerned market prices just reflected the labour that had gone into products, plus some meaningless statistical fuzz – and the Bolsheviks were mining Marx's analysis of capitalism for hints to follow. They were not assembling an elegant mathematical version of capitalism as described by its twentieth-century theorists. They were building a brutish, pragmatic simulacrum of what Marx and Engels had seen in the boom towns of the mid-nineteenth century, in Manchester when its sky was dark at noon with coal smoke. And they didn't easily do debate, either. In their hands, Marx's temporary Roman-style dictatorship had become permanent rule by the Party itself, never to be challenged, never to be questioned. There had been supposed to be a space preserved inside the Party for experiment and policy-making, but the police methods used on the rest of Russian society crept inexorably inward. The space for safe talk shrank with the list of candidates to succeed Lenin as the embodiment of infallibility, till, with Stalin's victory over the last of his rivals, it closed altogether, and the apparatus of votes, committee reports and 'discussion journals' became purely ceremonious, a kind of fetish of a departed civilisation. The only necessary ideas about economics – and the only acceptable ones – were those embodied in the particular programme of crash industrialisation on which Stalin rose to total power.

They were not very complicated, these ideas. Until 1928, the year of Stalin's 'Great Break', the Soviet Union was a mixed economy. Industry was in the hands of the state but tailors' shops and private cafes were still open, and farms still belonged to the peasant families

*who'd received them when the Bolsheviks broke up the great estates.
Investment for industry, therefore, had to come the slow way, by
taxing the farmers; meanwhile the farmers' incomes made them
dangerously independent, and food prices bounced disconcertingly
up and down. Collectivisation saw to all these problems at once.
It killed several million more people in the short term, and
permanently dislocated the Soviet food supply; but forcing the whole
country population into collective farms let the central government
set the purchase prices paid for crops, and so let it take as large a
surplus for investment as it liked. In effect, all but a fraction of
the proceeds of farming became suddenly available for industry. In
the same way, nationalising all shops and eating places allowed the
state to take direct control of the proportion of the USSR's income
that was spent on consumption: and to lower it drastically, in
favour of investment again. The diverted funds went to start the
production lines going, to feed industries picked out for superfast
growth in the new Five-Year Plans. Which industries? The heavy
ones, of course; the ones supplying goods like steel and coal and
concrete and machine tools, which in turn could be used to bootstrap
other industries into existence. Marx had helpfully pointed out that
capitalist economies grow fastest when they are producing to expand
the production base itself. Stalin took the hint. Managers of plants
turning out 'producer goods' were given dizzily increasing targets for
output. If they met them, by whatever means they could contrive,
they would be rewarded – and the targets would increase the next
year by another leap and a bound. If they failed to meet them, they'd
be punished, often by death. When things went wrong, in Stalin's
industrial revolution, someone was always to blame.*

*Between them, these policies created a society that was utterly
hierarchical. Metaphysically speaking, Russian workers owned the
entire economy, with the Party acting as their proxy. But in practice,
from 8.30 a.m. on Monday morning to 6 p.m. on Saturday night,
when the work week ended, they were expected simply to obey. At the
very bottom of the heap came the prisoner-labourers of the Gulag.*

Stalin appears to have believed that, since according to Marx all value was created by labour, slave labour was a tremendous bargain. You got all that value, all that Arctic nickel mined and timber cut and rail track laid, for no wages, just a little millet soup. Then came the collective farmers, in theory free, effectively returned to the serfdom of their grandfathers, since they weren't issued with the internal passports which they'd have needed ever to leave the kolkhoz. A decisive step above them, in turn, came the swelling army of factory workers, almost all recent escapees or refugees from the land. It was not an easy existence, crowded into squalor in cities built for populations half the size, systematically deprived of consumer goods, exposed to splashing molten metal and unguarded machines that ripped off arms and legs. The spare income workers couldn't spend was raked off through compulsory 'bond purchases' and fed back into even more investment. Discipline at work was enforced through the criminal code. Arrive late three times in a row, and you were a 'saboteur'. Sentence: ten years.

But from the factory workers on up, this was also a society in a state of very high mobility, with fairytale-rapid rises for those who could fill the Soviet state's insatiable hunger for skills. The economy needed whole categories of trained people to spring into existence in the twinkling of an eye: teachers, nurses, doctors, chemists, metallurgists, pharmacists, electricians, telephonists, journalists, architects, designers, book-keepers, aviators, car drivers, truck drivers, locomotive drivers, and engineers, engineers, engineers of every description. Every new factory needed its cadre of managers, every level of the new bureaucracies handling retail and food distribution needed its office staff, every part of the apparatus of control and surveillance needed its white-collar specialists. If you could fill a quota, if you could talk the talk convincingly as laid down in Stalin's Short Course, while negotiating the subtler personal politics of the hierarchy, then a middle-class life beckoned in short order.

Or something grander still, especially once Stalin started purging away all the original Bolsheviks, and opened up every job but his own to the ambitious. You could go to work as a foreman in a textile plant in 1935, and be the commissar for the whole textile industry four years later: that was the fairytale rise of Alexei Nikolaevich Kosygin, for example, who will come into this story later. You could be an ex-coal miner with a gift of the gab and the knack of making Stalin feel unthreatened, and go in two years from semi-literate rural apparatchik to deputy mayor of Moscow. That was the upward ride of Nikita Khrushchev. You could be the mayor of a city at twenty-five, a minister of the state at thirty; and then, if you were unlucky or maladroit, a corpse at thirty-two, or maybe a prisoner in the nickel mines, having slid from the top of the Soviet ladder right back down its longest snake. But mishaps apart, life was pretty good up at the top, with a salary twenty times, thirty times the wages on the shopfloor, as steep a relative reward as the spoils of any capitalist executive. There'd be a car and a cook and a housekeeper, and a fur coat for Mrs Red Plenty to wear when the frost bit. There'd be a dacha in the country, from whose verandah the favoured citizen could survey the new world growing down below.

And it did grow. It was designed to. Market economies, so far as they were 'designed' at all, by their institutions and their laws, were designed to match buyers and sellers. They grew, but only because the sellers might decide, from the eagerness of the buyers, to make a little more of what they were selling, or because the buyers might decide to use what they'd bought to sell something else. Growth wasn't intrinsic. It wasn't in the essence of a market economy that it should always do a little more this year than it had last year. The planned economy, on the other hand, was created to accomplish exactly that. It was explicitly and deliberately a ratchet, designed to effect a one-way passage from scarcity to plenty by stepping up output each year, every year, year after year. Nothing else mattered: not profit, not the rate of industrial accidents, not the effect of the factories on the land or the air. The planned economy measured its success in terms of the amount of physical things *it produced. Money was treated as secondary, merely a tool for accounting. Indeed, there was a philosophical issue involved here, a point on which it was important for Soviet planners to feel that they were keeping faith with Marx, even if in almost every other respect their post-revolutionary world parted company with his. Theirs was a system that generated use-values rather than exchange-values, tangible human benefits rather than the marketplace delusion of value turned independent and imperious. For a society to produce less than it could, because people could not 'afford' the extra production, was ridiculous. By counting actual bags of cement rather than the phantom of cash, the Soviet economy was voting for reality, for the material world as it truly was in itself, rather than for the ideological hallucination. It was holding to the plain truth that more stuff was better than less. Instead of calculating Gross Domestic Product, the sum of all the incomes earned in a country, the USSR calculated Net Material Product, the country's total output of stuff – expressed, for convenience, in roubles.*

This made it difficult to compare Soviet growth with growth elsewhere. After the Second World War, when the numbers coming out of the Soviet Union started to become more and more worryingly radiant, it became a major preoccupation of the newly-formed CIA to try to translate the official Soviet figures from NMP to GDP, discounting for propaganda, guessing at suitable weighting for the value of products in the Soviet environment, subtracting items 'double-counted' in the NMP, like the steel that appeared there once as its naked new-forged self, twice when panel-beaten into an automobile. The CIA figures were always lower than the glowing stats from Moscow. Yet they were still worrying enough to cause heart-searching among Western governments, and anxious editorialising in Western newspapers, especially once the launch of Sputnik in October 1957 provided a neat symbol for backward Russia's sudden technological lift-off. For a while, in the late 1950s and early 1960s, people in the West felt the same mesmerised disquiet over Soviet growth that they were going to feel for Japanese growth in the 1970s and 1980s, and for Chinese and Indian growth from the

1990s on. Nor were they just being deceived. Beneath several layers of varnish, the phenomenon was real. Since the fall of the Soviet Union, and the opening of its archives, historians from both Russia and the West have recalculated the Soviet growth record one more time: and even using the most pessimistic of these newest estimates, all lower again than both the Kremlin's numbers and the CIA's, the Soviet Union still shows up as growing faster, in the 1950s, than any other country in the world except Japan. Officially, the Soviet economy grew 10.1% a year; according to the CIA, it grew 7% a year; now the estimates range upwards from 5% a year. That was still enough to squeak past West Germany, the other growth star of the period, and to cruise past the US average of around 3.3% a year for the decade.

On the strength of this performance – which they probably valued at their own, higher figure – Stalin's successors set about civilising their savage growth machine. The prisoners (or most of them) were released from the labour camps. The collective farmers were allowed to earn incomes visible without a microscope, and eventually given old-age pensions. Workers' wages were raised, and the salaries of the elite were capped, creating a much more egalitarian spread of income. To compensate managers, the stick of terror driving them was discarded too: reporting a bad year's growth now meant only a lousy bonus. The work day shrank to eight hours, the work week to five days. The millions of families squeezed into juddering tsarist tenements, and damp ex-ballrooms subdivided by walls of cardboard, were finally housed in brand-new suburbs. It was clear that another wave of investment was going to be needed, bigger if anything than the one before, to build the next generation of industries. There'd need to be factories soon turning out plastics, and artificial fibres, and equipment for the just-emerging technologies of information: but it all seemed to be affordable, now. The Soviet Union could give its populace some jam today, and reinvest for tomorrow, and pay the weapons bill of a superpower, all at once. The Bolshevik simulation of capitalism had vindicated itself. The Party could even afford to experiment with a little gingerly discussion; a little closely-monitored blowing of the dust off the abandoned mechanisms for talking about aims and objectives, priorities and possibilities, the road already travelled and the way ahead.

And this was fortunate, because as it happened the board of USSR Incorporated was in need of some expert advice. The growth figures were marvellous, amazing, outstanding – but there was something faintly disturbing about them, even in their rosiest versions. For a start, at a point when the plans called for growth to rise faster still, it was in fact slowing from one plan period to the next, not much, but unmistakeably. And then there was a devil in the detail of the amazing growth, if you looked closely. For each extra unit of output it gained, the Soviet Union was far more dependent than other countries on throwing in extra inputs: extra labour, extra raw materials, extra investment. The USSR got 65% of its output growth from extra inputs, compared to the USA's 33% and the frugal 8% achieved by France. This kind of 'extensive' growth (as opposed to the 'intensive' growth of rising productivity) came with built-in limits, and the Soviet economy was already nearing them. There weren't that many more extra Soviet citizens to employ; timber and minerals couldn't be slung into the maw of industry very much faster than they already were; and investment was a problem in itself, even for a government that could choose what money meant. Whisper it quietly, but the capital productivity of the USSR was a disgrace. The Soviet Union already got less return for its investments, in terms of extra output, than any of its capitalist rivals. Between 1950 and 1960, for instance, it had sunk 9.4% of extra capital a year into the economy, to earn only 5.8% a year more actual production. In effect, they were spraying Soviet industry with the money they had so painfully extracted from the populace, and wasting more than a third of it in the process.

Yet somehow this economy had to grow, and go on growing, without a pause. It wasn't just a question of overtaking the Americans. There were still people in the Soviet Union, at the beginning of the 1960s, who believed in Marx's original idyll: and one of them was the First Secretary of the Party, Nikita Sergeyevich Khrushchev. Somehow, the economy had to carry the citizens of the Bolshevik corporation all the way up the steepening slope of growth to the point where the growing blended into indistinguishable plenty, where the work of capitalism and its surrogate were done at last, where history resumed its rightful course; where the hunting started, and the fishing, and the criticising after dinner, and the technology of abundance would purr in the background like a contented cat.

But how?

'Why do you weep?' asked the wise wife.

'How can I help weeping?' replied the archer. 'The king has commanded me to make apple trees grow on both sides of the bridge, with ripe apples hanging on them, birds of paradise singing in them, and strange kittens mewing beneath them; if all this is not done by tomorrow, he will cut off my head.'

I.

Shadow Prices, 1960

'Is this heresy?' said Leonid Vitalevich, no longer a prodigy, no longer a spectre of thought haunting an oversized suit. Time had thickened him; turned him solid and anchored him to the ground. A Stalin Prize for mathematics had brought the family eggs, cheese, ham and a private car. But the hard white light of creation still shone from time to time inside him, indifferent to the changes of the flesh. He settled his glasses on his nose and patted his notes. 'It is not an unimportant question. If it *is* heresy to use these mathematical methods, then work on them will wait, unpublished, for another ten or fifteen years – and the chance of applying them will be lost. But if it is not, as I hope our conference will show, a wide space will open for them to be applied and developed. Undoubtedly they will have a positive effect on the national economy. The opportunity exists to save, not tens or hundreds of millions of roubles, but tens and hundreds of billions.'

We have so little practice at this, thought Academician Nemchinov, watching from the back of the seminar room with his eyes lidded, his arms folded comfortably over his belly. Soviet scientists had learned to be good at telling when the party line in their subject was about to change, like birds who deduce from a particular subtle vibration that the firm earth is firm no longer, and take flight just before the earthquake. But until recently they had not often had to exercise the skill of deciding for themselves whether it was time for a change of mind. A peculiar tension was in the room now, the tension of ambiguity in what had been one of the most warily docile of the sciences. It was not clear, yet, who was going to win the present argument; therefore, not clear where the party of safety was going to lie.

The people he had brought together were a mixture: technologists intoxicated by the new power of electronic computers, cyberneticians gripped by the fashionable vision of the planned economy as a complex control system, economists tired of their subject resembling theology more than it did science. Leonid Vitalevich's specific mathematical ideas would not be what mattered most to them. What they had in common, or rather what they *ought* to have in common, if they could persuade themselves it was possible, was the need for the plug of dead thought to be removed that was preventing all their various projects alike from developing. He himself had a nice little practical plan: he wanted to get software written, in the next four or five years, which would run the economy better than the blundering, improvising, suboptimal decisions of human planners.

'Hey,' murmured a latecomer, slipping into the neighbouring seat in a cloud of better-than-Soviet cologne.

'Emil! Good to see you.'

'I was wondering: would you introduce me to –' and he nodded forwards, very charming, very confident his interest would be welcome, with a little lift of his pointed chin.

Now there was a perplexing combination on the face of it: Emil Arslanovich, sitting pretty in the apparat, hard at work on the favoured Kremlin project of standardising wage rates, but spontaneously educating himself in mathematics, to the point where, it was rumoured, he was thinking seriously about shifting sideways into academia; and Leonid Vitalevich, who had invented a large part of what Emil was excitedly learning, yet whose idea of a political manoeuvre was to write a letter of terrifying frankness to the most powerful person he could think of. In fact, thought Nemchinov, it might not be a bad combination at all, since by all accounts and by his own observation, Emil had the connections and the worldly wisdom but lacked the true lizard-brained coldness of those on their way to the very top, those for whom ideas and people were only ever useful. He suspected Emil, beneath the urbanity, of being secretly in earnest.

'Surely, surely,' he whispered back. 'If you wait after the session, we'll walk together.'

'Wonderful. And how's it going?'

'Well – I think the bombardment is about to start . . .'

'Let me give a simple demonstration', Leonid Vitalevich was saying, 'of how much it matters which variant is chosen in the national plans, and therefore, how much it matters that a method should exist for selecting the better variant. After all, for every individual decision there may exist two, three or four possibilities that look equally plausible, making, altogether, when they are multiplied, innumerable billions of possible plans. Suppose, then, that we wish to produce two products, A and B, in equal proportions, and must split the production among three different factories, each of which has its own level of efficiency at producing A and at producing B. It may be, that by simply sharing the production equally between the factories, we would obtain an output of 7,600 of A, 7,400 of B. Almost the same number, certainly close enough to count as successful plan-fulfilment under the present system. Yet it may also be that another plan can result in output of 8,400 A, plus 8,400 B, with just the same outlay of labour, materials and factory time. Simply by organising production differently, we obtain perfect fulfilment of the requirement for equal output of the two products – and 13% more production. Where has the 13% come from? "Out of nothing", "out of mathematics"; or, more accurately, out of the optimising of the system of production as it already exists. This is – yes?'

Nemchinov leaned forward. A hand had gone up; not a hand belonging to one of the big names in old-fashioned political economy, since they had declined to come to Nemchinov's conference, perhaps judging that in this new time their appeals to philosophical authority might sound a little like calls for the police. The doubts of the old guard were being represented by middle-rankers. Disapproval from them didn't carry the same force, didn't convey quite the same weight of conclusive judgement. This was Boyarskii the statistician.

'Yes?'

'Professor, you're effectively quoting from your own book, aren't you? The much-criticised *Best Use of Economic Resources*. Condemned by reviewer after reviewer for the same fault, your naive flirtation with theories familiar to us from the works of bourgeois apologists . . .'

Boyarskii hesitated. Ah yes, thought Nemchinov, you're waiting for the sky to fall, as it always used to do if anyone spoke words like that; and instead there's only this silence. You're actually going to have to make the argument, I'm afraid.

'Naturally,' Boyarskii continued with awkward politeness, 'I don't say a word against the strictly mathematical part of your work. I'm sure we're all aware that a greater degree of quantitative analysis is essential to the refinement of our planning; and you have provided tools which, in limited areas, can clearly be of great assistance. In the same way, it's a matter of pride for all of us, I'm sure, that you should have independently originated the principles of, of –'

'– linear programming –'

'Thank you, linear programming, here in the Soviet Union, before it was discovered by scientists in the imperialist countries. Yet economics is not a science of quantity alone, is it? It is pre-eminently a science of quality, *the* science of quality, in which the meaning of economic phenomena, not just their magnitude, is revealed; and revealed how? Of course, by the rigorous application of Marxism–Leninism. It follows that economics is particularly based on *partiinost*, party-mindedness.

Mathematical investigations can only succeed if they proceed from the economic content disclosed by political economy. For example, political economy teaches us that the plans for the development of the socialist economy are an objective expression of socialism's economic laws. Yet in your book you refer to them as being just "collections of numbers": an expression, if I may say so, of spectacular disrespect for the socialist system. You have declined to be guided by political economy, and that is why, above all, you have made the error of ascribing to your mathematical discoveries a universal significance which they could only have in the fantasy worlds of those writing apologias for capitalism. I am referring to your so-called "objectively derived valuations" –'

'– objectively determined valuations –'

'Thank you; which you have extended from the modest, useful function you first gave them, until they cease to describe one quantitative aspect of the production process in an individual factory, and become instead a challenge to political economy's central truth, its great foundation stone: that all value is created by labour. "Shadow prices", I believe they're also called – and they are shadowy indeed, are they not? I refer you to your book, to Conclusion Six, where you are arguing that your valuations are "dynamic". You write, "any increase in the requirements of some article entails a corresponding increase in costs and consequently in its o.d. valuation. A decrease in requirements entails a reduction in its o.d. valuation." What is this, what can this possibly be, but a suggestion that value is determined by supply and demand? Supply and demand, for heaven's sake: bourgeois ideology's most transparent disguise for exploitation! Academician Nemchinov here criticises you on this very point, in his actual introduction to your book –'

Yes, thought Nemchinov, because nobody would have published the book if I hadn't, and my making a fool of myself was a price worth paying to get the ideas into circulation.

"'It is impossible to agree with the author's point of view; it must be rejected.'"

Another silence.

'Well,' said Leonid Vitalevich, 'let me say in passing that I think Vasily Sergeyevich' – a nod to Nemchinov at the back of the room – 'is mistaken to think that these are considerations which I am somehow bringing in unnecessarily to the analysis, or thinking up: they are *mathematical consequences* of the situation.'

Ah, Lyonya: endlessly patient with your enemies, angry with your friends.

'But I should like to answer properly, because this is a vital point. Naturally I do not doubt the great truth that all economic value is created by human labour. This is apparent even to mathematicians. The question is only, how this truth is to be best applied; how it is to be applied in a society where we are not aiming, like Marx, just to diagnose economic relationships, and to criticise them, but must manage them too; where we are obliged to be concrete and detailed in our thinking. For example.' Leonid Vitalevich pressed his fist to his mouth, and banged it there gently a couple of times, making eye contact with no one in the room. Then he straightened the little finger on that hand, waved it slowly twice in the air, and fixed his gaze again on Boyarskii. 'For example! Do you see my tie?'

Nemchinov had seen Leonid Vitalevich do this before, in lectures; turn staccato, and seemingly wander off into disconnected thoughts. In fact, he always made perfect sense, when you reassembled the fragmentary statements you had been given, afterwards, but Nemchinov hoped that this was going to be one of those occasions when the coherence was obvious at the time.

'Yes?' said Boyarskii warily.

'Made of rayon. Dyed blue. Cut and sewn at the Mayak works, but the fabric must've come from a supplier, first. We agree, then, that the value of the tie is determined by the work that went into it?'

'Of course. That's elementary.'

'The value is determined by the labour of processing the cellulose, spinning the threads, dying them, weaving them, moving them to Mayak in Moscow, cutting and sewing?'

'Yes! I don't see –'

'What amount?'

'I'm sorry?'

'What amount of labour is in my tie, exactly?'

'Obviously, I'm not in a position to know –'

'Then how would you put yourself in a position to know? Are there tables, somewhere, that record standardised quantities of labour for each of the actions involved in creating a necktie? Does a calculus exist for reducing the different kinds of labour involved, the different levels of skill, the duration, intensity, efficiency and so on, to one common denominator of labour-time? No: of course not. It is not surprising you cannot answer,' said Leonid Vitalevich kindly, 'because as a society we do not, in fact, handle labour-value quantitatively. Or rather, we do not do so in a direct way. It is always expressed in some synthetic form. We track value through a variety of indicators. Through the production norms given to enterprises, which state that a plant employing such-and-such a number of workers can be expected to turn out such-a-such a number of finished items in such-and-such an amount of time. Or, most obviously, through prices. But prices are acknowledged to be highly imperfect indicators of value, since they are set at such long intervals; and so, I and other economists are arguing, are the enterprise indicators as they exist at present. At present, our system of norms frequently produces perverse results, perverse situations in which a plan that benefits an individual enterprise does not benefit the national economy as a whole; or vice versa. So what, in essence, I am proposing – I and others who are at work in this area – is a new form of indirect indicator for labour value which would allow us to calculate, easily and straightforwardly, plans that are optimal all around. These indicators will be no less synthetic than those we already use, but no more synthetic either, and there is no reason to believe that they will not capture the deep truth of labour-value just as well.'

'But what about the evident similarity between your "valuations" and the market prices of a capitalist economy?' asked Boyarskii, who was sounding rather strained.

'It's true that there is a formal resemblance,' said Leonid Vitalevich. 'But they have a completely different origin, and therefore a completely different meaning. Whereas market prices are formed spontaneously, objective valuations – shadow prices – must be computed on the basis of an optimal plan. As the plan targets change, the valuations change. They are subordinate to the very different production relationships of a socialist society. Yet, *yet*, the scope for their use is actually bigger under socialism. The capitalists actually agree with you, Dr Boyarskii, that the mathematical methods we're talking about should only be applied on the small scale, on the level of the individual firm. They have no choice: there is no larger structure, in the economy of West Germany or the United States, in which they can be set to work. They have had some success, I believe. I'm sorry to say that, since George Danzig and Tjalling Koopmans made their discoveries of "linear programming" in America during the war, the techniques have been adopted there far more eagerly, far more quickly, than in the Soviet Union. Linear programmers in the USA calculate routes for airlines, and devise the investment policies of Wall Street corporations. But we still have an opportunity before us which is closed to the capitalists. Capitalism cannot calculate an optimum for a whole economy at once. We can. There is a fundamental harmony between optimal planning and the nature of socialist society.

'We can,' repeated Leonid Vitalevich, 'and therefore we must. It is our intellectual responsibility. Academician Nemchinov, when he was introducing me, declared that I should be working out algorithms to manage the national economy. I would say, rather, that that is work for the entire collective of Soviet economists, mathematicians and specialists in computer technology.'

The applause seemed to shrivel Boyarskii where he sat.

'I will just say one more word, about computers.'

Good, thought Nemchinov. This coalition we're building needs the programmers, and the statistical bureaucrats who'll like the budgets the computers bring.

'In my opinion it is not the lack of them that has held up the development of mathematical methods. There are ways we could have calculated optimal plans by counting on our fingers.'

Oh.

'But there is no doubt that electronic computers will immeasurably strengthen our ability to handle large and complex problems. And they have, moreover, the great virtue of requiring clarity from us. I'm afraid that the computer cannot digest some of our economists' scholarly products. Long talks and articles which people think they understand prove impossible to put into logical, into algorithmic, form. It turns out that, once you remove everything that's said "in general", once you pour away all the water, there's nothing left. Well, either nothing . . . or one biq question mark . . .'

'Ouch!' hissed Emil appreciatively to Nemchinov, through the laughter. People began to gather up papers and briefcases. 'That's fierce stuff. He must be . . . quite an operator?'

'Oh no,' said Nemchinov, looking at him closely. 'To the contrary. To the *absolute* contrary.'

'Really?'

'Yes, really. Come on, and I'll tell you outside.'

*

Outside, a spring afternoon of white and grey was blowing itself out in a wind with a renewed edge of winter frost to it, like a blunt knife resharpened. The snow had gone, though, except for the last few tenacious mounds, blue-black with city dirt, and smoothed by repeated thawing and refreezing until they looked strangely dorsal; as if a pod of whales were swimming up Krasikov Street through the ground, breaching the asphalt here and there with their rounded backs. Emil and Nemchinov waited on the portico of the Academy, two men pulling black overcoats close around them. In fact, two men pulling close exactly the same black overcoat: 'coat, winter, men's, part-silk lining, wool worsted tricot, cloth group 29–32', as the Ministry of Trade's retail handbook put it. Despite the bite in the air, pigeons on the shoulders of the granite giants holding up the Academy's facade were throatily crooning, and stepping out shuffling dances, puffed up to soft balls of feather and claw. The taxis passing on Krasikova had their headlamps lit.

Emil found that Leonid Vitalevich's final joke was still affecting him, still somehow tickling him internally. He felt giddy, bemused, oddly happy. There seemed to be more open space around him than he had realised; more elbow room for ideas. He shook his head and offered Nemchinov an American cigarette.

'Thank you, I won't,' said the Academician. 'Look, the thing about Leonid Vitalevich is that he argues like that because he believes, he *genuinely* believes, that it's argument that settles the issue. He is not scoring political points, or pleasing his friends, or giving shrewd knocks to his enemies. He expects to persuade people. He thinks that scientists are rational beings who respond to logic if you show it to them. Of course, he judges everybody by himself. *He* makes his mind up according to induction and deduction. Therefore, everyone does.'

'An innocent, then?' said Emil, intensely curious; curious too that the patron of a cause in academic politics would be willing to talk like this, to a relative stranger, about the person whose reputation was one of his main assets. It seemed to be an invitation to intimacy; but not necessarily with Nemchinov.

'A passionate innocent. Who knows, maybe even a holy innocent. It makes him . . . a little *literal* in his dealings with the world. He tends to think that the rules on display truly are the rules of the game. His book – I don't know if you know, but he wrote it a long time ago now, it was certainly finished by the end of the war, and ever since he has been lobbying and lobbying, and not always in the most careful way, to get it printed. Well, *he* probably thought he was being careful. You've read *Best Use*, yes? The text is supposedly aimed at managers, so it's nice and simple, with lots of demonstrations of how you can do linear programming on your fingers, or at least on an office slide rule. All the implications are in the maths. But it's still, by definition, an unorthodox book, certainly for the time of the, ah, cult of personality. It's a piece of unrequested, unsponsored technical thinking, by an outsider, about a subject of, ah, *intense* political attention, and it's written in a way that pays almost no notice to the formulas of political economy. So what does our Leonid Vitalevich do, once it's become clear that, so far as the planners understand them, his ideas are as welcome as shit on a new carpet? He petitions, like a woman whose husband's been arrested, or a collective-farm worker with a grudge. He writes to Stalin.'

'You're kidding . . .'

'No; and more than once too; and his manuscript goes up and down in the world, round and round. It has *adventures*, this stack of pages. I don't know all of them, but I heard the story of what happened when it landed on the chairman's desk at Gosplan. "Better get some advice," he thinks, and he calls in the head of his prices department. "Read this" – and he hands him the book, which is probably a bit dog-eared by now. Couple of days later, back comes his guy. "So whaddaya think?" says the chairman, "should we be printing this?" "Oh no," comes the answer. "It's nothing important, and politically, it's impossible." "Oh?" says the chairman. "Well, should we be arresting the fellow, then?" "Hmm," says his guy. "No, I don't think so," he says; "I wouldn't really call him anti-Soviet. He obviously *means* well."'

'Shit . . .'

'Yes indeed, shit. Close enough to hear the whisper of the axe, as you might say.'

'Which chairman – ?'

'Voznesensky, before *he* got the chop from Stalin in '49.'

Emil stubbed out his cigarette, and absently lit another straight away, thinking about the great silence that had fallen in Soviet economics, and about the number of scholars who had been winnowed out of the subject without ever having done anything as obtrusive or spectacular as petitioning Stalin on behalf of a heretical book; who had softly and silently departed for short lives chipping at the permafrost in Norilsk or the Kolyma, despite having done everything in their power to avoid risk. It was not a comfortable train of thought, and this was clearly the moment to make his excuses and walk away. Nemchinov was waiting for him to do just that, if he wanted to. Emil's laughter was well quenched already. But something persisted, perhaps: a reckless ghost of the hilarity he had been feeling as the conversation began, a faint and uncalculating wish for the sensation of extra thinking room not to disappear as quickly as it had come. His thoughts skittered about.

'Why isn't he dead?' he said eventually.

'That is a good question. After all, meaning well hasn't been a completely adequate shield in this century of ours. I don't know. Maybe blind luck. Maybe because he did, let's say, a little work with Academician Sobolev when there was mathematical heavy lifting needed for *this*." Nemchinov clasped his elderly fingers together, popped them out into a fist-sized mushroom cloud. *Bouf*, his lips formed. 'Which brings a little gratitude with it, and consequently a little latitude. Ah, here he comes.'

Leonid Vitalevich had stepped out of the triple-glass main door, proof against Moscow blizzards, and was detaching himself from a group in animated conversation. Emil and Nemchinov watched him walk towards them along the colonnade of bowed stone titans.

'In my opinion,' said Nemchinov calmly, but with a clear sense of the closing distance, 'if you care for the ideas we discussed today, if you care about bringing a semblance of rationality back to our economics, then you are obliged to feel a duty to Leonid Vitalevich. He's cut out to be the citizen of a much more sensible world, and he needs the help of those of us who are better adapted to this one. Friendship with him is a trust. If you follow me.'

'I do,' said Emil.

'Good. Lyonya, well done, well done! I thought that went very well. I don't think you've met Emil, have you?'

'No, I don't think so,' said Leonid Vitalevich, putting down his briefcase. 'I know your work, of course, and . . . could I have seen you at the Institute of Electronic Control Machines?'

'Probably with a stack of punched cards in my hand,' Emil agreed, 'waiting my turn to feed the M-2. Yes, I do a bit of work there from time to time; we're trying to get a fuller picture of labour expenses into the model of the inter-branch balance. But you know how it is. You wait months for the processing time, you finally get assigned a slot and it's at 2.15 a.m., and then some valve or other blows and the system goes down.'

'Emil is resisting the temptations of the scholar's life, at the moment,' said Nemchinov. 'Probably because of experiences like that.'

'Actually,' Emil said, 'it's a temptation I've tried to give in to. I put in for a transfer to full-time research, but it was blocked; the old guys at the Committee for Labour won't let me go. "Come on, boy, science is two days' work and five days' holidays! What sort of life is that for a young man?" Nothing counts but epic toil among the paper clips.'

'Have you thought about going east?' said Leonid Vitalevich.

'East?' For an instant Emil thought that Leonid Vitalevich had somehow guessed the subject of the previous conversation, picked up a molecule of fear hanging about in the gusty air.

'To Novosibirsk,' explained Nemchinov. 'The Academy's new science city? Leonid Vitalevich is moving there later this year with a group of his graduate students, to set up a lab.'

'Yes; and the Academy's managed to get a special decree authorising release from any job – any job at all, I believe – if you're someone the Siberian Division wants to employ. Might be worth looking into, if you're really interested.'

'Quite a nice package,' said Nemchinov. 'Mimeo reports to be circulated without pre-approval; new journals if you want to start one; decent company to work in. Economics, maths, biology, geology, automation research, physics. A cyclotron or two for the physicists to play with; a computer centre for everyone else. Machine time on demand, apparently. Apartments half a hectare wide, to compensate for life on the banks of the Ob. No, ah, *nationality* issues. And political backing for useful results. We're expecting to see quite a piece of what we need come out of there.'

'We might get somewhere at last,' said Leonid Vitalevich. 'Without all the *nonsense*.'

'Without all the people like Boyarskii,' said Emil. 'All the economists who know the value of everything, and the price of nothing.'

'Oh – oh that's very good,' said Leonid Vitalevich. 'Forgive me, could I have one of your cigarettes?'

'Why Lyonya,' said Nemchinov, 'you don't smoke.'

'So I don't,' said Leonid Vitalevich.

He fished the filter-tip inexpertly out of the packet and leant forward to Emil's lighter, his hands cupped around the flame to block the wind. Emil, finding the wide tired eyes glistening so close to his own, also found that he did not agree with

Nemchinov, entirely. Leonid Vitalevich did not exactly look innocent; he looked like a man who knew the depths of the abysses beneath him, but whose nature compelled him always to be stepping ingenuously forward onto the wobbling plank bridges that spanned them. His fingers were trembling.

2.

From the Photograph, 1961

Electrons have no point of view. They form no opinions, make no judgements, commit no errors. Down at their scale, there are no opinions, judgements, or errors; only matter and energy, in a few configurations from which the whole lavish cosmos jigsaws itself together. Electrons move when forces act on their speck of negative electrical charge or on their infinitesimal pinpricks of mass. They do not choose to move; they do not *behave*, except in metaphor. Yet the metaphors creep in.

These electrons, for example, boil and jostle on the surface of their heated filament, as if it were a beach crowded by millions upon millions of sunbathers until the sand itself had vanished from sight. Normally, electrons in the atomic lattice of a piece of metal are free to flow along through the metal, creating a current. They can hop sideways from atom to atom. They can't jump off the metal altogether, because the positive charge in the nucleus of each atom holds them back. But the filament is glowing red-hot. It's being pumped up with extra energy in the form of heat, enough to break the bond that ties each electron to the metal, that grips each bather to the beach. They're scarcely attached to the lattice now. They're thronging its surface, ready to go if any other force sets them in motion.

And now a force does. Two centimetres away, an electrode flicks on. It's an anode, positively charged, and it pulls. The electrons surge forward off the filament in their millions: it's an exodus, it's a lemming-rush off the beach, it's an identical horde flinging itself into jabbering mass motion. To ensure that nothing gets in the way, that no electrons are batted off course by collisions with the gaseous soup of particles in air, the electrons fly into vacuum. In vacuum they surge, in vacuum they pour, through three electrified control grids. The grids smooth the motion out, and prevent any bouncing, or eddying, or unwanted reverse flows. They discipline the horde. Where electrons move there is by definition an electric current. So here, for the whole time the anode is switched on – one ten-thousandth of a second – a strictly one-way current flows to it across the vacuum. There is no build-up, no gentle curve of rising power. The current is either fully on, or it's fully off. A bulk process, full of statistical fuzz, where millions of particles mill around, has been converted into a completely determinate one, with just two states. Off or on. No voltage or high voltage. False or true. Zero or one.

Already, the flow of electrons is more than just mutely physical. It has been harnessed to the work of meaning, cajoled into making a picture that follows the simplest rule of picture-making imaginable, where there need only be a binary choice between showing a something or showing a nothing. Yet from this simplest yes–no choice, repeated and repeated, can mount up information's most complex structures, its most subtly shaded pictures, just as the few basic configurations of matter and energy, rightly arranged, can generate neutron stars, ice-cream cones and Politburo members. Here, the choice has been yes. This current, running for one ten-thousandth of a second, says yes. It says: on. It says: one.

We're inside a device which in American English is called a vacuum tube, and in British English a thermionic valve. To be precise, it's a pentode, so named because the filament and the anode and the three control grids make five powered components, inside the stumpy, evacuated cylinder of black glass. The pentode is one of forty-seven pentodes socketed into a big black circuit board; the circuit board is one of thirty-nine circuit boards arranged in a vertical rack; the rack is the arithmetical processor of the *Bystrodeystvuyushchaya Elektronno-Schyotnaya Mashina-2*;

and the BESM-2 is installed in the basement of the Institute of Precise Mechanics in Moscow, where it was designed. Midnight is long past. Hardly anyone is around. The night is trundling downwards towards that disconsolate moment of minimum when sheets of newspaper formerly used for wrapping fish blow about the deserted streets of Moscow, and human wishes all seem vain. But the BESM-2 is hard at work; and so is its designer Sergei Alexeievich Lebedev, sitting at his usual work-table and grinding out one after another of the cardboard butts of Kazbek-brand cigarettes. By now the night tastes of nothing but ash. But nicotine substitutes for food, nicotine substitutes for sleep, and there is so little time left for the future, once all the demands of the present are taken care of. Back in the war, when there were only his thoughts and no mechanism yet at all to vest them in, Lebedev sat up all night doing binary arithmetic by hand. How can he stop now, when computers exist – he built the first one in the Soviet Union himself, in 1951 – yet always fall so short of what might be? Every machine takes an age to perfect. Yet every machine leaves this maddening residue of new thoughts not acted on. Helpful toxins from the tobacco fields of Uzbekistan goad the blood in his veins to hurry. The BESM hums. There are more than four thousand vacuum tubes in there, all glowing red-hot behind smoked glass. Someone, somewhere, in the control room of this section of Moscow's power grid, is watching the BESM drain down as greedy a load as an average night-shift factory, all on its own – but for Lebedev the hum is a kindly womb of sound, provided by a machine of the present so that the machine of the future can come to birth.

Meanwhile, inside the BESM, the current that flowed through our pentode is triggering further currents in other pentodes on the same board, so that the binary 1 it represented is passed along through circuits representing logical operations on that digit. Not very complicated operations, not very abstruse logic. A pentode is plugged in line with another pentode, so both must be on for current to flow through from end to end. This is the logical relationship AND. A pentode is plugged in parallel with another pentode, so the current flows if either is on. This is the logical relationship OR. A pentode is plugged together with a signal inverter, so that the current switches off if it was on, and on if it was off. This is NOT. And that's all it takes. Wired together in the right order, these are the only moves required to mechanise the whole panoply of reasoning; to set the yes–no picture growing towards the complexity of a Rembrandt in the Hermitage. Sixteen of AND, six of OR and three of NOT, arranged in a branching tree, make this board capable of adding. It can add the 1 in our first pentode to a zero in another pentode, and produce (of course) 1; then add that 1 to another 1 carried over from a previous addition, and produce 0, with an extra 1 to be carried over in turn, down a wire to the circuit board next in the stack, where the next addition is about to commence. 1 plus 0 plus 1 equals 0, carry 1. Of course, Sergei Alexeievich, sitting up late in 1943 manipulating 1s and 0s with a pencil, could do this himself, and operations so much more demanding that the comparison is ridiculous. But he couldn't do it in one ten-thousandth of a second, and do it again ad infinitum every ten-thousandth of a second. Here's the power of the machine: that having broken arithmetic down into tiny idiot steps, it can then execute those steps at inhuman speed, forever. Or until a vacuum tube blows.

And in fact ten thousand operations per second is no longer so very fast, as these things go. The computer Lebedev is planning will, of course, use the new technology of transistors, and replace all of those red-hot filaments with modest semiconducting nuggets. But even with vacuum tubes, he can build a machine that runs far quicker. He has done it already: the BESM-2 is the cut-down civilian version of the M-20, so called because it works at twenty thousand operations a second. The M-20 has scarcely been glimpsed outside the laboratories run by the Ministry of

Middle Machine Building, whose middle machines are all the kind that have a blob of plutonium at their heart, and ride on top of missiles. Virtually the whole production run disappeared at once to the 'mailbox' towns you cannot find on any printed map. And, more secretly still, an M-40 exists, and an M-50 too. He built these to act as the brain of the USSR's embryo missile defence project. They sit at present in an air-conditioned bunker in the Kazakh desert, cabled up to six different radar installations as inputs, and to a ground-to-air rocket battery as an output. Silos over in the Ukraine lob dummy nukes eastward towards the test site. In the slim interval between detecting an incoming round and the moment it becomes too late to intercept it, Lebedev's computers have to calculate a course for the counter-missiles. Out in the desert a barbed-wire fence marks off a target zone exactly the size and shape of the city of Moscow. For two years, ICBMs dropped unmolested onto this imaginary metropolis; but then the machines started to score hits, putting the rocket streaking up from the ochre scrubland close enough, if it were loaded with its own live warhead, to have engulfed the attacker in a ball of nuclear fire. Lebedev isn't sure how practical he thinks it would be to defend the real Moscow with nuclear airbursts overhead. But some fine, demanding work has gone into making the system fast enough. Though it is only at the proof-of-concept stage, Khrushchev is already hinting and boasting about it at press conferences. 'We can shoot down a fly in outer space, you know,' says Mr K.

Tonight the BESM is calculating neither trajectories nor the destructive details of one of the Ministry's man-made suns. The stack of thirty-nine circuit boards finishes adding the string of binary digits it is working on; then does it again, and again, and again, because this is a multiplication, which the machine can only achieve by adding the amount it is multiplying, over and over, with lightning stupidity. A little over a hundredth of a second passes. The BESM has a result, and sends it out of the arithmetical processor altogether, a string of thirty-nine 1s and 0s to be parked in a row of the magnetised chunks of ferrite which serve as the BESM's memory. Another line of ferrite cores gives up another string of thirty-nine 1s and 0s, and sends it back to occupy the processor instead. This is not a number: it is the next line of the program the BESM is running. The first six digits are an instruction, telling the BESM to compare the result it just arrived at with a previous result, stored at an address in the memory indicated by the other thirty-three digits. Laboriously, shuffling numbers and pieces of program in and out of the one place where it can pay attention to them, like a person whose table-lamp illuminates only one little circle of a vast cluttered desk, the BESM discovers that the new number is larger than the old number. Now the program gives the BESM a command which is not absolute, but conditional, and we move from pure arithmetic into something different, into the world of supposition, of hypothesis, of what might be. If – says the program – the new number is larger, then twitch the figures slightly, by one pre-set increment, and go back; go back to an earlier step in the program itself, by fishing out of the line of the program to be found just *here*, and then proceed again through every step in between. The faithful idiot complies. Round it goes. It is executing a loop. Another hundredth of a second passes. And round it goes again; around and around. The BESM cycles tirelessly through the same instructions, working the same changes on very slightly different numbers. It will go on cycling round the loop till the comparison comes out differently. Ah: now it has. Meaning has been advanced. The picture has been dumbly refined. A picture of what?

Compared to the BESM's operations, so rapid and so simple, Sergei Alexievich's thoughts drift as slow as the blue twists curling up from his Kazbek, and expand in as many directions. He's reflecting, as he sometimes does, on the frustrations of working for the military. It's not that he has any problem with what his machines are used for, behind the wall of secrecy. He remembers – his generation can't forget – the locust advance of the Nazis in 1941 and 1942. He doesn't grudge any use of his time that helps prevent that terrible devouring from ever happening again. The trouble is that the secrecy is slowing down the technology. His own best work is sequestered. The military tuck it away where it cannot influence the state of the art; and since only a handful of finished machines are ever required, there is never the chance to find out what good things yet undreamed-of might come, if there were just the chance to *play* with the stupid power he creates. He has to admit, on the other hand, that there are compensations. The military are first in the queue for every scarce resource, and when you work for them, you borrow their standing as the country's most favoured customer. He smiles to himself, remembering the story his rival Izaak Bruk told him: a beautifully blatant demonstration, from ten years ago, of what military support could mean. Bruk had sent a graduate student to the Svetlana Vacuum Tube Factory in Leningrad to pick over the latest batch of pentodes, for with tube-based logic, the factor limiting the operating speed is the quality of the tubes. Plug-in rig to check the pentodes, letter of introduction – and the chief engineer at Svetlana still sent the boy away with a flea in his ear. But the physicists of the Soviet H-bomb project were clamouring for Bruk's machine at the Power Engineering Institute to be up and running, and he'd been given a phone number to ring in case of trouble, and a codeword flower to mention. The boy dialled the number. He said, 'I'm having some trouble buying my, er, tulips.' In an apartment on the Nevsky Prospekt, opposite a knitwear shop, polite people took down the details, and told the student to wait two days and try again. Two days, because 'We only act at the level of the Regional Party Committee', and it would take that long for the twisting of arms to work all the way back down to the Svetlana chief engineer. Sure enough, two days later the reception at the plant was all smiles. The Svetlana people couldn't do enough to load the student up with the very best they produced. This too, of course, was a loop; a very characteristic human loop in the Soviet economy. If the signal that a job's important isn't strong enough, it can be led away around a circuit of important human beings, each having a little word on the phone to the next, each boosting the signal, till it arrives back where it started, able to trigger action.

The BESM. A picture of what? Of potatoes. The electrons flowing through the vacuum tubes represent digits; and tonight the digits the BESM is processing represent potatoes. Not, of course, potatoes as they are in themselves, the actual tubers, so often frost-damaged or green with age or warty with sprouting tubercles – but potatoes abstracted, potatoes considered as information, travelling into Moscow from 348 delivering units to 215 consuming organisations. The BESM is applying Leonid Vitalevich's mathematics to the task of optimising potato delivery for the Moscow Regional Planning Agency. Seventy-five thousand different variables are involved, subject to 563 different constraints: this problem is out of reach of fingers and slide rules. But thanks to computers, thanks to the BESM's inhuman patience at iterating approximate answers over and over again, it is a problem that can be solved.

The BESM is using Leonid Vitalevich's shadow prices to do what a market in potatoes would do in a capitalist country – only better. When a market is matching supply with demand, it is the actual movement of the potatoes themselves from place to place, the actual sale of the potatoes at ever-shifting prices, which negotiates a solution, by trial and error. In the computer, the effect of a possible solution can be assessed without the wasteful real-world to-ing and fro-ing; and because the computer works at the speed of flying electrons, rather than the speed of a trundling vegetable truck, it can explore the whole of the mathematical space of possible solutions, and be sure to find the very best solution there is, instead of settling for the good-enough solution that would be all there was time for, in a working day with potatoes to deliver. You don't, in fact, have to look as far away as the capitalist countries to find a market for purposes of comparison. There is still a market in potatoes, right here in Moscow: the leftover scrap of capitalism represented by the capital's collective-farm bazaars, where individual kolkhozniks sell the produce from their private plots. Somehow, in the hardest times, there are always piles of green leeks here, and fat geese, and mushrooms smelling damply of the forest, and potatoes dug that morning; all so expensive you'd only shop here if money was no object, to stock up for a birthday or a wedding party. When the trade is briskest, the recording clerks sally out from the Ministry of Trade's little booths and walk among the stalls, carefully writing down prices. But how slow it is! How slowly things move, as customers jostle in these triangles of waste ground next to the city's bus stations and train stations, compared to the ten thousand operations per second of the BESM!

The market's clock speed is laughable. It computes at the rate of a babushka in a headscarf, laboriously breaking a two-rouble note for change and muttering the numbers under her breath. Its stock arrives one sack or basket at a time, clutched on a peasant lap. It calculates its prices on cardboard, with a stub of pencil. No wonder that Oskar Lange over in Warsaw gleefully calls the marketplace a 'primitive pre-electronic calculator'. In the age of the vacuum tube, it's an anachronism, good only for adding a small extra source of high-priced supply to the system, for those moments when the modern channels of distribution can't quite satisfy every consumer need. And now even that function is becoming obsolete. When Leonid Vitalevich's program reorganises Moscow's delivery system, the efficiency gains should fill the state shops with enough cheap potatoes for everyone. Now, as the seconds pass, the BESM is steadily shaving away the average potato delivery distance in the capital. At present, it seems, a spud must travel an average of 68.7 kilometres from cold-store to shop: but in the basement of the Institute of Precise Mechanics it is already clear that 61.3 kilometres is possible, 60.08 kilometres, 59.6 kilometres, and still the program is showing that the optimum has not yet been reached. The shorter the distance, the fresher the potato, the smaller the spoilage: this is the best index of success the programmers can come up with, since price as such is not available to them as a quantity to be minimised. The state selling price of potatoes has been fixed for many years. 57.9 km, 56.88 km. This is very nearly a 20% improvement. Soon Moscow's potato supply will be 20% better. 55.9 km, 54.6 km. It's a new world.

Ah, thinks Lebedev, the high-ups love this stuff. Always have done, since we turned the very first machine on. Nazarenko, from the Ukrainian Central Committee, came to see it, in the tumbledown monastery building outside Kiev where we built it. 'Sorcery!' he said, and winked, as if we'd just shown him the cleverest conjuring trick in the world. Which Lebedev supposes they had, in a way; thrown some wires and some vacuum tubes into a hat, and pulled free brainpower out of it. It was the kind of magic a good materialist could enjoy, certifiably the product of science even if it looked like a wonder out of the old tales. Ask the computer and it would obey, as ready as a genie in a bottle – and as intolerant of badly-framed wishes. At first the politicians had only wanted it to work its magic on weapons. Then, with Stalin dead, and a cautious pragmatism in the air, they'd been willing to see what else it might do; and now 'cybernetics' is universally caressed and endorsed, very nearly the official solution to every Soviet problem. Rumour has it that its magic will be brandished in the new Draft Programme for the Party, the document that is going to lay out Khrushchev's plan for reaching paradise. An obliging genie; a timely genie. If it can shoot down a fly in outer space, it can certainly sort out a few vegetables. And the best of the magic is, for the politicians, that computers promise to lend speed and decisiveness to what the Soviet Union does anyway. They'll make the plans run quicker. They won't require the digging up of what has already been achieved, or demand a reconfiguration of the world that might disturb things only just beneath the surface of this kinder time. Lebedev isn't so sure. He sees that new technology does need new forms of human organisation, to do it justice, to let it work the magic of which it is capable. The moment may come when the choice has to be made to accept the new machines' powers to disturb, or else to forgo what they can do. He hopes to be ready, with arguments and alliances, if that moment comes. Because, of course, his own choice is already long made.

It's time to call it a night. He gathers up his papers, slides them into the security briefcase he'll leave at the security post in the lobby. He cannot find his own work magical, not in any sense of the word that implies mystery. He knows its innards too well. And yet there's something about the way mute matter mounts up in his machines, and up and up, pattern upon pattern, until it manifests the patterns of thought, which still strikes him with reliable wonder. The earliest computer he built used sound waves echoing through mercury for a memory. The mercury is long gone, except in his imagination: where, with the logic of dreams, he knows his calling is to make thinking pools of quicksilver, with the world reflected in them.

In the bright pool of the BESM, images waver and crease of Moscow's 348 potato deliverers, its 215 potato consumers. The economists recognise the difficulty of getting a computer model to mirror the world truly. They distinguish between working *ot zadachi*, 'from the problem', and *ot fotografii*, 'from the photograph'. It would always be better to be able to work from the problem, and to make direct enquiries into how organisations really function, but usually it is only practical to work from the photograph, and to follow the data the organisations give you. This calculation, alas, is from the photograph. It deals with potato delivery as it has been reported to Leonid Vitalevich and his colleagues. There has been no time to visit the cold-stores, interview the managers, ride on the delivery trucks. But the program should still work. Conditionals, again: it will work, if the figures are reliable. It will work, if it is indeed possible to redirect the flows of potatoes at will in the way that the program decides is efficient. It will work, if the loops by which the program optimises are compatible with the loops in Soviet life that get things done.

It's a point of view.

3.

Stormy Applause, 1961

Lucky Sasha Galich. Lucky Sasha, with his cheekbones and his curly hair and his scarf tied loose round his neck like a banner of relaxation. Lucky Sasha, making it look easy, noodling at the keys of the piano in his flat full of antiques near Aeroflotkskaya, writing another hit song; or pecking out more witty dialogue on his neat little typewriter. A trifle grizzled as his forties began, but no less charming. Lucky Sasha, trusted and caressed, with his indulgent wife and his actress girlfriends and his trips to Paris. Foreigners liked him, but he knew his duty. He never crossed a line. He never caused unpleasantness. And so the rewards of talent showered down upon him. Lucky, lucky Sasha Galich.

He was early for lunch. He expected to wait, and having risen late with a slight legacy of the night before, was quite looking forward to a little indoor time, parked in the shade of a quiet corridor. But instead Morin's secretary ushered him straight across the main floor of the newspaper office to a glass-walled cube at the corner of the tower. The view down the boulevard pointed all the way to the Moscow River, and the clouds which had seemed to promise the first snow of autumn an hour ago had been driven back. Suddenly the city was roofed in bright air. Through the thick glass of windows, it looked as if it had been capped in a lens of blue.

Morin was in conference. A line of galley proofs was laid out on a long table, and he was steadying a particular page about two-thirds of the way along with his wide fingers, while a stringy woman in her late thirties bent over it, blue pencil in hand. As she spoke, a young man at Morin's elbow took rapid notes on a pad. There was another man in the room, much older, head sunk on his chest as he sat, not asleep but expressing inertia in his entire demeanour. This, Galich assumed, must be the paper's nominal editor, Morin's nominal boss: a relic, Morin had delicately hinted over the poker table, still grimly in post but reliant on Morin to handle the disconcerting ups and downs of the present. And the woman must be the in-house representative of Glavlit. Galich recognised the tableau from a thousand script meetings: Still Life, with Censor.

'Sasha!' said Morin. 'We're almost done. D'you want to take a seat for a minute or two? I'm sure no one will mind. Gentlemen, Marfa Timofeyevna, may I introduce Alexander Galich – author of many shows you've seen, and many songs I'm sure you whistle.'

Good grief, thought Sasha. The boy with the pad gave him a quick smile, from a face which close to had a sharp hungriness to it; an orphanage-grown face, maybe, once upon a time. The editor in the corner gave a grunt so neutral it was as if air had been expelled from a hole in the ground. Marfa Timofeyevna, though, smiled shyly, switched the blue pencil to her other hand and held out her right to be shaken, schoolgirl-wise.

'*The* Alexander Galich?' she said.

'Well,' said Sasha, 'the only one there is, at any rate.'

'I loved *Moscow Does Not Believe in Tears*,' she said. 'I thought it was just – so true. So understanding. And such a remarkable play for a man to have written.'

How wonderful, thought Sasha, the censor likes my work, the censor thinks I'm truthful. But immediately he found himself constructing lives for her, her with her carefully-chosen cardigan and her unfortunately large nose. *Lives with her mother, gallery-goer, takes along a miniature score to concerts. Never married. No: married once, but only for a year, and to a melancholic.* And automatically he gazed at her with warm eyes, and kept her hand in his for a moment longer than she was expecting.

'That's very kind of you,' he said. 'Of course, I mostly notice the imperfections in what I do. My women friends keep me on the straight and narrow; I find that simply listening to what they say is an enormous advantage for a writer who wants to create plausible female voices.' Skinny shanks, and probably hips like the bleached bones of a camel left in the desert to die. 'But look,' he went on, 'I mustn't keep you from your work.' He could see over their shoulders that the galleys bore a speech on them, a very long speech continuing in column after column of newsprint, and therefore probably the address that Khrushchev was due to give to the Party Congress today. Here and there the unspooling paragraphs were punctuated by italicised rapture. Simple '(*Applause*)' over and over; Khrushchev being Khrushchev an occasional outbreak of '(*Laughter*)'; but as the speech gathered pace, '(*Prolonged applause*)', and for the real peaks of excitement, the accolade a Soviet audience was never known to withhold, '(*Stormy applause*)'. The speech might be being printed before Mr K. actually gave it, but Galich felt certain that the orchestration indicated by the galleys could be relied on. Those were certainly the moments when the two thousand delegates under the great Kremlin dome would boom out their approval. Would that a theatre crowd was so easy.

'Please,' he repeated, 'don't mind me.'

'That's right,' said Morin smoothly. 'We had better just let Marfa Timofeyevna finish keeping *us* on the straight and narrow.'

Somehow his tone as he said this managed to suggest both that censorship was silly, and that it was silly to mind it. Galich conceded Morin a small internal round of (*Applause*), his headache whispering in his temples. He was highly accomplished himself at finding pleasure-giving, urbane descriptions of what couldn't be helped, but Morin, moreover, had hit the precise note of the moment, liberally-minded yet unchallenging, ironic yet inoffensive.

The three bent back to their task. Morin smacked his lips together, as they worked, in a series of cheerful little musical pops. It was the same sound he had made two nights before, contemplating the cards in his hand, and surprisingly effective at concealing how good they were. Galich dumped his satchel at the end of a long, deep, editorial sofa, and sat down, ready to make conversation if required with the discarded grey monolith in the corner: but the editor-in-name-only continued to stare dourly into space. His age put him in the right generation to have inherited the paper sometime in the late thirties, the Morin of his time perhaps, perfectly fluent in the brutish language of that moment and so ready to rise when all the intellectual types with funny-sounding surnames were shaken out of the Soviet newspaper business. Galich had been, what, twenty, riding the metro daily to his classes at the Stanislavsky Studio. Playing the guitar in the park. Falling in love. Getting laid. Getting elated. Getting his own first, all too successful sense of how to speak the dialect of the age, and how to bend it towards happy laughter.

Back issues of the paper were arranged in a rack. He pulled one out at random and shook it open like a screen in front of his face.

Letters; letters from readers across the whole double-page spread. This was an issue from a few weeks ago, he saw, during the famous consultation with the public over the Draft Programme. Like all the others, Morin's paper had been crammed. Rank by rank, column by column, eager citizens had written in with their tuppenyworth. Morin's paper being a metropolitan, enlightened affair, with an educated readership, a lot of the correspondence dwelt approvingly on the Draft's proposals to open up local Party elections to multiple candidates, and to impose term limits for officials. A Corresponding Member of the Academy, no less, had suggested that the Party should commit itself to 'protecting in every way the rights of Soviet citizens'. But there were suggestions on an incredible scattering of subjects. In the abundant future, there should be more planting of peas, please; more atheism; more tea-rooms; more television parlours in boarding-houses for single people; more labour-saving devices; more help for inventors; more defence lawyers; more deputies in the Supreme Soviet; more taxis. And all of the suggestions, on every subject, were enthusiastic. Galich had no idea how spontaneous the letters could possibly be. Some were clearly generated by local Party meetings obediently feeding back the chosen themes of the moment. But the effect was not quite the usual one of seeing the citizenry of the Soviet Union claim that their every happiness was already embodied in some policy or other. Here, people seemed to be trying to add their own wishes to the giant tower of wishes reared up by the Draft Programme. They were sticking their wishes to the surfaces, they were poking their wishes into the crannies of Mr K.'s promise to make them the richest people in the world. People were dreaming the dream along with him; they were worrying, worrying *helpfully*, over its details. Take the man who wanted more taxis. He'd noticed that the Draft guaranteed an automobile for every family, and not just any automobile either but one which, like all material blessings of full communism, would be 'of considerably higher quality than the best products of capitalism'. All well and good; but where would they be parked, these Zhigulis so creamily powerful they put Porsche to shame, these Ladas purring more quietly than any Rolls-Royce, these Volgas whose doors clunked shut with a heavy perfection that reduced Mercedes-Benz to impotent envy? Had the Party considered the number of garages that would be required? The 'deleterious effect on the hygienic conditions of city life'? The extra roadworks? The – Galich shut his eyes behind the newspaper, and let the traffic problems of the radiant future deliquesce into a field of orange and scarlet, criss-crossed with shadows.

'Done,' said Morin cheerfully. 'Where are we going, then, maestro?'

Galich rose renewed, face adjusted, from the foam of Soviet newsprint.

'I thought the Writers' Union? Not too far for you, and I've got to head out of town this afternoon.'

'Very good, very good,' said Morin, rubbing his hands in a pantomime of greed. 'I ate there last month, and it was dee-licious. Im-peccable. A real treat.'

Morin pulled on a raincoat and led him back through the newsroom, greeting, flirting, finger-pointing as he went, surprisingly light on his feet for a big man. Outside, the day had brightened one notch more; the snow cloud had retreated to the north-east corner of the heavens and was staying there, a knot of white held back by some invisible counter-attack of high pressure. The rest of the sky had the clean richness of high summer, only without heat or dazzle. It had become one of those days when everything looks its best. The walls of Moscow were dusted with light. New concrete, bricks and stucco, old plaster tinted in the edible palate of ice cream, mosaic on the merchants' mansions, ruddy statues of the gods and goddesses of Soviet plenty – all of a sudden, everything glowed.

'You seem to be on good terms with your Miss Marfa,' said Galich in the taxi.

'Not as good as you, my friend. I've been working with her for two years, but thirty seconds of your acquaintance, and whoosh, the air was turning to steam . . .'

They laughed.

'Not my type,' said Galich.

'Seriously,' Morin went on, 'I do think it's worth trying for as much, ah, mutual respect as possible. We all know how it can chafe at times. But you know the usual way things go, with the Glavlit rep as the perpetual outsider, always resented, always glanced at, always the bad guy who stops the writers doing what they want to do; and always knowing it too. In my experience, if you treat someone that way, they live up to it, or rather down to it. They'll say no out of spite. But this way, you show a little respect, you build up a little trust, and it's . . . money in the bank. Glavlit aren't unreasonable, if you approach them the right way. They have their responsibilities, of course, who doesn't, but there's always a certain amount of room for manoeuvre, if you've shown yourself trustworthy. And Marfa Timofeyevna is a woman with some sensibility, you saw that. I don't know if you saw the Yevtushenko poem we were able to run, last month? It was very good; very strong.'

'No, I must have missed that.'

'Ah well, the point is that when it mattered, when there was something I really needed to get through, I could. I could look after my writers: that's extremely important to me.'

Galich nodded sagely. Ah, that kind of lunch. But what if, he didn't say, the censor's spite was not just their own? What if the spite was shared and obdurate, and offered no room for manoeuvre, could be eased by no amount of charm? A couple of years back, judging that the spasm of hate stirred up by Stalin would have died away, and normal service been resumed, he'd dusted down an old play of his, about a typical Soviet family, by chance a Jewish one, and their struggles in the Patriotic War. In the stalls, at the rehearsal mounted for her, the censor turned to him and said, 'Oh, so the Jews won the war for us now, did they?' Nod and smile, nod and smile; back away from the misstep, Mr Sasha Ginzburg-working-as-Galich, before the contamination could spread. For a moment there, just a minute ago, he had thought that Morin meant to point out how convenient it was, always having the censor take the blame; and that would have been interesting, that might have been the seed from which more than a professional friendship could grow; but really, uncomfortable thoughts didn't seem to be in Morin's style.

'You're well yourself?' he said, smiling across the back seat.

'Oh, the usual ups and downs. My wife is trying to carry off the most complicated dacha-swap you could possibly imagine, and we keep having to have these cantankerous old bastards to dinner, from the committee; and my son finishes at MSU this next summer, and the grad school he wants is like gold dust – you know. Busy, busy, busy. Or, no,' went on Morin grinning, 'I suppose you *don't* know. It's bachelor freedom all the way with you, isn't it?'

'I'm married!' protested Galich.

'Well, technically. From what I hear, not in any way that, uh, slows you down,' said Morin. 'You probably can't even imagine these . . . domestic chains and shackles.'

'Oh, I do try to *imagine* them. For *material*, you see. I'm a very sympathetic person.'

'Mm-hmm, mm-hmm. Actually, talking of busy – I'd better say, I shouldn't stay out of the office for too long. It's quite a newsday.'

'The Congress, of course?'

'The Congress of course. And everything that goes with it. Not that I'm expecting too many surprises' – another finely calibrated twinkle – 'but there's a lot to cover today. Just look at it all.'

Galich looked. They were swinging around the Inner Ring, crossing Gorky Street, Nikitskaya Street, the Arbat, all the radial avenues that led inwards towards the Kremlin. Each of them was a corridor of flags. But where, in the past, the mood aimed for at Congress time had been spartan determination, now the effect was lighter. Happiness, said the city's decor; hope, it added; youth, it remarked. And for once the real Muscovites seemed to harmonise with the message, rather than letting it down with their lumpish private faces. This year, the Party Congress was promising a future, not of sacrifice, but of a myriad everyday satisfactions rolled together into one ball of achievable desire, and crowds who undoubtedly dreamed of flats and cars, televisions and fresh fruit salad, flowed along the sidewalks, stepping easy; welled up at metro signs from the underground kingdom of granite and chrome, rock crystal and gilt. Girls dressed for colder weather carried their coats, checked their reflections in shop windows. *Stilyagi* sauntered by, quiffed and narrow-lapelled, too cool to flirt. Taxis idled at red lights, gunned forward in unison on the green. And outside the hotels, middle-aged women with clipboards marshalled hordes of Africans in dashikis, slouching Cubans, Indonesians in little round red hats, Egyptians in dress uniform, angular Indians elegant in saris and Nehru jackets, Iranians and Arabs and Mongols and Koreans and Japanese. Moscow, capital of half the world; Moscow, with its best bib and tucker on. The skyline was spires and monoliths, Deco ziggurats and barbers'-pole chimneys belching smoke, all twinkling, all glittering, all shining in the sun. It should have made his heart lift. Lord knows, he preferred this version of his city to the ragged place in which he had first been one of the lucky ones. It almost looked like the hospitable home for a million separate stories which every great city was. It almost looked like Paris. But he had seen Paris. Moreover he worked in film: he saw this city, and he couldn't help but notice the way its surfaces habitually turned face-outward to be seen, instead of inwards for the comfort of the inhabitants. He recognised the thinness of the scrim, the cutting of corners where the audience would have its attention elsewhere and be content to register a general blur of grandeur. Those doors would be out of focus anyway: who needed to make sure they actually fitted their frames? The skyscrapers blocked out bold volumes of air, the walls of the city were receding planes, leading the eye back to a sky painted on glass. Moscow was a set, and like all sets looked more convincing from the middle distance than close up. He had started to brood lately on what was behind it; on what you would find if you peeled back a corner of the painted hardboard.

*

Some kind of international problem had broken out on the kerb outside the Writers' Union. Grigoriy, the doorman, was barring the way to two obvious foreigners. 'No – no – closed,' he kept saying, loud and simple and desperate, but they were gesturing angrily towards the dining room clearly visible through the ground-floor windows, where waiters were coming and going with steaming trays.

'Mr Galich,' said Grigoriy with relief, 'can you talk to these two? They don't understand a word I say.'

'Sh-sh-sh-sh. That's fine, that's no problem. Let's all just calm down. Er – *Deutsch? Italiano? Français? Ah, Français. Messieurs, je vous prie de nous excuser, mais ici, c'est pas un restaurant, c'est le club privé des écrivains sovietiques.* I'm telling them this isn't a restaurant.'

'*Ah merde,*' said the shorter of the Frenchmen, who had black bristles for hair and the jowls of a disappointed dog. '*Est-ce que ce ville ne contient pas vraiment un seul café ouvert, un seul petit bistro?*' Does this town really not possess one single open cafe, just one little bistro?

How to explain; how to explain that the doors of Moscow's eating-places indeed opened only to those entitled to pass through them, and that there were remarkably few places where you could hope to be fed simply by turning up with money. These two should be eating their lunch with the delegation they came with. They must have wandered enterprisingly off, to fend for themselves. Somewhere, a woman with a clipboard was tearing her hair out. Ah –

'*Par hasard, vous êtes peut-etre des journalistes?*'

'*Oui,*' said the Frenchman cautiously. '*Agence France-Presse.*'

'They're journalists. Grigoriy, I'm going to let them in. My responsibility: I'll sort it out upstairs. *En ce cas,*' he said smiling, '*vous vous trouvez chez vous. Un maison des écrivains, c'est aussi naturellement un maison des journalistes. Nous vous souhaitons la bienvenue, commes nos invités.*' And having told them that a house of writers was a house of journalists too, and welcomed them as guests, he ushered them up the steps, followed by Morin, amused but hanging unobtrusively behind.

'Is this really all right, Mr Galich?' said Grigoriy.

'Yes. Don't worry.'

In fact it took twenty minutes in the secretariat upstairs to clear what he had done, and to see to it that Intourist would send a car after lunch to collect the lost sheep. When he made it back down to the dining room – having been waylaid to sign a petition protesting some new slander broadcast by Radio Free Europe – the French pair were settled at an obscure table, eyeing the linen and the silverware and the painted panelling. He supposed they would get served eventually. Morin was waiting at a rather better table, and had been equipped with a glass of wine. He was taking in the celebrity floorshow – Ehrenburg holding court; Sholokhov, in town for the Congress, already rosy round the chops and a little loud – but also covertly glancing at his watch.

'I'm so sorry,' Sasha said, slipping into his seat. '– Yes, another glass of that for me, please. Are you still doing the veal? Good. Veal for us both.'

'It's all right,' said Morin. 'You're a man of impulse, that's all.'

'I don't know,' Galich said. 'It just seemed to me that two plates of lunch were a price worth paying for a favourable view of the Soviet Union.'

'There you are, you see,' said Morin, pointing a big finger at him, hairy-knuckled. '*That's* the kind of fearless thinking we need these days. Responsible, sincere –' More mottoes of the Thaw.

'Oh, shut up.'

'All right, all right. But I mean it. Listen, since time is tight: I do have a business proposition for you.'

'I thought you might. Go on.'

'Well. We're running a series. "Life in 1980". The idea being to put some, ah, meat on the bones of the future, to bring it to life for readers, from various different points of view. You know, political, economic, cultural, and so on.'

The veal arrived: escalopes in a cream sauce with peppercorns, on a bed of rice. Morin cut his up, speared a morsel and chewed blissfully. 'What did I say? Ex-quisite.' Galich waited. 'The problem', said Morin, waving his fork, 'is that they're all coming in a bit *dry*. Take a look at this – in confidence, of course,' and he reached under the table to his briefcase and rummaged out a few pages of typescript.

'The Universal Abundance of Products', read Galich. He took out a pair of reading glasses he preferred not to put on in public, and leafed forward through the papers. 'Food', he read, 'should be tasty, varied and healthy, and have nothing in common with the primitive gluttony of curs or the perverted gourmandism of plutocrats . . . Each member of society', he read, 'will obtain a sufficient amount of comfortable, practical and handsome clothing, undergarments, footwear, etc., but this in no way presupposes superfluousness or extravagance.' He began to laugh quietly, and went on laughing as the author explained how, in 1980, everyone's need for 'cultural goods' would be fully satisfied, but it would be sufficient to be able to borrow a musical instrument 'from the public store room'.

'That's it?' he said. 'That's *it*? The dream of the ages, and it comes down to mashed potatoes, woolly socks and shared use of a trombone?'

Morin smiled uneasily. 'As I said, it's a little dry; not very inspiring. That would be where you come in. We were thinking: a piece about the world of the future from the point of view of the human heart. How it will change us, how will it change the way we live and love, to be citizens of a time without scarcity? That sort of thing. The *private life* of the future – not a bad title, incidentally.'

'Come on, you don't need me. You want, what, a science-fiction writer.'

'No, no, we do *exactly* need you. We said to ourselves, we don't need anybody else who's an expert about the future; what we have to have is an expert in feeling. This' – he tapped the typescript – 'is all well and good, but it needs to be brought alive. It needs the little touches that say: real life is here. You can do that. You can make people believe in it.'

Oh Morin, fuck your mother.

'Do you believe it?' said Galich, and didn't realise for a moment that he had actually voiced it, this latest of the unaskable questions that lately ran in his head, through and beside and around the conversations he had aloud; reckless shadow repartee, plain and drastic instead of smoothly dabbed with nuance. There were ways to find out what people thought, and they were polite dances of implications, not this blunt public assault. It hadn't been a wish to know Morin's opinion that had caused the words to slip out of Galich's mouth now. But he had said them. There seemed little to do but to follow with a smile, as non-committal as possible, as sphinx-like, leaving Morin to wonder about his motives for the provocation.

Morin coloured. 'What a question!' he said. 'My subjective reactions are . . . I mean, we can have this conversation' – the poor boob really does want to be friends, thought Galich – 'but I don't think this is the time or the place, to, to . . . Yes, of course I do,' he went on angrily. 'Of course I believe it. This is a moment of justified optimism, based firmly on the foundations of science. The ascent towards communist abundance', he snapped, 'is a profound historical process in which, as a journalist, I am naturally proud to participate.' *Good enough for you?* said his eyes. He ran a hand back through the damp cow-lick on his forehead. 'Honestly! What has come over you?'

I don't know, Sasha thought. Embarrassing someone like that is the last thing I would do. It's dangerous, and worse still, it's naive. But I have to say, it doesn't feel bad.

The silence lengthened.

'Well,' said Morin, after a while. 'Will you do the piece?'

'I'll have to think about it,' he said.

Morin long gone, and another taxi, heading across the river in the stretching shadows of afternoon to his appointment at Mosfilm. The water swayed like dark-blue ink under the long bridges, crinkled here and there by the first licks of a breeze. Barges dragged triangles of churned white behind them. From the chocolate factory on the island opposite Christ the Saviour drifted clouds of insinuating sweetness, working their way through the seams of the cab and into the piebald upholstery. The driver had the radio on, relaying the opening speeches of the Congress and bursts of stormy applause, but Galich was gazing at his city again, and hearing the soundtrack it would have, if it were filmed on a day like today. Basso brass for the barges and the smokestacks, muted trumpets for the towers, tweedling clarinets for the pedestrians, skittering timpani for the traffic, all saying urgency, expectancy, hectic charm. Gorky Park unreeled to the right; offices and workshops, velodromes and slaughterhouses went by; at the bend of the river ahead, the ground curved up to a tree-lined ridge with the immense golden spike of the university rising behind it. What *has* come over me? thought Sasha. He remembered a joke. What is a question mark? An exclamation mark in middle age. Maybe that was all this was, just his arrival at a time of life when the muscles of certainty begin to go slack, and doubt naturally replaces vigour. Just the first delivery of the universal scepticism of old men. But then why did he find himself so much angrier than before?

It had been exciting, four or five years ago, to feel the space expand that a writer was allowed to work in. What could be said ballooned, not because it had become permissible to disagree about anything fundamental, but because suddenly it seemed that a huge area of human nature existed which could be explored without needing to jostle the orthodoxies. Possibility made Soviet literature dizzy for a while. You could write confused sons rather than authoritative fathers, disappointment rather than just contrasting shades of rapture, lyrical intimacy instead of monotonous epic. For a while, he scarcely cared about the limits of this new freedom, they were drawn so much further out than they had been, they pressed so much more lightly. But soon he found he had reached them all the same. The mere logic of devising characters more freely got him there. Why must the confusion of the sons always be dissolved away, at the end of the piece, into a goodwill felt by no person in particular, yet, somehow, all in general? Why, in a piece of work for grown-ups, must disappointment always be assuaged? Why must lyric defend nothing larger than the integrity of friendships round the kitchen table? If anything, the frustration was worse now than it had been before. He had not known what he was missing until he was arbitrarily allowed a fraction of it; that was part of it. And another part was that the reason for limits had departed. It had been acknowledged now, once for all, that life was not just the forward surge of a crowd, everyone singing and shouting, everyone moving with that tumbling impetuousness that in Soviet film made even showing up at the factory gate look like a spontaneous march on the Winter Palace. It had been admitted that other moods, other tones of voice, existed and were necessary. And with that, the rapture was gone.

The rapture had been real. He made himself remember that. He had had one of the happy childhoods Stalin had promised would someday be universal, and had ardently desired to defend it, to stop class enemies and kulaks and fascists from threatening the components of the good place he lived in, as he knew them: the hard earth path from the dacha to the lake, under the resiny pines, and the yellow oilcloth lampshade in his parents' book-filled apartment, and shovel-handed Masha the nanny, in whose name he loved all the peasant Mashas and Ivans populating the great cloudy landscape beyond the familiar streets. There was fear, too, as he got older; but never only fear. He and his friends admired their teachers, gazed up at the thrumming squadrons on Aviation Day, dreamed the approved dreams. He had been happy to serve. He had been happy to be squeezing up the aisles of the troop-trains, guitar held over his head, and to find that the stuff he'd practised really worked, compartments-full of tough and surly boys cracking into smiles at his teasing *chastushki*, singing along with 'The Little Blue Shawl', 'Lady Death' and his own 'Goodbye Mama, Don't Be Sad'. Tears in their eyes, some of them. Doubt had seemed a detail then; and he had moved through the dangerous world immune, encased in luck like a bullet-proof bubble. On one single occasion had he ever come close to danger, in '49, during the anti-cosmopolitan campaign, wandering on a vague impulse of solidarity into a meeting of the Writers' Union's Yiddish section. Suspicious faces turned towards him as he walked into the room; everyone there, of course, as good a Stalinist as him, but bearded, foreign, exuding a perfume of alien pickles. 'D'you speak Yiddish?' asked someone. 'No? Then fuck off, you louche little momzer. Visit your roots some other way. What, you think this is some kind of a Jew buffet? All the zhids you can eat? Out, out.' Two weeks later, the section was disbanded, and most of the people in the room were on their way to execution. Only then, reading the paper, did he understand that he'd been protected by the kindness of strangers.

Drip by drip, these last years, he had understood more of what had been happening in his own time, just around the corner, just behind the scenes, just out of his sight, as if he had been a child in a fairytale wood who sees only green leaves and songbirds ahead, because all the monsters are standing behind him. Quiet conversations with a returned choreographer, almost toothless, who'd survived his ten-year stretch on dancer's strength. Confidences from an uncle's friend, a secret policeman blurred by the bottle, who knew that young Sasha was *svoi*, one of us, and could be trusted; so talked, in a kind of laughing shame, a nightmare fit of giggles, about the famous year of 1937, when the vanloads came in so fast for the bullet that the drain in the floor of the basement corridor sometimes blocked, and some poor sod had to fish in it, and pull out mush and bonechips and hanks of human hair. Putting two and two together from the silences in old soldiers' talk. A little light reading done in Paris. The uncertain bursts of revelation in the newspapers at home, sanitised by code phrases about 'breaches of socialist legality'. Khrushchev's own secret speech of 1956, passed along to him in the little red booklet stamped NOT FOR THE PRESS. A drip of knowledge from here and a drip from there, till he saw that his lucky world was founded on horror. Like Peter the Great's city beside the Neva, his city was built upon a layer of crushed human beings, hundreds of thousands of them, or perhaps even millions. And you were not supposed to mind too much. It was enough to be assured that such things no longer happened, that mistakes had been made but were now corrected. It served no purpose to look back. It did no good to toss in bed in your elegant apartment and remember the ways in which you'd helped to give horror its showbiz smile, its interludes of song and dance.

And now, just when he was coming to hate his luck, it seemed to be spreading out, becoming general. He was not an economist; he had no idea what part of Khrushchev's promises was feasible. But the Sparrow Hills were one big building site. New boulevards marked out with pegs and string branched off a road that not long ago had been a one-lane strip of country blacktop. There were cranes on every rounded rise of ground, and concrete panels dangling from them swayed up to fill out the skeletons of endless new apartment buildings, blessed by the bright air today like every other surface. The pale panels were the hopeful white of clean pages. You could look at them and feel that cockroach days were nearly over for the people who didn't live among amber and inlay above Aeroflotskaya. No more scuttling in the dark and the damp for them. The city of light was rising in the Sparrow Hills.

'Lot going on,' said Galich, experimentally.

'Ah, Nikita Sergeyevich is a miracle worker!' said the taxi driver. Did he mean it? Or in other moods was he ready to pun on Mr K.'s name and the word for slums, and call these blocks *khrushchoby*? Impossible to tell; he'd said it in the deadpan style that refused to collapse into meaning just one thing. Normally Sasha admired this folk art of undecidedness, but today it only made him feel the more alone with his private clot of dark. Moscow glowed like an icon, the future shone, and only he was left out of the happy concord. At the next corner, a giant banner rippled and flapped against the end wall of a block, with the honest face of Yuri Gagarin on it, six storeys high, and underneath the words he was supposed to have said, back in April, when they lit the rocket beneath him: LET'S GO. Upwards with Yuri! Up to the stars; up Mr K.'s ladder to the heavens, whose foot stood in a mulch of blood and bone.

The radio roared its approval.

Lucky Sasha Galich. Lucky him, joking through the script conference; lucky him, chatting to the hoofers as they rehearse today's big number; lucky him, homeward bound with his latest beautiful young thing. Though later, after they've made love and he's asleep, she stands at his window overlooking Aeroflotskaya, smoking, and feeling that he withdrew from her into some place much further off than the slightly rueful place you always go, when joined skins separate back into two cooling island selves. '1980', blinks red neon in the distance, 1980, 1980, 1980, as if the figures were all the lullaby the city needs. It's started to rain. She'd meant to discuss with him a part she'd been offered, out of town, but the lead, and a good director; but somehow Sasha's charm never let up long enough to give her an opening. Yes, she thinks, she will go to Minsk. There's not much to keep her here.

'Do not worry, my soul,' said the wise wife. 'Go to sleep. The morning is wiser than the evening.'

PART III

In 1930 the Bolsheviks abolished universities. Only the two famous ones at Moscow and Leningrad survived, drastically truncated. But this was not an attack on education as such, as in Maoist China later, or still more so in Khmer Rouge Cambodia, where the authorities would aim at burning away intellectual life altogether and leaving a level plain of pure ignorance as the foundation for a new society. Nor was it an attempt to do without an intelligentsia. The universities were closed in order to open them again, massively expanded and redesigned as factories for the production of a new kind of intellectual.

The Bolsheviks had been having trouble with the old kind of intellectual ever since the revolution. The tiny professoriat they inherited – a fraction of an educated class which was itself a small fraction of Russia's literate minority – was shaped by an ethical tradition more than a century old. Pre-revolutionary Russian intellectuals felt a sense of public obligation not shared by their equivalents abroad. Since the beginning of the nineteenth century, it had been obvious to anyone educated that the tsarist regime was an embarrassing, oppressive anachronism. To be one of the lucky few who could read about the world outside therefore gave you a responsibility to try and do something about Russia; usually not in a directly political way, unless you were one of those with a very pronounced bump of idealism, but by building up an alternative Russia in culture, in novels and poetry and art where stupidity was not enthroned. Above all, to be an intellectual was to feel that you were, at least potentially, one of those who spoke truth to power. By teaching and learning at all, reading and writing at all, you were implicitly acting as a witness, as a prophet of a larger life.

These attitudes meant that while intellectuals largely welcomed the Revolution as the end of tsarism, very few of them signed up for Lenin's brand of Marxism, even when – or especially when – it had state power behind it. Indeed, a number of scholars who had been happy to teach Marxism before the Revolution, as a way of sticking a finger in the eye of power, promptly started offering courses in religious philosophy after it, to achieve the same effect. Most of the Party's own intellectuals were needed, in the early years, to keep the improvised apparatus of the Soviet Union going, so for a decade the universities were essentially left in the hands of the academics. The scholars were purged and sometimes deported; they had university rectors and department heads imposed on them; experiments with the admissions system gave them, some years, mostly war veterans or factory workers to teach; but they continued to offer an education in criticism and argument. College buildings were among the last places in the Soviet Union where it was still possible to find printed leaflets issued by the Central Committee, not of the Bolsheviks, but of the dying Mensheviks, forlornly calling for social democracy without dictatorship.

By the end of the 1920s, however, the Party was in a position to enforce ideological conformity. The first Five-Year Plan had just begun, and 'bourgeois specialists' were being hunted out of industry and government. With Narkompros, the 'Commissariat of Enlightenment', in the hands of Stalin's allies, the bourgeois specialists of education were next. 'It is time for Bolsheviks themselves to become specialists,' said Stalin in a speech. And 'the working class must create its own productive-technical intelligentsia'. He had in mind something very different from its predecessor: a service class, speedily and narrowly trained in the disciplines required to operate heavy industry, with membership held out as a reward for the loyal and the ambitious.

First, the universities were abolished. Then, they were replaced by a multitude of 'VUZy' and 'VTUZy', 'schools of higher learning' and 'schools of higher technical learning', usually all chaotically time-

sharing the same old buildings to maximise throughput. From the Agricultural College of Voronezh, for example, the Poultry Insitute of Voronezh inherited 'eight small benches, a corridor, and one lecture room (shared with the Mechanisation Institute)'. Students were drafted in in bulk from the Party itself, from its tame labour unions, from newly established shopfloors and the newly starving countryside. These vydvizhentsy, *'promotees', were indeed working-class, but mostly not in the European or American sense that they belonged to an existing, urbanised, long-disadvantaged mass of the industrial poor; they were representatives of a class that the Party's own policy of crash industrialisation was calling into being. Their numbers swelled the system enormously. Where there had been around thirty thousand old-style graduates a year before the change, there were getting on for a hundred thousand a year by the second half of the 1930s. In the Party alone, more than 110,000 people had studied for a degree, including Nikita Khrushchev, Alexei Kosygin and Leonid Brezhnev.*

By that time, things had settled down in higher education, from some points of view. Though spending was skimped – like spending on all present-tense human needs – enough money was put in to end the jostling scenes at the back of every lecture theatre, where twenty or thirty students had struggled to share a single textbook. Entry was, once again, by examination, and not just by political recommendation. The universities' traditional names and styles crept back, in line with Stalin's own preference for respectability and hierarchy. Stalin had been willing to work with educational radicals, as part of his meticulous campaign to destroy all the independent factions within the Party by feeding them to each other, one at a time, but once he was in a position to impose his tastes, he wanted to see tidy tsarist-style uniforms on high-school boys again. He wanted learning to look august and venerable. The Party's rival to the old autonomous Academy of Sciences was abandoned, and effort directed instead into making sure that the Academy became a pliable, reliable instrument of prestige.

But the change in the subject-matter of education was permanent. The old universities had taught the European liberal arts curriculum. All of that vanished, and technology took over. Almost half of all students now studied engineering, following a fiercely utilitarian curriculum designed to feed the economy with specific skills. When they graduated, they were supposed to know everything they required to go out solo and kick-start a power station, or a metals refinery, or a rail line. Next came the pure sciences, with physics and maths leading the way, chemistry a surprising poor relation, and biology in deep ideological trouble; then medicine, disproportionately studied by women, and 'agricultural science', intended to provide expertise to collective farms. Humanities departments were closed down altogether – though a few historians then had to be put back in business, in order to prepare school texts stuffed with figures and dates, and praise for previous centralising rulers. Literature became 'philology', a technical subject mainly devoted to teaching the many languages required to rule the Soviet Union. Philosophy died, anthropology died, sociology died, law and economics withered: the Party regarded 'social science' as its own private technology, to be taught to cadres within the Party itself, and dispensed to college students in the form of compulsory courses in Marxism–Leninism.

Culture ceased to be the responsibility of professors. New films, plays, books and poems emerged from the Film-Makers' Union and the Writers' Union; the old stuff, reduced to a conservative selection of classics, it became the duty of every ambitious citizen to know. The Party wished the Soviet public to be kulturny, *a term which stretched from brushing your teeth regularly to reading Pushkin and Tolstoy. There was an irony here. A hard-working promotee, with a nice clean background as a worker or a 'poor peasant', would get on in the world by carefully reading stories about aristocrats and princes and bourgeois functionaries – exactly the kind of people who would have been defined as 'socially alien', as 'enemies', if they were alive in the present. But it mattered far more that* War and Peace *or* Eugene Onegin *represented objects of guaranteed quality which ordinary people were now entitled to possess. None of that avant-garde hooting and face-pulling, thank you very much; just the best, the great works of the Russian past, in gold-stamped bindings you'd be proud to have on the shelf of your new apartment. And it wasn't as if continuity with the past was completely lacking. There was indeed a strand in the old intellectual tradition – half of its coiled DNA – which could be adapted as a credo for these rising Stalinist graduates. The Russian intelligentsia had always been committed to modernising Russia: and what were these chimneys but modernity on the march? It had always thought of culture as something operating top-down, an enlightenment spread to the many by the educated few: and what was the Bolshevik mission but an elite's twentieth-century effort to raise lumpish Russia high? It had always been prone to believing in panaceas, in ideas that could solve every problem all at once: and what was Bolshevism but the ultimate key to open all locks, the last and best and greatest system of human knowledge? Believing these things, the new technological intellectuals were willing to be told, were willing to believe, that the task of speaking truth to power was now redundant, because truth was in power. By definition, friends of truth, friends of thought and reason and humanity and beauty, were friends of the Party; friends of Stalin. To be opposed to the Party would be to become an enemy of truth, and to break the intellectual's reponsibility to truth.*

With a reliable substitute in place for the old intelligentsia, Stalin could afford to sweep away most of its surviving members in the purges of the late 1930s, along with most of his own political generation within the Party, and most of the people, formed by the pre-revolutionary world, who had risen to lead industry, the army, the state bureaucracies. He was left with the promotees: grateful, incurious, ignorant of the world outside the Soviet Union, and willing to accept the Stalinist order as the order of reality itself. A great silence reigned about the parts of intellectual life that had disappeared. Soon, young people were unaware that things had ever been otherwise. In the new curriculum, different subjects experienced different fates. The closer a science was to practicality, the more it was co-opted into serving the practical needs of power. The closer it was to the dangerous ground of social science, on the other hand, the more distorted by ideology it tended to become. And the more abstract it was, the more intellectually uncorrupted it was likely to remain. The result was a landscape of intellectual lives laid out very differently from its counterparts abroad. Where the United States (for example) was a society ruled by lawyers, with a deep well of campus idealism among literature professors and sociologists, the Soviet Union was a society ruled by engineers, with a well of idealism among mathematicians and physicists. Law, economics, history were sterile, insignificant fiefdoms, ruled by 'little Stalins', pint-sized intellectual stand-ins for the great mind in the Kremlin. After Stalin's death, these subjects had to be revived by incomers from engineering and the pure sciences – who brought with them the engineers' faith in the solvability of problems, and the scientists' uncompromising delight in pure pattern. Biology continued to be a disaster area. The little Stalin it had been handed to, Trofim Lysenko, was an anti-Darwinist charlatan who managed to adapt himself in the 1950s to playing on Khrushchev's insecurities.

By the 1960s, the Soviet Union had gone from being one of the most illiterate places on the planet to being, by some measures, one of the best educated. It turned out more graduates per head of population than any of the European countries; only the American college system, with its tradition of mass participation, did better. Entry was by competitive examination, set locally so that institutions could pick and choose exactly the intake they wanted. Courses lasted for four or five years, and students were expected to work steadily for thirty-five to forty-five hours a week, digesting the whole relevant body of knowledge in their subject. Nothing was dumbed-down except the Marxism – for having eliminated the tradition of independent Marxist thought in the 1930s, there was nowhere in the sciences to reignite it from. The drop-out rate was high, understandably; but every year almost half a million young men and women completed the ordeal, and stood in the corridors of their university searching through the thousands upon thousands of job offers posted there.

Universities were only for teaching, though. Research usually happened elsewhere, in special institutes operated by the Academy of Sciences or the various industrial ministries, with scholars flitting back and forth between their professorships and their labs. At the crown of the system were the 'science towns' built to house research work that had been designated as a strategic priority, from nuclear physics and aeronautics through to computer science and mathematical economics. The people who lived here were among the most privileged of Soviet citizens – and they were held up as well, in popular culture, as forerunners of the coming world of abundance. Not only did they live, right now, as all Soviet citizens were shortly going to live, with commodious flats and lavish food supplies and green spaces all around. They also worked, right now, in the way that everyone was supposed to, when abundance came – for the voluntary love of it, treating the working week as their playground rather than their burden. For the most part, scientists accepted the idolising, just as they mostly accepted the legitimacy of the arrangements of power in their society. Physicists themselves enjoyed Mikhail Romm's 1962 hit film, Nine Days in One Year, *about a driven, wisecracking nuclear researcher who irradiates himself so that humanity can have energy. A little later, they smiled at the gentle satire of the Strugatsky brothers' 1965 novel* Monday Begins on Saturday, *in which a secret department investigates, appropriately enough, the magical objects in Russian fairytales. The scientists were confident; and in a curious way, they were also innocent. By now, they usually didn't know what it was that they didn't know, about the non-Soviet experience of mankind. International contacts were opening back up, but from a very low level; 'special collections' of foreign material were available in libraries to senior scholars, but a separate permit was required on each visit, and you needed to know exactly what you were looking for. So they evolved their ideas with almost no reference to analogies, to parallel cases, to the accumulated mass of situations in history in which someone might have tried something similar. Above all, they had very little access to pessimism. Stories of good intentions turning out badly were in short supply where they lived – published, written-down stories, at any rate.*

But there were frustrations. All of a sudden, for example, in 1958, Khrushchev had announced that far too many of those getting into universities were themselves the children of intellectuals and white-collar workers – and passed a law that harked back to the wild old times of the First Five-Year Plan. School-leavers now had to do two years of work experience before they were let in. This was unpopular with students, unpopular with parents, and unpopular with academics, whose first-year physics students now had their fading knowledge from school overlaid by two years of semi-skilled drudgery in a warehouse or a factory. It also rankled with the intelligentsia that, having forsworn the more brutal methods of ensuring conformity, Khrushchev was now trying to achieve it by exhortation. Which meant that, from 1961 on, groups of intellectuals were gathered together to be shouted at; sometimes by Khrushchev's aide L. F. Ilichev, head of the Central Committee's Ideological Commission, and surprisingly often, in crude and ungrammatical Russian, by the man himself. (Contemporary joke: Khrushchev asks a friend to look over the text of one of his speeches. 'I can't deny, Nikita Sergeyevich, that I did find some errors. "Up yours" should be two separate words, and "shit-ass" is hyphenated.') There were more specific grievances if you were a serious biologist, obliged to disguise your real research behind screens of dissimulation; or if you were Jewish. In the 1930s, Soviet Jews had been perhaps the most spectacularly mobile and high-achieving group in the population, but the wave of official anti-Semitism from the late 1940s on had brought restrictions and quotas. Seen in absolute terms, more Jews than ever before were employed in the sciences in 1960 – 33,500 out of 350,000 Soviet 'scientific workers', or 9.5% of the total, when Jews made up only 1% of the Soviet population – but certain specialisms and certain elite institutions were closed to Jewish candidates altogether, and, on the whole, the route to the very top was blocked. You had to be unignorably brilliant, now, as a Jew, to be promoted as far as your ordinarily diligent and distinguished ethnically Russian colleagues – which left behind it the peculiar sting of a prize confiscated after it had once been given, of an acceptance turning conditional when you'd believed it was permanent.

Gradually, something unexpected was begining to happen. These frustrations, small and large, had started to draw the scientists' attention to a difference between the kind of educated they were, and the kind the vydvizhentsy *engineers running the Party were. The scientific method itself taught lessons, and so, in fact, did reading all that compulsory Tolstoy. When they reflected on the idiocy of anti-Semitism in the country that defeated Nazi Germany, when they heard of Khrushchev's red-faced rage over the Academy rejecting one of Lysenko's stooges, they started to suspect that truth and power might not be so united; that what was enthroned in Russia, after all, might be stupidity.*

These old men were not ordinary people; they were the Freezer, the Glutton, and the Magician. The Magician drew a picture of a boat on the sand, and said: 'Brothers, do you see this boat?' 'We see it.' 'Sit in it.' All of them sat in the boat. The Magician said: 'Now, little light boat, serve me as you have served me before.' Suddenly the boat rose in the air . . .

I.

Midsummer Night, 1962

It had all taken longer than it needed to, of course. The super at the block in which the institute thought it had booked her an apartment had no record of her, and when she followed the trail back to the central office for the allocation of housing, it turned out that there had been, a few months back, a dust-up between institutes over rights in the next blocks to be completed – and poor Cytology and Genetics had lost out, unofficially, to the physicists. Her promised flat had disappeared into a file. Instead of simply collecting the keys, she had had to get the Director's secretary to call the housing office, and to ask, as a special gesture of goodwill, for an apartment to be released. But it was done. The stairwell in the new building might be finished to roughly the look and standard of a coal cellar, but it led, up four flights, to a front door she could call her own; with, beyond it, quiet rooms filled only by late-afternoon sunlight and the shadows of leaves.

Dizzy with change she walked through her domain. Here would be her bed. Through here Max would sleep, with the door open a chink so he'd know his mama was still within reach, even though they were no longer sharing the fold-up couch under the oil painting. A room of his own: she could paint the alphabet on the wall, some cheerful animals maybe. Here they'd live, with the books lining the wall opposite the window, and a worktable like so, in the good light, which could be cleared for mealtimes. In the kitchen, predictably, only the cold tap worked. But you could manage perfectly well without piped hot water in summer; plenty of time to get things fixed up before Siberia began to show a less friendly face. She sat on the new linoleum of the kitchen floor and drew up knees to her chin. Too late today to start hustling for furniture, or to spy out the kindergarten situation; nothing she could be doing at the institute, till they issued her with a pass tomorrow. Max and her mother were still almost two days away, chugging east safe aboard the train she'd put them on in Leningrad, before making her own disbelieving way to the airport to present the institute's extravagant ticket. She hoped the other people in the compartment were making nice. A four-year-old with a habit of questions was not the easiest companion for a long journey. But there was nothing she could do about it if they weren't. She'd deal with the aftermath of the experience, whatever it had been like, when they arrived, and Max came out grubby and upset, or grubby and smiling, onto the platform in Novosibirsk; till then, they were out of reach, in a capsule that could not be opened for another two days. They were in suspension, and so till then must be the whole hyperactive part of her that schemed and fended and smoothed Max's path through the world, and explained (a big item recently) the different colours of sunlight and moonlight. Suspended; unneeded. It was the strangest feeling. She couldn't remember a time since Max had been born – certainly since his father had skedaddled – when nothing was expected of her. But now the impetus of the journey had run out, and deposited her, with nothing she ought to be attending to, in these empty rooms. The leaf shadows tossed slowly on the wall behind her. There seemed no particular reason why she should not go on sitting under them in vegetative silence until night fell and eased the dappling into the general dark. But she supposed she had better get up and do something about finding herself supper. In her bedroom-to-be, she opened her case and hesitated. Well, it was summer. She picked out the armless green dress; brushed her hair; went out.

Not knowing quite where she was going, she strolled. Men with briefcases, and a few women, were threading their way homeward around the brick-stacks and duckboards of a landscape that was still mainly a construction site. The concrete cliff-face of her block stood, with its trees, on a gentle slope grubbed full of holes for foundations not yet laid. Most of the labourers had already knocked off for the day; the last ones were closing down the drills and steam-shovels, and setting off downhill, smoking and talking. Probably, she thought, there was a model somewhere showing how the Academy's city of science was going to look when it was finished, all terribly clean and modern, the buildings immaculate white solids – but midway through the process, entropy was definitely defeating geometry. Mud was winning so far. Living in Leningrad, unfortunately, made a visual snob of you. If you were used to the casual beauty of the old capital, there was not much to get excited about in what she'd seen today. The flats were flats, no different from the blocks going up on muddy fields everywhere, and the institutes were standard lumps of public architecture, nondescript and undecorated. From close up, the wide grey frontage of Geology, where Cytology and Genetics had squatters' rights till a building of its own should appear, resolved into wavering courses of mud-grey blocks, alternating with mud-grey tiles, as if a clay mound in the approximate shape of a scientific institute had been reared up from the earth by termites. The clumsy corridors inside ignored the scale of the human body. They were sized for the convenience of giants. The doors of labs and offices came less than halfway up the slab walls. No, not much to please the eye in Akademgorodok. Not much beauty in Academyville.

But then the path she was following turned in among a denser group of trees, and delivered her, only a hundred metres on, into forest hush. Suddenly the path beneath her feet was carpeted with dry pine needles; suddenly the world was roofed with a speckled canopy of leaf and sky through which the sinking sun filtered only as a focus of greater brightness. Sounds were filtered too.

Now and again she could still hear the grinding of construction machinery, but it had become as tiny and unimportant as the buzz of the occasional bees that cruised between the tree trunks. The wood was a mix of pine and silver birch. The pines rose straight and slender as ship's masts, while the birches all tilted a few degrees away from the vertical, in different directions, like a vast game of spillikins. The pines' bark was a creased ruddy brown. The birches were paper white, marked with endlessly varying squiggled lesions of black: cuneiform, to go with the mud-brick monuments of the town, or magnified chromosomes, the chromosomes whose existence the Lysenkoists denied. The air smelled cleanly of resin. Knee-high, the undergrowth of bracken glowed with chlorophyll in the evening light, each frond a complex green lamp. Oh, now this was something. This was really something, this tall place of birdcage delicacy on the doorstep of the termite mound. She would need to adjust her idea of the town, if this was here to refresh the spirit on the way to every day in the lab, on the way back from every workplace tussle in the grey corridors. She tilted her head back and let the speckled sieve above shake photons gently down on her face.

'Excuse me,' said a voice behind her, male, elderly, patient, amused. She was blocking the path.

'Sorry,' she said, moving to one side. He stepped courteously by, a thin-necked sage holding a cardboard map tube, then paused; two young men backed up behind him paused in turn. It really was a commuter route, this path.

'Just arrived?'

'Yes.'

'Well then, welcome,' he said, with a bestowing nod. 'Welcome to the island' – and moved on. As the little column of three rounded the next corner of the path, one of the young men looked back over his shoulder and gave her an assessing stare. He was saying something to his friend as they went out of sight. 'Island?' she thought.

Beyond the wood, it turned out, lay the street with the town's services on it. Hotel, post office, movie theatre, central stores offering MILK and MEAT and VEGETABLES on their shopfronts, all more or less finished. Little buses and delivery vans came and went; the occasional car. And over here, by some minor but definite adjustment in the fall of the light, some invisible line ticked past on the clockface of the day, it was evening. The homeward stream of walking intellectuals had been joined by a contraflow of the intelligentsia coming back out again, combed and washed and in a fresh shirt, to take the air. *Progulka*, going for a wander: however much the government tried to fill up people's leisure time with bicycle races and extension classes and boxing clubs, you couldn't stop Russians heading out of doors in summer for a chat and a drink. Scientists were no different. Clusters of people had gathered around the noticeboards of the cinema, looking at the black-and-white stills from forthcoming attractions, and settling into the comfortable to-and-fro of colleagues off duty. She joined them. Somewhere around here there would be a cafeteria, the trick being to talk her way in without the institute pass.

'What *is* that supposed to be?' a man to her left was saying, pointing at a tacked-up glossy.

'A woman, you ape. Dear, dear, has it been that long?' said his friend.

'No, idiot, the machine behind her. The thing they're supposed to be working with in this, quote, "portrayal of the lives and hearts of our young scientists".'

The group peered.

'Part of an electricity sub-station?'

'An automated milk steriliser?'

'The illegitimate offspring of a cement mixer and your cyclotron.'

'For shame! Our cyclotron is a good girl, and would never consort with a ruffian like that.'

'And has she presented you with the plasma of your dreams yet?'

'Well, no.'

'Ah, you see, that's because she's sneaking out of the lab at night and having it away with agricultural equipment. She may say she cares for you and your tedious particles, but when it really comes down to it, she can't resist the masculine dribble of concrete from his enormous bucket.'

'You're a sick, sick man, Pavel.'

'Thank you.'

'They'll never make a movie about you.'

'I know.'

'Too disgusting.'

'Quite.'

'Actually, we did get some interesting results today. Budker thinks he may have found a way around the power fluctuations . . .'

'Hello, beautiful.' She assumed for a moment that this must be more of the physicists flirting with their experimental apparatus, but then a finger tapped her politely on the shoulder. She turned round. It was the two boys from the wood, spruced up slightly: one blond and bouffant, the speaker, and one dark, with his fringe lying on his forehead.

'Yes?' she said warily. 'What?'

'No offence,' he said. 'No offence, no problem, no difficulty at all –' all this said as fast as he if were performing a tonguetwister, with a consciously charming smile pulling up the corners of the lips he was moving prestissimo – 'don't want to bother you, particularly if for some reason you're not at ease with your own good looks' – momentary pause, eyes wide with comical sympathy – 'although you should know that we can help you with that –'

'*What?*'

'Nothing. Nothing at all. Just that me and my friend, we

overheard back there, and we thought, oh dear, new to town, doesn't know anybody yet, we really ought to show you around. Maybe you'd like to come to a party?'

'Valentin,' said the dark one, warningly. Not being the one responsible for discharging this flood-tide of blether, he had been looking at her, and had started to smile; not, she got the impression, at her expense, but at his friend's.

'It's a service', went on Valentin regardless, 'that we like to offer to new students; especially the pretty ones, I must confess, but there is, you know, real altruism in it too –'

'New *students?*' she said, beginning to laugh. 'How old do you think I am, exactly?'

'Er –'

'Tried to tell you,' put in the friend, helpfully.

'I'm sure this works brilliantly on eighteen-year-olds,' she said, 'but I am in fact a thirty-one-year-old. A thirty-one-year-old fruit-fly biologist, exhausted by plane travel and bureaucrats. Got any lines that work on one of those?'

Touchingly, Valentin blushed: a proper pink sunrise in both cheeks.

'Don't mind us,' said the friend, putting an arm round Valentin's shoulders and rotating him gently. 'We'll just creep away, embarrassed. Welcome!'

She looked back at the glass box of photographs. It made a dim mirror. That refracted blur in there, with the dark bob and the bare arms, that was her, and it was, she realised, all that the boys had seen, a face and a body unconnected to anything else. The fine chain-links of her commitments were quite invisible. They had not perceived her in relation to Max, or to her chosen position of elusive scorn in the politics of biology. They had had nothing to go on but *this*. She frowned; the woman in the glass, the girl in the glass, frowned back. No, it was impossible to take her for eighteen, if you were paying attention at all. But what else might you guess about this face if you could only guess?

Nothing it said about her was positively untrue, of course, but it only told partial truths, and she was out of practice at dealing with approaches that came unconditioned by knowledge of the rest of her. A couple of streetlamps had come on behind the mirror-woman's head, two blobs of blue-white that instantly organised the fading light into proper twilight, and the leaves around them into pierced balls of green. They loomed at the reflection's shoulders like will o' the wisps, night spirits come to orbit the black hair, the black eyes, the green dress. She'd be known here too, soon enough. This was only an interlude, and no time to make a fool of oneself. But the evening air was nice, cooler than the stale heat of the summertime city, and she was also, she discovered, suddenly very hungry.

The boys had not got very far up the sidewalk. Valentin's humiliated droop was already straightening out: she suspected that it never lasted very long.

'Wait!' she called. 'This party of yours – any food at it?'

'Should be,' said the friend. 'It's an official candidate-degree bash. Booze, dancing, banquet, the works. I'm Kostya, by the way.'

'Zoya.' They exchanged a comradely handshake.

'And Valentin, you've met.'

'Madame,' said Valentin, with a sketch of a bow.

'Hey, I'm not that old,' she said.

They were economists, or graduate students in economics to be precise, twenty-three and twenty-four, one in the economics lab at the Institute of Mathematics, one in the mathematical research lab at the Institute of Economics, both members of a seminar intended to train up the economic and the mathematical alike into cyberneticians. On this subject if on no other Valentin, she was interested to see, became gravely enthusiastic; Kostya seemed to be quiet and ironic on all subjects. When they weren't working, they hung out in their dorm rooms at the State

University a little further along under the trees, playing records, listening to the jazz programmes on Radio Iran, and trying to impress young girls.

'And what is your field?' asked Valentin politely.

'Mutagenesis,' she said. It was one of her rules that she would always name her research honestly, when asked about it. But it was up to the hearer what they were able to make of it. She saw no obligation to make life easy for the world's legion of fools.

'Meaning . . . change? Change in – ?'

'In the units of hereditary information.'

Valentin smiled. 'Around here, you know, you can just say "genes" and no one will faint with shock.'

'Hardly anyone,' corrected Kostya.

'All right. Hardly anyone. But you're mostly among friends. So, go on,' he prompted, 'change in the genes. What sort of change?'

Both of them were looking at her with an expression of sympathy she had sometimes encountered on the faces of senior physicists. It meant, *dear colleague, your subject is afflicted by the plague, and I pity you.* But was she really supposed to spill her guts to two complete strangers?

'Get used to it,' said Kostya. 'This town chatters, and it expects chatter in return.'

'I do *not* chatter,' said Valentin indignantly. 'I converse. I probe, I enquire; on occasion, I query –'

'All right, all right,' she said. 'I work on the genes that determine the mutation rate when an organism is under environmental pressure. Happy now?'

'I thought it was Lysenko's mob who claim that environment affects heredity?'

'They do. They say environmental influences rewrite the germline, which is rubbish. Changes always go from the genes to the body, not the other way around. But whether the body survives decides whether the genes survive, so the environment ultimately selects the genes, and it turns out that one thing a stressful environment selects for is a set of genes which encourage mutation.'

'There,' said Kostya. 'Was that so bad?'

'I don't know,' she said. 'Let's wait and see what happens because I said it.'

'It's a feedback loop, then?' said Valentin.

'If you like.'

'And there are genes that, what, tell other genes what to do? A kind of higher-level control system?'

'Yes. The mutator genes seem to turn mutation in other genes on and off.'

'Do you realise that's binary? This is great! You should come and tell us about it properly, the seminar I mean; give us some biological cybernetics to get our teeth into. I love the way this happens! Cybernetics as the universal language, translating between the sciences!'

'Is he serious?' she asked, glancing at Kostya.

'Oh yes.'

'Well, get me an invitation, and I'll give you a paper.'

'Done,' said Valentin. 'We'll get you invited before the evening's out.'

'And what do you work on, then?' she said to Kostya.

'Oh, you know,' he said, 'saving the world. Bringing about the golden age. Building the material-technical basis of full communism. The usual things. And here we are.'

The party, it seemed, was being held in the restaurant of the hotel. She expected that her deficit in ID would become a problem at the door, and require some fast talking, but no one asked for passes.

'On the whole, people don't,' said Kostya. 'It's fairly free and easy. Even in the institutes, if your face looks familiar you can come and go pretty much as you please.'

The tables had been pushed back against the walls to create a dancefloor. There was a crowd around the buffet, and another one in front of the gleaming battalion of bottles and glasses. Here, she saw, getting on for half the company were female, but if her experience of scientific life back in the city was anything to go by, the women would almost all fall into the species-categories *wife* or *girlfriend*, not *colleague*. If they worked in the institutes, it would be as secretaries or junior lab staff; otherwise, they'd be low-status riffraff like primary-school teachers or medical doctors. The green dress, she was glad to confirm from a rapid eye-gulp at the room, more than held up in comparison to the rose-print outfits favoured here by the middle-aged, and the predictable plumage of youth, innocence and availability adopted by the rest; as well it should, considering its painstaking relationship to a copy of Italian *Vogue* which had floated out of Moscow in the wake of the Party Congress last autumn and been captured by her circle of friends. Not that she had had many occasions till now to wear it; not that this wasn't the first evening in four years that she had spent out of reach of the sound of Max breathing; but a little sneer can be a comfort on the threshold of a roomful of strangers, in a strange town far from home. A blue roof of smoke was already thickening overhead, fed by the separate spires of many cigarettes. A jazz band was tuning up in the corner. Probably not professionals, honking and parping and twanging over there. They were the same age as Valentin and Kostya, and had the same look of seriousness at play.

'Why don't you grab yourself a plateful before the good stuff goes?' said Kostya. 'We'll get the drinks.'

Sliced beef, pickles, black bread, a hardboiled egg, a pyramidal salad of tinned peas and diced apple held together with mayonnaise. Manoeuvring clear of the queue she stuck a mixed forkful into her mouth, and was startled by her body's gratitude. The boys were still over by the bottles, arguing. She could guess the problem. If she had been one of the impressionable students they were used to moving in on, the protocol for the evening would have been to stick to her like glue, while steadily getting her drunk. But now they were in unknown territory. Should they release her into the company of other elderly people, should they do the whole Dr-X-meet-Dr-Y thing, or was there still a faint possibility of Plan A left in the air? They were coming back. Kostya had three glasses precariously held in front of him.

'We weren't sure what you wanted,' said Valentin, 'so we got you some of everything.' Everything was a shot glass of vodka, a wine glass of something red and a tumbler containing a soft drink of a sinister yellow.

'That's a question in liquid form, if ever I saw one,' she said.

'Ouch!' said Valentin.

'Come on, now,' said Kostya. 'We don't know you. Really, that's all. We're trying to be good guys here.'

'I'm sorry, I'm sorry,' she said, rubbing her face. 'I'm a little rusty at this. Look, I will say yes please to the vodka, as a chaser for the pickles –'

'– and not in any sense as an indicator of floozy-hood –' put in Valentin helpfully.

'– and also yes please to the wine, because, as a matter of fact, that is what I like. Thank you.'

'Think nothing of it.'

She drank off the vodka, and it lit its little sun in her belly. The jazz band blew a brassy chord for attention and launched into a tune that even she, musical know-nothing that she was, could tell was old-sounding: one of the kind of things that you used to get on the radio during the war, when Eddie Rosner's big band was serenading the Red Army, now lovingly polished and recreated. The crowd sorted itself into dancers and non-dancers. She moved off with the boys to a section of tabletop where she could balance the plate and the wine glass and they could fit food of their own.

'So,' she said, pitching her voice to pierce the swoony wa-wa of muted trumpets, 'so – who are all these people? And what do you really work on, specifically?'

'Hmm,' said Kostya. 'Here's the thing. We really do work on saving the world.'

'Really, truly, specifically,' said Valentin.

'I think I could probably handle a few more specifics than that,' she said.

'We're working on ways to improve the economic mechanism?'

'With you so far.'

'We're building a dynamic system of planning algorithms, using the techniques of linear programming in the light of the theorem that the equilibrium point in a many-person non-coalition game must be an optimum.'

'Ah – too much.'

'The lady has passed from a state of insufficient bafflement to one of excessive bafflement, without stopping at the point of optimal bafflement in between. For God's sake, Kostya – help her, help her.' Valentin bit into a slice of sausage and beamed.

'All right, all right. Let me think. Let's agree', said Kostya slowly, 'that the world is finite. Whatever they say about limitless nature in dialectical materialism classes, the amount of something that you can actually lay your hands on, at any one moment, is always limited, yes? Organisms have a limited food supply, mines contain a limited amount of iron ore, factories have a limited supply of raw materials to work with. The fundamental economic situation is one of scarcity.'

'Yes.'

'Yet we mean to get from scarcity to plenty. So the economic task is to allocate our limited resources in the most efficient way possible. The socialist economy tries to do that by pushing factories to do more every year. But here's the catch. We don't want them to do more. We really want them to do the *least* they can possibly do that will still fulfil the plan. Yet the targets they're given don't make that possible. The target for a transport enterprise, for example, is given in ton-kilometres. They're supposed to move the greatest weight they can over the greatest distance they can – which is hopeless, it should be exactly the other way around, so long as everyone who needs stuff moved is happy. We need new targets. And luckily, thanks to Valentin's boss, Professor Kantorovich, who is standing just over there, the mathematical means exist to create them.'

'Not ton-kilometres.'

'No; and not kilowatt-hours of electricity either, or litres of refined gasoline, or square metres of spun nylon. Did you know that last year more than half of the hosiery delivered to shops was sub-standard?'

'Let's say that I had an anecdotal appreciation of that fact, from trying to put some of it on.'

'Kostya really knows how to talk to girls, don't you think?' said Valentin. 'No, no, go on: league after league of malformed stockings . . .'

'The point being that it was incredibly hard for the stores to send the bad stuff back to the knitting mills, because it all counted towards their output targets. What we need is a planning system that counts the *value* of production rather the quantity. But that, in turn, requires prices which express the value of what's produced.'

'The value to whom?'

'Good question,' said Valentin.

'Not just the value to the producer, or even to the consumer, because that only gives you capitalism again, surging to and fro, doing everything by trial and error. It's got to be the value to the whole system; the amount it helps with what the whole economy is trying to do in the present plan period. And it turns out that a set of prices exist which will do that. But –'

'But,' agreed Valentin.

'But – in order to work, they have to be active. They have

to keep changing along with the changing possibilities of the economy; they can't be fixed by an administrator in an office somewhere. So, in order to get them –'

'– you have to automate the management of the economy,' said Valentin, forgetting to be frivolous. 'You have to take away the discretion of the bureaucrats, and treat the economy as –'

'Ta-dah!' said Kostya.

'– one big connected cybernetic system. With software –'

'Ta-dah!'

'– written by us.'

'Or at any rate, written by great minds whom we are, from time to time, honoured to be able to help out.'

'In our obscure and menial way.'

'Hang on,' she said. 'Doesn't that mean that the economy has to be completely centralised? I mean, *perfectly* centralised?'

'Ah,' said Valentin, 'no. It *could* mean that; and in fact Academician Glushkov of the Ukrainian Academy has proposed a rival system in which the computers really do track every single nut and bolt that come off the production line, and take every single decision. But –'

'– but –' said Kostya, smiling.

'– this is where the game theory comes in. That stuff about the many-person non-coalition game? It turns out that the mathematics is indifferent to whether the optimal level of production is organised hierarchically or happens in many distributed, autonomous units. So long as the prices generated by the algorithms are correct, all of the decisions can be made locally. There's no loss of efficiency.'

'And this is good because . . . ?'

'Because it means you can have a society dedicated to maximising the total social benefits of production, without everyone having to obey orders all the time.'

'Do you like obeying orders?' said Kostya.

'No.'

'Well then.'

They were joking about; but still, in joke, they were talking as if the heaviest, most inevitable parts of the order of things had suddenly lost the awful mass that strained the earth beneath them, and risen up to be played with, soap-bubble-easy. It was as if gravity had failed. They were talking as if having the right idea stole away the weight of refineries and textile works, department stores and ministries, technologies and social systems, and set them floating where they stood, to be switched and swivelled about at the touch of a hand, to be tried out at will in experimental configurations, now like this, now like that. Usually she would have scoffed. Not overtly, of course: by asking them how the great work was going, and leading them with gentle malignity to the point where they had to confess complications, frustrations, disappointment. She did not quite think of herself as a bitch, but the last few years had not been fun, and she had developed a certain sour pleasure in easing awkward facts into view. But the boys were grinning at her, most charmingly, and it occured to her that they really might not, yet, have been disappointed. And she was finding, too, that gravity did not seem to have its whole grip on her. Tonight, without Max nearby, and her attention constantly extended into the entire zone around her where he orbited, there seemed to be less of her than she was used to, and what was left was, exactly, lighter. Lighter, less responsible, more prone to bob and shift if the breath of circumstance blew on her. She grinned back.

'So which ones are your great minds, again?' she asked.

'All right,' said Kostya. 'Just there by the buffet is our Leonid Vitalevich. Resident genius.'

'Candidate member of the Academy. King of mathematical economics. Prince of cybernetics. Rabbi of functional analysis. Master of algorithms. The White Crow himself,' said Valentin.

The genius was a short man, becoming tubby, with a nose that didn't seem large enough to explain the nickname, though she could see that it was probably growing beakier in effect as the rest of his head got more convex.

'And the person he's talking to' – slight, ascetic, horn-rimmed glasses – 'is Professor Ershov of the computer centre.'

'Who says –'

'Who famously says –'

'"A programmer"', they chorused together, '"must combine the accuracy of a bank clerk with the acumen of an Indian tracker, and add in the imagination of a crime writer and the practicality of a businessman."'

'And then,' Kostya went on, 'if you look right a little bit, that's my boss, the other chair of the seminar, Dr Shaidullin. Ah, he's coming over.'

Yes, he was: slight but sleek, full of the assumption of power, with delicate features and a long narrow skull down whose sides the curly hair was retreating. Whatever else was different in Akademgorodok, this was not. Strangers get the once-over from someone in authority. It was a law of life, an almost biological law, for it was how institutions protected themselves, how they operated an immune system. When an interloper appeared, so must the human equivalent of a white blood cell, to see if what had arrived in the social bloodstream was a pathogen. Watch, children, she thought, if you don't know how this is done. You'll be doing it yourselves before very long.

'A face I don't know,' Shaidullin remarked, giving her a look that mixed one part of carnal consideration with many parts of suspicion. He held out his hand, and she shook it, but as the opening formality of an examination. She told him her name, he asked her where she would be working in Akademgorodok. She told him that, he asked her where she had come from. She told them that, and told him where she had been before, and who had taught her, and who had taught them, until in a few minutes he had an academic lineage for her. The mood perceptibly relaxed as it became clear that she came from the untainted part of the biological family tree, and became almost cordial when she mentioned the name of Nemchinov, her supervisor's supervisor – who had, come to think of it, left genetics to go off and do something to do with economics.

Shaidullin, of course, wanted a milder, less urgent version of the assurance that the Director of her institute had been after, when she went through a similar interrogation with him earlier in the day. 'And will you be a good comrade?' the Director had ended. Meaning, we wanted you because you were a real geneticist, but will you be tactful about it? Will you lie when lying is necessary, will you be silent when silence is necessary, will you obfuscate when obfuscation is necessary? Will you back us up when we do these things? Meaning, above all: are you going to be trouble? It seemed to her that it would take an unlikely kind of honesty to give anything but the answer the question asked for, but perhaps the art here, the art of vigilance, lay in judging how people gave the inevitable answer, obligingly or otherwise, convincingly or otherwise. She couldn't tell how convincing she had been, herself, for the truthful reply would have been that she didn't know; that she was not sure, any more, how good a comrade she had it in her to be.

At last Shaidullin smiled – a provisional smile. She was in, or in enough for the purposes of the evening. Valentin and Kostya had said nothing, because there would have been no point in offering any endorsement of her till she had been judged worth endorsing. Now, with the signal given, they brought up the seminar, and to her surprise Shaidullin took the suggestion that she be booked to speak entirely seriously. They were talking about dates before she knew it. Shaidullin exhibited an easy, impressive, tactful familiarity with the current anguishes of her subject, as if it were only normal for an educated person to know a smattering of every science; and an easy familiarity, too, with its big names, as if that were his natural company and (he flatteringly implied) hers as well. He raised his eyebrows at her enquiringly, as Valentin launched into another breathless riff. *What are you doing with these little boys?* She gave him the eyebrow lift back, wide-eyed and uninformative. *Mind your own business, sir.* Playing, she thought. I'm playing. It's a summer night and I'm playing. Shaidullin put on, for one split comical second, a long face that must have come from some ancestral store: it was a commercial expression, a bazaar merchant's good-humoured dumbshow of disappointment, to be deployed when you turned down his very reasonable offer. She smiled at him properly, and turned to egg Valentin on as he climbed up his new mound of rhetoric.

And the invisible fissure which had separated her from the rest of the party closed. The crowd thickened around her. More drinks appeared. Shaidullin, as he moved smoothly away, snagged a passing physicist with a mossy, nineteenth-century beard and sent him back to make conversation with her about the theory of automata. It turned out that he had attended one of Timofeev-Ressovsky's famous genetics summer schools in the Urals: it was, he said, quite true that the audience was encouraged to sit in the lake in their swimsuits, while the lecturer scribbled at a blackboard set up on the shore. Valentin and Kostya were joined by a gaggle of their friends, including, she was amused to see, a girl in a hairband who laughed enthusiastically at everything Valentin said, and shot poisonous glances in her own direction.

'"Tahiti",' announced the boy leading the band, and Hairband Girl swiftly grabbed Valentin and pulled him onto the dancefloor. Kostya made a face.

'You're not dancing?' she said.

'All this old stuff gives me the shits,' he said. 'I don't see the point.'

She wondered whether Historical Beard might be in the mood to dance, but before she could find out, another voice said, 'Excuse me. May I?' It was the genius.

The Master of Algorithms only came up to her chin, but when the foxtrot started he clasped her firmly round the shoulders with one pudgy arm, shot the other one straight out with his hand round hers and was off with pace and attack, leaning back slightly so she could see a little more of him than just the bald crown of his head. Ba-ba-ba, BA, ba, went the band. Oh, he had mastered the algorithm for this, all right; they whirled, the room whirled, and he put her through the turns with precise glee. As the faces of the onlookers and the other dancers went by, she saw the same look directed at the pair of them over and over: a sort of affectionate satisfaction. It was, she saw, part of the genius's legend that he should do this, that he should like to do this. She wondered, for a moment, what she had let herself in for, but the touch of his hands was entirely correct, in the old-fashioned sense, and his expression was nothing but friendly. She had the impression, too, that if she had surrendered to her pressing urge to giggle, it would not have mattered to Leonid Vitalevich very much; perhaps he was not so far from giggling himself.

'Thank you,' he said afterwards. 'I enjoyed that very much.'

'So did I,' she said, truthfully.

'Emil tells me you'll be coming to talk to us? Good. I find myself more and more interested by the robust homeostasis of biological systems.'

They talked for a little while about cellular self-regulation, and then he went. He had his eye, she could see, on another tall woman on the other side of the room.

'Comrades, ladies and gentlemen, the White Crow!' cried Valentin, crowing himself.

'He likes to dance, doesn't he.'

'He *loves* to dance. And always with good-looking women. But there's a moral here, you know. I've seen old photographs of him, and he was good-looking himself, not too long ago. A nice, brown-eyed boy.'

'What's your moral?'

'Simple. Brown-eyed boys don't last very long. That's why you have to pluck us while we're ripe. During our brief flowering.'

'Yeah, yeah,' said Kostya.

'"Blue Horizon",' declared the band leader. A clarinet began to hoist the sorrows of the world skyward, by patient stages.

'Does this suit you any better?' she asked Kostya.

'Not really. I don't like Dixieland any more than I like swing.'

'Kostya's a bebop man,' said Valentin. 'He's strict in his loyalties.'

'If you want to hear good jazz round here,' Kostya said, 'the only place is Under the Integral. Even these guys experiment a bit, there. It's a club,' he added, seeing her looking blank. 'You know, like Aelita in Moscow.'

'I'm afraid I don't know much about music.' Or care much, she politely didn't say. She could never hold patterns of sound in her memory for very long. Probably some specialised protein was missing. 'You probably don't want to dance to this, then?'

'Kostya doesn't, on the whole,' said Valentin. 'Generally he prefers to just stand around, inhaling the vapours of the cool.'

She looked at Kostya.

'Thank you but no,' he said.

'I, on the other hand, am very much available,' said Valentin. Hairband Girl vibrated with indignation at his shoulder.

She did dance with Valentin, but not for a slow number. She also danced with the bashful, newly-anointed Candidate of Science whose party it was; and then again for a second time with Leonid Vitalevich, once a sufficiently venerable and sufficiently rule-defined dance step came up. She chatted with Kostya's economist colleagues and Valentin's mathematical ones, wandering away from the pair of them on long looping arcs, but always intercepting them again; or perhaps always being intercepted again. She even made an effort to talk to Hairband

Girl, but got back only hostile monosyllables and a face of rabbitlike defiance. The food ran out but the drink did not.

'A bunch of us are going on,' said Valentin, as the party wound up. 'Are you coming? Leonid Vitalevich is holding open house, and he said to invite you.'

Better not, she thought. 'All right,' she said. The group of young people burst out of the hotel in the genius's wake. The warm air dried her damp forehead. Crickets chirred in the dark beyond the street lamps.

'Which way we do walk?' she asked.

'Walk? Pfah!' said Valentin. 'Our White Crow is famous for lots of things; and one them is for just how much he likes the car they gave him.'

Leonid Vitalevich had stepped to the kerb and raised his hand with a conjurer's solemnity: a long green Volga slid obediently out of the shadows. He opened the passenger-side door and sat down next to the driver.

'Now we fit the rest of us into the back,' Valentin said. 'It's a topological exercise, tricky but not impossible. If you just sit on my knee –'

'I don't think so,' she said. 'Perhaps you should sit on mine –'

But the others ignored both of them and crowded straight in, carrying her to a position topologically quite separate from Valentin's, halfway down a tangled wedge of arms and legs in the far corner of the big back seat. So far as anyone was on her knee, Hairband Girl was, angrily shifting about, and in the end sticking her feet out of the open window. The weight was quite something. But there it was again, even with gravity doing its worst: that lightness, that sense of pressing on the world with less than the whole of herself. Kostya looked in without envy through the other window.

'See you there,' he said. 'I'm just going to go and get something.'

The car pulled away, full of laughter. Someone towards the bottom of the heap started to sing, and the rest joined in raggedly, with grunts of discomfort as the car jolted on the unfinished roadways. The glow of the lighted piece of street holding the hotel and the cinema dwindled behind them, and they entered a black zone with no lamp standards at all. Her eyes adjusted, and she began to make out the bulks of buildings going by, spiky with scaffolding, against a sky absurdly thick with stars.

'Professor,' she asked, 'won't your wife mind us all dropping on her in the middle of the night?'

'Oh, she isn't here,' said Leonid Vitalevich. 'She doesn't get along very well with Siberia, you see.'

The car rounded a corner, then another corner. Trees blocked out the stars. 'Not far now,' said someone at the bottom of the heap. Streetlamps returned, and the driver pulled over. The knot on the back seat unknotted itself; she spilled out with the rest into meadow-grass, feathery and thigh-high. It smelt of summer. There were ferns in it, and clover, and flowers with delicate little bells, of what colour she couldn't tell, because in this dimness they showed only as a silvery glimmer. Grasshoppers sang all around. The trees arched overhead, hanging down their tresses of small leaves into the street lighting; and beyond a white wooden fence, a row of houses stood, bigger and solider than any dacha. Somehow they were familiar though, and so was the layout of the wide, quiet road, with its twin sidewalks set back in the long grass. As Leonid Vitalevich led them through the gate in the fence, and up the garden path, she got it: familiarity resolved into a memory, not of anything she had ever seen herself, but of that brilliantly insidious filmshow at the exhibition in Sokoloniki Park, three years ago. This was what American suburbs looked like, more or less. Here, in the middle of a Siberian wood, as a reward to its geniuses, the Academy of Sciences had apparently recreated a piece of the good life as defined far, far away, on the world's other shore; recreated it, she could see when she got closer to the house, in the same standard concrete panels as her apartment block, trimmed with wood. But the local materials scarcely took away from the inspiring comedy of the idea.

Light and a hubbub of voices came from the screen door on the porch. Leonid Vitalevich's open house had clearly been running without him for several hours already; in effect, a parallel party, attended by an older contingent that preferred talking to dancing, and liked to do its drinking sitting down. Little groups were scattered through the house. Shaidullin was leaning on the mantelpiece, talking to a couple of grandees. As the professor bustled to find a bottle and glasses for his gaggle of newcomers, she walked from room to room. Through room, after room, after room. It was the biggest private dwelling she had ever seen, easily five or six times the floor area of her new flat. And he lived here alone. At the same time it was almost as empty as her new flat, except for the books. A few chairs in the kitchen, a brand-new dining table set, a desk. The walls were huge and bare. Many of the conversations were taking place at floor level, for want of seating. Leonid Vitalevich seemed to be camping out in his mansion. He must roll around in its spaces like a pea in an empty coffee can.

There was a philosophical argument going on in the kitchen, between a man in his forties, leaning down low from his seat with his elbows on his knees, long fingers palping the back of his neck, and a floor-dweller of the same age propped against the white-tiled wall, his face gleeful. They were both glitter-eyed and slightly ruddy from the booze; still under control but definitely lit up, suffused. Probably she looked the same way herself.

'Look, I'm not saying your plenty is impossible,' jabbed the man on the floor. 'Maybe it is, maybe it isn't. How would I know. Pure maths, me, every time. None of your murky compromises. No, what I'm saying is that plenty is an *intrinsically vulgar* idea. It is, in itself, a stupid response to human needs. "Oh look, there's someone unhappy. Let's overwhelm him!" Real human needs are always specific. No one ever feels a generic hunger or a generic loneliness, and no one ever requires a generic solution to those things. Your plenty is like a bucket of plaster of Paris you want to pour over people's heads. It's a way of not paying human attention to them.'

'Bullshit, Mo,' said the man in the chair. 'Bullshit, bullshit, bullshit. Plenty is the condition that will let us distinguish, for the first time, between avoidable and unavoidable suffering. We solve the avoidable stuff – which seems pretty bloody generic to me, given that a bowl of soup cures everybody's hunger and a painkiller cures everybody's headache – and then we know that what's left is real tragedy, boo-hoo, write a play about it. Who the hell ever said that plenty was supposed to abolish unhappiness? But what it will do is free our hands to concentrate on unhappiness. If we're so minded. If we're as as pure as you. And I don't see how that can be anything but a humane goal. A humanist goal, if you like. Plenty will let a truly human life begin.'

'Oh, bullshit yourself! "Let human life begin"? What d'you think we're living now, for God's sake?' He cupped his hands around his mouth. 'Hey, is there a biologist in the house?'

She couldn't help herself, and raised a finger silently, where she stood in the kitchen doorway.

'Excellent!' said Mo. 'You know about animal behaviour?'

'Not so much,' she said. 'I'm a microscope biologist.'

'Ah well, pretend you do. Dear old Sobchak here will never be able to tell the difference. Right! What does squirrel behaviour consist of?'

'Oh, I dunno,' she said. 'Gathering nuts . . . scampering around in trees . . . making baby squirrels . . .'

'Exactly,' said Mo. 'And this has been uniformly true of squirrels at all times and on all continents, am I right? So, if somebody said to you – Sobchak, for example – that the *true* behaviour of squirrels was to ride around on little bicycles while singing selections from Verdi, even though no squirrel to date had ever, ever done those things, this would be – ?'

'Untrue.'

'Oh, worse than that. It would be rubbish, it would be nonsense; just like Sobchak's claim that true human behaviour consists of living in a way that no one has yet experienced.'

'You could always try pouring your drink over his head,' she suggested to Sobchak.

'Don't think I'm not tempted,' said Sobchak, mournfully.

She went away.

Leonid Vitalevich caught up with her to give her a glass just as Shaidullin caught up with him.

'It's going to happen,' said Shaidullin. 'The news just came in on the teletypes, apparently: an announcement to be printed on the front page of every paper tomorrow morning.'

'Have you got a copy?' asked Leonid Vitalevich.

'No. We'll have to wait for the printed version. But the outline is – small cuts on rayon and sugar, 25% rise on butter, 30% rise on meat.'

'And how much of the retail increase gets passed on?'

'10% for butter, virtually all of it for meat.'

The two of them smiled at each other.

'I don't understand,' she said. *Nor need you understand*, said Shaidullin's expression. But her host was obviously the kind of man who responded by reflex to statements of ignorance.

'The price of meat is going up,' he said kindly.

'And . . . you're pleased by this? You want people to pay more?'

'Well, yes: in this case.'

'That seems rather callous.'

Valentin had appeared at Shaidullin's elbow, as if summoned out of the air by the exchange of secret knowledge.

'I'll tell you what,' said Shaidullin sharply. 'Why don't we have Valentin here explain it to you?' He waved them off with his well-kept fingers.

The boy looked irritated. Impressing her obviously dropped precipitously down his list of priorities, if there was a chance to be on the inside track of something important. But he accepted the assignment, of course. He led her through the house to the porch steps, where someone was strumming a guitar in the starlight. She looked back as they went: Shaidullin and Kantorovich were touching their glasses together, like men solemnly saluting a success.

'Where's Kostya?' she said.

'I don't know. I haven't seen him. Don't you think', he said when they had sat down, 'that you were a bit rude back there? Those are people whose good opinion is valuable. You can't go round just saying whatever comes into your head, you know.'

She opened her mouth and shut it again.

'I just didn't see what there was to be glad about.'

'That's because you're not thinking cybernetically. You're not thinking in terms of the whole system.'

'No, I'm thinking in terms of seventy million families who will wake up tomorrow morning and find they can't afford beef any more.'

'Yes, but it isn't a straight loss of something they really possessed, is it? How many of those families do you think were actually able to find any beef to buy today, or in the last week, even, at the old price? It's been in deficit for years, compared to the demand for it, and there's a relationship between the degree of the shortage and the level of the price. The national economy is one of the most complex cybernetic systems ever created, you know, with an enormous variety of different feedback mechanisms at work in it, from low-level autonomic loops all the way up through the planning system to the meta-mechanisms of political oversight. You're smiling.'

'I've just never come across a Party secretary who'd be glad to be described as a meta-mechanism.'

'Well, meet your first.'

'What – you?' *Oh, Valentin.*

'On a very small scale. I'm second secretary of the Komsomol group in our institute. It makes sense; we're under the Academy so we're exempt from supervision by the county committee, and the more the Komsomol and the institute committees are run by scientists, the more, in effect, we supervise ourselves. Very meta-mechanical. Anyway, beef, if you still want me to tell you?'

'All right.'

'Well,' said Valentin, 'the thing is that, till now, the procurement price the state pays to collective farms for meat hasn't been enough to cover the farms' costs for producing it. They've been losing money with every cow. It costs eighty-eight roubles to produce a hundred kilos of usable meat, and for this the state paid them R59.10. That's why the drive to increase meat production hasn't got anywhere. The farms didn't have any incentive to go along. But if the retail price of beef goes up by 30%, and the slice taken out by meatpackers and wholesalers stays the same, then the state can pay the kolkhozniks ninety roubles for the hundred kilos. And suddenly, as of tomorrow, they'll be in profit, and their incomes will go up. Which is good news, because farm workers are the poorest people in the Soviet Union.'

'Ye-es, but then the good news for them is bad news for everyone else.'

'Well, there will be some benefit for the consumer. There'll be much more beef in shops. I know, I know, people won't be able to afford it – but in a way, like I was saying, there's no real new bad news there, is there? There isn't much logical difference between *not* being able to find something you *can* afford, and being *able* to find something you *cannot* afford. Is there?'

Spoken like somebody who doesn't do the shopping, she thought.

'At least, this way, the production level for beef will be up, which is the essential first step towards getting beef that's both cheap and available. If we had optimal pricing, then once the higher level of meat production was established, the unit cost would drop, and the selling price would go down again with it, automatically.'

'But we don't have optimal pricing.'

'No. This is just another old-style administrative change.'

'So those two in there aren't celebrating a victory for the stuff you told me about.'

'Actually, they sort of are. You see, if the idea is to get prices which can function as useful signals in the economy, then this counts as a step in the right direction. What's more' – he lowered his voice impressively – 'it's a sign that we can win the political argument for active pricing.'

'Your geniuses in there were pushing for the price increase?'

'Economists all over the Soviet Union advised it, but we certainly added our weight to the recommendation.'

All of a sudden she could hear the middle-aged man that Valentin was going to become, sooner than he imagined. A good teacher, but a slightly pompous one, inclined to wrap himself in borrowed dignity. Oh, Valentin.

'All right,' she said, and held up the brimming shot of hooch Leonid Vitalevich had given her. 'To brown-eyed boys and expensive beef.' She drank it down.

Valentin smiled uncertainly.

'You're laughing at me,' he said. But then Shaidullin called him, from inside the house, and he jumped to his feet. 'You do know', he said, hovering, 'that *you* won't be paying the new beef price? You're on the Academy's special list, now. Cheap meat, cheap butter, cheap eggs, and cans of salmon on public holidays.'

No one else on the steps seemed inclined to draw her into their conversation when Valentin had gone. She laid her cheek against the cool wood of Leonid Vitalevich's porch, and gazed into the glimmering dark, and listened to the grasshoppers. Perhaps, she thought, it followed from feeling all the gargantuan furnishings of this world lose their grip on the ground, at least in thought, and bob in place obedient as soap bubbles, that you would then take the emotions of your fellow creatures just as lightly. But who was she to talk. If she was immune to this particular dream, it was through no particular virtue of hers. She had her own professional vision which removed her, in some ways, even further from everyday human sympathies, when she was looking through her science's eyes. She too was a believer in a world that could be reduced, along one dimension of its existence, to information: only in her case, it was the information of the genes, not the information of the computing circuit, which stood as the pattern of patterns. And once you had seen it, once you had parted the curtains of the visible world and seen that human beings were only temporary expressions of ancient information, dimly seen in tiny glimpses by the light of science's deductive flashlight, but glimpsed enough to tell that it was vast, and intricate, and slowly changing by indifferent rules of its own as it went on its way into a far future – then all the laws and plans of the self-important present looked like momentary tics and jitters in comparison. A dark message, posted from the past to the future; a dark armada, floating through time. Dark masses, moving in the dark. Dark water. Dark ocean swell.

'Don't wake her up,' said Hairband Girl. 'Can't you see how tired she is?'

A trumpet blew in her ear.

'Hello,' said Kostya. He lifted whorled metal to his mouth and did it again. 'I'm sorry I was so long. It took forever to find someone who'd lend me it.'

Another blast.

She looked round wildly. Embers of the party were still alight, but two or three hours of the short summer night had passed. The moon was up, scorching the mock-suburb with explicit silver; her cheek was corrugated.

'Oh now really,' said Leonid Vitalevich, arriving on the porch flustered, more like a hen than a crow. 'Now really, Kostya. That's just too loud. Take it outside. Take it away, take it into the *forest*.'

'Sorry, Professor,' said Kostya, quite amicable. 'Well, what do you say to a little concert under the trees?'

'Excellent plan, you madman,' said Valentin, coming to see the commotion. He and Hairband Girl had their arms round each other's waists. 'In fact, why don't we collect everybody up, listen to you do your thing, and then go down to the sea for sun-up?'

'The sea,' she said stupidly. A children's-atlas outline of Asia drew itself in her mind's eye, with their present position marked by a flag, halfway across the blob and almost halfway down: about as far from an ocean shore as it was possible for a human being to be.

'You really haven't had time to look round yet, have you?' said Kostya. The momentary look of annoyance on his face had already disappeared.

'Nobody say anything,' Valentin commanded. 'Let's keep it as a surprise.'

The guitarist, the girl leaning on his shoulder, sleepy leavetakers emerging from the house: nine or ten people straggled up the sidewalk in the moonlight. She walked with Kostya, yawning. They crossed a wide avenue lined with unfinished apartment houses, the glassless windows black gaps in silver. Nothing moved in either direction as far as the eye could see, as if the bright gaze of the moon had pinned the earth into stillness. Kostya was humming something over to himself, under his breath. She wondered, irritably, how much simulated music appreciation was going to be required of her to keep the male ego happy. *Go home*, she instructed her legs, but they kept on walking with the group through the silent town, past the shops, past the cinema, past the hotel. The weightless feeling was gone. She was just tired. And she was finding the moonlight curiously oppressive. It shone hard enough to cast shadows, to throw a pale bleak certainty over foolishness. *Why is moonlight different from sunlight, mama?* Sometimes it isn't different enough. 'What am I doing here?' she thought.

But then they stepped back under the trees, and the moon receded as the sun had done, into a faraway source only sifting speckles of light down into dimness. Under the pines and the birches the night turned indefinite again. Black shapes of the walkers slipped between black masts, black birdcage spars. Somebody laughed. Small rustles propagated in the resinous air, origin unknown, destination unknown. Here and there a thinning in the canopy made a patch of dappled paleness on the leafmould floor of the forest, and in one of these they came to a halt around Kostya, whose trumpet, when he lifted it, became an abstract knot of shine and shadow.

'Comrades,' crooned Valentin, 'I give you –'

'Shut up,' said Kostya, 'before I forget what I'm trying to do. "Blue in Green",' he announced, 'by Mr Miles Davis.' He nodded to her. 'This is what I like.'

Then he lifted the horn and began to blow high, exact phrases. There was nothing to anchor them into the rest of a song, and you could tell, anyway, that they were carefully refusing expectation, declining sweetly to close or to resolve, to fall in with the hints of structure they themselves were constantly giving. Yet they were familiar all the while. They were still hoisting the sorrows of the world, only the sorrows had been unpicked from the old sense woven of them and let go to dart though the dark in single threads. All this, to her surprise, she heard in the thirty seconds after he started to play. The first phrases laid an elusive pattern, in pieces, in the air; the second set of them complicated it by adding another layer athwart or at an angle to it; and after that, it exceeded her power to keep track of it.

When Kostya had finished, the circle surrounded him with whoops and murmurs of praise, then quickly drifted off downhill through the trees in separate threes and twos. Only Valentin and his reluctant partner lingered.

'Well?' said Kostya. He seemed to be smiling, but what if anything he expected was as hard to settle as his song.

'Do you suppose this could be a magic wood?' she asked. 'You know, the story kind.'

'Could be,' said Kostya.

'What kind of magic do you suppose it would do, a wood round here?' she asked.

'What kind do you want?' said Valentin, too late and too fast; for after all, it would be in the nature of a genuinely enchanted forest that it would give you what you didn't know you wanted, rather than granting dreary wishes as familiar to you as the lacks they were supposed to fill.

'You know, I don't think I understand this place at all,' she told Kostya.

Kostya looked at her. 'Why don't you go on ahead,' he said to Valentin. 'We'll catch you up.'

'Yes,' she said, 'why don't you?'

Very briefly, annoyance and pure amazement chased each other across Valentin's expression, before amused good humour caught them both and wiped them away.

'All right,' he said. 'See you on the beach,' and he was gone, with Hairband Girl beside him exuding sudden, rabbity benevolence.

Alone, Kostya was no more shy but no less shy either. He unscrewed parts of the trumpet, and put it away in the bag he had slung over his shoulder. 'Let's walk down after them, but slowly,' he said, 'and you can tell me what it is you don't understand.'

They moved off through the trees.

'You all talk so much,' she said. 'Well: not you, individually. But collectively! As if it's going out of style. I've heard things said tonight in public that I thought were strictly whispers for the kitchen.'

'It's very simple,' said Kostya. 'This is a privileged place, and one of the privileges is speaking freely. Or more freely. You live here, and you get a flat and a fridge and food delivered to your door, all exactly in accordance with your seniority, and you also get to talk. I'm not sure they know why we like it, the powers that be. They just know we do like it, and they want to keep us happy, within reason. But within reason, you see. There are limits. You mustn't ever question the fundamentals. It's like the paths in the wood: wander about on them as much as you like, but don't step off them.'

'Don't step off the paths?'

'Nobody's told you? There's a nasty little Siberian tick that lives in the undergrowth.'

'Oh, marvellous. Can't they spray, or something?'

'They did, two years ago. Dusted off the whole area with DDT, using a jet engine for a fan. But apparently the little fuckers are back. You're still puzzled,' he observed.

'It's not just the talking,' she said. 'It's what you say. You all sound like – I don't know. I couldn't work out, back there, whether I was listening to bohemians disguised as good boys, or good boys disguised as bohemians. You babble like dreamers, and then it turns out you're dreaming of the Five-Year Plan. You seem to be saying whatever the hell you like, but . . . Maybe you've already answered me. Maybe it's just . . . keeping to the paths?'

'I hope not,' said Kostya carefully. 'Not the way you mean, anyway. I think it's something about economists, probably. We're used to reasoning as if we had our hands on the levers of power – change this, change that, see how it looks the new way. But that's not necessarily megalomania. The ideas truly are powerful. Once they're put in practice, there'll be no stopping them, they'll be having effects no one can take back again. Laugh if you like.'

'I'm not even smiling.'

'Some people here', he offered, 'call this place "the island". You know, not a real island, a conceptual one; as if we were living just offshore of what is, a little way out on the water towards what might be.'

'Like the man last night. When I first bumped into you? He said "Welcome to the island", and I didn't know what he was talking about, so far away from the ocean.'

'Oh, but we have ocean. A toy ocean, all our own. Five more minutes, and you'll see.'

'Yes, Mr Mystery.'

'I'm far less mysterious than you.'

They emerged suddenly from the trees into open space. It was a highway, silent in both directions. The moonlight was giving way to the very first, faint grey tinge of dawn. On the other side, the trees resumed, and so did the path, steeper and more ceremonious, with electric lamp standards glowing at the turns, and making the blackness between blacker once more. She shivered, and yawned.

'Can I ask you something, then?' said Kostya.

'All right.'

'You have family, don't you?'

'Yes.'

'A husband?'

'No.'

Then, when Kostya only padded along again in comfortable silence beside her, she said, 'That's it? You don't want to know anything else?'

'Not just now,' he said.

The path crossed a railroad track on a footbridge, and became stairs, splitting and recombining at a descending series of concrete platforms like an outdoor sketch of the grand staircase into a ballroom. At the bottom, she stepped, disbelieving, onto sand. It was, indeed, a beach, dim and pale, under an abruptly wide sky just beginning to blush with colour. Dark headlands ran out to left and right. And from ahead came the quiet glock and splosh of waves, and voices calling.

'It's a reservoir?' she said.

'It's the Ob Sea, thank you very much,' said Kostya. 'Sixty kilometres long, twenty kilometres wide, ten metres deep. Nature metamorphosed. Nature moulded like putty by the builders of socialism. Best seen from this spot, manufactured for the pleasure of the intelligentsia. Yachting, water-skiing. Swimming. Will you come?'

They ran to the water's edge and undressed hastily among the other little piles of clothes, not looking at each other. Glassy little breakers rolled in, and she launched herself through the dark face of one, expecting a shock of cold to break in on her daze and her incipient headache; but it was only cool, under the surface, and saltless like the river water it was, with an unclassifiable other taste to it which, for the first time in the whole day and night that she had been here, really persuaded her that she had arrived far, far away from home, in strange Asia. This cool envelope of liquid, stroking her like a multitude of hands, had trickled down from mountains where yak-herds followed the bells of their flocks; and here she was in it, bobbing about, a head among the other heads breaking the smooth steel-coloured surface. She turned onto her back, and looking past her nipples and her toes at the horizon of the toy ocean, she laughed out loud with pure childish pleasure. Real life would resume, Max's train was already descending the foothills of the Urals, soon daybreak would turn the water transparent: but there were little islands out there coming into view with the dawn, a puff of trees on a sandbank and no more, absurdly like the desert isles of picture books.

'What now?' called Valentin, across the water.

'Well –' she said.

2.

The Price of Meat, 1962

Volodya stood by the parapet at the edge of the flat roof of the city procuracy, and fought against the urge to crouch. He had been frightened since yesterday morning, and now he was terrified. The crowd was coming into view around the bend of Moscow Street. They should have been stopped by the line of tanks on the bridge at the edge of town, but somehow they had not been; they should have been stopped by the fire engines posted in the side streets along Herzen Hill, but somehow they had not been; and now the front rank of the strikers was almost here, red flags flying, portraits of Lenin held high, looking extraordinarily like the virtuous mob in every film about the Revolution, except that among the stores for the May Day Parade they'd raided, they were waving homemade placards of their own, as indecorous as farts in church, which said MEAT, BUTTER & A PAY RISE or, worst of all, CUT KHRUSHCHEV UP FOR SAUSAGES. And as they neared the square, the noise grew, an insistent buzz of anger Volodya had never in his life heard before. It was good-humoured anger, so far, a kind of carnival fury, because it was the sound of people who thought they they were winning. All along the street the shops were still open, windows glinting and flashing in the sun, unbroken, even the windows of the empty-shelved food shops, and the workers had brought their families, dressed up in holiday clothes. Students from the Polytechnical Institute were along too, seizing the chance to protest the grey pea soup and gristle served in their canteen. Excited children were running up and down on the sidewalks. It looked like a parade to them, Volodya supposed, and the weather was right for a parade, only the dust and the haze clouding the hard southern blue of the sky. The tarpaper roof of the procuracy exuded a sluggish summer perfume. But no one was in charge, down there. Ten thousand voices were talking at once, ten thousand voices merging into human static, from which you could pick out only the anger they were voicing in common. And they were all, in effect, angry with him.

'Silly sods,' said the white-haired man Volodya had just unlocked the rooftop door for, along with five or six soldiers. 'Where *do* they think they are.' Almost affectionate. The soldiers did what he told them to, but he was a civilian, dressed in a flat workman's cap, a waistcoat and watch-chain. He had a monk's face, red and jovial and sad-eyed.

'All right, son,' he said to Volodya. 'That's us settled. Off you go. Chop-chop.'

Volodya took the stairs in threes, gulping his breaths, glad to be out of sight of the crowd but still hearing its wrathful mutter through the stairwell walls. Out of the backdoor, across the courtyard, over the cross-street behind the police cordon, to the rear of the gorkom – only to see the visitors from Moscow pouring out of the building themselves, trotting in hasty retreat to the line of black cars parked there in the dust. Basov, the regional first secretary, spotted him and jerked his head at the last car. Volodya piled in and found himself squeezed among the silent senior members of the regional apparat; men who, till yesterday, he'd have schemed to be noticed by, but who now gazed hungrily at him, too junior to have caught their contagion, and therefore still able, if he played his cards right, to come out of this with a career intact. They were unshaven and sweat-stained after their night held captive at the plant. The special forces squad had rescued them at dawn, but they had not been allowed to go home and freshen up; Basov and his cronies were required to tag along behind the Muscovites, humiliated and silent, as an object-lesson in blame. Volodya, on the other hand, was allowed to run errands. Basov had a sick look of disaster in his eye, and the others looked just as defeated, except perhaps Kurochkin the plant manager, who Volodya believed was quite possibly too stupid to take in the scale of the reverse that had just hit his life.

Basov cleared his throat.

'I trust', he said, 'that you're offering every assistance to our friends.'

'Every assistance I can, Comrade Basov.'

'If there's any local knowledge they require, any resource they wish to draw on – well, I'm sure you won't hang back. In a certain sense, you now represent the Party's authority, locally. I hope you understand that.'

Meaning, thought Volodya, that I have a responsibility to throw you any lifeline I can think of. Thanks for nothing. In any case, all they require of me is running up and down flights of stairs. But he nodded gravely.

'Do you know,' said Kurochkin, too eagerly, 'can you tell us, whether the comrades have given, uh, any indication yet of their thinking?'

'Oh, leave it alone, can't you,' snapped one of the others, and wretched silence fell in the car. The convoy barrelled through traffic signals as if they were invisible. Volodya turned his face away from the plague victims and stared out of the window, still breathing fast, trying to shake off the touch of nightmare he'd felt on the roof.

This shitty town. He shouldn't even be here. He didn't really understand why he was. They had been sitting pretty two years ago for a life in Moscow, he and Galina; contacts made, dues paid, friendships lined up to let him start his Party career with a metropolitan bounce, and them their marriage. He still missed her. She had seemed so matter-of-fact. But suddenly she had grown reticent, embarrassed, evasive, and all about what, she wouldn't say. She wouldn't say and he couldn't tell. Something had happened, though; something, it became clear, bad enough to cast a shadow over her reliability, and by extension over his judgement for pairing up with her. Nothing to do then but to break things off. And still, it turned out, the doors he had so painstakingly opened remained shut. If he wanted to be a Party full-timer, there was no question now of easy acceleration up a ministry, or even of putting in his footsoldier-time at some convenient raikom or gorkom in the Moscow region. It was back out to the provinces again, for him; back down to the bloody South, 'because you'll know the territory', only a couple of hundred kilometres from where he'd started, with all the ground to make up again that had so mysteriously been lost.

Down south to dusty trees, and a boarding-house life conducted from a suitcase under the bed, and perpetual mild hunger. Even with his spets for the Party store, a lot of the time he was subsisting on cans of anonymous fish, spooned up stone cold after work. He was doing up his belt two holes tighter than he had last autumn. He didn't know whether the town really did run particularly badly. It felt as if it did. The supply system had it moronically misclassified, on the basis of the Polytechnical Institute, as a college town, in need of the calorific intake required to lift pencils and wipe blackboards; but there were forty thousand people living and working in the industrial zone out by the tracks now, and between the students and the loco workers, a locust would have been hard put to it to find a spare crumb. White bread was a distant memory, milk was dispensed only at the head of enormous queues. Sausages were as rare as comets. Pea soup and porridge powered the place, usually served on half-washed plates. He'd spent his days, this last year, trying to get people motivated for the cost-cutting competition with Rostselmash in Rostov. The productivity charts in his briefcase were waxy along the crease-lines from folding and unfolding. But you never saw one spark of enthusiasm from the workers for the pledges the labour union and the management and the Komsomol branches had signed them up to; just coarse faces looking back, lumpy with impulses not voiced. Other activists could at least kindle a guffaw with the right joke, but he didn't have the touch. He didn't see how it was done, no matter how often he watched it, that particular sleight-of-hand, that conjuring trick which extorted liking from a crowd even while you were picking their pockets. Perhaps the secret was just expecting to be liked, in your suit, with your chart, when the foreman called a break and you hopped up onto the chair or the box. It was a world of managers he had meant to join: he had never, particularly, stopped to think about his relationship to these others he was supposed to be able to control, to cajole. In theory, they were the body, and he was supposed to be the agitating consciousness; but it didn't feel like that. Most evenings, he walked. He'd start thinking about something in the park, burping back the taste of fish, and find his feet had carried him wishfully to the train station again. Hot slate-coloured sky; the caboose lights of departing trains wavering to nothing in the distance like pennies falling to a stream-bed. A bit of music would have helped. But if anyone played live here, it was only ever oompah-oompah.

The cars bounced hard on their springs as the convoy shot under the raised barrier at the entrance to the barracks. Security men spilled out of the lead vehicle and made a double line of protection in the courtyard, up which they beckoned the two grandees in the next limo, followed by scurrying aides and officers and, last, the carload of the disgraced. Volodya moved ahead of them as quickly as he could during the race back along the corridors to the conference room where the day had begun: he had a place to stand, now, over against the wall behind the end of the table with the telephones on it, and he wanted to be back in it.

But Kurochkin, to his horror, had followed him, and now lurched past, sweating with desperate amiability, to bother the men from the Presidium. They had only just sat down, Mikoyan as dapper as ever, Kozlov radiating heat of his own from his pink jowls and his brilliantined wave of white hair.

'Comrades!' said Kurochkin, 'if I might be permitted to suggest –'

'Who's this?' said Kozlov. 'Which one of the idiots is this?' An aide whispered in his ear. 'Ah, the Director himself. The Marie fucking Antoinette of Novocherkassk. You're uglier than your picture, Marie.'

'I don't understand,' said Kurochkin, stretching his cheeks into a grin painful to see, as if a joke might be coming that he, too, could laugh at.

'No? Aren't you the one who told 'em to eat cake, yesterday? Aren't you the one who thinks, angry crowd, how can I make things worse, how can I fuck up a well-fucked situation so it's even more fucked: oh, I know, why don't I add insult to injury. Why don't I say some fucking stupid thing that will really rub in the salt. That's you, Marie, isn't it? Isn't that you?'

Yes, that was him. Volodya still had trouble believing what had come out of Kurochkin's mouth when he remembered it. It had been a little after eight o'clock yesterday morning, and a couple of hundred workers from the first shift had left the steel foundry and gathered in the square in front of the admin building to complain about the price rises just announced. Nobody could call this good; the crowd had already ignored two orders to get back to the job, and workers from other divisions were beginning to stream into the square too as word got around. But neither was it completely out of hand yet. Volodya and the trusties of the plant's Party branch and the Militia auxiliaries were already out in the crowd trying to dampen things down one small knot of listeners at a time, trying to smooth shouting back into discussion and thence into obedience again; and the mood was only excited and aggrieved, not drunk yet on the pleasures of defiance. Maybe it would have been enough if the crowd had felt it had been heard, that it had been taken seriously. After all, by going to the admin building the workers had, in a sense, been taking their complaint to authority. When Kurochkin came out, the crowd tried to hush, so that he and they could be heard. Everyone twitched around, Volodya remembered, to try and face the pilastered frontage of the offices, where he was standing. There was no PA system, so what was said was amplified by being relayed in shouts back over people's shoulders. It travelled outwards in ring-shaped waves, picking up commentary as it travelled. And then picking up fury. Volodya was close enough in to glimpse Kurochkin's nervous bulk, and to hear his actual voice bleating away. Accusations were raining on him, about the wages, and the norms, and the apartment shortage, and the broken stoves in the canteens, and the missing safety equipment, and Kurochkin was denying everything: not making promises, not expressing sympathy, just flat-out refusing to proceed on the basis that anything, anywhere, was less than perfect. Then a woman worker in a headscarf, really upset, said, 'How are we supposed to manage, if meat costs two roubles a kilo? That's more than it costs at the market. What are we supposed to give the kids?' And Kurochkin replied, 'Let them eat *pirozhki*,' and laughed, and added something about liver still being nice and cheap. 'He said, "Let them eat pies",' the bucket-chain of shouts repeated. 'Feed your kids on pies.' 'Give them liver pies to eat.' A tiny pause, for digestion. Someone roared: 'The bastards are mocking us.' Then the shouting was continuous. The shouting, the surging to and fro, the eruption out of the plant grounds, the blocked railroad, the daylong carnival of forbidden statements down on the waste ground by the tracks, the sucking in of the students and the townspeople, the whole unrolling catastrophe.

'So I'll tell you what you're permitted to do,' crooned Kozlov, 'since it was your big mouth that got us into this. You're permitted, comrade, to sit down over there, and to *shut the fuck up*. Is that simple enough for you? Is that something you can understand, you dopey fuck?'

Kurochkin backed away, white; Kozlov sank into his chair, blowing out air in a long disgusted stream. Volodya understood that he was frightened too, and needed to pass it on. He was not what Volodya had expected to find, at the top of the organisational tree. He'd thought the caste of professionals he'd joined would grow more and more subtle the further up you went. The brutishness was all supposed to be down below, as he understood things. Mikoyan resembled his idea of Party seniority much better. During the tirade, he'd winced but made no move to interrupt. Now he sat with his fist in front of his mouth, stroking his narrow moustache up and down with a knuckle.

'I still think we should have talked to them,' Mikoyan said. 'We're all Soviet people here. This isn't enemy action.'

'You don't know that,' said Kozlov. 'We're in Cossack country. This could be irredentism, this could be a provocation, it could be any number of things. If "we're all Soviet people here"' – he made Mikoyan's formula sound prim and weak – 'tell me why this one town has gone apeshit. Everywhere else, a bit of angry graffiti, a few nasty jokes, the odd arrest. Here, they're seizing the town hall. Tell me you see a difference.'

'Oh, come on,' said Mikoyan. 'The reason this is the only place that's had an explosion is, this is the only place that had the price rise right on top of a pay cut. Have you looked at the figures? Our trembling friend over there decided to bring in the new work-norms all at once, instead of phasing them in once he'd got productivity raised. There are people in that crowd who've lost 30% of their pay packets. Come on, there's room for manoeuvre here. The price rise stays, but we offer some hope on the norms. We should talk to them.'

'What, with a gun to our heads?' said Kozlov. *You wouldn't even think about talking if there weren't*, pointed out an unruly voice deep inside Volodya. 'I don't think so.'

They glared at each other.

'Nikita Sergeyevich will be expecting our report,' Kozlov said, and reached for the phone between them. Mikoyan's hand had come out too, but it was a tentative movement, checked almost immediately. Kozlov jiggled the handset, barked at an operator and then abruptly became deferential and solemn, like a doctor giving bad news. The disorder, he said, was severe and increasing. From the receiver, Volodya could hear the thready murmur of a voice familiar from newsreels and the television. It was surreal: as if Khrushchev had entered the room, but reduced to the size of a paperclip.

Kozlov was describing the march of the strikers into town, without actually exaggerating the scene but with the terror Volodya had felt somehow daubed directly onto the crowd – 'troublemakers and hooligans, Nikita Sergeyevich' – when a runner in uniform burst into the room and carried a piece of paper to the generals from the North Caucasus Military District. They bent their heads over it, and then one of the generals stepped forward, tapped Kozlov's arm and held the message before him.

'Excuse me, Nikita Sergeyevich,' said Kozlov. 'I'm just being told that shots have been fired at the central police station. Apparently, a part of the mob are storming it, and are trying to seize automatic weapons from the militia.'

Pause. Thready murmur.

'My recommendation is for decisive action,' said Kozlov.

Pause. Murmur.

'Yes, I'm sure,' said Kozlov. 'The time for talking's gone.'

Pause. Murmur.

Kozlov said to Mikoyan: 'Nikita Sergeyevich wants to know if you concur.'

'Surely –' began Mikoyan.

Kozlov muffled the receiver against his shoulder.

'You know this is over the line,' he said to Mikoyan. 'This is so far over the fucking line I can't believe you think there's even anything to discuss.'

Mikoyan dropped his gaze to his lap, looked up again; nodded.

'He concurs,' said Kozlov into the phone. 'We'll get on it immediately. Don't worry, it'll all be sorted by sundown. Yes. Yes. As soon as we know anything.'

Volodya felt an instant and deep relief. The end was in sight; it was all going to be sorted out. The troops would break up the crowd. Things would be normal again. He could feel the knot in his guts unclenching.

Kozlov put the phone down. He beckoned. Aides gathered round him and Mikoyan in a muttering huddle, and quickly generated a mass of orders, scribbled on little bits of folded paper. One of the scribblers pointed at Volodya.

'You,' he said. 'You're the local guy, aren't you? Take this back where you just came from.'

Volodya's heart sank. 'In the car?' he said stupidly.

'Take a dromedary, for all I care,' said the aide. 'Just be quick. We're on a timetable now.'

Volodya lurched off the wall and forced his feet to carry him out of the smoky safety of the conference room, back up the barracks corridor towards the roaring world. The last thing he heard was Kozlov's voice. 'And get me some real grub,' he was saying. 'This place is such a fucking hole . . .'

Back through the corridors, back to the courtyard. No need to pull rank on a driver; he was part of a gaggle of jog-trotting emissaries, it turned out, military and civil, all clutching their piece of folded paper, all piling together into the two Chaikas nearest the gate, all sitting in sweaty silence together on the ride back through the strangely ordinary streets; all piling out in the cross-street and scattering on their errands.

Volodya panted up the procuracy stairs, crowd noise growing, and came out under the unprotected sky with his head ducked.

The sun was the same, the smell was the same. The noise, in fact, was remarkably much the same. He gave the note to the monk-faced man, who was leaning on the parapet and smoking as if he had all the time in the world, and gingerly looked over himself. He had expected a riot, or something like it; but whatever was going on at the police station, the square only held a mass of people in the same state of calm wrath that he had seen before. Some were chanting and shouting at the empty balcony of the gorkom building: 'Send out Mikoyan!' 'Give us Mikoyan!' Many had sat down on the grass of the public garden, as if on a foodless picnic. The upturned faces shone like grains of rice.

'Someone's got their balls back, I see,' said the civilian. 'Here we go, then, lads. Not long now. You know the drill.' The soldiers picked up their gear and started to line up along the parapet.

'Cigarette?' he said to Volodya.

'I don't,' Volodya said. 'It's bad for the chest.'

'No shit,' said monk-face. He had a metal eye-tooth which showed when he grinned.

On rooftops all around the square, Volodya could see similar movement. A few people down below looked up and pointed, presumably seeing armed silhouettes appear against the rooflines. But most of the attention was reserved for the double line of soldiers filing in at the gorkom end of the square, to take up position on the steps. They had an officer with them, carrying a loudhailer.

'All soldiers out of the crowd,' he squawked. 'All Komsomol out of the crowd. All militia out of the crowd. All comrades from the organs of security, out of the crowd.' Trickles of faces started to work their way out of the mass, rice grains in motion, and shook themselves free at the square's edges, walking away in the different greens of the Red Army and the police, in shirtsleeves and leather jackets and overalls. Some were carrying cameras and notebooks. The officer waited till they were clear. Then he lifted the bullhorn again.

'This is an illegal demonstration. You are ordered to disperse immediately. Your grievances will be addressed.'

'Calm down, general,' someone shouted, and there was laughter.

'Disperse *immediately*,' said the officer.

'Not till they speak to us,' shouted another voice, and a roar of approval echoed off the buildings, dwindling into separate hubbubs, then into many different cries. 'C'mon, you're not going to shoot us!' 'You disperse!' 'Who are you to give orders?' 'Stand with the workers!' 'Send us Mikoyan!' '*Meat* and *milk* and a *pay rise*!'

'Go home,' said the officer. Some new element in his voice made part of the crowd laugh again, but another part shifted nervously. 'I will count to three,' he said, 'and if you do not begin to disperse, I will have no alternative and I will order my men to fire. One.'

The front rank of the soldiers on the gorkom stairs dropped to one knee and lifted their rifles till they pointed, not at the crowd, but at the sky overhead, like an honour guard at a very rowdy funeral. At this the collective voice of the crowd did change pitch; it dropped to an alarmed bass murmur, and those who were sitting on the grass scrambled to their feet. The edge of the crowd nearest the gorkom even fell back a few metres, shrinking away from the line of guns.

'Two,' shouted the officer. 'For God's sake, go home!'

The crowd wavered, but then someone cried out, 'They won't shoot at the people,' and forward surged the strikers again, the people at the front less enthusiastic but borne on by the press from behind.

'Three,' bellowed the officer, into sudden silence. The crowd stood. The soldiers waited. The officer helplessly pulled out his pistol and fired it into the air over his head, a tinny little *crack*; at the signal the kneeling troopers let off a rolling volley, much louder, and puffs of gun-smoke rose up from the gorkom steps.

Cries of fear, backwards stumbling in the square, then confused realisation that no one was hurt. Calls to and fro, shouts front to back in the crowd, like the telegraph of voices that had broadcast Kurochkin's offence yesterday morning; and the calls turning, unbelievably, nightmarishly, to reassurance. 'Stand firm!' 'They won't shoot the people!' 'It's only blanks!' Volodya heard one woman directly below crying, 'They're shooting, they'll kill us,' but immediately a male voice answered, 'Are you out of your mind? In our time?' And the crowd, which had looked as if it might shiver apart, solidified again.

'Tsk, tsk,' said monk-face. 'Much too brave.'

Volodya craned forward, looking for the reinforcements who must surely now pour out of the side streets to shove the strikers back by main force, to beat them back with batons maybe, but a hammer-blow of sound fell on his right ear, dazing him. The world rang; then rang again, monstrously loud, and dulling as the hammerblows came over and over, on top of one another. Someone else was shooting. Not the soldiers on the gorkom steps: they were reeling too, looking wildly around from side to side, trying to work out where the new gunfire was coming from. It was the crew on Volodya's rooftop who were doing it, and the crews on the other rooftops, kneeling up at the parapets and firing down, spent cartridge cases spinning out of their rifles in slow fountains of brass. And these bullets were not disappearing into the blue, they were being drilled deliberately into the flesh of the crowd – which shook, which fissured, which fell apart and revealed that it was made only of the single bodies of men and women and children. A man of sixtysomething, grey beard, drinker's cheeks, was turning baffled on the spot just where Volodya was looking, everyone around him lurching into motion. Just where one of his neighbours with the guns was looking too, evidently: the near side of the old man's head caved in, the far side blew out in a geyser of red and grey. A woman holding a baby got the spray in her face and began to scream, but no sound reached Volodya at all. He screamed himself; he turned around and waved his arms in the face of the monk-faced man, and shouted 'Stop! Stop! What are you doing?'

The monk-faced man reached out big, soft, well-cared-for hands and seized Volodya's wrists; pulled him close so that he could speak into Volodya's ear.

'Sit down,' he said. 'Sit down, son, and shut up. Be grateful you're up here, and not down there.'

Volodya folded up against the parapet, but he could still see through the gap between the plaster pillars. He could see people trying to run, now, but moving with dream slowness, with mouths working to push out syllables of fear one by one, while the bullets tore along, perfectly brisk; tore along, and through. He saw a man stumble and fall because his leg now hinged in a new place, at a crater halfway up his thigh. He saw blood running from ears. He saw blood with teeth in it. He saw a face pulped. He saw a knee burst. It made no sense. Was the mind supposed to attack the body? Did the head reach down and start chewing at the fibres of the arm? It made no sense! Volodya had wondered – you always wondered, if you were in the lucky generation born later – how he would have done in the war; and always suspected that he might be a usefully cold fish in battle, able to choose not to care much about suffering, if it wasn't his own, since what he felt for other people was so much more often annoyance than anything stronger. But he'd been wrong. There was no choosing in it. He saw, and something dreadful built in his face, sorrow or fear (was there any difference) pumping all the tissues round his eyes up to a pressure that tears didn't relieve. They ran down his face, but they would have had to break out of him as hard and fast as the rounds from the rifles to make any difference. Windows were breaking now, at the corners of the square with Moscow Street and Podtelkov Street, as the guns chased the crowd in the direction it had come. The plate glass of the hairdressing salon shattered. A middle-aged hairdresser blew across the room and ceased to be. The shooting went on, and on, and on. And Volodya wrapped his arms around his head, and was, indeed, grateful.

When the shooting stopped, the square was empty, except for the bodies, some moving, some not. Two new smells ruled in it now: the burnt smell of cordite and a fresh hot reek like a butcher's shop just after the stock van arrives. Volodya dragged back to the stairway in the wake of the descending soldiers, his feet jingling on spent brass. At the first landing he was abruptly sick. The monk-faced man companionably waited for him, and lit another cigarette.

'You'll get used to it,' he said.

No, I won't, vowed Volodya. No I won't.

The old man took the bag in his teeth, and began to climb to heaven. He climbed and climbed – he climbed for a long time. The old woman asked: 'Is it still far, old man?' He was about to say 'Not far', when the bag dropped out of his teeth. The old woman fell to the ground and was smashed to bits. The old man climbed down from the cabbage stalk and picked up the bag, but in it there were only bones, and even they were broken into little pieces.

PART IV

The same afternoon that twenty-eight people died on the square in Novocherkassk, Khrushchev gave a speech to an audience of Soviet and Cuban teenagers. He was supposed to be talking about something quite different: instead, compulsively, he talked about the price rise. He told the young people what he'd hoped Mikoyan and Kozlov would be able to make the strikers believe, that having more expensive meat and butter would make agriculture 'rise as if on yeast!' He turned it and turned it about. 'What were we supposed to do?' He said the government had trusted in the good sense of citizens. 'We decided to tell the people and the party the truth.' Knowing what we know now, it is hard not to hear a confused anger. The Politburo's announcement had come as a shock to a population which had been trained to expect prices only ever to fall, but it represented one of the few occasions in Soviet history where the decision-makers genuinely tried to share their reasoning with the public. Khrushchev had taken the advice of experts. He had tried to do the virtuous thing, the anti-Stalinist thing, and it had just made him a mass-murderer again.

The teenagers may have been puzzled by his mood, but no one detected any incongruity, that day or the next day, or for many years after, because, of course, the Soviet people were certainly not told the truth about what had happened at Novocherkassk. Fire hoses were used to wash the blood off the ground, and when stains still remained, the square was repaved overnight with a fresh layer of asphalt. The bodies were distributed to five different cemeteries, and buried anonymously, in graves already filled with more peaceful bones. Relatives were never told what had become of the dead. It was as if they had suddenly evaporated. Not a word about the massacre appeared in the newspapers, or on the radio or television; and great pressure was applied to the students and workers of the town to doubt the evidence of their senses, or, if they stubbornly insisted on remembering, to do so at least in silence and in private. There had been some unrest, provoked by a handful of troublemakers, now all tried and convicted for their crimes. The authorities had stepped in, calm had been restored, end of story.

Since no one knew different, except in Novocherkassk itself, and later on in samizdat whisperings, the massacre damaged nobody's reputation. Frol Kozlov continued as Khrushchev's heir apparent till he had a stroke the following April. Anastas Mikoyan went on being the civilised man of Soviet politics. Far more powerful in their effect were the events played out, unignorably, in public: the missile crisis Khrushchev blundered into in the autumn, which killed nobody but might have killed billions, and the next year's atrocious wheat crop, which put paid to his predictions of yeast-like success in agriculture. Khrushchev was by this time gleamingly bald, except for a white fuzz above each ear. Contemporary joke: What do you call Khrushchev's hairdo? 'Harvest of 1963'. Compared to these, the massacre at Novocherkassk caused nothing to happen. It had no consequences anywhere – except in the thinking of the Politburo.

By 1963, almost all the elements seemed to be coming together in Academician Nemchinov's scheme to reform the Soviet economy mathematically. New cybernetics institutes and departments had sprung up right across the Soviet Union, and were hurrying to complete pieces of the puzzle; or perhaps of several different puzzles. Mathematical models were being built for supply, demand, production, transportation, factory location, short-term planning, long-term planning, sectoral and regional and national and international planning. Automated control systems for factories had been commissioned. A group of Red Army cyberneticians were proposing an all-Union data network that could be used by civilians and the military alike. But Nemchinov himself was no longer in charge. Another casualty of 1963, he was now too ill to go on acting as patron and progress-chaser-in-chief to the proliferating, multiplying discipline he'd helped to guide into existence. When his own base of operations in the Academy expanded into the fully autonomous TSEMI, the Central Economic-Mathematical Institute, with a building out among the muddy new boulevards of the Sparrow Hills and a banner in the hall reading 'Comrades, Let's Optimise!', he could not be its director. The alliances he had created would have to work by themselves. 'The main task', he had told a new conference at Akademgorodok, was now 'the widespread introduction of the results of research'. Others were less sure that the research was ready, or that it all pointed in the same direction. Academician Glushkov's group down in Kiev favoured the direct cybernetic control of the entire economy, eliminating the need for money altogether. The Akademgorodok crowd called for rational pricing. An economist from Kharkov by the name of Evsei Liberman had made a big splash in Pravda *by urging for profit to become the main indicator of industrial success. But the premise of the whole intellectual effort was the practical improvement, very soon, of the Soviet economy; of all its ten thousand enterprises, and of the systems that integrated and co-ordinated them. The countdown to paradise in the Party Programme required the economy to grow, through the 1960s, at the rate it had in the official figures for the 1950s: 10.1%. The economists had undertaken to support this by bringing theory swiftly down to the shopfloor. Mines, department stores, chemical plants, fur farms, freight depots: all of it had to be optimised.*

Every year, every enterprise in the Soviet Union had to agree a tekhpromfinplan *with the organisation it reported to. The* tekhpromfinplan *covered finance for the enterprise, and the technology it would be using over the next twelve months, but most importantly it stated targets for production. It specified what the enterprise must produce, and in what quantity, and at what quality, in order to fulfil its plan. There were bonuses for the managers if they overfulfilled the plan, penalties if they underfulfilled it. Exactly how the* tekhpromfinplan *was worked out kept changing, as initiatives from the top restlessly rejigged the Soviet Union's bureaucracy. But there were always three main players. There was the enterprise, down at the bottom; there was Gosplan, up at the top; and in the middle, there would be an intermediary. Sometimes the intermediary gathered together all the enterprises working in one particular area of industry, and then it would be called a 'ministry'. Minradioprom, for instance, the Ministry for Radio Production. But at the time we are talking about, the intermediary was a* sovnarkhoz, *a regional economic council, which gathered together all the enterprises in one geographical zone of the country, no matter what products they made.*

If you were reading the official descriptions of the system published by Gosplan, you would think it worked liked this. Every spring, as the Soviet Union's rivers broke up into granitas of wet ice, Gosplan analysed last year's performance figures, paying close attention to the strategic priorities for the economy, and the big picture of the march to communist abundance. But before it had quite finished – alas, there was never enough time to do things in strict sequence, and the year's work tended all to proceed via estimates, later corrected – the zaiavki, *the 'indents', had already been sent out to the enterprises. On these printed forms, the enterprises requested the supplies they would need for next year's production. But the enterprise, of course, did not yet know how much it was going to be asked to manufacture. So management would estimate how much coal, gas, electricity, wool, ammonia, copper piping, polystyrene etc. it might need, one material per printed form, on the basis of a plausible percentage rise from its output last year. Around about the end of June, Gosplan would complete the set of draft production targets. They, descending from Gosplan, would arrive in the offices of the* sovnarkhoz *at the same time as the ascending mass of* zaiavki *and production proposals from the enterprises, and a period of negotiation then followed in which the* sovnarkhoz *and the enterprises together explored the true productive possibilities of the enterprises. Gosplan's 'control figures' came in a highly aggregated form, for ease of handling: general categories of production, from ferrous metals to foodstuffs. It was up to the* sovnarkhoz *to disaggregate them into the actual products its region produced, and to divide the making of them between its enterprises. Needless to say, the management of the enterprise might prefer a looser plan, and a more generous flow of materials, than suited the overall interests of the economy. Negotiation continued until the* sovnarkhoz *had imposed on the enterprise a taut but not impossible level of output and a lean but not impossible level of inputs. Then, around the end of September, the* sovnarkhoz *combined all of the adjusted* zaiavki *and production targets for its region and sent them on to Gosplan.*

Gosplan added up all of the zaiavki *from round the country to give a figure for the total demand for each commodity, and added up all of the production targets to give a figure for each commodity's total supply. This was called 'the method of balances'. It ensured that, at every upward step of the socialist economy, the quantity of each product the USSR produced always balanced the quantity of each product that was required. But it might be that the two figures, at first, did not quite match. Then there would follow a second period of negotiation, this time between Gosplan and the various* sovnarkhozy, *with Gosplan doing its best to limit demand (or at least to prioritise it on the most strategic sectors) and to expand supply. Negotiation continued until Gosplan had agreed with the* sovnarkhozy, *in turn, a challenging but manageable programme of production. The economy once balanced, the Council of Ministers signed off Gosplan's work in late October, just allowing time for the final production targets and supply quotas to be passed down to the* sovnarkhozy, *for the* sovnarkhozy *to divide them between the enterprises, and for the enterprises to go shopping for their needs in the coming year in the vast compendium of the 'specified classification', which listed every item produced anywhere in the Soviet Union. This last pulse of paperwork passed through the economy in early December. With their order-books now filled firmly for the coming year, managers could dot the i's and cross the t's on their* tekhpromfinplan, *and (precious document in hand) board the train to deliver it to the* sovnarkhoz *just before New Year, in a spirit of justified celebration.*

All clear so far?

'I want the lovely Swan Maiden to stand before me, and through her feathers let her body be seen, and through her body let her bones be seen, and through her bones let it be seen how from bone to bone the marrow flows, like pearls poured from one vessel to another.'

The Method of Balances, 1963

Maksim Maksimovich Mokhov was a very kind man. All of his colleagues remarked on it. When he travelled on business to the Comecon countries or beyond, he would always bring back a thoughtful little present, and by no means the stereotyped or obvious things for which those places were known. From Bulgaria, for example, he brought back for his secretary a small flask of the genuine attar of roses, presented with a little bow: too strong to be used as perfume in the ordinary way of things, but nevertheless delightful. When she uncorked it, a heavy richness soaked the air of Gosplan, like crimson dye sinking into a bowl of water. From Poland he brought ceramic plaques of kings and knights, as thin and brittle as iced biscuits. From Sweden came children's toys, beautifully made from wood. Not having any children himself, he gave these to his deputies in the department; and when the seven-year-old daughter of one wrote him a thank-you letter, he replied, covering a sheet of paper in careful script, and replacing many of the nouns with charming little pictures. A horse instead of 'horse', for example.

The same consideration, it was said, applied in his private life. His wife had been killed in the siege of Leningrad, when they were both in their later twenties. Although he had never remarried, he had been attached virtually since the end of the war to a woman in a similar position, a young widow then, a rather older widow now. This lady had suffered some sort of street accident a couple of years ago which had injured her face, causing great problems to her and, apparently, ruining what was left of her looks. Maksim Maksimovich had remained devoted throughout, securing the services of the best doctors for her, and taking no steps to replace her with a new mistress, even though it would not have been difficult for a man in his position to do so. A number of young women in the building would in fact have been willing, impressed by his fidelity. He received looks of sympathy and admiration when he handed out the traditional bouquets on Women's Day. But he seemed content to leave things as they were. Tuesday evenings were the regular time for him and his lady friend to hear a concert, or to go to the opera together. He could be seen standing at the mirror in his office, just before he left, tidying his brilliantined hair and making efforts to reduce the diabolical appearance of his bushy eyebrows. Then he would hook his coat jauntily off the hatstand, check the envelope of tickets in his inside pocket and be off down the long corridors, bending his dark head and his spindly shoulders obligingly to acquaintances.

What a mind, though. As sharp as a razor. Even in his kindness, you might feel that he was amused by what he understood of you, and perhaps also by what he understood of himself. In times alike of frenzy, denunciation, desperation, triumph, complaisance and anxiety, he had made himself valuable. He had risen as high as you could go at Gosplan before the posts became purely political appointments; to the top, in other words, of one of its industrial departments, but not into the general policy apparatus at the apex of the pyramid, which tended to be staffed from the Central Committee. Yet, since his was the level at which competence was known to reach its ceiling, people at it were sometimes, paradoxically, a good deal more important than their job title suggested. On paper, Maksim Maksimovich was Deputy Director of the Sector of Chemical and Rubber Goods, responsible for the forty-one strategic commodities in the chemical and synthetic-rubber industries which the notional Directors of the sector rarely had time to contemplate in detail, being (as they were) apparatchiks in a hurry, and often unable to find their arses with both hands, let alone to analyse the accounts of a chemical factory. And this was significant enough, for chemicals were a vital sector at present, growing so fast that it took all the planners' agility to keep the expansion under control. But in practice much of the day-to-day running of the department was handled, in turn, by Maksim Maksimovich's trusted assistants, because he himself was now being called on flatteringly often by Minister Kosygin, poised right on the very point of the Gosplan pyramid, to act as one of his kitchen cabinet of advisers.

Year by year Maksim Maksimovich understood the stress points, the secret path dependences, of the plan. On a whole range of subjects, he could give you a view of the most refined realism about what was likely to work and what to run into apparently unforeseeable trouble. Moreover, he kept up (so far as Gosplan's library let him) with Western commentary on the plan, which he could translate into Soviet terms. He could tell you, with beautiful ideological tact, what foreigners meant when they said the Soviet system suffered from 'suppressed inflation' or a 'permanent sellers' market'. Conversely, he could see where the unfolding developments of the plan might create business opportunities for the Soviet Union in the West. Hence the trips he now found he was taking, not to Romania to talk about nylon, but to Stockholm to help Kosygin talk to the capitalists, riding along in a jump seat of the ministerial Zil, other competent persons from Trade and Finance and Gosbank perched around him. Then an unobtrusive conference room, with the Soviet Union's technicians of money on one side and the West's on the other: loans, credits, wheat purchases, petroleum sales. It was impossible for Maksim Maksimovich not to notice that, on the other side of the table, the intelligence types and security men served the bankers, while on his it was the bankers who whispered advice to the commissar. In the West, he saw, the limousine would have been his own. You may be sure that this thought manifested itself only as an invisible addition to the irony of his gaze.

Maksim Maksimovich would probably not have been working the balances himself, this particular October morning, if a plague of flu had not swept through the Gosplan tower, felling several of his subordinates just as the frantic final weeks of plan revision began. The situation was a nuisance: yet how exhilarating to get back into the specifics of the system again, with its never-ending judgement calls, its hidden little psychological games, its lateral complexities. He whistled under his breath as he trundled his famous chair in front of him across the herringbone parquet of the eighteenth floor. The chair was famous because he could trundle it. It was an ingenious East German contrivance, terribly comfortable to sit in, which had four little castors at the end of legs curving out from a central metal column. He had brought it back himself, by train from Berlin, and used it to spin to and fro across his office at alarming speeds. On its seat, two volumes of chemical-industry input co-efficients were weighing down a thin file of correspondence.

'Going into battle?' said a passer-by from Non-Ferrous.

'That's how the steel was tempered,' he said.

'How many down with it, with you?'

'Eleven so far, and two more suspiciously green. You?'

'Worse!'

The balances were kept in a long, library-like room lined with filing cabinets, watched over by a librarian-like gorgon at a central desk. Mokhov showed his pass – though in his case, it was not strictly necessary – and seated himself at a workspace where there was a convenient spare abacus. He shot his cuffs with a touch of theatre, and opened the file. This room had been his playground for many years, and it stimulated him still. In its grey metal drawers this year were 373 folders, each holding work-in-progress on the balance for a commodity. Three hundred and seventy-three commodities: represented, for the most part, in the highest possible state of generality, so that each one of them rolled together under a single heading what was in practice a mass of different products. Yet still they cast only the loosest and most imperfect conceptual net over the prodigious output of the economy as a whole. There were quarter of a million separate items listed in the specified classification of the electro-technical industry alone. You could never capture the activity of something so huge, so irredeemably multiple, in 373 folders. It would have been an absurd error, therefore, to suppose that the room in any substantial sense contained the economy. The best that could be said was that it contained a kind of strategic outline of it. No; that was not quite true. The best that could be said about the room was that it worked, and had done for thirty years. Some of the folders tracked the basics of industrial life: steel, concrete, coal, oil, lumber, electric power. Some were devoted to the food supply, and to agriculture's inputs of tractors and fertiliser. Some attended to sensitive military items. Some followed the production of very specific pieces of critical machinery, because these were the tools on which whole other sectors depended for their existence. Some paid special attention to new technologies just now being bootstrapped into being. Some concentrated on things many different industries used. It was an ad hoc apparatus, not one generated predictably from a set of axioms. It was not the result of any economic theory. But it functioned. It provided the economy with something necessary: a place where the incompatible demands made on it would reveal themselves, where they finally rose up and required to be reconciled, with whatever finesse a planner could muster. And finesse it needed to be, for the 373 commodities did not exist independently. They were interconnected. A change to the output of one might send ripples of change through many others. At this time of year, teams from the different department were all pursuing the consequences of their own last-minute revisions from folder to folder, trying to make the balances compatible with each other, trying to make the balances balance; before the time ran out, and the revisions had to end, and a summary of the state of the room had to be sent on up to the Council of Ministers for approval, in the form of twenty-two typed volumes of figures, four thousand pages or thereabouts, loaded onto a trolley.

So. Maksim Maksimovich spread documents and telegrams with his long fingers. A little problem with Solkemfib, the viscose plant at Solovets, away off in the green gloom of the north-eastern forests. It was one of Maksim Maksimovich's new generation of chemical-fibre operations, along with the big new installations at Barnaul and Svetlogorsk, and it ought not to have been causing trouble at this point in its life-cycle, with machines only four years old and the trials of running them in safely behind. It had its own wood-pulp mill, to provide cellulose, and a nice big lake for water. Power came by 220-kilovolt line from one of the hydro stations on the upper Volga. Everything else arrived and departed on a railroad spur. Really, it was only salt, sulphur and coal in, viscose out. That was the particular simplicity of viscose production from the planner's point of view. None of the more complex chemical inputs the process required – sulphuric acid, lye, carbon disulphide – could easily be transported in bulk. They all had to be manufactured on the spot, at the plant itself; which meant that, to the remote and abstracting eye of someone chiefly concerned with supply chains, a viscose plant could be treated as robust. It was relatively insensitive to disruption. It could be supplied from multiple sources. It was not a hostage to problems elsewhere. Feed it its raw materials, and it chugged along, an economic black box, busily turning trees into sweaters and cellophane and high-strength cord for car tyres. This always struck Maksim Maksimovich as a very obliging way for a physical process to work – and charmingly close to the political textbooks too. Trees into sweaters! Brute matter uplifted to serve human purposes! What could be more dialectical? Who knows, perhaps this thought had figured in

Mr K.'s decision that the citizens of his radiant future should, mainly, be wearing viscose and polyester. Yes, a viscose plant was an activist. It woke nature from its idle sleep and set it to work. Unfortunately, it also created a mighty run-off of lignins and poisonous sulphide compounds, but Solovets was a good long way from anywhere else.

Yet somehow Solkemfib had contrived to fumble. The week before last, according to the report in front of him, a piece of heavy earth-moving equipment had been left overnight on a hilltop beside the plant where construction was due to begin. Sometime in the small hours, the clutch had slipped. The behemoth rolled downhill, gathering speed as it jolted over tree stumps, until by the time it reached the bottom it had acquired the momentum of a wrecking ball at full swing. It rolled straight through the thin brick wall of Solkemfib's No. 2 Stretching and Spinning Shop and crashed into the delicate machinery for stretching the fresh viscose filament as it emerged from spin baths of sulphuric acid. Since the line was running at the time, the collision caused considerable spillage of acid, and it was some time before workers were able to separate the wreckage. At this point it became clear that, between the impact and the spill, the stretching machine was beyond the reach of even the most ingenious repair. The plant's mechanical engineer had submitted a list of the crushed and damaged parts. Inspectors from the *sovnarkhoz* confirmed that the machine was, indeed, a write-off. Local police investigating the accident, with the help of the same Solkemfib engineer, had found that the brakes and clutch had been properly set when the earth-mover was parked. A flaw in its hydraulic system was to blame.

Enterprise-level difficulties were supposed to be dealt with at the *sovnarkhoz*, and the stage for bargaining over them was definitively over for this year. But the *sovnarkhoz* had behaved quite correctly in passing this particular problem straight on up. It had the potential to cause serious disruption. Without the stretching machine, the whole No. 2 line at Solovets was out of action. Half the capacity of the plant had suddenly become unavailable; and it was the half that produced tyre cord, not the half that turned out viscose fibre for clothing. Without Solkemfib's contribution of tyre cord, the tyre cord balance would sink into deficit on the supply side; and that could have a knock-on effect on the output of tyres; and that in turn could cause a fall in the output of cars and trucks and buses; and so on, and so on, the original shortfall leaping from commodity to commodity, from folder to folder, propagating itself around the room and therefore around the economy, branching and multiplying and creating chaos. So many of the strategic commodities were themselves inputs in the production of other strategic commodities that a big change in the availability of one could, in theory, ripple on undamped, or perhaps even amplified, through areas of the plan utterly removed from the starting point, seeding all the balances it passed through with incompatibilities that would themselves require further disruptive waves of revision to deal with. In theory – Maksim Maksimovich had seen the mathematical demonstrations – you would need to revise all the balances a minimum of six times over, and a maximum of thirteen times, to make them consistent with one another again, and if all 373 commodities were evenly interconnected, each iteration would require 373 x 373, or 139,129 separate calculations. The academic would-be reformers of the economy made much play with this. It was the basis for Emil Shaidullin's entertaining prediction that, by 1980, the entire population would have to work full-time on balancing the plan.

But here, thought Maksim Maksimovich, was precisely where the reformers showed their naivety. They missed the point entirely of the planner's task; which was not to adjust passively to disrupting developments, but to take active steps to limit their effect. The art of the planner was to lead away a ripple of change through the balances in such a direction that it died down, with the minimum of consequences, in the minimum number of steps. Gosplan did not deal with alterations in the plan by repeatedly revising all 373 balances, or anything like it. And nor was he going to chase the consequences of a shortfall of tyre cord meekly through balance after balance. He would cut off the forward-running shortage before it could seriously affect tyre production, let alone run on into the balance for vehicles. Tyre cord could be made of other things than viscose, and quick orders for the substitutes would make up part of the gap. The rest he would fill by last-minute increases to the tyre-cord target for all the other viscose producers. They would groan and strain, but they would probably manage to cover most of the increase, and he could sweeten the situation for them by generosity with viscose's handily generic raw materials; also, perhaps, with extra dollops of cash, under some suitable heading, to make up for the fulfilment bonuses those plants would probably lose. Alas, the effect of moves like these was always to tighten the plan a notch or two further than anyone had originally intended. It would be pushed (everywhere, as other colleagues did what he was doing) that bit more towards a state where its goals could only just barely be achieved. Thus it would be more vulnerable to bad luck, and even more susceptible to proliferating gridlock should anything *else* go wrong. But the alternative was the incoherent wonderland of the mathematicians.

First, though, he had to know just how big the shortfall of tyre cord was going to be. It depended, of course, on how long the No. 2 line at Solovets stayed down; which in turn depended very much on what he, Maksim Maksimovich, now decided to do about it. Again, not at all a mathematical problem. He had been sent numbers, but his task was to descry, through them, the human situation behind. What was going on at Solovets? The accident made him instinctively suspicious. He counted the pieces of bad luck required for it to have happened. Earth-mover parked just so; fault in the hydraulics; treeless path down the hillside; entry point through the wall exactly beside the machine; acid spill. Five separate unlikelihoods all lined up in a row, one after the other. Very neat. In the old days, heads would have rolled over this on principle. It would have been labelled as sabotage just to close the books on it. The organs of security would swiftly have uncovered a conspiracy of wreckers, vilely determined to cheat the people of their rightful viscose. But the policy now was not to compound the effects of an accident by losing, in addition, the expertise of skilled workers over it. After all, accidents did happen. It was not a very satisfactory objection to an event that it was unlikely, for in the nature of probability, unlikely things took place all the time. And then, to set against his suspicions, there was the one great counteracting factor that he could not for the life of him see what motive there could be for deliberately doing such a thing. The risk would be enormous, even now. You would have to be desperate. A personal grudge of some kind, a disaffected individual? Hard to believe that they could have covered their tracks so well. Management? Hard to see what cause the management at Solkemfib would have for desperation. He slid the relevant page in front of him. Some teething troubles with the tyre-cord line last year, and as a result a mix of output slightly awry from what the plan had called for, with a good gross output but too much ordinary yarn in it. But this year, solid progress: tyre cord output 2% above target in the first quarter, 3% in the second quarter, smack in the golden zone of plan overfulfilment which brought bonuses raining down. You wouldn't imperil that voluntarily.

Mokhov sighed. The gorgon, whose hair was rinsed the red of old blood, smiled at him. He kicked off gracefully from the table and his wheeled chair flew backwards across the room towards the rank of cabinets where the balances for 133 types of machinery were kept. The replacement stretching machine Solkemfib was requesting, urgently backed up by the *sovnarkhoz*, was itself a strategic commodity. He riffled through a drawer and found it: the PNSh-180-14S continuous-action engine for viscose, exclusively produced in Sverdlovsk by a division of Uralmash, the giant of machine-building enterprises. Recent technological upgrade. The folder was thin, which suggested that this balance had hardly been altered at all. He was not surprised. With just one manufacturer, and a take-up determined by the rate new viscose plants opened, there would not be much volatility in the call for a PNSh-180-14S, unless something like this happened. But that might make it all the worse to introduce an alteration now. A viscose stretching-machine was not some handy lathe-sized object, three metres by two. It was a metal porcupine the width of a subway hall. Building one was a sizeable commitment of resources in itself, and for that matter a major capital cost too. He picked out the folder and propelled himself across the floor again, with paddling motions of his shining black shoes.

Ah yes: a total production of only seventeen machines for the whole USSR, and no revisions paperclipped to the original balance. The page in front of him was simplicity itself compared to some balances. On the left, under 'SOURCES', it gave production as 17, imports as nil, suppliers' stocks as nil. On the right, on the 'DISTRIBUTION' side, it listed the plants receiving the machines, in order of their *sovnarkhoz*. Nil distribution for export, nil for suppliers' stocks, nil for the special reserve of the Council of Ministers. Nil nil nil. Crisply pencilled words and numbers inside the smudgy boxes of the form; departmental authorisation code and operator's initials down at the bottom. Maksim Maksimovich hesitated. If he added one more to the production side, he would be condemning the Uralmash division in question to squeeze out the equivalent of a 6% output boost, on top of the agreed growth for next year, just by that act. It would certainly stress their operations and disarrange their timetable for the year. But the alternative would be to lose one of the seventeen machines already on order, and with it a chunk of the longer-term output growth in viscose he needed to satisfy the targets of the Seven-Year Plan. He was supposed to get chemical-fibre production up to four hundred thousand tonnes per annum by 1965.

He could have wished that Solkemfib's No. 1 line had broken down instead. True, clothing manufacturers were waiting for the ordinary yarn it made, but compared to the tire plants they were a distinctly low priority; because, one single step beyond them, you arrived at the consumer, and the consumer was an end-point of the system, and therefore a natural sink for shortages. All that consumers did with viscose was to wear it. No one stood beyond them in the chain, so there were no consequences whatsoever for inconveniencing them, no farther balances to consider. You could inconvenience the consumer with impunity.

He cast himself off once more, shuttling sideways to the central desk. The gorgon gave him a blank balance form, fresh from the mimeograph, and he signed for it. Then he sailed back to where the papers were spread out. He poised his pencil. He would, he decided, do a little something to keep Solkemfib's minds on the job, by tautening their coal and salt and sulphur supplies a tad. Bad luck might spring from carelessness, and should be discouraged. A reminder of plan discipline would do no harm. But they would have their PNSh-180-14S, and so would all of his enterprises that were already expecting one. Uralmash could be soothed some other way. In the box next to the word 'production' on the left-hand side of the new page, he wrote firmly, '18'. There; there was the budget of pain shared out, and shared out more or less evenly, since there must be a budget of pain.

Maksim Maksimovich Mokhov was a very kind man.

2.

Prisoner's Dilemma, 1963

The light was fading as the train from Solovets left the forests behind, and snow swept past the window in bluish swathes. Out on the Moscow plain, factory walls rose higgledy-piggledy, first a few and then more and more, unstoppably, as if a sorcerer's apprentice had been let loose to build industry and had just kept going, a coking plant here and a fractionating tower there, reduction gears here and solvents there, tractors and rifles, lathes and electro-plate, steel and brass and zinc and cement, da da da da-da-da dadada, the countermanding spell never uttered, until the same sights repeated all the way along the railroad; the same dark clustered silhouettes of chimneys, the same girdered rooflines, the same gridded windows, the same branching tracks of rusty wagons, the same blocks of workers' flats, with the snow rushing through and between, thick and soft, smoothing to blankness the churned mud and ice from which so many pipes, stakes, poles, reinforcing rods protruded, on which so many sacks, pallets, drums, bundles were piled. The snow rushed through, the train whirled by. Arkhipov pulled the curtains closed and turned back to the compartment.

'Well,' he said, slapping his knees, 'who wants another drink?'

The flasks were out, and a chunk of sweating ham wrapped in newspaper, and a whole sausage, to be carved with a penknife. Arkhipov, Kosoy and Mitrenko; they were all getting pleasantly steamed, there in the prickly heat of the soft-class car. Mitrenko, Arkhipov and Kosoy; three big men, tightly filling their skins, all in high good humour. The *tekhpromfinplan* was in Arkhipov's briefcase, up in the luggage rack, and they were off to the fleshpots together for the annual jamboree. Mitrenko's wife and Kosoy's had given their men shopping lists, detailed plans of campaign calling for raids on GUM and Gastronom No. 1 and Moda. Arkhipov's lady was a little too high-minded, or absent-minded, to manage that kind of thing; but he had already resolved that when they boarded the train home he would be wrestling a new top-of-the-line radiogram up the steps for her, with an armful of discs to play. They might shop on their own account too, when the meetings and the hand-shaking were done. Late at night, in the bar of the Ukraina, you could meet obliging professional girls, offering the kind of entertainment in such short, such lamentably short supply in Solovets, where everyone knew everyone, and the hotel Icebound Sea faced across the town square in dismal competition with a closed ice-cream kiosk, the household goods store and a teashop run by the fisheries trust. Oh, the sorrows of provincial life! But, till next Thursday, they were out of it, and they grinned at each other, Kosoy and Mitrenko and Arkhipov, their moods buoyed up, as if by thousands of little bubbles, with the knowledge of boldness rewarded.

This time last year, how dismal they had been. Solkemfib, the three of them had understood by then, was a career-killer. For a while they had been able to kid themselves that there was something else to try, but now the truth had sunk in. Ahead of them lay the ignominious destiny of the failed executive. First would come the reprimands and the censures, then the newspaper article in that special voice of wide-eyed sarcasm. 'Why has Director Arkhipov failed to fulfill his socialist pledges? His attitude can hardly be termed commendable. We asked Chief Accountant Kosoy to enlighten us, but he proved tongue-tied. Chief-of-Planning Mitrenko was no more helpful . . .' Doors would slam shut whenever they needed the slightest favour, suppliers would sneer and shit on them with impunity, making things so humiliating and disagreeable that it would almost be a mercy when the final blow fell, and they were banished to run fertiliser sales in Buttfuckistan.

Maddening, that was the word for it; maddening that the path to career death was separated by only a few percentage points of plan fulfilment from the other one, the upward path, the road to glory and local fame, where the press printed photos of you looking resolute, and the regional secretary pinned the Red Banner to your lapel while the hall applauded, and the bonuses swelled. That was the incentive, of course; that was why the bonuses were highly geared, so that the difference to a manager between hitting 99% of the plan target and hitting 103% was not an extra 4% on the salary, but more like 40%. They wanted your whole attention on pushing the plant to do that little bit more that made the difference between failure and success. Hence the utter importance of plan bargaining; hence the necessity, in normal times, of low-balling your first production estimate, so that the *sovnarkhoz*'s reflexive upward correction would put the target back in the band you had privately calculated was achievable. The *sovnarkhoz*, needless to say, knew what you were doing, knew the first estimate was always going to be deceptive. The trick was to make the deception seem transparent, thus gently flattering them in their sense that they knew what was *really* going on. It should seem to be offering them a hint about where you thought the true figure ought to lie. Then they'd go a couple of points up on your implicit suggestion, and feel like winners if you went along with it; which you would, after a certain amount of nominal shrieking and groaning, because you'd been low-balling the implied suggestion too. The gameplay varied, depending on who, exactly, you were facing off with this year. You might have to get subtler, or get cruder; you might have to do something unexpected, if you found things had settled into a rut which made your moves too easy to predict. But the game went on, within bounds roughly agreed between the players. With good luck, you'd have a comfortable year, with bad luck you'd have an uncomfortable one. You ought not to have an impossible year.

But what if you found yourself stuck – fixed – nailed to the fucking floor – on the wrong side of the hair-thin line between glory and ignominy? What if your private knowledge of your plant's true capacity told you that you had a problem beyond the scope of the game? Solkemfib was new, but it was not that new; by now, its managers were intimately clear about what they could and could not expect from the lovely new machinery. The viscose yarn line worked fine, the tyre cord line . . . did not. Or rather, it worked, and the wormlike filaments of viscose were stretched and strengthened as required as they were drawn out of the acid baths, and led away to be washed and dried and coiled onto wall-high racks of humming bobbins: but too slowly, altogether too slowly for Solkemfib's PNSh-180-14S to satisfy any plan for tyre cord they might be able to bargain out of the *sovnarkhoz*. The *sovnarkhoz* would base its reasoning on the paper rating for the machine's capacity, and the paper rating was simply too high, by an amount that added up to several hundred tonnes of tyre cord over a year. It might be that there was some kind of defect in their particular machine, though the mechanical engineer Ponomarev had climbed all over it looking, ingenious little goblin that he was, and not found anything; or it might be that the whole class of machines had been optimistically misrated by Uralmash. There was no way of knowing. For obvious reasons, it wasn't possible to contact another viscose plant and compare notes. That would have revealed the disastrous weakness of their hand, at a point where one of their few advantages was their ability to keep things dark.

So they'd been low, this time last year, quiet and morose on the Moscow train, all too aware that their stopgap answer, the best they could do, was no answer at all, really. They'd hit the gross target for the year 1962 dead on, 100% delivered of the 14,100 tonnes of viscose planned, only with the mix of production deliberately skewed towards plain ordinary clothing yarn off Line No. 1. Whoops, so sorry, slight technical difficulties with No. 2, now resolved. In other circumstances you could run for years turning out the wrong assortment mix, but not this way around, when you were pleasing your consumer-facing customers, who had no clout at all, and pissing off the industrial ones, who could shout good and loud when their tyre machines had to power down for lack of cord to mould the rubber to. No doubt it was nice that Mayak and the other Moscow textile outfits were happy with their Solkemfib yarn, woven into rayon scarves and neckties etc. etc.; but Arkhipov, Mitrenko and Kosoy would have cheerfully seen them struggling to sew socks out of spoiled stock if they had been able to keep the auto combines smiling instead. Anything else would have been flat contrary to common sense. As it was, they knew that they had drawn on a very limited supply of indulgence, on the planners' part; and the plan they had had to agree for this year had committed them to output from No. 2 that they were never going to achieve, no matter how many corners they cut. They could lean on Ponomarev all they liked to overclock the machines, they could 'storm' night after night. Still the chickens were coming home to roost.

And the thing of it was, the most maddening part of the whole clusterfuck was, that a simple technical fix existed. Uralmash now produced, apparently, an upgraded PNSh-180-14S which, even allowing for the righteous scepticism recently implanted in the breasts of Kosoy, Mitrenko and Arkhipov, ought to make the fulfilment of present plans a breeze. But Solkemfib had a plant full of shiny, virtually mint equipment. Solkemfib would be so far to the back of the priority line in getting the upgrade that it would probably be two decades before the planners decided it was replacement time for the career-killing piece of shit in Spinning and Stretching Shop No. 2. There seemed to be no way of getting from where they were to where they needed to be; to the solution hovering just out of reach. No way, at any rate, within the terms of the planning game as they were used to playing it, with the usual level of risk and the usual level of fiddling, and the usual understanding between themselves and the *sovnarkhoz* over what the *sovnarkhoz* wouldn't dig too deep into, as long as the viscose kept flowing.

Perhaps having to lie blandly in Moscow, last year, had encouraged creative thought. Maybe there had been something about sitting in the *sovnarkhoz* offices, and making promises they had no idea how to fulfil, which shook inspiration loose in them. Because it had been after that dismal journey that they began to see what they had to do, what a barefaced defection from the usual understanding was going to be required to sort this one out. What would be needed was a move in the game so outrageous that the planners would not recognise it as a move at all. They found it hard to believe what they were planning, at first. Certainly, they would never even have considered it, in the old days; and even now, they scarcely named it out loud to each other. And yet they understood each other very well.

Which of them first thought of Ponomarev? The mechanical engineer's name came up, that was all, during one of the nightly card games at Arkhipov's place, while the three of them were obsessively chewing the situation over, and over and over; and then, when he had been raised to mind, all three of them at the table under the hanging lamp had slowly smiled, all seeing the possibilities, all liking what they saw. Ponomarev was a funny fellow, a grizzled little creature with protruding eyes and skin so pale you could see the forked blue veins in his temples. 'A real Siberian tan,' said Mitrenko knowledgeably. He had been useful enough already, as an engineer. It was hard to get qualified staff to relocate to a hole like Solovets, let alone to tolerate the signature stink of the viscose process, now that Mr K. had removed most of the restrictions on workers' mobility; so it had seemed like straightforward good luck when Arkhipov ran into him at a chemical-fibre conference in Almaty and discovered in him somebody who, for his own particular reasons, was willing, even eager, to endure the northern forest. Not that Ponomarev was attending the conference. He was repairing the hotel's lift, and he happened to be there when Arkhipov, making a note of something, pulled out his fountain pen and found that it had leaked. 'I can fix that for you,' he said. 'It'll be the reservoir.' 'What, you're a pen expert?' said Arkhipov. 'Any little thing,' said Ponomarev. And he held out his hand. 'How do I know you won't run off with it?' Arkhipov asked. 'This is a good pen.' Ponomarev shrugged. The pen was waiting at the front desk next morning, neatly mended with a little piece of rubber tubing from an eyedropper. When Arkhipov, curious, asked questions, and found that the handyman was more than a handyman, was in fact a trained engineer, and in the right specialism too, Ponomarev explained his situation in a voice of extraordinary, colourless neutrality. If the Comrade Director wanted him, he would endeavour to justify the Comrade Director's trust; but the Comrade Director would need to sponsor him for residence in European Russia. He had been imprisoned, but was now released; he had been under sentence of indefinite administrative exile, but was now free to travel, if he were given somewhere to travel to. From where he was standing, lost in the dust of Central Asia, Solovets was virtually on Moscow's doorstep. It was a step almost all the way home. Arkhipov made enquiries, found no obstacles, and brought Ponomarev back to use his surprisingly illustrious education for Solkemfib's benefit.

The goblin was as good as his word. He worked with silent zeal and made no complaints, whatever shifts he was assigned. But he was not popular. He spoke in clipped, telegraphic style, spending as few words as possible on each utterance. He had a way of meeting the eye of the person he was talking to the whole time the conversation lasted, unremittingly, as if he scorned to do otherwise. He lived alone in a hostel room. 'Shacked up with a slide rule,' said Kosoy. He never joked, he never smiled. He was never seen to take a drink. For recreation, he wrote long letters and posted them. The most animated you might see him was on the nights just before the quarters ended, when No. 1 and No. 2 were storming. Then, when every cause that stopped the lines or cramped their speed had been pushed, somehow, to one side, and the digesters were shaking as they churned the cellulose crumbs with carbon disulphide, and the air was thick with the smell of putrefied cabbage, and the lines were quivering end-to-end with work being done – then, Ponomarev quivered too, and patted the surfaces of the machines with his fingertips.

'Won't he have our balls in a vice, afterward?' said Mitrenko.

'Who's going to believe him?' said Kosoy.

'Who'd take his word over ours?' said Arkhipov.

In fact when they told him what he had to do, if he wanted to keep his residence permit, he said nothing at all. He only gazed from face to face. Then he took his good time to act. In fact, he played it bloody close to the limit. They'd backdated so much production on No. 2 to pad out the earlier quarters' figures – some of Q2 assigned to Q1, more of Q3 asssigned to Q2, all of Q4's production so far assigned to Q3 – that there was very little margin left; No. 2 had to go down soon. Arkhipov was more relieved than he could remember being since the war when the emergency klaxons woke him in the middle of the night and he could go off in overcoat and fur hat to tour the carnage Ponomarev had contrived, gravely shaking his head. Give the little fucker his due, he had done a beautiful job, 'prepared in depth' as they used to say of battle plans. And he conducted himself through the investigation that followed as if he had ice water in his veins, and it was the furthest thought from his mind that he was basically staked out in front of the Solkemfib administration building, waiting to be grabbed, quick and easy, if the word came down from above that a culprit was required. But Moscow, it turned out, did not require a culprit. Moscow scowled, and dispensed happy endings all round. An attachment order arrived, entitling the Solovets Chemical Fibre Trust to take emergency delivery of one Uralmash PNSh-180-14S (upgrade model). Ponomarev could slink back to his hostel room, and Arkhipov, Mitrenko and Kosoy could climb aboard the express, knowing that one year of reduced bonus lay ahead of them, rather than unlimited ignominy.

'Now look what I've got here,' said Arkhipov, reaching into his suit pockets like a meaty-fingered magician. 'Gentlemen, take a look at these. C'mon, Mitrenko, leave the kid alone.'

Mitrenko had the door into the corridor open. He was baiting a young soldier trying to get by.

'Please move your leg, mister,' said the boy.

'Suck my cock,' remarked Mitrenko, pleasantly.

'Get out of the way!'

'Or what?'

'Get out of the way!'

'Or what?'

'Get out of the way, you old fart!'

'Ooh!' said Mitrenko, and blew in the boy's face. In a minute, the boy would lose it and take a swipe; then the militiamen in the next compartment would rise up, take the side of authority against youth, and, delightfully, sling him off the train at the last stop before Moscow, where he could expect to spend the night shivering on the platform, this being the last inbound service.

'Come on,' said Arkhipov. 'Never mind that.' He was holding up three fat cigars. 'Remember the Cuban delegation?'

Mitrenko slammed the compartment door in the kid's face and reached for his stogie. They smelled of dry brown summer far away, with a tickle of spices. He and Kosoy and Arkhipov bit the ends off and took turns to draw at the flame of Kosoy's steel lighter, tongues curled. Suck-suck-suck. And blow. 'Here's to us,' said Arkhipov. In the rattling heat of the compartment the rich smoke rose in spirals, blue as the wild snow outside where the sorcerer's apprentice rampaged.

Back at Solovets, the snow had barely begun. Only the first dotting of powdered diamond hung in the cones of the arc-lights where Ponomarev was walking, in dark, in light, in dark, in light, up the cinder road past the lumber stacks and the moulding shop, up the hill overlooking the poisoned lake, to the director's house where Mrs Arkhipov was waiting for him, with her pink nose and her nervous hands. He was carrying sheet music for a piano duet. He, too, had decided to defect from the usual rules of the game.

3.

Favours, 1964

Toreador pants were hard to come by on the eastern slope of the Urals, and so Chekuskin was wearing his suit trousers, with a plum-coloured shirt: but when Señora Lopez began to pound out the paso doble on the Palace of Culture's piano, he cocked his hip and he was off with the rest of the class, small feet stomping. Over the ridge where the floor heaved up they danced, over the other side and down to the level again. Darrarrum, darrarrum, darrarrum said the piano. Somewhere far below one of the mines wormholing the earth under Sverdlovsk had given way, and the buildings on the surface just here had all been stretched and creased in unpredictable ways. The class were used to it; they rose up over the bulge like a wave of the sea.

Darrarrum darrarrum darrarrum. Chekuskin spun neatly, head tilted back, and gilded mirrors flew across his field of vision, with ochre plasterwork, and the teacher's ravaged face at the piano. It must be strange for her, he thought, to be so far from home, a real Spaniard marooned here, in a crude cold steel town beyond the bounds of Europe. He had pieced together a little of her story: husband a refugee from the Fascists in Spain, husband meeting the usual fate of mouthy foreign communists not too long after; then deportation east, a quarter of a century of music teaching, the Palace of Culture piano. He pieced together all stories, if he could. It was his business to do so, he made his living snapping up these trifles. Not to pass judgement; to try to see what, in each case, might be the quickest way to sympathy with that person, and what they might have and what they might need in this life. Even the most unpromising individual might turn out to possess, unknown to themselves, the key to some stranger's dilemma. In Chekuskin's experience it was never wasted time to make a new friend. Señora Lopez, for example, knew him as a gentlemanly, assiduous regular, a little comical by reason of his height but a true aficionado of the Latin style. She would not refuse if he brought her – tentatively, with a proper diffidence – a request for Spanish lessons from a lady he knew whose husband was soon to be posted to the Caribbean. As it happened, he knew, at the moment, of no such person. But he might do tomorrow, or next week, or next year, and there in his stock-in-trade now sat the Spanish language, waiting to be exchanged for something else entirely, and for that matter too the tango, the rumba and the cha-cha-cha. Chekuskin's small feet flew.

Afterward, he towelled his head dry and changed back into his everyday shirt, putting the purple one in his almost empty briefcase. A touch of pomade on his grey hair; tie, jacket, coat, scarf, gloves, fur hat, and out onto the January street. It was bitterly cold, with last night's snow drifted deep against the buildings and the weight of more bellying down the leaden sky. But the city was at work. Smoke shovelled itself out from chimney stacks, a burly cacophony shouldered aside the snow-hush. The air tasted brackish as it warmed on his tongue. Traffic steadily churned onward towards the cream-and-rust vanishing points where the horizons ate the straight street, and pedestrians tramped head down along the flattened strips in the centre of the sidewalks. No one was looking at Chekuskin, but even if they had been, there was nothing worth remembering about him. His face was an obliging oval. He must have had eyes, and a nose, and mouth, but the moment you turned away from him, the details began to slip your mind. 'He looked like –' you might say to someone, and then pause, stumped. What *did* he look like? Along with the bright shirt had disappeared his only distinctiveness. He was short, that was true, very short; but apart from that, he looked as much as possible like everyone else. His suit was neither particularly old nor particularly new, neither a particularly good fit nor a particularly bad one, although the tailor who made it for him would have been glad to cut it any way he chose. He looked like a librarian as he joined the crowd waiting at the streetcar stop; or a teacher, or a clerk. One of the world's nondescripts. Across the way, two men with ladders had stripped HAPPY NEW YEAR off a billboard and were pasting up its successor in sections. Gradually, a moustached fellow of improbable brawn appeared, in overalls, holding out his big bare arms for a hug. A MAN TO A MAN, said the poster, IS A FRIEND, COMRADE AND BROTHER. Hatted and mufflered, blue in the cheeks, breathing out clouds of steam, the crowd gazed back impassively; Chekuskin too.

He got off the streetcar at the central post office. Under the clangorous dome, there were lines for the counters and lines for the row of phone booths. Mildly, courteously, he ignored them all, and as if he had a perfect right, interrupted the transaction in progress at the third window along by leaning forward with one of the few items in the briefcase presented in his outstretched hand: a little bunch of violets. 'Mr Chekuskin!' said the woman serving, and beamed at him. 'Wait!' she said to the customer, turning off the smile as if it had never been. She slid off her stool, and rummaged on the shelves behind her. 'Here we are. Your letters, and one – two – three telegrams today. I'll bring them around.' Chekuskin bowed, and moved to the door at the end of the counter to meet her. She led the way across the main floor to the telephones and unlocked the varnished door of the last booth with a key from a bunch as big as a prison warder's. Ceremoniously, she removed the OUT OF ORDER sign that had been threaded through the door handles; she patted the seat inside with a rapid little to-and-fro motion as if dusting it for him. 'There,' she said, handing him his mail. 'Are you better?'

'Oh, I can't complain,' he said. 'A few sniffles, but it's the season, isn't it? And yourself?' 'The same,' she said, 'awful aching. I suppose you didn't –' 'Do you know,' he said, 'I did? I spoke to the friend I mentioned, and he said you should certainly consult a specialist. I took the liberty of writing down the name and address of the lady he suggested. She's very good, apparently; very understanding.' And he passed over a slip of folded paper, which went straight into a skirt pocket. 'I really can't imagine', she said, 'how you manage to find flowers in January.' 'My secret,' he said.

In the booth he organised himself. Stack of ten-kopeck pieces on the shelf, case on his knees to serve as a desk. The door opened again a crack, and a glass of tea, steaming, appeared at his elbow, in a tin holder ornamented with flowers and cosmonauts. Bless her. And so to work. He slit envelopes. Numbers he wrote down in pencil in his notebook, but words, and especially names, he preferred to remember. He had an excellent memory, developed over the years until it resembled the interior equivalent of a whole card index, and it was in here, on the phantoms of file cards that no one could read but him, that he stored his true stock-in-trade, his ever-expanding contacts list, without which the pencilled figures, he trusted, would mean very little indeed. His clients paid him to solve problems, not to create them. Today, six of the fifteen firms he represented had sent messages, though a couple of them were only expressions of anxiety, reiterated statements that they were depending on him for the timely despatch of this item or that. He couldn't blame them. They were only acting in accordance with his own great principle that, when you need something from someone, you should never quit their consciousness, you should always make sure to be there on the edge of their attention, pleasantly maintaining the need to deal with you and your request, soon; and he was the person whom his firms could bother. Rapidly, he built a running order for the day's calls.

'Hello, Chekuskin here. Yep, colder than a witch's tit, isn't it? Listen, about that sand . . .'

'Hello, is that Masha? Did the tickets arrive? They did? I'm so glad. Yes, one of his best performances I think; real magnetism. Oh now, sweetheart, as if I would ever want anything in return. Oh you cynic. God preserve us from cynics. Shame on you. We-ell, there is just one thing . . .'

'Hello, may I please speak to Deputy Director Sorov? My name is E. M. Chekuskin, representing the surgical equipment division of Odessa Saws and Cutlery, we have an order in with you for Grade 12 low-carbon steel billets, and we have a suggestion to make about the delivery schedule which we think will considerably ease things for you in the first quarter. Yes, I'll hold . . .'

'Chekuskin. Where are the vehicles, Andrei? Where are the bloody vehicles? We're trying to be good guys about this, we've worked with you a long time and you know we're reasonable people, but you need to understand the shit you're getting into here, you really do . . .'

'You don't know me, sir, but Secretary Belaev recommended me to get in touch. He's very well, sir; he sends his greetings and his congratulations, sir. Now, the reason I'm calling . . .'

'Good morning, angel-face. Is Himself in? No? Well don't be sorry; that's good news. Because it gives me a chance to talk to you, of course . . .'

'Morning! Yes, Chekuskin again. On the phone and in your face every day, I promise, till you release our shipment. But here's the deal. Every time I ring up, I'm going to tell you a joke I guarantee you haven't heard before. Don't groan, I'm very funny. And if you want to cut the chuckles short, you know what you have to do, don't you? All right: a flying saucer swoops down over the earth and grabs a Russian, a German and a Frenchman . . .'

And so on, and so forth. Leaving only the telegram from

Solkemfib, who ought to be in a state of calm contentment, because he'd just found them a trainload of iron pyrites to solve their sulphur shortfall, but who were not calm, distinctly not calm at all. Chekuskin rubbed his throat, coughed, sucked a peppermint lozenge. He kept a packet of papiroshki in one pocket and a pack of filter-tipped Java in the other, for offering to people, but almost alone among his acquaintance, he didn't smoke; he found it made his voice phlegmy and unappealing. URALMASH DECLINES SUPPLY UPGRADED STRETCHER STOP URGENTEST SEEK EXPLANATION COMMA REMEDY STOP ARKHIPOV. This would be the PNSh-something-or-other stretching machine they were getting to replace the one lost in their accident; a big, big item for whose transportation away off to cheery Solovets he had already begun to spin a few ideas. Uralmash were not pleased to have had it added to their quota at the last moment, but this was the first he had heard of any trouble getting it built. There ought not to be, given the priority ranking the job had been given. Chekuskin considered. Especially, he considered the word DECLINES, and its worrying finality. It had the sound of policy about it. There were implications for who he should call. No point in starting too far down the Uralmash hierarchy, if a decision of some kind had already been taken at the top. No point in talking to a secretary or a foreman on this one. On the other hand, till he could work out what was going on, he should also avoid speaking to anyone so senior that they might have prestige at stake. Nothing solidified a problem like making some grandee feel that they'd have to eat dirt to change their mind. What he needed here was the bottom of the top, someone with a junior post in senior management. Riffle riffle went the invisible card index. Ah yes, Ryszard: early forties, Pole from the Ukraine, wife religious, lots of children. Pleasant chap. Drinking problem. Probably not destined to rise. Chekuskin put the coin in the slot and dialled.

'Ryszard, yes, hello?' Harried-sounding voice; a man in the middle of something.

'Chekuskin here. Sorry to bother you –'

'I can't really talk. Later would be better.'

'Of course, of course, whenever you can. Maybe a drink this evening?'

'I don't know. I've a family do. God, this is the Solkemfib thing, isn't it?'

'Well, yes. There's some puzzlement at this end –'

'I'm sorry, Chekuskin, but really, that's one to leave alone. No joy to be had there. And honestly, that's all I can say. Your friends will just have to make do with the old model. They're lucky we can fit them in at all.'

'Wait a minute, wait a minute. You're saying, their order is going through, then, but they can't have the upgraded version?'

'Uh, yes. There really is some puzzlement over there, isn't there?'

'Actually, I think it's mine. I've only just been brought into this, and I'm sorry, I think I got the wrong end of the stick. Look, if you could spare a minute this evening to clear things up a bit, I'd take it as a personal favour. Just to get me oriented a little.'

'Oh, I don't know, Chekuskin. Like I said, I shouldn't be running my mouth about it at all.'

'Just five minutes, strictly off the record. To stop me making a fool of myself.'

'Well –'

'Say at the station bar, at six. So it's on your way home anyway.'

'It would have to be a very quick one.'

'As quick as you like. That's wonderful, that's all I ask. See you later!'

And he put the phone down, quick-sharp. Looking at his watch, Chekuskin found that he was almost in danger of being late for his lunch appointment. Hastily he gathered his paperwork and exited, aiming a bow of general-purpose gratitude across the hall before he pushed back out into the cold. The letters and telegrams went into a trash-can fire being tended by a couple of drinkers at the corner of the next block. Round the corner he trotted, stepping high where the snow was less trampled, and over the intersection to the big portico of the Central Hotel. Puffs of breath hung in the air where he'd passed as if a diminutive steam locomotive had gone by.

'Is my guest here?' he asked Viktor at the front desk. Viktor pointed through the bronze doors into the restaurant, where pale snow-light from the tall windows made the dusty napery on the tables look as if it had congealed in place. The Central's restaurant had hardly any custom at lunchtime – and indeed the staff would have resented serving anyone who simply wandered in and sat down – but the combination of grandeur and privacy seemed to Chekuskin to strike the right note when he was meeting a client for the first time. He hurried in, arms held out, then paused, because the fidgeting man in his early thirties who was sitting as uncomfortably bolt-upright at a table as if he had ironwork inside his shirt, and polishing his eyeglasses on the tablecloth, was not at all what he had been expecting.

'Mr Konev?' said Chekuskin, uncertainly, feeling a certain wavering in his legs, as if they were anticipating a sudden need to flee.

'No. I'm Stepovoi. His deputy. He's ill,' said the man in a succession of nervous bleats.

'Well then,' said Chekuskin, recovering himself, and sitting down, 'you're very welcome, Mr Stepovoi. Nothing too serious, I hope, Mr Konev's illness?'

'Just flu. But he has given me. Full authority.'

'Good, good,' said Chekuskin. 'What a day, eh? Cold enough to turn your spit to icicles.' He would have said *piss* not *spit* but he suspected it would have made Stepovoi blush.

'I can't say. That I am very comfortable, With the situation. That I. Altogether approve.'

'Mr Stepovoi,' said Chekuskin, steepling his fingers and looking at this alarming fool with careful warmth, 'I believe you are under a misapprehension. I believe you think you are speaking to some kind of a . . . of a *black marketeer*. If that were the case, you would be right to be alarmed, because you would be committing an illegal act by doing business with me. In fact, you would already have entered into a criminal conspiracy just by sitting down with me here.' Think about that, you self-righteous little fucker. 'But of course, nothing could be further from the truth. In a minute, you will see that, because I will explain it to you, and then we will laugh over the misunderstanding together. And we will also have lunch, because I don't know about you, but I am starving.' Without looking, Chekuskin raised a finger in the air and circled it near his right ear, which was all the signal he needed to activate the Central's solitary lunchtime waiter and cook.

'What do I do. Mr Stepovoi? I am a servant of the Plan, that's what. I make what's supposed to happen, happen. You can call me a purchasing agent, you can call me an expediter, you can be crude and call me a pusher. It's all the same thing. I help things along in the direction the Plan says they should be going. I don't steal. I don't give bribes or take bribes. I persuade the wheels to go round. That's all. Here, have a glass of wine, it's not bad, it's Azerbaijani.'

'I don't usually drink alcohol. So early,' bleated Stepovoi.

'Of course you don't. You're at your desk, you want to concentrate. But now you're not at your desk, you're travelling on business for the firm, and you're interviewing someone who is going to be very useful to you, believe me. So a little sip won't hurt. There. Cheers.'

'But,' said Stepovoi. 'But if. But if you only do what the Plan says. Then I don't see what we're going to pay you for. We have the purchase orders. They have to give us the goods.'

'You're right, you're quite right. Indeed they do have to give you the goods. But *when*, that's the question, isn't it? You want them now, toot sweet, because your line is waiting; but why should they care? They've got a whole fistful of purchase orders to fill, this time of year, and why should they care about yours? What makes you so special that they should want to serve you first, or at least, serve you soon?'

'You do?' said Stepovoi.

'Correct, old son. But there's a little more to it than that. Now, eat up, while it's still hot. Mmm, I do like a good dumpling. The thing is' – gesturing with his loaded fork – 'in any set-up there's always what you might call a resistance to be overcome. If you want to get anything done, there's always something to get past, right? I learned this a long time ago, probably before you were born, when the world was very different; but I'll tell you the story anyway, because it is interesting, and because, strangely enough, it is relevant to the troubles of you and me right here and now. You see, I got my start in this business as a salesman. You don't know what that is.'

'Yes I do –'

'No, you don't. You're thinking of some fellow who works in a sales administration, sits by his phone all day long like a little king, licks his finger when he feels like it and says, "You can have a little bit." He licks his finger again; "So can you," he says, "but you can't, I don't feel like it today." And the customers go, "Oh, thank you sir, thank you sir, may I kiss your arse sir?"'

Stepovoi grinned: a narrow grin, still gummed up by virtue, but a grin nevertheless.

'That's *not* a salesman. You see, the world used to be the other way up, and it used to be the buyers who sat around examining their fingernails, hard though that is to imagine. A salesman was a poor hungry bastard with a suitcase, trying to shift something that people probably didn't want, 'cause back in those days, people didn't just get out the money and buy anything they could get their hands on. They had to be talked into it. And that was me, that was my first job, aged sixteen, a poor hungry bastard with a suitcase working for a gentleman named Gersh, who did pickled herrings in jars. "Gersh's best, spiced and brined." Yeah, he owned the company; like I said, this was a long time ago. It was on its last legs, and it was tiny, you wouldn't believe what a tiny operation it was, now. But I did the circuit for him, for a little while. I went round the towns, and I went into the state stores, and I went into the private grocers which also still existed then, and I'd open my case, and I'd bring out my jar, and I'd do my little spiel. And do you know, do you know what I learned?'

'Er . . .'

'I learned that it was never about the bloody herrings. The herrings were the least important part of the whole thing. Always, every time, it was about whether I could make a connection with the person I was talking to, in that couple of minutes I was hovering there with the case open. If they liked you, if they *enjoyed* you, maybe they'd buy. If they didn't, they definitely wouldn't. And *that*, you see, is what I carried away from that situation, when Mr Gersh came to his sad end not very much later, and the world changed, and nobody needed salesmen any more. That was the lesson that stayed valuable, that was the little jewel I picked up. Back then, people didn't want to buy. Now, they don't want to sell. There's always that resistance to get past. But the trick of it stays the same: make a connection, build a relationship. Chekuskin's First Law, my friend. Everything Is Personal. Everything – is – personal. Have another glass. And repeat after me. Everything . . .'

'. . . is personal.'

'Good boy. So what you get, you see, when you and Mr Konev sign me up, is all my relationships. I know everyone in this town that you need. I'm not kidding: *everyone*. And they regard me as a friend, they deal with me as a friend; and if I'm representing you, they deal with you as a friend too. Tell me this, all right: if you're a canteen cook, and you're handing out the soup through the hatch, and you've got one bowl left, and in all that crowd of faces there's someone you know, who're you going to give the soup to?'

'Well, the friend –'

'Exactly –'

'But what if there's two people you know, in the crowd?'

'Fair point,' said Chekuskin, holding up his hands like someone stumped by a chess move. 'A very fair point. Then, all other things being equal, the advantage goes, doesn't it, to the friend who's going to be able to do you a good turn back, one of these days. And again, that's an advantage we want you to have in this case. Which is why, when you sign up with me, I will not just be asking you to pay me a monthly retainer which will make your eyes water, but which you will pay, because I am worth every kopeck; and my expenses, which will be large. I will also be asking you to trust me, and to make just a little bit of your output available, now and again, when I ask you to ship it somewhere. Because friends look after friends; and when you're with me, you aren't just friends with the people you do business with direct, you're friends with everyone I'm friends with. And that's enough people, I promise you, to solve virtually any problem you may have. So tell me, while we get another bottle of this good sweet wine here – what are you worrying about, just now? What can I help you with?'

And Stepovoi, oiled by Azerbaijani red, began to talk. Chekuskin relaxed a little, for once the confidences were flowing, the danger was usually past. He had told the story of Mr Gersh's herrings so many times now he barely remembered the experience, as opposed to the anecdote; or the particular nature of Gersh's sad end, and the part played in it by his own need to extricate himself. Depending on the audience, he called Gersh a 'gentleman' sometimes, sometimes a 'capitalist', sometimes a 'yid'.

By three, he was free, leaving Stepovoi with the promise of tickets for the theatre that night. The clouds had not yet unzipped their bellies and let down the snow, but the short day was dimming to a grey murk, in which the red tail-lights of the traffic gleamed. He was in a hurry again. Viktor called him a taxi, and he rode eastward, between warehouse walls, to the zone of new construction, his briefcase banging hollow on his knee. He sucked a peppermint as he checked the other item inside it, a good fat bankroll secured by rubber bands, with a brown hundred on the outside. He was not, himself, a great believer in money. You could hardly get anything important with it, by itself. But there were a few places it was indispensable. He thought a bit, and then, screened by the opened case, took apart the roll and moved a plum-coloured twenty-five to the outside. In the company he was going to, money boasted, money bragged, money swaggered, and the hundred-rouble bill, though it represented a month's wages for a drone in an office, was the same dull brown as the lowly one-rouble, and only a little bit larger. In the company he was going to, it was wise to avoid creating even a momentary disappointment. The taxi had started to labour: the snow was deeper here, out among the half-finished buildings where only construction vehicles passed. Chekuskin tapped the driver on the shoulder to stop, and got out. Even on foot the going was hard. His short legs sank into the drifts past his knees, and where they rose to smooth little crests he had to clamber, with his gloved hands outstretched and the briefcase dragging flat over the soft fresh surfaces like an inefficient leather snowshoe. The cluster of cranes against the sky ahead were not working today; snowfall had thickened their outlines, bulked them out with cornices of white, till they looked birdlike, looming over the snow-choked building site like giant herons or storks, long beaks pointing. Beyond, in the tight gap between two new concrete blocks, an old little wooden building still stood. It had been slated for demolition, but it had not been knocked down, and now would not be. Chekuskin had helped to get it designated as the bathhouse for the neighbourhood rising around it. Whether the future flat-dwellers would ever see the inside of it was another matter. A bullyboy in a leather coat was leaning against the door, slowly chewing. He watched Chekuskin's slow progress without moving, and did not offer a hand up the steps when he pulled free of the last drift, and paused to stamp and to beat at his coat-tails. 'You're late,' he said, although Chekuskin was not. 'So don't keep me waiting,' said Chekuskin, with as much snap as he could muster. 'Steady there, little man,' said the gatekeeper. He cracked the grey front door a few scant centimetres, and Chekuskin sidled through into sweltering heat.

Inside the banya was lit not by electricity but by a few hissing hurricane lamps which gleamed on moist flesh and left the rest of the place in ruddy gloom. It smelt of shredded leaves and old wood rotting. Steam licked at Chekuskin's pores; even here, in the cooler, outer room, he felt himself begin to liquefy, to ooze, inside his clothes. He unwound his scarf and degloved, but undressing here was definitely by invitation only, and no one was suggesting he should hang his suit up and trip onward to the hot room in a towel alone. In a curious way, as he knew from previous appointments here, being the only clothed one among the naked left you feeling as vulnerable as if you were the only naked person in a roomful of the clothed. It was the difference that did the work. No, no one was making any invitations, no one was speaking at all; the rumble of male chat had stopped the moment he came in, they had looked up from the card games and were gazing at Chekuskin as if a dog turd had had the impudence to walk in. Up bare arms, across bare chests, tattoos wriggled in such profusion, blue on Russian winter white, that their skins looked like willow-pattern china. Except that the lines of the tattooing wandered amateurishly, and blurred beneath scrims of fat; and no one would have printed on a cup or a bowl what these citizens had imprinted on themselves, not the swastikas, not a Madonna off an icon right next to some detailed gynaecology, not the bleeding knives and the garlands of cocks and the homemade kama sutras. A kid with a broken nose, less heavily illustrated than the others, and less musclebound, jerked his head toward the inner door and reluctantly led him through.

The leaf-smell strengthened; so did the heat and the wet, till at the inmost heart of the banya the air seemed virtually unbreathable, a thick gruel of steam and shadows. Chekuskin came to the alert. Around the iron stove, Kolya's chief cronies were lounging on tiered benches. Enormous in the midst of them, shining with sweat, bright-eyed, wholly naked, sat the thief-king himself, every part of him from his neck down engraved with artwork. But someone was sobbing in the corner, down in the dark where Chekuskin could make out nothing of them but knees and hair, not even their gender, only that they were young. Every time he had come before, he had been received with a kind of parody of courtliness, a slightly bored and slightly contemptuous approximation to a business manner, interrupted by laughter. But this time the mood was quite different. Kolya was swollen with good humour, as if the sobs were something he was eating, and fattening on. It was a hopeless sound: whatever had been done to the person in the corner, it had come as no surprise. And now Kolya had turned to Chekuskin as toward the next amusement the day had brought him. He might have been drunk or high; he was certainly excited. His grin let you see all his teeth. His gaze was an omnivore's. There were cards in his hand, and in the hands of the cronies too, but while they had little piles of jewellery and damp bills in front of them, he had nothing at all except a folded razor.

'Little man!' he roared. 'My little man! Hey, what d'you think, boys? Is my little man in the game? What's he worth, would you say?'

Chekuskin's mouth had dried. He had heard about the thieves' marathon card sessions. They were famous. They had run on and on, it was said, through the Arctic night in the camps, and when the money ran out, the stakes only grew wilder, with the players pumped up on the pleasures of risk and betting fingers, ears, eyes, lives. Usually not their own. God knows how long Kolya had been on this particular jag. Chekuskin reached for all the swagger he could find. He did not look in the corner again. He gave his best grin back, though his teeth were the small regular grinders of some minor mammalian scavenger, a rat at best.

'Worth this,' he said, and tossed the bankroll through the steam. Kolya grabbed it from the air and brought it close to his face. He didn't look at it though. He held it next to his ear, lifting his chin to give Chekuskin a beautiful view of the picture across his collarbones, where a blonde in tears was choking on the monster cock of a goatish commissar with a star of David on his forehead, and horns. Kolya palped the money once, twice, and stuck a red tongue out, testing the ambient molecules of wealth with his taste buds. Rumour had it that Kolya had, in fact, once pulled the walking-larder stunt on a political he persuaded to escape with him in the dawn of his greatness fifteen years ago, and dined at his leisure on intellectual during the long walk home. The cronies waited. Chekuskin waited. Then the bright eyes fixed upon him crinkled and seemed to dim a little. Kolya looked down. When he looked up again, self-interest and calculation, thank God, were back. Kolya put the bankroll carefully down in front of him on its end – opened the razor – shut the razor – balanced it on top of the cylinder of cash.

'Nah,' he said regretfully. 'You're all right. Well, Mis-ter Che-kus-kin,' drawing out the syllables, 'was there anything you needed?'

'Copper pipe,' said Chekuskin, and he was pleased his voice was steady.

'See Ali outside. He'll sort you out. Anything else?'

'No.'

'Good. Fuck off, now, there's a nice little man. Not you!' added Kolya, as the boy with a broken nose made to follow. 'C'mere, kid.' Chekuskin didn't look back.

Now they gave him a towel, and he rubbed at his sodden scalp and neck while he gave his order to the Tatar who handled Kolya's trade in stolen building supplies. He had been telling the truth when he told Stepovoi that he was not a black marketeer; but just as his corporate business necessarily merged on one side into the ordinary world of individual favours, so it bordered on the other with the kingdom of the thieves, and now and again there needed to be traffic across that border. Sometimes there was just no other speedy way to find the small critical quantity of something a client needed to get a construction job finished, to get a facility up and going. Kolya's men controlled the building sites and gathered together for onward sale all the stuff that walked away with the workers when the day ended, all the tools, all the paint, all the cement, all the wood, all the plumbing. The monthly payment to Kolya bought him shopping rights to the loot. Although, in truth, before it was payment it was tribute; it bought him permission to operate at all in Kolya's city, and protection, should any other 'boxing club' be stupid enough to try and put the squeeze on him. What use they found for the money, he didn't know. The thieves were literal people. Sometimes they even robbed banks. For sure the cash circulated between them, as a marker of status, and if you cared about only the most immediate components of the good life, as opposed to housing and healthcare and foreign holidays and so on, there were certainly things you could buy with it to eat, and to drink, and to smoke, and to wear. He guessed that Kolya's boys didn't queue much.

Outside the night was coming on for real, and the snow had finally begun, spiralling down in slow goosefeather clumps; but the smoothing hummocks of the unfinished city were still wide and white and calm after the little inferno of the banya, and he floundered over them with relief. Through the flurries, he saw the shape of a car pulled over by the main road and was glad the taxi had waited. He got closer; his heart sank. Not the taxi. The Moskvitch that was waiting with its lights off, snow-spatter caking the word on its side, the embers of two lit cigarettes coming and going in the front seat, was a squad car.

The front window wound down with a judder as he approached.

'Lieutenant,' said Chekuskin, more reckless in tone than he would have been if not for Kolya. 'What a treat.'

'Button your mouth, you little cunt,' said the policeman. 'Get in. We're giving you a lift.'

The car was not in good shape. The muffler banged and the gears stridulated as it lurched off the snowbank and away. Also, someone had been sick in the back and the mess had been incompletely cleaned up. Chekuskin pulled the tails of his overcoat up and sat as far as he could from it.

'Yeah, sorry about that,' said the lieutenant. 'Not what you're used to, right? Not your usual, uh, travelling carriage. You see,' he said to the cop driving, 'Chekuskin here is used to the good life. He likes to have things nice. He lives in a hotel and he drinks fucking champagne. And he eats fucking caviar, am I right? And he makes more in one fucking afternoon than you or I will see in a month. And do you know why that is, son? Tell the boy why that is, Chekuskin.'

'I'm –'

'Shut the fuck up. The *reason* is, that Chekuskin here is an honest-to-goodness parasite. A louse. Just like in the papers! A real one! A soft-handed, profiteering, piece-of-shit parasite who thinks he's too good to do a day's work.'

The driver grunted. It was time to stop this: the lieutenant's voice had the dangerous sound of someone working themselves up.

'You do remember,' said Chekuskin, 'that I have an understanding with your captain?'

'Oh, you do. I know that. He's a friend of yours, isn't he? Everyone's a friend of Chekuskin's,' the lieutenant told the driver. 'You can't turn round in this city without bumping into a friend of Chekuskin's. Look under a rock and what do you see wriggling there? Some friends of –'

'Where are you taking me?' said Chekuskin, urgently. They had just turned the wrong way at the junction, and were heading east out of the city on the Tyumen road. The red oval glow of the sunset swung into place in the rear window, obscured by moving veils of snowfall, sinking down behind the city's spike-forest of pylons and cranes and gantries. The wipers laboured ineffectually on the windscreen. There was nothing ahead on the highway but snow and dark.

'For a little ride,' said the lieutenant. The driver grunted. 'Where was I?' said the lieutenant. 'Oh yeah. Chekuskin's friends. Now, Chekuskin does favours for all his friends. So what do you think he does for the captain? I will tell you. Our good old parasite here, wriggle wriggle, is also, what do you know, a snitch. You should see his file. He's been helping us out for twenty-eight whole years. And not just us, either. The security boys up the street, too. Very laudable. Very civic-minded. Of course, some people might call that ratting out your friends. Some people might say that meant you couldn't trust Chekuskin any further than you could throw him. But Chekuskin knows which side his bread is buttered. He gives us a titbit here and a titbit there, enough to keep us happy; but he looks after himself first of all, doesn't he. Doesn't he, Mr Chekuskin? He rats out everyone just enough to get along.'

'I have an *arrangement* –' said Chekuskin.

'Yeah, yeah. With the captain. But you don't have an arrangement with me. And the thing is, I've been thinking. I've been thinking about you, and all your friends; and I said to myself, now, if those were *real* friends, you'd be a very well-protected man, you'd be the last person anyone would want to fuck with, because think how upset all those powerful friends of yours would be, if anything happened to you. Then I said to myself, pull yourself together, here. This is a parasite and a snitch we're talking about. And everyone who ever deals with him has got to know it, has got to have a little bit of a feeling of what a weasel he is. Real friends, they'd die for you. Your friends – well, I doubt they care whether *you* live or die, do they, really. They'd be, what, mildly pissed off if they didn't get their next favour from you. And that'd be about it. Where are we?' he asked the driver. 'About Kilometre 8?'

'Just gone,' said the driver.

'This'll do.'

The Moskvitch slewed, clanking, to the side of the highway. A single pair of blue-white truck headlights was in sight in the distance. Otherwise, all was quiet.

'So I thought to myself,' said the lieutenant, 'I could do some clean-up. I could wipe away just a little bit of the shit that clings to this shitty world. Nothing to stop me.'

This has got be a bluff, thought Chekuskin. This has got to be theatre. It's just a shakedown. But the lieutenant got out of the car, ripped the back door open and dragged Chekuskin out by his collar. Vodka-breath came off him, close to, and he moved like someone who was very drunk. He took toppling strides away from the road, with Chekuskin pulling along behind, hooked onto one big fist. His toes dug two white runnels. Snow descended million-fold. The driver followed more cautiously. The lieutenant puffed and blew.

On the far side of a row of fir trees, the lieutenant stopped. He pulled Chekuskin to his feet, then on up, hoisted by the fist under his chin, till his short legs in their nondescript trousers dangled in mid-air and he was looking down into the policeman's red, bristling face, into bloodshot eyes blinking convulsively as flakes spangled them again and again.

'What do you *want*?' squeaked Chekuskin.

The lieutenant hit him; punched him in the gut with his free hand. It hurt amazingly much.

'Piece-of-shit life,' said the lieutenant meditatively, as if taking inventory. 'Piece-of-shit flat. Piece-of-shit job. Piece-of-shit car.'

'Tell me what you want!'

'. . . piece-of-shit car.'

'I can get you a new car!'

'You can, can you?'

'Yes!'

The lieutenant pulled him close, nose to nose. The two bloodshot eyes swam together, and it took Chekuskin a moment to realise that the cyclopean shuttering he was seeing a centimetre away was, in fact, a wink.

'Much obliged,' whispered the lieutenant, and dropped Chekuskin into a snowdrift.

It seemed better not to get up. He lay there, gasping and leaking tears, with his coat rucked over him and the scald of the snow on his neck, till he was sure the theatre was finished. It was. The footsteps moved away from him, crunch and sough, crunch and sough; a burst of laughter ended in door slams; the Moskvitch hacked into life; the engine-note rose, and receded. Then he rolled over onto his face. That way up, gravity squeezed the soft sac of his abused stomach: he threw his lunch up in three watery gushes, and it sank away through the fresh fluff on the surface of the drift. When he rose onto all fours, his weight pushed his hands down to the hard old crust beneath, as rough and granular as a cold coral reef. It took a backwards scrabble and twist to get him out. He wobbled to his knees, spat, wiped his mouth with snow; stayed there with his hands over his face in the dark, as if he were praying, though he was not, nor devising a revenge, nor making a plan, nor doing anything but attend to his breath blowing shakily in and out through his palms. The breath still moving. The world's air still feeding the life in him, whatever he deserved. No black bundle under the pines, leaking dark blood, soon covered over with the new fall and dropping away, dropping deep, into the geologic layers of winter, into the cold, into the past, into the dark. No. Instead, a little more of this moving wind, a little more breathing; a little more jinking and weaving and dodging, in the bright world.

But it was not bright out now. It was full dark, and damn near as thick with snow as in a blizzard, albeit the fall was all a slow vertical tumble rather than a horizontal blow. He was disappearing just kneeling here. The lieutenant had only meant to give him a scare, but he might have killed him anyway, by accident, if Chekuskin didn't stir himself and get to shelter. Dizzily, he stood, and waded back to the highway, beating at the litter of perfect mathematical beauty which had dropped from the sky to his hair and his shoulders and his arms.

No traffic at all was visible on the Tyumen road. He tottered across to the other side and set off walking, his city shoes slipping where the sludge in the wheel-tracks had refrozen. He tried to calculate. Kilometre 8, or thereabouts, so only three or four kilometres to the edge of the construction zone, and only four or five kilometres to buildings that were warm and inhabited. But he was feeling quite strange. He ached from the blow. It seemed to have spread out from where it had landed, and to be suffusing itself into his whole upper body. Also, with nothing in his guts he was remarkably cold. It took effort just to keep following the roadway. He could feel the flakes whispering down onto his bare head, though he couldn't see them in the black ahead, except as a flickering of the darkness itself, a pulsed flutter like the static on a television screen. Where was his hat? In the back seat of the police car, he realised, along with the briefcase. That was all right: there was nothing left in it anyhow, the notebook was safe in his pocket. He thought he probably wouldn't go and ask for them back. The idea made him giggle. He tottered on, and on. Nothing shone through the fluttering static ahead to tell him the city was there; no streetlamps, no red warning lights on cranes. Very gradually though, he saw, the static was brightening, rising from black on black, to grey on grey, to cream on cream, to a busy variegated gold, as if someone were adjusting a knob on the television. The volume was increasing too, all the way from the whisper up to a roar. The phenomenon was so interesting that he forgot to walk. He swayed and contemplated it, till the giant MAZ truck right behind him sounded its horn and made him jump.

'What the fuck are you doing, man?' said the driver, with his head out of the side window. Then, incredulously, 'Mr Chekuskin?'

He let solicitous hands help him up the step into the cab, settle him in blissful warmth in the corner of the big front seat. The driver's face swam up, young, moustached, curious.

'Man, you look really rough,' he said.

The card index spat out a card.

'Hello, Vassily,' croaked Chekuskin. Vassily drove quarry materials, sometimes sold petrol from his tank to Kolya's lot. Vassily was a serious Spartak fan. He should talk football – but the glowing comfort of the cab undid him, the flush of heat in his face made it necessary that his eyes be shut, and he slipped into instant, irresistible sleep. Vassily shrugged, and put the MAZ in gear.

'Mr Chekuskin? Mr Chekuskin?'

'What –'

'Where can I drop you?

The truck was grinding along one of the city avenues, streetlamps jerking past. Things looked suddenly different in the cab, and not just because sodium light was shining in, shuffling its dull orange fingers across the plastic of the seat and the metal of the dash. Ordinariness had resumed; the world had gone ordinary again. For a confused instant, he could remember the cab as a place like a rich little jewel box, blazing with fierce beads of colour, but already the memory was elusive, in the face of the magazine pictures of Spartak's 1964 team line-up pasted to the dashboard; already it was shrivelling, it had dwindled, it had skittered to nothing like a drop of water on a hotplate. He wished he could say the same for the memory of the scene with the lieutenant, but only a thin skin of indifference had formed over it during his brief sleep. He wanted very much to duck straight back into oblivion and let that skin thicken, so that he shouldn't feel, anywhere nearby, what he had felt as he dangled. He could go home – he didn't live in a hotel – and he could climb into bed, and the widow lady he rented from, as round and comfortable as a pouter pigeon, might climb in with him, as she had been known to do from time to time. He could –

'Mister?'

Chekuskin looked at his watch. Improbably, it was only five past six. He wavered. The bed called. It pulled at him like gravity. He felt unready for anything else. But he was alive, and living creatures work. He could certainly use a drink.

'The station, please,' he said, and the rest of the way he made himself make conversation, trying to warm up the instrument again.

'What on earth were you doing out there?' asked Vassily.

'Long story,' said Chekuskin.

'Bit of a mishap, eh?'

'Something like that.'

Vassily was still puzzled, but he had the egocentricity of youth, and when he found he wasn't going to get a tale out of Chekuskin, he let him change the subject happily enough to his, Vassily's, own life and opinions.

'Here you are then,' he said, pulling over at the base of the stone steps up to the main doors of the railroad station. 'Need a hand?'

'No thank you,' said Chekuskin determinedly, though he winced as he negotiated the drop to the ground. He had stiffened up: a sore tightness ran from his knees to his neck. Citizens heading homeward poured past him. He took the steps one at a time. The snow was falling just as fast, but it seemed a tamer creature here. By the time he levered himself to the top, it was 6.15. Ryszard might still be there, or he might not. He almost hoped he wasn't. The bar was off the ticket hall, an aquarium of smoke behind a glass door. No one paid him any attention as he limped at half-speed through the crowd, but the reflection he saw swimming up in the glass, shoulder-height to all the other men, seemed horribly memorable. The librarian had been out on a bender. He looked like a depraved old midget. His hair was wild, his face was blotchy, his neck was bruise-purple, his suit was wrenched and split at the shoulder, showing the lining. He would have turned away but there, indeed, was Ryszard, sitting at the bar with his back to the door, shoulders miserably rounded, pulling with one hand at the black spikes of hair on his scalp.

Chekuskin limped in, parting blue eddies, and tapped the Pole on the arm.

'There you are,' said Ryszard. 'I was just – good grief, man, what's happened to you?'

Chekuskin considered the task of ascending a bar stool and rejected it.

'Could we move to a booth, do you think?' he said. 'I really need to sit on something with a back.' He passed a banknote to the barman, also gazing at him agog, and led the way to an empty alcove with padded banquettes.

'Oof,' he said, settling himself. 'That's better. Mugged. I was mugged. About an hour ago. Couple of *stilyagi*. Really stomped me, the little bastards. Knocked the breath right out of me.'

'Dear oh dear oh dear. How awful,' said Ryszard sympathetically, but with a certain gloomy relish. He had brought his beer over; not his first, by the look of it. 'Did they get much?'

'Cigarette case. Bit of cash.'

'Ouch. You should get yourself home, you know – put your feet up.'

'I will, but I think I deserve a drink first, if you know what I mean. You'll join me?'

Ryszard waved his beer.

'I meant a *real* drink. Ah, here we go.'

Ryszard's eyes widened. The station bar had no finesse. It slopped booze into travellers who needed help to endure the evening at home ahead of them. Every tabletop was encrusted with olympiads of rings. But now through the yeasty murk a vision was gliding, a waiter ceremoniously holding out a sparkling-clean tray with a new bottle of Stolichnaya on it, in ice; and clean glasses, and tempting little saucers of gherkin, and ham, and red caviar, and pancake, and pickled mushroom.

'I didn't think they did *zakuski* here,' said Ryszard.

'They don't,' said Chekuskin. 'Cheers.'

'Cheers. All right, I'll just stay for a couple, but then I better move. I'm expected.'

'Of course. Cheers.'

'Cheers. Mm, that's the stuff.'

It was making Chekuskin feel better too. This loosening of the grimy little knots tied in him by fear was the next best thing to bed. His policy was always to make clients feel he was matching them drink for drink, convivially, while truly consuming a fraction as much, but this time he tore into the bottle on his account, recklessly, only ensuring that he put a healthy spoonful of food into him for each slug. Ryszard was dabbing his empty little glass back across the table towards the bottle for more, with a flirtatious touch of one index finger on it, then the other, like a schoolboy dribbling a sugar-cube for a soccer ball, or Charlie Chaplin making his supper dance. He gave Chekuskin a smile that was already slightly muzzy. He had been good-looking not long ago; perhaps was still found so by his wife, judging by the rate at which they seemed to be reproducing; but the skin round his eyes was moist all the time now, like damp white suede, and he blinked a lot. Chekuskin poured him another one.

'How's the family?' he asked, judging that the moment was passed when this would trigger thoughts of departure. It didn't; it triggered storytelling, a morosely jokey account of life in wintertime in a two-bedroom flat with four children under seven and his mother-in-law, diapers constantly drying, the ammoniac tang of infant urine constantly in the air, green trails of snot constantly hanging from four noses.

'I tell you,' he said, 'I love 'em, but I leave in the morning, and it's like a weight being lifted off, I swear I get taller just going down the stairs to the street door.'

Chekuskin nodded sympathetically, but he didn't say anything. Too risky, to stake out a position on someone else's private life, when the tide of a drinker's confidences might turn at any minute and flow back the other way, leaving you as the guy who criticised his nearest and dearest. A friend might do it. A friend, maybe, would speak up with an opinion here, or maybe take Ryszard by the ear and bundle him downstairs to his suburban train. But the lieutenant had been right about one thing. These careful connections weren't friendships, quite, but imitations of them running in parallel to the real thing, always with an end in view, always lacking the commitment required to piss someone off and not care about it. The vodka couldn't make Chekuskin as reckless as that. He poured himself another, and it burned.

'About the Solkemfib order,' he said, and hoped Stolichnaya would do most of the persuading. He seemed to have misplaced his own subtlety somewhat. 'You promised to fill me in.'

'I did?' Ryszard's hand was in his hair again, tugging. 'God, must we? It's been a long day.'

Hasn't it just, thought Chekuskin. But he coaxed together a firm smile – a firm, definite, adult smile, since Ryszard seemed to want to play at boyish sulks.

'Come on,' he said. 'Give.'

'I dunno,' said Ryszard. 'I dunno if there's any point. You are a magician, I concede that freely' – patting the empty space above the neck of the bottle – 'but this is beyond your powers. It's out of reach. And it's confidential.'

'Everything's confidential,' said Chekuskin sharply. 'That never stopped you before. I'll tell you what, we'll do this the other way around. I'll tell you what the problem is, and you confirm it or deny it, all right? Production problem.'

'No.'

'Supply problem.'

'No.'

'Political problem.'

'No.'

'Personality problem?'

'No – and you're not going to guess it this way, I assure you. This is . . . a fuck-up from off the map. From out of nowhere. A new and unique style of fuck-up.'

'*What*, then?'

'You can't fix it, Chekuskin. What's the point in telling you about it, if you can't fix it?'

'Where's the harm in telling me about it, if I can't fix it?'

'Oh, give me a break. All the harm in the fucking world. Do you know how public this is? Your precious clients break their machine – the only plant in the whole Union that has managed to do that, by the way – and suddenly, the whole world is watching. The fucking curtain has been lifted, don't you get that? None of your ingenious little arrangements under cover of darkness will fly, even if you could find the money.'

Chekuskin sat very still.

'The money,' he repeated.

Ryszard wrapped his arms despairingly round his head. 'Oh God,' he said, from within the ball of wrists and hair, 'I should have gone home. Give me another drink.'

Chekuskin poured. The bottle was nearly empty.

'The money,' he said again, baffled. 'This is a *budget* problem? Nobody cares about those.'

'They do this time. They do this time. Because thanks to the special soddding circumstances, and the last-minute increase in the quota, Gosplan is trying to help us out with a budget increase. Which we have to justify by hitting the money targets this year as well as the physical ones. It's not enough to just turn out eighteen machines; we've got to meet the sales target too. And so, although your clients want the upgrade, and believe me, we would like to give them the upgrade, because it is in fact easier to manufacture, we cannot give them the upgrade, because there is a little itty-bitty price difference between the upgrade and the original.'

Price difference. Chekuskin could not think of an occasion in thirty years where this kind of thing had been an issue. He struggled to apply his mind through the analgesic fug.

'All right, the upgrade costs more,' he said. 'Where's the problem? It's not as if my guys are going to pay for it themselves. It all comes out of the *sovnarkhoz* capital account anyway.'

'Ah, ah, ah. But it doesn't cost more. That's the delightful essence of the problem; that's what you're not going to be able to solve. It costs less. It costs 112,000 roubles less. Every one that leaves the factory would rip a great big gaping fucking hole in the sales target, which this year, courtesy of your guys, we're going to have to care about. Gosplan is pressing its collective nose up against our workshop windows trying to see what's going on.'

'I still don't get it,' said Chekuskin. 'Why should the upgrade cost less?'

'We didn't get it either,' said Ryszard. 'We asked for clarification. We said, why is our lovely new machine worth less than our old one? And do you know what they said, the *sovnarkhoz*? No? They pointed out that the new one weighs less. They said, and I'm quoting, "Pricing of equipment in the chemical industry is calculated chiefly by weight."

'And no,' went on Ryszard, 'I am not joking. I am in dismal earnest. So, you see, unless you can devise a way to compensate us invisibly, in plain sight, with the whole world watching, your clients will be receiving back the good old original PNSh-180-14S which they were so careless with in the first place.'

Ryszard went home. Chekuskin made to get up too, after a decent pause, but something dreadful had happened to his body while he sat. Under cover of the vodka, his aches had set like cement. He had stiffened in place, from his neck right down to the dangling soles of his shoes. His legs wouldn't move properly at all. He had to get the barman and the waiter to lift him from the booth and chair him down the outer stairs to a taxi. They let him know by their resentful eyes what a bum he looked, and how very much this service was not included in his present deal with them. All the way down the steps in the snow, limp arms draped round their necks, he felt his debts mount.

Nor was the widow glad to see him, when the taxi-driver dumped him at her threshold. It was understood between them that he would frequently need to return with a drink or two in him, but showing up incapable was a different story. She gave him a minimal arm to shuffle to the bathroom, past the guardian photos of her husband. No friendly blancmange-pink flesh to cuddle up to tonight. In the mirror, the halves of his shirt split centimetre by fumbling centimetre to reveal a dingy rainbow of bruise. He lay down in the dark and his head spun. Round and round the bed tilted, round and round reeled images of the day, a windmill whirl of them: Kolya's illustrations, Mr Gersh and his pickled herrings, vomit on the snow, the paso doble, the lieutenant, the lieutenant, the lieutenant.

Chekuskin dreamed. He was in a factory, sidling up the walkspace beside some immense machine. But when he put his hand on it to steady himself, instead of cold metal the surface he felt was leathery and warm. Little tremors ran through it, but not mechanical ones. The machine, he saw, was vilely alive. Beneath a membrane of purplish black, fluids were pulsing thickly from chamber to chamber. He stepped back, but his hand would not come free. It had stuck to the machine, and now, he realised, there was no real palm to his hand any more. He could no more pull away than he could pull his arm off. His arm, his whole body, were outgrowths of the machine, just a siphon in a man's shape through which the same fluids sluggishly circulated. Then the walls were gone, but the machine remained. It stretched away into snowy darkness. Somehow, because he was part of it, he could feel its vastness. At its edges it was tirelessly eating whatever remained in the world that was not yet it, and it consumed its own wastes too. It was warm and poisonous, and it grew, and grew, and grew.

But in the morning he felt much better. The dream washed off him in a hot shower, the widow smiled at him forgivingly. Over coffee an inkling came to him of a solution to the Solkemfib problem, a first mental draft of a complex scheme of favours, arranged in a braided circle. By 8.30, he was waiting at the main entrance of Uralmash, his spare briefcase loaded with one or two carefully chosen items. Uralmash! A treasury of possibilities! The snow had stopped, and the world was as white as meringue, beneath a sky of eggshell blue. The gate swung open – 'Morning, Yuri,' he cried to the guard, 'how's your mother?' – and through he danced on his neat little feet.

Straight away the archer was seized as if by an impetuous breeze, and carried into the air so fast his cap fell off. 'Hey, genie, stop for a minute!' he cried. 'Too late, master,' said the genie, 'your cap is now five thousand versts behind us.' Towns and villages, rivers and forests flashed before his eyes . . .

PART V

Baggy two-piece suits are not the obvious costume for philosopher kings: but that, in theory, was what the apparatchiks who ruled the Soviet Union in the 1960s were supposed to be. Lenin's state made the same bet that Plato had twenty-five centuries earlier, when he proposed that enlightened intelligence given absolute powers would serve the public good better than the grubby politicking of republics. On paper the USSR was a republic, a grand multi-ethnic federation of republics indeed, and its constitutions (there were several) guaranteed its citizens all manner of civil rights. But in truth the Soviet system was utterly unsympathetic to the idea of rights, if you meant by them any suggestion that the two hundred million men, women and children who inhabited the Soviet Union should be autonomously fixing on two hundred million separate directions in which to pursue happiness. This was a society with just one programme for happiness, which had been declared to be scientific and therefore – the people were told – was as factual as gravity. It had originated in a profound discovery, the programme: an unveiling of the entire logic of human history. Then it had been clarified, codified, simplified and finally brought down to a headful of maxims, all without losing its completeness or its authority.

To carry it out, those in whom the knowledge was installed were authorised to act on it directly, unrestrained by laws or by any moral code of the old style. So, alongside the nominal structures of state and society in the USSR, the Party existed, its hierarchy shadowing all other hierarchies, its organisation chart mapping the true nervous system for the country. Every factory, every army unit, every university faculty, every town council, had its corresponding

Party committee, staffed with people who might not, on paper, outrank the soldiers or professors or managers or functionaries they worked among; but who possessed, in fact, an unlimited authority to guide, nudge, cajole, threaten, intervene, overrule. Up at the top the arrangement became explicit. The Presidium which ruled the Soviet Union was not the cabinet of the Soviet state. It was the Presidium of the Central Committee of the Party; it was the court of the First Secretary, chief and principal among all the philosophical kings of the USSR. Sometimes the First Secretary was also prime minister of the Soviet Union, sometimes he wasn't. It didn't matter much. The notional premiership was a second-order position, a nice bauble to hang round the neck of real power.

The ordinary apparatchiks were not, of course, allowed to do freelance philosophy on their own account. Ideological direction was set at the top, and passed down, by conference resolutions and newspaper editorials, as a 'Party line' which only needed to be applied. But on the kingship side of things, even junior apparatchiks had considerable discretion – or perhaps it would be better to say, they were obliged to improvise. They had to make endless, quick, unappealable decisions about the fate of the human beings in front of them. The theory in their heads was universal in its reach, and their expertise was supposed to be universal too. They were the agents of humanity's future, which they were to manufacture by being, in the present, experts in human nature. In this sense, even the grimmest of them was, professionally, a people person. They acted as progress-chasers, fixers, censors, seducers, talent-scouts, comedians, therapists, judges, executioners, inspirational speakers, coaches, and even from time to time as politicians of the representative variety, carrying a concern of their constituents to the centre for attention. It was a quality deliberately designed into their power that it should be unlimited, that it should have the weight of the whole project behind it, in whatever unforeseeable situation the little monarchs found themselves. There had been a period, under Stalin, when the security police seemed to be supplanting them, but Khrushchev had restored the supremacy of the apparat. Here was another reason for the baggy suits. Earlier, at the turbulent beginning of Lenin's state, the Party's operatives had signified their power by using the direct iconography of force. They wore leather jackets and cavalry coats, they carried visible revolvers. Stalin's Party, later, dressed with a vaguely military austerity. Stalin himself had favoured plain tunics, unlimited by badges of rank; at the very end of his life, when he was being hailed as the strategic genius of the Great Patriotic War, he enjoyed wearing the fantasy uniforms of an ice-cream generalissimo. Now, by contrast, the symbolism was emphatically civil, managerial. The Party suit of the 1960s declared that the wearer was not a soldier, not a policeman. He was the person who could give the soldier and the policeman orders. The philosopher kings were back on top.

But the Soviet experiment had run into exactly the difficulty that Plato's admirers encountered, back in the fifth century BC, when they attempted to mould philosophical monarchies for Syracuse and Macedonia. The recipe called for rule by heavily-armed virtue – or in the Leninist case, not exactly virtue, but a sort of intentionally post-ethical counterpart to it, self-righteously brutal. Wisdom was to be set where it could be ruthless. Once such a system existed, though, the qualities required to rise in it had much more to do with ruthlessness than with wisdom. Lenin's core of original Bolsheviks, and the socialists like Trotsky who joined them, were many of them highly educated people, literate in multiple European languages, learned in the scholastic traditions of Marxism; and they preserved these attributes even as they murdered and lied and tortured and terrorised. They were social scientists who thought principle required them to behave like gangsters. But their successors – the vydvizhentsy *who refilled the Central Committee in the thirties – were not the most selfless people in Soviet society, or the most principled, or the most scrupulous. They were the most ambitious, the most domineering, the most manipulative, the most greedy, the most sycophantic; people whose adherence to Bolshevik ideas was inseparable from the power that came with them. Gradually their loyalty to the ideas became more and more instrumental, more and more a matter of what the ideas would let them grip in their two hands. High-level Party meetings became extravagantly foul-mouthed from the 1930s on, as a way of signalling that practical people were now in charge, down-to-earth people: and honest Russians too, not those dubious Balzac-readers with funny foreign names. 'Ladies, cover your ears!' became the traditional start-of-meeting announcement.*

In a way, the surprise is that Bolshevik idealism lasted as long as it did. Stalin took his philosophical obligations entirely seriously. The time he spent in his Kremlin library was time spent reading. He held forth on linguistics, and genetics, and economics, and the proper writing of history, because he believed that intellectual decision-making was the duty of power. His associates, too, tended to possess treasured collections of Marxist literature. It was one of Molotov's complaints, after Stalin's death, that by sending him off to be ambassador to Outer Mongolia, Khrushchev had parted him from his books. And Khrushchev, in his turn, tried his best to talk like the great theoretician one magically became by elbowing and conniving one's way to the First Secretaryship. It came even less easily to him, but the transition to utopia by 1980 was all his own work, and so was the idea of peaceful competition with the capitalists. He was not a cynic. The idea that he might be committing an imposture bothered him deeply: he worried away at it, out loud, in public, busily denying and denying. A sculptor dared to tell him he didn't understand art: 'When I was a miner,' he snapped, 'they said I didn't understand. When I was a political worker in the army, they said I didn't understand. When I was this and that, they said I didn't understand. Well, now I'm party leader and premier, and you mean to say I still don't understand? Who are you working for, anyway?' Stalin had been a gangster who really believed he was a social scientist. Khrushchev was a gangster who hoped he was a social scientist. But the moment was drawing irresistibly closer when the idealism would rot away by one more degree, and the Soviet Union would be governed by gangsters who were only pretending to be social scientists.

In 1964, Khrushchev was entirely surrounded by people he had appointed himself. Initially, he had had to share power with the other survivors of Stalin's inner circle. With the backing of Marshal Zhukov and the army, he and Malenkov and Molotov had been able to arrest and kill the most dangerous of their colleagues, Stalin's rapist police chief Beria. Then with Zhukov's help Khrushchev outmanoeuvred Malenkov and Molotov. Then he sacked Zhukov, and after that he had a free hand. The rivals he had competed with for Stalin's favour were all gone. Only his ally Mikoyan remained. He restocked the Presidium from the Central Committee, with apparatchiks whose life histories had followed paths like his own. Half of them were vydvizhentsy, the other half were the postwar equivalent. So when he looked along the table – at Brezhnev, Kosygin of Gosplan, Andropov, Podgorny, the rising stars Shelepin and Kirichenko, the culture minister Furtseva – he saw people he had hoisted to power personally. He had made them. They were his.

But he was starting to frighten them. Not in the sense of making them fear for their individual safety – he had banished that fear from the top of Soviet politics – but because the fervour of his true belief now seemed to be making him take bigger and bigger risks with exactly the order of things exemplified by the baggy, two-piece Party suit. He had made alarmingly specific, alarmingly verifiable economic promises, and given these promises a redemption date only sixteen years away. It might yet be that the mathematicians would come to the rescue and wave their cybernetic wand over Gosplan, but for now the growth rate continued to drift on gently down. Khrushchev had made a vast public fuss over the reform of agriculture, filling the newspapers with his pet initiatives; now drought and falling yields had pushed the Soviet Union to the brink of bread rationing and forced them to waste precious foreign currency on importing wheat, *ten million humiliating tonnes of it. He had tried to stick his thumb in the scales of the strategic balance by putting the missiles in Cuba; and the world had nearly burned. He was getting angrier and angrier, more and more impatient, more and more puzzled. 'You'd think as first secretary I could change anything in this country,' he told Fidel Castro. 'The hell I can! No matter what changes I propose and carry out, everything stays the same. Russia's like a tub full of dough . . .' The yeasty mass kept pushing back, and all he knew how to do was to keep trying the same methods, more and more frantically, more and more frenziedly, announcing new policies, rejigging the organisation chart, tinkering and revising, even to the point of messing with the basis of philosophical kingship itself. He had split the Party into separate agricultural and industrial sections, for no very apparent reason. He was taking away apparat privileges. He was talking about running multi-candidate elections for Party posts – although only the low-level ones. Meanwhile, he listened less. He mocked his colleagues to their faces. He sent Mikoyan to Cuba while his wife was dying, then failed to turn up to her funeral. He absent-mindedly alienated supporter after supporter, till by October 1964 there was a solid majority around the Presidium table for replacing him.*

Which left the question of what to do about his promises.

Once a turnip said, 'I taste very good with honey.' 'Get away, you boaster,' replied the honey. 'I taste good without you.'

I.

Trading Down, 1964

The Zil had disappeared in the night and so had the familiar bodyguards. The new guard captain stopped him in the wet grass by the garage door.

'You're the driver, right?' he said. 'Not much use looking in there, I'm afraid.'

He cranked up the garage door anyway, and looked at the bare concrete floor where the Zil had been parked. His workbench looked small against the rear wall without the big black bulk of the limo filling the space. The Zil was a marvellous car. It was a copy of the Cadillac Eldorado. In the whole country, only three men were entitled to ride in one. Which meant that when he drove the boss, he was one of only three people getting to feel the burbling surge when you gave its six-litre engine some gas, one of only three getting to guide its chromed immensity down the highway's special lane. Which had meant that.

'Too bad,' said the captain. The driver looked at him, expecting a taste of the impersonal relish with which, on the whole, bystanders watch the great go down, and their retinue with them: payback time for lording it before. But he didn't seem to be enjoying himself, particularly. 'There'll be a replacement along any minute. It's on the day sheet.'

There were new faces in the guard box by the gate, and a couple of men he didn't know over by the front door of the main house. But the strangest thing was how quiet things were, this morning. The air was scarcely moving, just the lightest little autumn breeze. The birches along the path by the high yellow wall trembled where they stood. The sad red leaves of the cherry trees trembled where they drooped. The noise of Moscow beyond the wall seemed further away than usual. By now, on every other day that the boss had lived here, there would have been a vortex of bustle emanating from the house. Mr K. would already have been on the steps, looking at his watch, talking nineteen to the dozen to a stenographer while Mrs K. straightened his tie, drawing into the knot of people around him tributary streams from the households of the other high-ups in the leadership compound, who had come through the connecting door in the tall yellow wall to snatch a moment of his time before the ride to the Kremlin. And the Zil would have been waiting for him at the bottom of the steps, purring, its brightwork immaculate, its leather soft, ready to go. The boss liked to be on his way at 8.30 sharp; and he always was, even in midwinter, even on the really cold days when the driver rose at six in the iron-hard dark to warm the Zil's engine block with a blow-lamp. But today the doors of the house stayed closed. The many telephones inside it were silent. One of the new security men over there was even smoking, perhaps not knowing how much the boss detested the smell. Or perhaps not caring.

'Yes, here we are,' said the captain. The barrier was rising. A long shape in black and silver nosed through the gate. A Chaika: this was not so bad. The Chaika was a fine car. It was a copy of the Packard Patrician. It did not quite have the broad, overwhelming presence of the Zil, with the radiator grille wrapping all the way across the front fender to the headlights. It was not quite the barge of state the Zil was. But it still had muscle, it still had eminence. If the Zil was transport for the highest powers, the Chaika was the next step down, the magic-carpet ride for the rest of the Presidium, and for regional chiefs. The stylised wings of the seagull it was named for spread, shining, across the grille. The big black hood, between humped tunnels for the lights, stretched back and back. Really, things could be worse.

The Chaika only lacked 10 kph of the Zil's top speed; still speed enough to feel the metal fly.

One of his colleagues from the motor pool was at the wheel – got out with eyes averted, and stepped away, once the paperwork was signed, as fast as if he stood on poisoned ground. The driver ignored him, took jealous possession, eased the Chaika through the garage doors. Then he took inventory. He squinted at the polish job, checked out the tyres. He found flecks of chipping paint beside the chrome rails that ran along the sides, swooping and rising again, gull-like, on the rear doors. There was autumn mud spatter on the side panels and the tail. Salt had corroded the underside a little, nothing too bad. He popped the hood. Sparks all right, the V8 a little worn-looking; again, nothing too bad, but the Chaika had not been cherished, that was clear. It had come straight from the general service pool. Well, he thought, a wash and a polish and an oil change, at a minimum. Then we'll see. He put on his overalls.

He was on his back on the dolly-board, under the Chaika, when he felt a polite tap on his ankle. He slid out. It was the guard captain again, expression still neutral; but the motor-pool colleague was back too, and he was openly smirking.

'Sorry,' said the captain. 'Change of plan.'

He finished the oil change – had to, or the Chaika wasn't driveable – and then watched it driven away, rising and dipping over the bump by the guard box, showing a last gleam of its black flank as it turned onto the Vorobyovskoe Chaussée.

'Somebody changed their mind?' he said.

'I'd say,' said the captain.

In place of the Chaika, he had now been brought a Volga. It also was black: but what a difference. It was a car, on the whole, for people who drove themselves around: obkom third secretaries, raikom chairmen, factory accountants. Thousands of them were in use as taxis. It was even for sale to the public, if you had the life expectancy required to survive the waiting list. The driver stared at it. It was not a bad car. It was a copy of the Ford Crestline. But compared to the Zil it was a tin can. And who was to say that he would even be the one driving it?

'Comrade Captain,' said the driver, formally, 'may I ask if a decision has been made about the personal staff?'

'I haven't heard anything.'

The driver considered. 'Excuse me,' he said. The captain nodded. The driver took off his overalls and went into the house by the servants' entrance. Perhaps by the time he came back, the Volga would have metamorphosed into a Moskvitch. Or a bicycle.

In the kitchen he found the cook unnaturally at rest, sitting on a stool beside the table and gazing at the remains of the family's breakfast, by the look of it hardly touched. In here she had prepared the banquet for the boss's seventieth birthday. She had made canapés for the President of Finland and the Chinese Foreign Minister. She had had access to the best scraps in the country; what Mr K. ate, her husband ate two nights later.

'Heard anything?' asked the driver.

'No,' she said. She might not be in the same boat as him. She had been cooking for Mr K. since '54, he had been driving for him since '48, but it might well be that she stayed with the house while he followed the man, or vice versa.

'Any chance of a drink?' he said experimentally.

'In the cupboard,' she said. 'You can pour me one too.'

They drained a glass each.

'They say he didn't fight,' she said. 'Just gave it up.'

The driver grunted. No one knew how this was supposed to go, this so-called retirement. There had hardly ever been one before. The big bosses died on the job, or got arrested. They didn't – they hadn't – taken a pension and stepped into obscurity, before. Everyone understood how the old style of fall dragged a household along with it, wife and relatives and aides and staff, circling the plughole their *vozhd* had gone down; but what kind of suction had this new fate? Where would they be going, because the boss had decided not to fight?

The drink had muzzed the edge of anxiety, at least. He went back outside. The Volga was still there. Someone was making a point with it, he guessed. There'd been a fuss a little while back when the boss had had an economy drive and tried to cut down the number of limos the apparat used; it was going to be Volgas, Volgas, Volgas all the way for all the middle-sized cadres around the country. *Let's see how you like it*, someone was saying.

He had better clean the damn thing. He was just getting the bucket when the front door of the house opened, and everyone in the yard turned and looked. The boss came out, with his son holding an arm under his elbow and seeming to be guiding him. Mr K. looked grey in the face, and stunned – the muscles slack around his mouth and his eyes. He moved uncertainly. To the driver, he had always been the embodiment of power, thick forefinger stabbing the air to make his points, or the shoulder of the person he was talking to; voice the loudest in any room. Suddenly a fat old man was standing in his place. Fat and tentative. He had his pants hoisted up over his belly like a peasant grandad come to town. The driver threw the dry chamois in his hand into the empty bucket; it hit the bottom with an angry clang.

The guard captain trotted over. He was much taller than Mr K., but he bent his head respectfully.

'Good morning, Nikita Sergeyevich,' he said. 'Melnikov, your new *kommendant*. You don't remember me, but I worked in the government box at the Sports Palace. I used to see you there. What are your orders?' He waved his hand at the Volga. 'Perhaps you'd like to take a drive to your dacha?'

'Hello,' said the boss, leadenly. He shook Melnikov's hand. 'You've got a tedious job cut out for you. I'm a loafer now. I don't know what to do with myself. You'll waste away from boredom with me. But you may be right. Why sit around here? Let's go.'

And they all piled into the Volga, Khrushchev and his son the aeroplane engineer in the back, Melnikov in front next to the driver. The Volga was a fair-sized sedan, but it was no limousine, and the car felt very full with the four men packed into it. Everyone was squeezed together more than Mr K. was used to. The driver saw him, in the mirror, moving his shoulders around and glancing from side to side in a surprised way, like an animal in an unfamiliar enclosure. The driver fumbled with the keys. The truth was, he had grown used to the beautiful automatic gearbox on the Zil. It was a while since he had driven a stick shift. He tried his best, but there was a grind and a scrape as he pulled out through the arch onto the Vorobyovskoe Chaussée. The hood was much shorter than he was used to, too, and sloped down more. Virtually straight in front of him, just over the leaping stag ornament of the Gaz company, he could see every crack in the asphalt going by. And feel them: the Volga wasn't sprung, like a Zil or a Chaika, to cancel out the road surface. Around the corner, up to the junction with the predictable surrealism of Mosfilmskaya Street where, today, a party of extras dressed in SS uniforms were chatting to ringletted ladies in ball gowns. And he stalled at the lights! The starter motor chugged fruitlessly, he pumped at the choke, and the engine only started as the lights turned back to red. When they went green, the Volga, released, bounded forwards in a series of humiliating hiccoughs.

'What a balls-up!' he muttered, meaning more than the junction.

'Steady on,' said Melnikov, looking at him sharply.

'Leave him be,' said the boss, from the back seat.

Then over the river bridges, and northward out of town. He was suddenly unsure whether to use the special lane, but Melnikov made no face, gave no signal, so he swung across between the white lines of privilege, and put his foot down. The Volga accelerated with a plaintive whine.

At the dacha, Melnikov politely tried to walk behind the Khrushchevs as they took Mr K.'s favourite walk, but the boss summoned him forward. The driver leant against the car and watched them go, over to the brook, then across to the cornfields of the state farm next door. Mr K.'s hands rose; he began to gesture; without a doubt, he was lecturing to Melnikov about the proper cultivation of maize. He was himself. But abruptly his hands dropped to his sides and he shrank again. After a moment he turned away, and came picking his way back toward the car, in the pale autumn sun. The other two followed more slowly, Melnikov's head attentively inclined.

Mr K. arrived and leant against the car next to the driver.

'No one needs me now,' he said to the air straight in front of him. 'What am I going to do without work? How am I going to live?'

It was unbearable seeing him so reduced. The driver pulled out his cigarettes.

'Would you care for a smoke, Nikita Sergeyevich?' he asked.

'I've lost my job, not my senses,' the boss snapped. 'Put that crap away.'

That was better.

2.

Ladies, Cover Your Ears! 1965

Emil splashed his head with cold water from the basin and chased the stinging rivulets down the bare dome of his scalp. He had sunburn. His skull was a baked egg, hideously pink, with limp wings of curl on each side. Usually, he flattered himself, his early baldness looked distinguished; a form of cerebral display, even, showing off the smooth casing of the mind that had made him, while still so young, the head of a lab, the head of an institute, a corresponding member of the Academy. Women didn't seem to mind the change. And students, if anything, deferred to him more. But now he seemed suddenly ridiculous to himself. He mopped himself with a towel. Insects whose names he still had no idea of were belting out the music of July in the meadow around the government dacha, and from the main room came the equally tireless buzz of the minister's aides, amplifying whatever it was they took to be the minister's mood just at this moment. He blotted his eyebrows. He should go back in.

He had felt sure straight away, last year, that Khrushchev's fall was something to welcome. This time around, it was quite possible to imagine other states that the world might be in; and from everything he heard through his Moscow contacts, it had become urgent that the world be put into a state where Mr K. was no longer in charge, because the craziness was getting out of hand, and something needed to be done to protect the reform agenda from its own erratic patron. A task with the delicacy of reforming the planning system required a safe pair of hands. Rumour had it that towards the end Mr K. had slipped into real puce-faced spittle-streaked raving – threatening to abolish

the Red Army, the Academy of Sciences, heaven knows what.
So when he went the overwhelming sensation was relief. The
new Presidium, led by Brezhnev and Kosygin, immediately
confirmed that the main lines of policy would not change.
Only what the *Pravda* editorial called the 'harebrained schemes'
would disappear. The new men exuded a deliberate, welcome
calm. You are ruled, they indicated, by professionals now, steady
and businesslike people who will not trip the country up on
a banana skin and pitch it down an open manhole cover. The
clowning was over. No more of that crass voice on the radio,
talking on and on, making grammatical errors at the rate of
approximately one per sentence. No more speeches in which Mr
K. told generals how to fight wars, novelists how to write books
and plumbers how to fix pipes. Or, worse, in which he told
geneticists how to do genetics. It was goodbye to the snorter, the
ranter, the joker, the table-pounder. Goodbye to the man who
you always felt might break wind while addressing the United
Nations, and would probably guffaw if he did. Even the movies
got better, in the months after Khrushchev fell. A backlog of
good stuff had built up, it turned out, which had fallen foul
one way or another of Mr K.'s recent cultural brainstorms, and
now out they came, release after release. At the picturehouse in
Akademgorodok, Emil sat in the crowded dark with students
and scientists and watched the smoke-billowed bundle of blue
rays over his head paint the screen again with recognisable life.
It felt as if hopeful times were back.

Only a couple of things gave him pause. Small things; crumbs
of straw lifted and dropped again before you could decide
whether there was a true current in the air or just stray gusts.
Directly after the switchover, a peculiar and discordant piece had
been printed in *Ekonomicheskaya Gazeta*, warning economists
'not to comment on decisions that have already been taken'.
A call to order, clearly, but why? It was the reformist line that
had been decided on. And then, this year, just as the building

work at Akademgorodok was more or less finished, there came a reorganisation of the lacework of Party committees within all the institutes. Now, instead of reporting to the Academy's own main Party committee for the Siberian section, they all answered directly to the district committee of the town. It didn't sound like much, and it was done very quietly and unemphatically, but if you considered it suspiciously, it was true that it would have the effect of cutting out the layers of scientists through which directives used to have to go. It stopped the scholars from policing themselves. He had put out feelers but again there seemed to be no sign of any intention to use the new structure for any particular purpose. It might just be one of the periodic assertions of control the system was prone to; a signal to tighten up generated almost vegetatively. Wherever it came from it was certainly far more benign than some frenzied attack on the actual existence of the Academy, and Emil had to say, now that he was one of the institute directors who ran the town, that he had not himself been inconvenienced or interfered with in any way.

He might have worried more if he had not been so excited. For months, he had been in a condition of trembling anticipation which felt very similar to anxiety. When he woke up in the morning, there it was, a tautness in his chest, gripping on again with a lurch as if it were bad news not good that he remembered anew each day and carried with him to the sluicing water of the shower, to the breakfast table with the children, to the walk to work under the big trees. (For now that he was a corresponding member and so to speak halfway to full Academician-hood, he had been assigned exactly half a house for the family, and lived near Leonid Vitalevich among the foxgloves and the tall Siberian grasses.) He couldn't have talked himself out of his excitement if he'd wanted to. How could your heart not race, to know that the consummation of your working life was rushing on towards you, closer and closer? This was the time, this was the year, this was the moment, when history at last sent out the call for the conscious arrangers; and it just so happened that it had come when he had himself risen high enough to answer, when he was known in the land, as a name, as a new star of the Academy, as the public face of the newly mathematised economics. It had grown clearer and clearer that Kosygin was serious about the upcoming reform of the economy. When good reports came back, in December, from an experiment in letting clothing stores determine the output of two textile factories, Kosygin instantly extended the experiment to four hundred factories, bang, just like that. When he gave a speech on the reform to Gosplan in March, he sounded like one of Emil's own circle. 'We have to free ourselves completely', he said, 'from everything that used to tie down the planning officials and obliged them to draft plans otherwise than in accordance with the interests of the economy.' Away with ideology at last, and at last, in its place, a blank slate on which to write the technical solution for plenty.

And at the same time, gloriously, it was growing clearer and clearer that of all the various reform proposals, only the Akademgorodok group's was still a contender. A beautiful paper at the end of last year had skewered Academician Glushkov's hypercentralised rival scheme for an all-seeing, all-knowing computer which would rule the physical economy direct, with no need for money. The author had simply calculated how long it would take the best machine presently available to execute the needful program, if the Soviet economy were taken to be a system of equations with fifty million variables and five million constraints. Round about a hundred million years, was the answer. Beautiful. So the only game in town, now, was their own civilised, decentralised idea for optimal pricing, in which shadow prices calculated from opportunity costs would harmonise the plan without anyone needing to possess impossibly complete information. The signals from on high all showed that Kosygin accepted the logic. The minister had listened to the arguments of the mathematical economists, the minister was using the language of the mathematical economists, the minister meant to act on the ideas of the mathematical economists. Daily, Emil expected the call to come, for the reform was palpably under construction within Gosplan by now, and the time was short to get the economists involved.

Yet the call had not come, and not come, and not come, right through the spring, while he felt the clamp of hope tighten his chest every day. And then, surprisingly late in the game, it had: an invitation to Moscow, to consult with Minister Kosygin. The invitation had left room for Leonid Vitalevich to come along if he chose. They had decided he'd better not, for obvious reasons. And Emil had boarded the plane with a briefcase full of position papers and a head full of persuasive arguments, and flown west. And he had been met at the airport in style, and chauffered out of roasting Moscow to the country retreat where Kosygin did business in summertime. And he had been greeted warmly. And now he was baffled.

Emil felt the sting of burnt skin tighten again on his forehead the minute he stepped back into the dacha's main room, but the minister looked as cool and self-contained as ever, in his seat at the front of the three rows of chairs facing the blackboard. The screen door out onto the verandah was open to let the air circulate, but the air would not oblige. It hung in place, thick and still, flavoured by the wheatfields outside with a smell like bakery dust. Yet the white of the minister's shirt had not crumpled; the black knot of his tie was drawn up high and tight under his grizzled chin. Alexei Nikolaevich Kosygin was a neat old, solid old, dry old pol, with deep lines running from his nose to the outside corners of his upper lip, which lifted his cheeks, when he smiled, into little sardonic bunches of muscle as round as billiard balls. He sat at his ease with an arm along the back of the empty wooden chair next to him and gazed at Emil with a bright-eyed curiosity. He was supposed to be very intelligent, for a commissar, and Emil believed it. You could imagine him easily enough as the factory foreman he had once been, so long as you pictured him wearing overalls just the way he wore his suit now: as a costume, within which the man himself remained detached and observant.

'Are you ready to resume?' said an aide, contriving to suggest that Emil had paused the meeting for hours rather than minutes. Perhaps his long experience of the minister enabled him to detect the tiniest trace quantities of impatience in Kosygin: Emil couldn't see any, though what he could see was bad enough.

'You were just telling us, Professor,' said Kosygin, 'how we had got everything wrong.'

'Of course not –'

'Good,' said Kosygin, 'because so far as I can see, the measure as we've outlined it to you contains almost nothing you didn't recommend. This would be a peculiar moment to change your mind, don't you think?' The aides snickered. He counted off on his pale hand. 'An interest rate to allow the future benefit of investment decisions to be properly discounted. Yes. A new way of calculating enterprise profits which includes a rent charge for using machinery and resources. Yes. Plan fulfilment to be *based* on profits, not on physical output. Yes. All ideas promoted by your group. So what is it you don't like? What stupidity do you think you have caught us out in?'

'None at all, Minister. Of course not,' said Emil. 'These are all excellent practical applications of mathematical economics.'

'Thank you so much,' said Kosygin. The aides laughed.

'It's just that something is missing; something essential.'

'Yes? Go on.'

'Well,' said Emil, trying not to lecture, 'it's a question of . . . rationality. Why is it advantageous to shift our planning from the quantity of an enterprise's output to the profit the enterprise makes? Because profit is a better measure of how useful the output is, as well as of how efficiently the enterprise works. As our Leonid Vitalevich has put it, "an optimal plan is by definition a profitable plan".'

'Yes, yes,' said Kosygin. 'That argument is won. Move on. What's your point?'

'My point, Minister, is that this is only true under certain conditions. Profit only gives a rational indication of success if it is, itself, generated from selling goods at rational prices. We will be telling enterprises to maximise their profits. At the same time we will be telling them to supply the goods their customers require. But they will only be able to do both these things at once if the goods in greatest demand are priced so that they give the greatest profit; otherwise, they will have a choice between giving the customers what they want and failing to earn the profit level in their plan, or meeting their planned profit target by palming off the most profitable goods on the customer, whether they want them or not. Profit is only rational if price is rational. I can give you an example,' said Emil, and flipped through his notebook, his fingers leaving moist smears on the corners of the pages. 'Take the experiment at the Bolshevichka and Mayak factories last year. There was a report in January in *Ekonomicheskaya Gazeta* –'

'I read it.'

'Of course, Minister. Then perhaps you remember the section about profits. During the six-month period when the factories produced only what the stores ordered, sales went up, but profits actually went down, compared to the six months before. At the Bolshevichka plant, from 1.66 million roubles to 1.29 million; at the Mayak plant, from 3.15 million to 2.3 million. And as the report pointed out, this was not because of any defect in the work of the two plants. It was entirely a phenomenon of irrational pricing. It turned out, for instance, that virtually identical men's suits – the same size, made of the same cloth – had quite different prices.'

'You really want to talk about the price of trousers?' asked Kosygin. The aides began to laugh again, but he held up his hand for quiet, and went on, 'I don't see a serious problem here, Professor. These are the little difficulties of a change from one rulebook to another, surely; nothing more. They may make for a bumpy ride in the short run, but the price revision scheduled for '67 will iron them out. You can be assured that when the Price Bureau reviews the retail and wholesale lists they will take all this into account. That's what the run-in period is for. Now, let's move on. What is the next item of your, ah, critique?'

'I'm sorry,' said Emil with a flustered tenacity, 'but I have to insist on this point. Irrational pricing is not a transitional difficulty. It is a fundamental issue. I'd thought this was understood. It won't go away by itself, and it can't be dealt with by the Price Bureau. There are hundreds of thousands of commodities in the specified classifications. How is a committee – forgive me, how is even the best-informed committee going to know what price point for all those myriad things will reflect the true state of the possibilities of producing each one, and the true need for each one? It's impossible, it's quite impossible. And the consequences are not trivial! If managers have only profit to guide them, but prices do not give them reliable information about the priorities of the plan as a whole, then the priorities of the plan as a whole will not be maintained. Output will wander off God knows where.'

'We've thought of that,' said one of the aides. 'That's why we're modifying the production-to-order system before extending it to the whole economy. Detailed selections will still come from customers, but the total volume of the enterprise's output will now be set by Gosplan.'

'What?' said Emil.

'The total volume of output will be set by Gosplan, and raw materials will be centrally allocated, as before.'

'But . . . that defeats the entire object of the reform,' said Emil, whose hands had risen all by themselves and were now clasped over the sore apex of his head, as if incredulity might pop the top off his cranium, if he didn't hold it on.

'What on earth do you mean by that?' said Kosygin. His face was too impassive to be startled, but his eyebrows had risen; and around him, the aides were acting out astonishment.

'Minister,' said Emil. 'Minister! If you reimpose control of that kind, you will have a system whose components fight against each other. Part of the system will encourage managers to think in terms of profit, and part of it will encourage them to think in the old way, about getting hold of materials whatever they cost. And they'll know that they can't do both, so they'll reckon up which is most important. They'll say to themselves, "Profit is all very nice, but if we have to stop the line because the aluminium has run out, then we'll really be in trouble." So they'll concentrate their efforts on supply problems, and the reformed elements of the system will shrivel and die. They'll slough off like a snakeskin, Minister.'

'Professor, Professor,' said Kosygin. 'That's a little hysterical, don't you think? There are always multiple factors for a manager to consider. It's a complicated world. And you admit yourself, some kind of guidance is necessary, or there's no telling whether they'll produce what the plan requires.'

'Yes,' said Emil desperately, 'but I meant, give them guidance by giving them prices which make sense. We have done the work on this, Minister. The mathematics is clear. It is perfectly feasible to calculate a price for every product which reflects its value to the plan. Then all the manager has to do is to make the biggest profit he can, at those prices, and his output is guaranteed to accord with the plan. It's automatic! I thought', he said again, 'that this was understood.'

His hands were down from his head, and were making big fervent sweeps as he spoke: not very urbane. Kosygin's hands were up too, tapping one set of dry fingertips against the other. But he said nothing.

'It's true,' added Emil, 'that the prices would have to be active. They'd have to be recalculated frequently –'

'Like the prices in a market economy,' said one of the aides.

'No!' said Emil. 'This would be an alternative to a market economy. The prices would represent genuine social utility. And calculating them would be well within the powers of existing technology. We have the software ready! Most of it, anyway. This is not like Glushkov's scheme –' He stopped. Smiles had appeared on the faces of the aides which made it horribly plain that, to them, optimal pricing was indeed just like Glushkov's scheme.

Tap, tap, tap went Kosygin's fingers. Then he said:

'It's a very pretty idea. Very clever. But not practical. Not a serious proposition.'

'You haven't even considered it,' said Emil, wonderingly. 'Have you?'

'Watch your tone, Professor,' said Kosygin sharply. 'I don't answer to you.' The aides hissed. Kosygin's mouth, which had thinned to a flat line, curled upwards into his smile. His cheeks bunched. 'Really, how can we consider it?' he went on, as if Emil ought to be able to share the absurdity of the idea. 'How can we possibly take you seriously when you're telling us we should let a machine take over a job as sensitive as deciding prices?'

'Within the bounds you set in the plan!'

'Pfft,' said Kosygin. 'As if people would blame the machine and not us, when it suddenly doubled the price of heating oil in December. Sorry, no. We'll just have to muddle along with the prices we've got. We're not going to tear up a working system for the sake of some little theoretical gain in efficiency. Now, *move on*. I don't know why you've got such a bee in your bonnet about this one detail of the reform, and I don't much care. I do know that I don't want to hear any more about fucking prices. Move on.'

'It's not a detail,' said Emil, with a wretched stubbornness. 'The wrong prices will ruin everything.'

Kosygin sighed.

'Oh, Professor,' he said. 'You have no idea what the wrong price can do.'

'I have no idea?' said Emil. '*I* have no idea?'

The aides gasped.

'I think you had better leave the room,' said Kosygin, slow and steady and calm as a glacier.

Oh God, what have I done to myself? thought Emil, leaning on his elbows on the wooden balustrade of the verandah with his hands clutched to his sore temples. And: *What the hell is going on?* The two thoughts scrambled over each other, like puppies in a too-narrow box, each trying to be the uppermost. The security men had stirred when he came stumbling out and pitched up against the railing; one spoke into a walkie-talkie. Whatever the answer was, it made the agent laugh, and the ring of suited muscle had dispersed again, back to the shade of the trees and of the parked limousines. The wild-looking professor was to be left alone. Emil stared down at the long yellow grass where the sun roared, and tried to collect himself. He saw vistas of disgrace among the dry stalks.

After a while the voices inside changed tempo, back from the spikes of shock and outrage to the sine-wave hum of business being transacted. They were going on without him. Presumably someone would come out to tell him his fate when the meeting ended. Emil took out his cigarettes and shakily tapped a filter tip out of the pack; then the screen door clicked. He stood up straight and scrubbed his hands against the pockets of his jacket, accidentally rubbing the unlit smoke he was holding into a mess of torn paper and tobacco, but the man coming out made pacifying flaps of his long hands at him, and came to lean against the rail beside him, almost companionably. He was the black beanpole of a fellow, fiftyish or so, thin to the point of emaciation, who had sat in the back row during Emil's humiliation, his legs spiderishly tucked up. So far as Emil remembered, he had not spoken and nor, probably, had he snickered.

'Mokhov; Gosplan,' he said, holding out a hand bristled with dark hairs right down to the knuckles. 'You've dropped your cigarette. Have one of mine instead. They're Swedish; not bad.'

Ceremoniously, he held up his lighter for Emil and then for himself. The blue flame was almost dissolved into the blueness of the day, and the smoke only tasted like an intensification of the hot summer air, but it was soothing. Emil breathed in a welcome numbness from it. Mokhov arranged himself on the railing in an arch of spindly black segments, and waited. He looked like an allegory of famine. When he judged that Emil had got himself back, he said:

'Academician, the Minister has the highest opinion of you.'

'Really,' said Emil.

'Really,' Mokhov insisted. 'He's just a little surprised that you got so upset. If it had been someone who's been tucked up in a college all his life – then, sure; but you've been in the apparat. You know how these things go. You were a staffer for the Committee on Labour, I think?'

'Yes; under Kaganovich.'

'Quite a pungent personality.'

'He liked to smash telephones,' said Emil. 'And deal out black eyes, on bad days.'

'And did he think well of you?'

'Reasonably.'

'Well then,' said Mokhov. 'Broken phones, the occasional left hook, the Minister's little bit of sarcasm: you know better than to take any of it personally. It's the way they do things. That's all. The Minister wants you to know that you may be assured of his continuing goodwill.'

It was embarrassing how relieved Emil felt. He studied the burning end of the cigarette.

'You know,' said Mokhov, speaking much more lightly, even teasingly, 'you should be grateful that it isn't Brezhnev you're trying to brief. By all accounts, how can I put this, he's a man who can get out of his depth in a puddle. They say that if you tell him something he doesn't understand he goes' – Mokhov adopted an expression of amiable cretinism – '"Hmm, not really my *area*. I specialise more in, uh, *organisation*, and, uh, *psychology*."'

Emil smiled warily. Now that fear was quieted, the other puppy, anger, was climbing on top. Mokhov looked at his face, and evidently failed to find there what he was expecting.

'But why bring me all this way,' said Emil, 'if the Minister doesn't want what we have to offer? I don't understand why you'd want to carry out the reform we suggested without the part that makes sense of it.'

'Oh dear,' said Mokhov.

'I just don't understand what I'm doing here.'

'I see that,' said Mokhov. He bent down and extinguished his cigarette carefully on the sole of his shoe. Then he lit another one. 'Why don't we go for a little walk?' he said.

'But shouldn't we – ?' said Emil, indicating the door of the dacha.

'They won't need us for a while,' said Mokhov. 'Truly; it's all right. Come on.'

He unfolded himself and led the way off the verandah. Security came over, but rubbery gabbling and squeaking from the walkie-talkie confirmed that they were permitted to stroll, and Emil followed Mokhov toward the avenue of trees running in the direction of the gatehouse; not the spindly pines and birches of Akademgorodok but gnarled old deciduous monsters, with canopies as thick as cauliflowers, and green gloom beneath. The air in there felt like slow-moving lukewarm water. Mokhov waited till they were out of earshot of the guards behind, and then raised his black brows at Emil encouragingly.

'I thought there was *backing*,' Emil burst out. 'Real backing for the reform, at the top.'

'And so there is,' said Mokhov. 'The Minister has spent real political capital on it. He is favour of the reform right up to the point where it collides with something more important.'

'Which is – ?'

'Stability, of course. The Minister, being a sensible and cautious man, cares more about securing what we have already achieved than he does about any experiment that might endanger it. He agrees with you that it would nice to be richer. He would certainly like the growth rates you promise. But his priority is to preserve the disciplined functioning of our economy.'

'Even if the disciplined functioning of our economy is inadequate to satisfy human needs? I mean the needs we already have. Grossly inadequate to the needs we will have.'

'My experience of human needs is that they grow at the exact speed of the resources available to feed them,' said Mokhov comfortably. 'Take your eyes off the radiant future for a minute, and look around. Our economy has its faults but it feeds and clothes our citizens better than the large majority of the people on the planet. Look at the Indians. Look at the Chinese. Compared to them the average Russian is as rich as Croesus.'

'And compared to the Americans? Compared to the Europeans?'

'Ah well,' said Mokhov.

'You're saying we've given up on overtaking the capitalists?'

'I'm pointing out to you that the Minister and his colleagues are nervous of anything that might lose what we've already got.'

'And optimal pricing falls into that category.'

'Indeed it does.'

'For God's sake,' said Emil. '*Why?*

'You really don't know?' said Mokhov. 'Look, your prices aren't just prices. They're policies in themselves. They're little pieces of the plan. And yet you keep telling us that nobody will decide on them. They'll be generated – what was your word? – *automatically*, by some mathematical black box we just have to take on trust. They won't be under control, and neither will their consequences.'

Emil was exasperated. 'This is exactly the illusion that does most damage,' he said. 'Do you really suppose that the consequences of *bad* prices are under control, just because the prices are chosen by a committee? They cause a parade of perversities that stretches all the way to the horizon!'

'Granted,' said Mokhov calmly. 'Granted. But it's up to you to prove that you've got a solution which wouldn't be worse than the problem. Bad prices have consequences we know how to deal with. We can intervene; we can ease things a bit; we can react when problems arise. We know the machine. We know how the parts connect – and they do all connect, you know, they are all of a piece, the prices and the supply system and the plan targets. They interlock. And we know that the thing that stops the machine from seizing up is our ability to be pragmatic; our discretion. What do you want to do? You want to take our discretion away. You want the plan targets for ten thousand enterprises to come straight out of the computer. And then there'd be no way of correcting errors. Whatever mistakes were built into your prices would stay there, locked in for ever, multiplying and multiplying until the machine shook itself to pieces. No, thank you.'

'But optimal prices don't contain errors.'

'Don't they? They're only as good as the data they're based on. If I understand correctly, they're calculated from the efficiency of the enterprises' equipment. In other words, they depend on managers submitting completely truthful information about what their enterprises are capable of. Speaking as somebody who has been trying to get them to do just that for nearly thirty years, I have to say it strikes me as a trifle unlikely that they'll change their ways just because you've sent them a new form to fill in. Assume, instead, an average degree of duplicity and self-interest, and your lovely new prices have just as many errors in them as our nasty old ones – with no way of cutting off the mischief they'll do.'

Emil stopped walking. He closed his eyes and pressed his fingertips against the lids. Squares of golden light pulsed against green in his personal dark. This was not a view of the economy he had expected to have to argue against. It was so cynical.

'Is this what Kosygin thinks?' he asked.

'How would I know?' said Mokhov, smiling. 'Probably not in so many words. But he does seem to have a lively sense that our system had better not be broken by well-meaning experiments. So he'll give the reform a try, and he'll invest his new power in it, but he will not take risks with the system itself. I'm afraid,' said Mokhov, looking at Emil, 'that if it was risk-taking you were after, Mr K. was your man.'

'Surely though,' said Emil, 'there is an urgency here. We have only a very limited window in which to achieve the growth rates required for –'

'I wouldn't worry too much about that,' said Mokhov. 'There's plenty of time.'

'But 1980 is only – wait a minute,' said Emil slowly. 'Are you telling me that the goals set down in the Party Programme are being abandoned?'

'Of course not!' said Mokhov. 'How could we possibly abandon the idea of building communism? It would be an existential absurdity. I'm just saying, there's plenty of time.'

Emil thought back, head spinning, to the restatements of the promise of abundance he had seen since Khrushchev fell. Perhaps they *were* growing more infrequent, more nominal. He had let himself think the policy must still have the passion attached to it that Khrushchev had put in, just because it was still being mentioned. But if it only remained on the books to give the new bosses a figleaf of continuity, then all his assumptions were wrong. He would have to rethink the world; which he did not feel at all inclined to do any more in the company of this malicious stick insect, who didn't bother to hide how much he was enjoying his chance to put an academic right.

'What does the Minister want me here for, then?' said Emil flatly.

'To arrange a series of articles by economists promoting the reform. Endorsements, explanations, popularisations: the usual thing. They'll give you the details when we get back. And perhaps we should be turning round,' said Mokhov, looking at his watch. He rotated on his axis in a swivel of black limbs and faced the way they had come.

'Do you know what my first job was, when I got back from the war?' Mokhov asked cheerfully, when they had been walking for a minute or two and Emil had not spoken. 'Burning bonds. You won't have heard about this, because it was – still is – highly confidential. But there was a decision in '45 to simplify the finances by getting rid of all the bond certificates which had ended up in our hands, for one reason or other, during the war. I was on a rota, with some staff at the same level over at Gosbank and the Ministry of Finance, because it was going to take weeks. There was a lot of paper to dispose of. So every evening that it was my turn, a delivery van collected me from Gosplan at the end of the day, and we rode on out to one of the city incinerators where the night shift had been told to stoke up and then mind their own business, with box after box of ten-rouble bonds in the back. A thousand or so to the box. The security detail humped them in from the loading dock and I checked them off on that night's list: war bonds, the normal mass subscription bonds from before the war, the 1938 conversion issue – on and on. Every bond that had been donated to the war effort, every bond pledged to the savings bank as security for a loan, every bond held by a dead soldier, every bond that was ever confiscated. And into the flames they went. There was a little glass panel beside the door of the furnace, so you could watch. And I did. It was hypnotic, believe me. You might expect paper to go up in a flash, *woof!*, like that, but it turns out that it doesn't burn very well when it's stacked together in bulk. It scorched and it smouldered and it ate away slowly from the edges, unevenly; just these little creeping fronts of fire, no wider than a thread, working in across the figures and the curlicues, the engravings of power stations and skyscrapers. You remember what the bonds looked like – I'm sure you had to buy enough of them. All the brown and blue and the fine print scorching away. Until there was nothing left of the stack but a kind of rack of ash, and it sank down in flakes on the incinerator floor.' Mokhov smiled reminiscently. It was not difficult to imagine the glow from the incinerator peephole reflected twofold in his fascinated eyes.

'Ten roubles face value,' he said. 'A thousand to a box. We got through a couple of million roubles' worth a night. Burned hundred of millions in the end. Now: in theory all of that paper represented liabilities of the state we had no business disposing of. Some of it had been given over voluntarily for the sake of the motherland, true, but most of those bonds belonged to someone, in theory. The loan-holders would have paid back their loans, the dead soldiers would have had heirs, who could have been tracked down, if we had wanted to, and told they still had a claim on the state for the roubles of income they had forgone, over the years, because we forced them to buy bonds. That's what the bonds represented, in theory. Income not paid to workers, work done but not paid for, because there weren't enough consumer goods for them to spend the whole of their wages on, and we had to get the liquidity out of the system somehow. Those bonds should have been going into the draws for prize money, not into the incinerator. They were promises.

But we burned them anyway, because the theory was only theory, and it counted for nothing against the logic of tidying up the state budget when we could. If I ever believed that we would let ourselves be constrained by roubles and kopecks, I had it burned out of me then. Slowly,' said Mokhov with a smile. 'Sheet by sheet. Ten roubles at a time. That's when I learned something which, forgive me, you too should have learned years ago, Academician. Money will never be allowed to have the last word here. It will never be allowed to be "active". It will never be permitted to become an autonomous power.'

'I'm surprised you didn't go for Glushkov's scheme then,' said Emil bitterly.

'Ah, but that would be just as bad. You wanted money that means too much. He wanted none of it at all. But we need *something* to keep score with, something we can control, or how would we ever be able to declare victory? And we must always be able to do that. Cigarette? No?'

Mokhov inhaled, and blew a long thin stream of smoke out upward, toward the motionless branches overhead. They were almost back in the blaze of light at the end of the avenue.

'Have you heard what's happened to Glushkov's proposal?' he said. 'His universal network of computers, all talking to each other? They've given it to the Central Statistical Administration, to "finalise". Which means it'll shrink and shrink. You know, Professor, you should count your blessings. For you, I foresee a shower of prizes and honours. And you have your research! Fascinating research on a subject which – who knows? – may someday be of enormous importance.'

'Can I hope, then?' said Emil, despite himself.

'Oh, you can always hope,' said Mokhov warmly. 'Be my guest.'

3.

Psychoprophylaxis, 1966

Fyodor's mother, unfortunately, was still attractive to men. When they got the new flat and she moved in with them, forty-seven years old and skinny as a schoolgirl, with black eyes snapping up what they saw and black arcs of eyebrow pencilled above, along came Ivanov, a foreman from the plant where she worked, though he had a family of his own in a building nearby. They sat at the new kitchen table, the two of them, drinking and laughing and making up to each other as if they were teenagers. Ivanov was forever wiping his mouth with his fingers, and then wiping his fingers on the edge of the tablecloth. Fyodor didn't mind; he laughed along with them. It was normal to him. When he was growing up she'd always had boyfriends, his father being out of the picture, usually men with some leverage to offer in the thousand skirmishes of *communalka* life, and since they were all packed in six or seven to a room, there was not much mystery to what Mama got up to under the blanket with her latest beau. The only time he put his foot down was when he needed peace for his Party paperwork, or to do his homework for his law course. He was registered with the All-Union Legal Correspondence Institute, and there was an essay a week for him to write, left hand propping his forehead and tugging at his clean black hair, textbooks spread out round him on the tabletop. This, his mother respected. Fyodor was on the rise; he was going to be a big man someday, a judge or maybe something at the obkom. On the whole she approved of Galina as a trophy of that rise, a fancy wife for a working boy made good, though speaking personally rather than categorically she made it clear enough she thought her soft-headed and impractical. On essay nights she tiptoed round Fyodor, snatching the little plates of nuts or salami Galina had made so that she could be the one to slide them reverently into his peripheral vision.

'All right, son?'

'Thanks, ma.'

But the noise she made when she and Ivanov were at it in the bedroom! It came right through the thin walls. Galina could hardly bear to meet any of their eyes in the mornings, when they all packed round the stove to slurp black tea and jam before work, as if Fyodor and his mother and Ivanov belonged to some slightly different species which by nature clustered close, at ease in the straw, pushing into the envelope of heat and noise and smell made by each other's bodies. Galina had not spent her childhood nights in the shared sweat of a *communalka*. She had slept in clean sheets in her own room in the manager's little house by the railroad line, with a doll dressed in a embroidered gown leaning against the mirror and her Pioneer uniform hanging neatly from a hook in the wall. The coal trains had clanked out mineral lullabies. When she tried to raise the matter, in a delicate and tactful way, her mother-in-law only said, 'D'you think we can't hear the two of you?'

They probably could. She did not think about it when it was not happening, but in bed Fyodor made her tremble and shake and break loose from herself in a way she had no idea how to fit together with the person she was in daylight. It had been true right from the beginning, from the first time she saw him again, six months after the disaster at the American exhibition. Fyodor's report had got her into the trouble that had lost her Volodya; then it had got her out of trouble again, or at least limited the trouble so that the way she had behaved could be put down as nothing more damaging than a character flaw. The word 'hysterical' appeared several times. She was a hysteric rather than a security risk, forever on file now as somebody too panicky for the kind of joint Party career she and Volodya had imagined, but still quite acceptable as, for example, a Party wife for someone starting a little lower down. Fyodor was good at pressing exactly the right buttons, it seemed, when he saw something he wanted. And what he wanted, it turned out, was her. 'Give us a kiss then,' he said, when she stammered her thanks. They were on the river embankment, a place where kisses were unremarkable, so she stepped forward to give him a dry-mouthed peck of gratitude and he ran a finger down her spine while she was doing it. A quite new and disturbing ripple of feeling followed his finger; she shivered and choked, because her mouth was suddenly wet. 'Oh,' said Fyodor, grinning at her, squinting at her from close up; 'Oho,' he said, as if his suspicion had been confirmed. And he pulled off her beret and put it in his jacket pocket.

So they were married; so she had a life in Moscow, after all. It just didn't quite seem to be hers. She worked as a nutritionist at the office supervising workplace meals for the north-western sector of the city, and at the end of the day she walked back to the flat from the new metro station, across the gouged earth of the micro-region, carrying a string bag of food, some bought, some taken as her share from the model kitchen in the office where recipes were tested. Fyodor brought home luxuries, thanks to his contacts: a washing machine, a telephone along with a man to install it. 'D'you want a piano?' he said. 'I've got a line on one.' She shrugged; she had never really cared one way or the other about music. But he got the piano anyway, for everyone knew that it was part of the good life to have a piano, and there it sat unplayed in its dust cover, brown and gold.

Fyodor was as ambitious as Volodya had been, but in a very different vein; not with the placid determination to better something he already had, but scrambling up, pushing himself up the slope before him with his elbows out and his legs kicking and his hands grabbing at whatever seemed to offer a purchase. There was something untidy about his energy; careless, even. He never seemed to have to compose himself, as she and her university friends had done, to say the things that would make the right impression. He said the right things copiously, effortlessly, it having apparently never occured to him that you could care enough about the content of politics to say anything except what you were supposed to say. There was nothing to be careful about, as far as he was concerned. The world was what it was. That was that.

He laughed a lot, and he hung out with other men who laughed easily too; beefy men a little older than him, mostly; back-slappers, drink-standers, middle-rankers, who looked out for chances to do each other some good. Sometimes he needed her to come along when he and his cronies went junketing, and she'd dance with Fyodor on the darkened little dancefloor of a restaurant, feeling inside the stir of helpless reaction to him as they boogied about, and on her skin the eyes of the other men appraising her as they circled by holding their wives, solid ladies from Accounting or Procurement with beehive hairdos and party frocks in orange or lime-green orlon. Galina was the youngest one. Then back to the table for saucers of pineapple chunks and interminable toasts in sticky liqueur. Fyodor didn't seem to mind the way the gazes ate her up. She turned round one time in a restaurant, coming back from the buffet, and found him and one of the friends staring at her thighs together, with their heads tilted at exactly the same angle and identical appreciative smirks on their faces, as if her flesh were something good on TV. She didn't see her own friends any more. Her parents came to visit once, and she watched Fyodor working like a safecracker on her gruff father, who had expected better for her, till he too grinned and guffawed and started to say what a good fellow she'd found. Her mother gave her one look of helpless anxiety as they were going. And that was that.

But it bothered Fyodor that laughter didn't work on her. On a night at the flat when he and his mother and Ivanov were roaring at some comedy show on the television in the corner – that got used, all right – and her face was aching from smiling politely for so long, he chased her into the kitchen as she was clearing a tray of glasses away, and tried to tickle her. The prodding fingers put her in a panic. Far from relaxing she drew back into a crouch; she cowered, covering her head with her hands. Somehow his pulls and grabs to make her come back out grew angrier and angrier, as if he thought she was acting this way to spite him, and then he punched her. It hurt less than she would have guessed a fist would, at first – just a numb jolt to the eyesocket. He backed away staring. Then he made a gesture as if he were throwing a disgusted double handful of air at her, and went back to the hilarity next door. Not knowing what else to do, she went to bed. The sounds from the living room seemed no different from usual, and he didn't come to bed until after she was asleep.

'About last night,' he said in the hall next morning, not meeting her eye. 'That's not how I want things to be. It won't happen again. But it would help if you didn't needle me when I'm plastered. Have a bit of sense, eh?' She nodded, though she didn't remember needling him.

'You missed a bit,' said a woman at the office she'd never liked, and drew her into the toilet to dab powder onto her cheekbone where the bruise-purple was showing through. 'There.'

Sometimes she had the urge to run. She thought about just going to the station and buying a ticket home; letting Moscow dwindle to a departing view from the window of the long green train east, folding itself up, tucking itself back to nothing, like a paper sculpture being put away; just an idea that hadn't worked out. But then what would she have to show for any of it? So she stayed, and she stayed. And now it was too late. The baby was coming. Everyone knew that youth ended with the first child, and she had waited as long as she dared – two more abortions – but Fyodor said the time was right to start a family. They had the space, and his degree would be done with in just a few more months, and then he'd be out of the electric plant for ever. She felt the orange orlon descending towards her like a shroud.

'Listen to this,' said Fyodor one Sunday morning in November. He was reading the court reports in the newspaper. 'This is great. A nice little puzzle.'

'What?' she said, turning from the sink and crossing her wet hands over her belly.

'Apparently, the deputy director of a pig farm's on trial for speculation under Article 154, because he used farm funds to buy a load of timber that the quarry next door was going to burn off. He said he needed the wood to build sties or the pigs would all snuff it this winter. Quote, "When arrested he claimed he had been acting in the interests of the state." What d'you think the story was there, then?'

'You mean, why he really did it?' she offered.

'No,' said Fyodor impatiently. 'It's obvious why he *did* it. He'd've been in the shit if the pigs had died. Not as much shit as he's in now, but he didn't know that. Anyone would have *done* it. It stands to reason. The question is –'

'Why it's in the news?'

'*No*. Shut up a minute, can't you? The question is, why he got caught. Now, if I were on the panel for a case like this, I'd be looking at the guy, and I'd be thinking: dimwit, blabbermouth or pain in the ass? Because this is simple stuff, this is just your most basic supply swap. So either this guy is too stupid to pull it off – and I'd say that the money was a point in favour of this theory, because he could have paid in bacon, for heaven's sake – or else he's incredibly indiscreet, and he's been talking about his dear old pigs freezing to death so loud and so long in the wrong kind of places that someone virtually had to look into it. Or, option three, he's annoyed somebody, he's just the kind of fellow who pisses people off, and now the word has come down, make a bit of an example of someone in your district this quarter, so that the thievery doesn't get out of hand, everyone thinks, who *deserves* to be in the shit, who's been making a nuisance of himself. So, I'd be looking at him for the little signs –'

And Fyodor was off, his hands on the tabletop in quick motion, his face full of the pleasure of attending to his own clear grasp of the world; and Galina found it easy to picture him in a few years' time, sitting on the bench with two other judges, blank and dignified of expression then of course, yet still alert, interested, inclining his head to detect the traces of the crime the court had really gathered to punish. Culpable lack of smarts, is it? Or culpable excess of speech; or culpable failure to be likeable. He was going to look good in a robe.

'So which d'you think?' Fyodor was saying. 'Hello?'

'Oh,' said Galina, painfully certain of being disappointing. 'I –' But she was saved from having to answer by a gush of liquid pattering on the floor around her feet.

'What's that?' said Fyodor.

'I think my waters have broken,' she said. And then a sensation assailed her that she had never felt before; quite faint, but definite, a tightening, gripping motion of muscles deep inside her that had never, in her whole life, sent her a signal before, but which now wished to announce that they were present, and would be squeezing when they felt like it, irrespective of the softness of what they squeezed.

'Oh,' she said.

'Oh shit,' said Fyodor. 'Ma!'

His mother sat with her while he rang to call for the ambulance, and while he ran downstairs to wait for it at the front door of the block.

'Don't worry, Princess,' she said. 'You won't remember it afterwards.'

Galina had rhesus-negative blood, and Fyodor had pulled strings to book her into one of the three Moscow maternity homes that specialised in Rh-neg patients. It was a long drive, even with the city quiet for Sunday afternoon. Fyodor looked nervously at his watch several times, as if they might be late for something; he held her hand but said very little. Neither did the midwife who had come with the neat little white ambulance van, once she had satisfied herself that nothing urgent was happening. She spent the journey writing something lengthy on many pages of lined paper. Galina assumed it must be medical records the woman was writing up but when she stole a look over her shoulder it turned out to be a letter, a dreary series of complaints about slights she had received from various people. As her pencil moved her head in its white cap like a fabric flowerpot nodded up and down. Galina felt most strange. The contractions only came at long intervals yet even in the spaces between them her body felt indefinably different; or perhaps the world did. Everything that was not her body seemed to have moved further away, into a state of floating inconsequence. She looked out of the ambulance window at low clouds roofing the city in dirty pearl, and she felt a kind of hungriness for the life going quietly on out there, for the putting on of gloves and the greeting of acquaintances, but she had already left it, it had already receded; it was flowing along in a separate stream, distant and unreachable on the other side of the glass.

At the maternity home Fyodor positively jumped out, and bustled around while she was being signed in and changed into a hospital gown. As soon as he had her street clothes bundled up on his arm he darted forward to kiss her cheek and stroke her head – and then he was backing, dwindling, absenting himself from the scene, with an expression of obvious relief on his face. Out through the doors; gone. She didn't blame him. She would have liked to be able to step away herself, and let the birth happen to someone else.

'Well, you got a good-looking one,' said the new midwife who had taken charge of her, a big woman in her fifties with a face beneath the white flowerpot that seemed to disapprove of the world, and to disapprove of it with a perfect right, as if she were everyone's righteous, put-upon auntie. 'Two of a kind, I suppose,' she said, looking at Galina. She didn't make it sound like a compliment. 'Right, follow me.' She led Galina along a corridor, and round a corner into a room with shower stalls and toilets in it, and a pair of examination couches. Everything was white tiles, but not very clean ones, once you got close up to them; there was a speckling of brown mould on the grout, and when Galina had to stop and lean on a wall, her hand came away slightly sticky.

'Come on now, don't make a fuss,' said the angry aunt. 'You've barely begun.'

She let the midwife take back the gown and put her under a sluggish blood-warm shower – and then do something utterly disgusting to her with a length of rubber tube which sent her scurrying crabwise to a toilet – and then lay her on one of the couches and shave her pubic hair. It was peculiar: ordinarily she would have hated every moment, and she still did but again remotely, with the strength of the signal turned way down. To be treated like this felt as if it were of a piece with the way that her body, which had expanded to fill the whole significant portion of the globe, was also turning impersonal on her. It had stopped being hers to direct. It was in the grip of a process in which she had no say. There was something comforting in the thought that it knew what it was doing even if she didn't. And if the nurses knew what they were doing too, that was good. She was being looked after. The midwife painted her down below with an orange disinfectant that stung the newly scraped skin. It looked as if she'd spilled a soft drink in her lap. Then Angry Aunt tossed the hospital gown over the top half of her, and went to fetch a doctor, a woman with a face ironed slack by tiredness. Her eyelids drooped and fluttered as she snapped on rubber gloves, and though she gave Galina an exhausted smile her fingers seemed clumsy and mechanical as she did the pelvic exam.

'Primipara,' she said to the Angry Aunt, standing by with a clipboard. 'Twenty-six years old. Labour not yet urgent. Early rupture of amnion. Longitudinal position of fetus. Left occiput anterior. Normal course; cervix at two centimetres; initial dilatation phase now at – when did you start, dear?'

'About eleven o'clock this morning,' said Galina.

'Three hours, then,' said the doctor. 'Now, my dear,' she said, hoisting the tired smile, 'everything is going perfectly normally, so don't worry at all. Inna Olegovna here will take you through to the labour ward, and then it's just a question of remembering your exercises when the contractions strengthen. Room B3,' she told the Angry Aunt.

'I think it's full.'

'Is it? G1 then – but she shouldn't really be climbing stairs, not with waters broken. Is the elevator working?'

'No.'

'Oh well. Can't be helped. Goodbye, my dear.'

'Wait a minute, please, wait a minute,' said Galina, but the doctor was almost gone and only turned her head in the doorway. 'Sorry,' Galina said, 'but – what exercises?'

'You didn't do the psychoprophylaxis classes?'

'The what?'

The doctor stifled a yawn with her hand. 'You should have had a letter,' she said. 'Didn't you get a letter?'

'Yes – but that was about childcare and things, wasn't it? I couldn't go, I didn't have time.'

'Well,' said the doctor, 'You had nine months. I'm sorry, but I'm afraid that at this moment I don't have time either. I was due off shift at six this morning and I have family waiting. Inna Olegovna will explain things to you. Goodbye.'

But the Angry Aunt didn't say much as they were making their way along more tiled corridors and up a stair where open windows slotted the steamy warmth with shafts of cold. She only muttered about the doctor loading her up with chores. A contraction came when Galina was on the landing, the hardest yet, and Inna Olegovna was resentfully obliged to prop her up. Galina panted, and not just from the squeezing and the clenching inside of her. She had worked out that that sound she could hear, the noise like seagulls in the distance, was actually the rising and falling cacophony of a flock of female voices, crying out. Screaming, in fact, some of them. At the top of the stairs the cries grew louder, with a particular focus, a particular clot of decibels, coming from the far end of the new corridor in front of her.

'Please,' Galina made herself say, 'what is this thing I'm supposed to know about?'

'You girls,' said Inna Olegovna with satisfaction. 'You girls get everything handed to you on a plate.'

'But how am I supposed –'

'In here,' said the Angry Aunt, and showed her through the first doorway on the left, into a white-tiled room with six beds in it, four of them already occcupied. Galina was so relieved not to be sent to the room with the screaming, which she imagined must be a kind of a bedlam judging by the noise, a place of dreadful abandon, that she grasped at the reassuring signs of order here – the big clock that the rows of beds all faced, the stack of clean sheets on the trolley by the door – though there were groans too, and cries, and grunted sounds, as the women in the beds struggled through their internal surges and ebbs, or lay big-eyed and sweating, waiting for the next round.

'Hello,' said Galina. Nobody answered. She sat on the edge of an empty bed and levered herself round and back onto the pillows. There was a big light-fitting directly above her head, a wide white bowl strangely pock-marked with black. The Angry Aunt twitched a thin grey bedspread over her legs.

'Now,' she said. 'Pay attention. When the contractions come, breathe deeply. Breathe in through your nose and out through your mouth. If you need extra help, rub the skin of your belly in circles. Use the clock to time the contractions. You'll know you're reaching the next stage when they come a minute or less apart. How much it hurts depends on how well you conduct yourself.'

'Is that really all you can tell me?' said Galina.

'Huh. Better than nothing,' said the Angry Aunt.

'I wouldn't worry,' said the woman on the right of Galina, when she'd gone; a thin woman in her thirties with curls stuck to her forehead. She kept her eyes on the second hand of the clock as she spoke. 'You didn't miss much.'

'You went to the classes?'

'Yes, but it was only stuff about taking lots of walks, you know, and how to prepare baby food, and then there were five minutes at the end about labour pain being an illusion promoted by capitalist doctors, and how it was really only messages from the subcortex of the brain which you could turn off by stimulating the cortex. Or maybe the other way around.'

'I don't know what that means,' said Galina.

'Neither do I,' said the woman.

'I do,' said her neighbour on the other side, a sturdy-looking teenager. 'It means they're not going to give us any painkillers.' And she started to laugh, but her next contraction arrived. 'Oh shit,' she said. 'Here we go again. Oh you bastard, how did I let you talk me into this? Oh you cocksucker. Oh. You. Motherfucker.'

'Must you talk like that?' said Galina. 'It's very vulgar.'

'You stuck-up bitch,' said the girl, through clenched teeth. 'Just you wait.'

The girl was right. Galina did wait, faithfully counting the interval between contractions, five minutes, four minutes, and trying rather self-consciously to breathe in through her nose and out through her mouth, while her new muscles worked, and perhaps it did help, sort of; but after a while, a long while or a short while, the feelings changed, in quantity of discomfort and therefore in quality too, until they began to stab holes in her deep breaths, and to leave her gasping, with the breath forced up into a tiny bouncing flutter in her throat, and everything further down surging along out of control. It was not squeezing that she felt, any more: it was a crushing, a pulping. It was not stretching now, but tearing. It put her in mind of what she'd seen butchers doing in the big meat lockers, twisting apart joints against the angle of the bones, the cartilage popping, the fibres of the meat pulling out in red strings. And the Angry Aunt did nothing to help. The first time she came back, Galina watched her hungrily, expecting that there would be a pill to swallow or an injection to take, but she had only brought a bowl of water, and briskly wiped all the foreheads in the room with it, like a person scrubbing tabletops.

Galina had never in her adult life experienced anything that really hurt, a physical sensation that would be up there in intensity of unpleasantness with sorrow or humiliation, and the discovery was astonishing. When each contraction reached its peak, she found that she would gladly have re-endured any awful emotion she had ever known, if it had just meant that she didn't have to experience the next instant of this. She would rather be back in the conversation she had had with Volodya when she came home from Sokolniki Park. She would rather be lying in the dark with one hand over her eye and the pillow wet and the TV braying through the wall. No contest. But no one was interested in making the swap. The next instant came, and then another one, and another, though the pain that filled each one up made it impossible to imagine that she would be able to endure any continuation whatsoever of this sharpness, this blade slicing in the tissue, this lightning-fork running through the nerves, until she did, and she had, and she was facing the impossibility of an instant further on. She didn't want to stroke her belly or her back. She didn't want to touch anywhere down there, where her body was not her own any more, and some kind of terrible misunderstanding had arisen about sizes and volumes and the feasibility of getting an object as big as a city bus out through narrow flesh. She wanted to watch from the other side of the glass. But that was the other discovery. It had been a ridiculous illusion to suppose that some detached bit of her would be able to watch her body getting on with it. The contractions sucked her down into flesh and bone. While they lasted, her body was all there was. Only her body existed. She was all body.

Now she too watched the clock, pushing at the second hand with her eyes, as if the thin red wand creeping round the dial directly controlled what she was feeling. It was the last thing in the room that made sense. The seconds tugged and dragged at it as it passed – they were viscous gulfs, they were treacly hectares of wasteland, they were wet mouths – but it went on moving. It pushed on. Nothing else helped. The time the hour and minute hands measured went away. People went away. Fyodor seemed as remote as the stars; the baby was unimaginable. The woman in the right-hand bed disappeared, then the teenager, wheeled away up the hall in a kind of thrashing paroxysm. It didn't matter. Nothing was real except her and the second hand. Because if she clung to it for two whole revolutions, every black division round the face a separate passage through an experience worse than sorrow or humiliation, it would arrive, in the end, at the second that ended the contraction, and make the pain drain abruptly down like water in a holed mug, and she would be briefly her recognisable self again, panting and trembling, with luxurious seconds of respite ahead of her. Gradually the respites ended sooner and sooner: three circuits of the second hand, two, one and a half. But it was all there was to hold onto, and it gave her just enough strength to bite her teeth together and stop herself making those dreadful groaning noises coming from the other beds. She could just, just manage it. Her and the second hand.

And then the second hand let her down. Two minutes of pain, and she waited for the end, she waited and waited, while the red needle crept onwards, up and over the top of the dial, and round the bottom again, and through two more whole turns before she understood that the respite wasn't coming, this time; wasn't coming any more. And the pain of the contraction changed shape too. It had come, before, in gathering waves, rocking in and rising higher and higher, all surging so to speak in one direction, all stretching and tightening – all tearing and crushing – towards the one goal, the one object. She'd been being opened. She couldn't help knowing that. But now there seemed to be no object, no pattern. If the pain was a sea, it was a choppy mess of froth now, churned by waves running every which way and slapping into each other. The butchers' hands forgot what they were doing and ripped at her at random. Things had gone mad inside her. And the seconds were just as hard to get through, and now they were going to come at her forever and ever, without stopping, with no order or logic or justification at all. *This can't be right*, she thought. *I can't do this.*

'Nurse,' she called, her voice a squeak. And again. And again. In the end Inna Olegovna came, wiping red hands on a towel.

'What is it?' she said.

'I think something is wrong,' Galina whispered.

The Angry Aunt sighed and rummaged in the parts of Galina for which she had never found a name she was comfortable saying out loud.

'Nothing's wrong,' she said. 'It's just the second stage. Perfectly normal. A couple more hours, maybe.'

Two hours maybe. A hundred and twenty minutes maybe. Seven thousand two hundred seconds maybe. Forever and ever.

'Please,' said Galina, '*please*. Can't you give me something? This is torture. I can't bear it.'

'We don't have anything like that,' said the Angry Aunt. 'It's against policy. You aren't ill, you know.'

'But I can't bear it,' Galina said, and helplessly began to cry, not in sobs, but in weak streams from the outside corners of her eyes. Down in the salt water dripped the awful liquor of everything: her body's betrayals, her ruined plans, her utter loneliness. 'I can't,' she wept. 'I can't, I can't, I can't.'

'Well, you have to,' said Inna Olegovna. 'You have no choice. You're not helping yourself with this kind of attitude, you know. It's all in how you think about it. So pull yourself together and breathe right, or you'll kill the baby.'

Oh, she knew this game. All her life it had been the cure-all. *Pretend the world better.* If you weep, pretend you're smiling. If you're puzzled, pretend you're certain. If you're hungry, pretend you're full. If you see chaos, pretend there's a plan. If today stinks, pretend it's tomorrow. If it hurts – psychoprophylaxis. The butchers' hands worked without cease. Behind Inna Olegovna's head the black splotches on the light shade swam into focus. Stalactites of black mucus with little legs and wings in them: they were all mashed flies, swatted and left to fester. *But why should I pretend this doesn't hurt?* she thought, and was all of a sudden angrier than she could ever remember being before.

The Angry Aunt was going.

'Nurse!' shouted Galina, and found she could throw the pain into her voice if she stopped trying to make it hurt less. Into the shout, the whole thing, the whole experience of being scraped out alive into a bloody tunnel. 'Nurse!'

The midwife came back, looking surprised.

'Now what?' she said.

'My husband', croaked Galina, baring her teeth, 'is the Komsomol secretary at Elektrozavodskaya.'

'All the more reason you should set a good example,' said the Angry Aunt, but she was cautious now.

'He has friends everywhere. Good friends. At the City Soviet, at the Party Control Commission. Some of them supervise the hospitals,' she said, and the word *hospitals* came out with a hiss.

'They would be very upset if he were upset. Do you understand me?'

'It's policy to –'

'Do you understand me?'

'Yes.'

'So go and get me something for the pain. This is a *hospital*.' Hiss. 'You'll have some morphine on a shelf somewhere. Go and get it.'

'But –'

'But nothing. Do what you're told!'

Inna Olegovna scurried.

Well, they did have a little injection of something tucked away on a shelf, and it just about lasted her until the last stage began, and they moved her down the corridor to the bedlam of the delivery room, not caring at that point about the shouts and screams because she was adding to them herself as she started to push. The teenager was in the next bed, all done, white and quiet and stunned, baby already papoosed up and whisked away; but she laughed when she heard the words that Galina was shouting. *I am going to get his mother out of that flat if it's the last thing I do*, thought Galina, and prepared to meet her future.

'No my boys,' said the merchant, 'it is hard to live by right, it is easier to live by wrong. We are cheated, and we must cheat others too.'

PART VI

The 'Kosygin reforms' of 1965 put a lot more money in factory managers' pockets, but they did almost nothing to stop the slowing of the Soviet growth rate. Even according to the generous official figures, there was only a 0.5% upward blip in growth during the Five-Year Plan that ran from 1966 to 1970. CIA estimates put the effect at only 0.2%, and recalculations later suggest there may have been no improvement at all. Whatever the effect, it was momentary: in every set of figures, official and unofficial, the growth rate then went on inexorably falling and falling, plan period after plan period, trending grimly downwards towards zero. The growth machine was grinding to a halt. Leviathan's gears had jammed. This was one of the reasons for Kosygin's own relative loss of power in the government. He and Brezhnev had been equals when they deposed Khrushchev. By the end of the 1960s, Kosygin was just one of Brezhnev's ministers, a definite underling to the placidly wily specialist in 'organisation and psychology'. In political terms, it turned out that the winning response to the problem was not even to try.

For help was arriving from an unexpected direction. In 1961, the first oilfield had been discovered in western Siberia, and by 1969 geologists – many working out of Akademgorodok – had identified almost sixty of them, brimming with saleable crude. They were just about all on-line and pumping in time for the 1973 oil shock, when the world price for petroleum rose by 400%. Suddenly, instead of being a giant autarchy, trying to bootstrap its way to prosperity, the Soviet Union was a producer for the world market, and it was awash with petrodollars. Suddenly, it was possible for the Soviet leadership to buy its way out of some of the deficiencies of the economy. If the collective farms still couldn't feed the country, then food could be *quietly imported. If the people wanted consumer goods, you could buy the technology to produce them, like the complete Fiat car plant assembled on the banks of the Volga. The Brezhnev regime managed to make some everyday luxuries available. There were thirty million TV sets in Soviet homes in 1968, and ninety million at the end of the 1970s; by which time, too, most Soviet families owned a fridge and a majority had a washing machine. Vacations to the sunny beaches of the Black Sea became ordinary. Cigarettes and vodka and chocolate and perfume were usually on the shelves, even when milk and meat were not.*

But the oil windfall was nowhere near big enough to pay for the threefold commitment that Khrushchev had made: to superpower-sized military spending, plus abundant consumption, plus a complete new industrial revolution. They could afford the guns — the Politburo made it a priority to funnel the oil dollars into fighter planes and aircraft carriers and helicopter gunships – and they could contrive to find a certain amount of butter; but the limitless, utopian plenty that Khrushchev had promised for 1980 had depended (so far as it was plausible at all) on successfully reconstructing the economy at the next level of technology and productivity, and it was this that did not get funded.

The Soviet economy did not move on from coal and steel and cement to plastics and microelectronics and software design, except in a very few military applications. It continued to compete with what capitalism had been doing in the 1930s, not with what it was doing now. It continued to suck resources and human labour in vast quantities into a heavy-industrial sector which had once been intended to exist as a springboard for something else, but which by now had become its own justification. Soviet industry in its last decades existed because it existed, an empire of inertia expanding ever more slowly, yet attaining the wretched distinction of absorbing more of the total effort of the economy that hosted it than heavy industry has ever done anywhere else in human history, before or since. Every year it produced goods that less and less corresponded to human needs, and whatever it once started producing, it tended to go on producing ad infinitum, since it possessed no effective stop signals except ruthless commands from above, and the people at the top no longer did ruthless, in the economic sphere. The control system for industry grew more and more erratic, the information flowing back to the planners grew more and more corrupt. And the activity of industry, all that human time and machine time it used up, added less and less value to the raw materials it sucked in. Maybe no value. Maybe less than none. One economist has argued that, by the end, it was actively destroying value; it had become a system for spoiling perfectly good materials by turning them into objects no one wanted.

The gap with American living standards widened again, precipitously. It became clear by any measurement that the Soviet Union was not going to overtake and surpass. All talk of full communism was abandoned, and in its place Brezhnev's government promoted the idea of 'developed socialism', an era in which the USSR could comfortably announce it had already arrived. Developed socialism was due to last a nice long time, with no awkward timetable. There only remained the problem of the 1961 Party Programme. Convenient official amnesia engulfed it. It was buried in silence, never to be dug up again. Indeed an émigré journal reported the rumour that when a couple of citizens in Balashov who really had buried the Programme in a home-made time capsule exhumed it in 1980 and read it aloud in public, they were promptly arrested under Article 190 of the Criminal Code, for 'spreading fabrications and defaming the Soviet social and state order'.

Suspiciously neat, this may be an example, not of a Brezhnev-era event but of Brezhnev-era Soviet joke-telling, which was sometimes difficult to tell apart from a reality that constantly verged on satire. If it did happen though it would have been of a piece with the Brezhnev answer to anything that seemed to offer an explicit challenge in the realm of ideas: always and every time, the police. Brezhnev had abolished the Ideological Commission as soon as he took over. There were to be be no more of Khrushchev's shouting matches. But what replaced exhortation was enforcement. Gradually, all of the relatively liberal areas of life during the Thaw were closed down. After a last burst of adventurous releases in 1964–6, Soviet film became a steady progression of conformist comedies and tub-thumping war spectaculars. Literature shrivelled. Science, said the Central Committee secretary responsible for it, was to be 'administered' not 'supported'. Universities became infested with the discreet little unmarked offices of the security service's Fifth Department, which scholars were encouraged to drop into to denounce their colleagues. This was the era when the psychiatric hospital was pioneered as a place of punishment for people who made a nuisance of themselves; this was the time when a minute fraction of the intelligentsia gave up on the Soviet system altogether and became 'dissidents'.

On the other hand, Brezhnev's government was conciliatory towards labour unrest. Several times in the late 1960s and 1970s there were strikes, especially in the oil industry, where the workers lured out east to work the Siberian wells knew their own bargaining power. Never again was the Novocherkassk solution applied. Each time, a Politburo member flew promptly out and negotiated. After all, what the workers were doing was no different, really, from what the waiter was up to in the restaurant when he wanted a little something before giving you a decent table, or what the saleswoman in the department store meant when she needed you to make it worth her while to look for your shoe size. There was nothing troubling in it; no threat, no malice. They were good Soviet citizens; they were just looking out for a little reciprocity in their dealings with their fellow creatures, ty-mne, ya-tebe, 'you to me and I to you'. All the indicators suggest that the vast majority of the Soviet population were, indeed, basically contented with their government. This was not history's end, with every obstacle to human fulfilment dissolved in the gush from the horn of plenty, but it was quite comfortable, *especially compared to earlier Soviet decades. The work was pointless but not hard. The environment was increasingly toxic, but the concrete flats were cosy boxes of warmth. The spectacle of Soviet power on the telly was gratifying, and after the news was over and the missile launchers had rolled by, it'd be time for KVN, Klub veselykh i nakhodchivykh, 'the club of the gay and the witty'. Life was not bad. Nobody bothered you if you didn't bother them. Things seemed to have settled into a status quo that could last forever.*

And if you were one of the real elite, you had a little personal exemption from some of the constraints of the world you ruled over. You could command the command economy to simulate, just for you, a little bit of what you had admired on your trips abroad. Brezhnev himself, for example, was very taken with denim jackets when he visited America, despite being a bulky sixty-something at the time. When he came home he summoned his tailor, Aleksandr Igmand, and had one made to measure. The problem was the metal buttons. The USSR didn't manufacture the right kind. So a special order was put in to a steel foundry, and back came just enough round American-type metal buttons to ornament one jacket. As a procedure, it was the absolute opposite of the dream of harnessing the fecundity of mass production: but as Brezhnev drove out of Moscow on a summer evening in his jean jacket, black coiffure shining, a tyrant without a cause, he could tell himself that the promise of abundance had been kept for him, at least.

After a long time or a short time – for speedily a tale is spun, with much less speed a deed is done –

The Unified System, 1970

A cell. A lung cell. Tobacco smoke swirls by in the spired and foliated channel the cell faces. Its job is to take in oxygen from breath and keep out everything else, and on the whole it does well filtering the usual impurities in air: but this is not a designed mechanism, put together for a function by conscious plan, it is a dumb iteration of all the features which have proved by trial and error to serve lung cells well in the past. The past did not include deliberately-breathed smoke. We could count an amazing number of different chemicals in the blue-grey vapour snaking through the tissue, altogether too many of which the cell does not know how to exclude. Formaldehyde, acetaldehyde, catechol, isoprene, ethylene oxide, nitric oxide, nitrosamine, the aromatic amines – not to mention the quinones, the semiquinones, the hydroquinones, a whole family of polycyclic aromatic hydrocarbons. We are watching for one of these last. Here it comes now, a drifting, tumbling molecule of benzopyrene. It sails into the cell's bulging curtain wall of fats and sticks there, like an insect caught in glue; then, worse, is dragged through, because the fat curtain is spiked here and there by receptors, and one of these has the benzopyrene in its grip. The receptor winches the benzopyrene through the curtain, hand over hand, atom over atom, wrapping it as it comes in a fold of the curtain, and then closing the fold behind it, so that when it reaches the inside, a little fatty envelope buds off from the inner wall of the cell with the benzopyrene sealed inside it. And floats free, into the warm liquid workspace where the body builds its proteins.

But it's all right. The cell has no specific defence against benzopyrene, but it is not defenceless. It has the powerful standard equipment all mammalian cells deploy when foreign bodies turn up where they're not supposed to. The package of fat is a flag, a label, an alert. Detecting it, up comes an enzyme to metabolise the contents. The enzyme munchs the benzopyrene into pieces of epoxide which other bits of the cellular machinery can flush safely away.

This has happened over and over again, every time Sergei Alexeyevich Lebedev lights a cigarette. There are billions of cells in the lungs. Lebedev has smoked sixty unfiltered Kazbek a day for fifty years. So this has happened thousands of billions of times.

Lebedev is wearing his medals. They jingle on his jacket like a drawerful of cutlery. Hero of Socialist Labour, Order of the Red Banner of Labour, two Orders of Lenin, assorted military and scientific honours. Red enamel, nickel, ribbons. So many of them that they drag down his suit on that side. He'd swear he can feel their weight. He used to have more chest to hang them on. The flesh is coming off him so fast now that he seems to be all teetering superstructure, just bones leaning together. A wobbling tower. A tripod grating in a cold wind.

The medals are supposed to be a claim for respect. And outside, they work. They get him a pension, rent reductions, lower taxes, a seat on the metro when it's standing room only. His life has been easier than the overwhelming majority of Soviet lives, because of them. But in here of all places, in this lightless corridor of the Kremlin, they're a devalued currency. Everyone has some. The General Secretary has so many, he's on the TV so frequently being awarded the Order of This or That or The Other, that, as the joke says, if a crocodile ate him, the poor creature would be shitting medals for a fortnight.

'The Minister does know I'm waiting, doesn't he?' says Lebedev.

*

Another lung cell. The machines that Lebedev has made all build up their complicated behaviours from absolutely predictable little events, from valves and then transistors turning on and off. Definitely on; definitely off. Without any shading of degree. Without any ambiguity. The machine that makes Lebedev is different. The base layer of its behaviour, from which all the rest emerges, is various and multiple and uncertain. There is no binary simplicity. There is the slow bubble of many chemical reactions all happening at once, each continuing until a task is mostly done, probably done, done enough to satisfy a programme which was itself only whittled out of randomness just well enough to get by. The enzyme's destruction of benzopyrene, for example, only flushes most of it away. A fraction of the epoxides react again with the enzyme and become diol epoxides. That's what's happened here; instead of nice, inert, detoxified molecules, we have a version of the same thing which is lacking one electron on one of its atoms, and which consequently yearns to stick to any other molecule which will share an electron with it. The diol epoxides are aggressive gloop. Aggressive? One electron's worth of electric charge doesn't tow a molecule very fast through the soupy interior of a cell: it doesn't send the diol epoxides streaming along at the speed of light like the electrons in a vacuum tube. But it does exert a tiny, persistent pull on them. It draws them along towards molecules they might stick to. It draws them everywhere in the cell, and so it draws some of them towards the cell nucleus, which has another wall of fats around it, but unfortunately is designed to let molecules rather like the diol epoxides in and out on the cell's ordinary business. The hungry, electron-seeking blob of gloop slips through, and there in front of it are floating twenty-three pairs of tempting targets: the huge, fat, friendly, electron-rich chromosomes of human DNA.

No one in the world in 1970 understands in any detail how

they work, and the ignorance is particularly bad in the Soviet Union, thanks to Lysenko. But the chromosomes work whether they are understood or not. The gloop drifts in; and at any and every point along the endless coiled helix where it happens to make contact, the gloop locks on. Where it jostles forward with its missing electron to embrace one of the DNA's electrons, there's a little chemical reaction, and the electron in question bonds to both the DNA and the gloop. The gloop is now an 'adduct', glued to the helix. But the helix is changed too, by having the blob of tobacco residue stuck to it. At the position where the adduct sits, the information in the DNA has been corrupted. Instead of the G, T, C or A that should be there, in the four-letter alphabet of the genome, it reads as one of the other letters instead. The adduct has written an error into the code.

But it's all right. In the vast majority of positions along the genome where goo might attach itself at random, altering one letter won't produce any significant mutation, even if the alteration lasts. The genome is Lebedev's software, but unlike software written by humans, it is not a set of procedures packed end-to-end, all of which at least purport to do something. It is a jumble of legacy code spread out in fragments through a whole voluminous library of nonsense. Almost always, a random change of letter will either hit some existing nonsense, or turn some sense into new nonsense. And because the chromosomes come in pairs, with a version of every chromosome contributed by Lebedev's mother floating there opposite a version from his father, if some sense on the version on one side turns to nonsense, the equivalent piece on the other version will go on making sense just fine. Dangerous mutations usually only happen in the rare cases where sense is accidentally turned into different sense. Which is not what has happened here. Here, the arriving molecule has glued itself where it makes no difference at all.

This has happened billions of times.

*

'Minister Kosygin is extremely busy,' says the woman behind the desk. She is in her late thirties, with a cynical droop to her mouth. Nevertheless, she is made up like a plump doll, with pink circles on her cheeks and eyelids painted metallic blue. The curls of her hairdo shine as if they were parts of a single piece of plastic. 'As I told you, he can't say when he will be free. He apologises for not keeping your appointment, but suggests you might prefer to return another day.' Almost word for word, she is repeating what she said when Lebedev arrived, an hour or more ago.

'It's fine,' said Lebedev. 'I'm happy to wait.'

She compresses her lips; sniffs. The door she keeps is at the end of a panelled passage lost to sunlight. When it opens, as it does occasionally, some pale reminder of day slips out, and the sound of typing, but the rest of the time it might as well be midnight where Lebedev is sitting, on a bench by the wall. The lamp on her desk glows in the gloom like the lantern radiating at the centre of some very brown old painting, the kind where the human figures almost vanish into the soot and the varnish. Lebedev wishes the thin cushion beneath him were thicker, for these days his buttocks seem to have been replaced, for sitting, by two sore angles of bone like the outer corners of a coat hanger. He aches. He waits. There isn't much to look at. It's a wonder that the rubber plant survives down here: perhaps it has found some alternative to photosynthesis. On her desk she has only the appointment book, a telephone and a bowl of peppermints to be offered to favoured passers-by. He has not been given one. She turns the pages of her magazine with short pink fingers. When he coughs she clicks her tongue disgustedly. True, it is a disgusting noise he makes. It begins as a commonplace wheeze in his throat, but tumbles down into his chest where it hacks and rattles and audibly moves clots of viscous wet stuff around, till the wet stuff has been dragged up into his airway, and he's in a gasping, gargling struggle to get it off his epiglottis, and out, so that he can breathe again. He spits into his handkerchief, clean this morning, now stiff and crusty, stained with nameless emulsions. He's been bringing up the traditional jade mayonnaise of bronchitis every winter for as long as he can remember, but this is something different, something thicker and redder and meatier, like liquescent liver. He folds the handkerchief away, and tries to muster his persuasive powers.

Another lung cell. The soft rainfall of gloop onto Lebedev's DNA continues. By chance, this particular sticky drop in the statistical rain is one of the small minority that is going to land somewhere that matters. By chance, it is falling onto a stretch of code on Chromosome number 11 which scientists will know later as the gene *ras*, or *hRas*. The electrophile noses in; it suckers on; the guanine (G) it has suckered onto on the helix now reads, for all intents and purposes, as cytosine (C). And this time, it happens that changing G to C creates sense, not nonsense, in the code. *Ras* with a C in it at this specific position is a viable and functional piece of software. But much more of a change is in prospect than there would be if someone substituted a new programme for the one that was supposed to be running in a computer. Human-made software is only an informational ghost, temporarily given possession of the machine and allowed to change os to 1s and vice versa. The software of humans, on the other hand, actually builds the hardware it runs on. It creates the machine. So a mutation in the code means a mutation in the body too, if the error endures.

Ras is one of the genes that control cell growth and cell division. In adults, it switches on and off periodically to govern the normal cycle of the cell's existence. You wouldn't want it switched on all the time. Foetuses in the womb run *ras* continually to generate all the new tissue that the Build-A-Human programme demands when a human is being first assembled. Otherwise, cell multiplication must happen when, and only when, the body part the cell is in needs a new cell. But it's the switch that has been altered by having C where G used to be in this mutant version of *ras*. C instead of G at this one particular point jams the *ras* gene at 'on' – throws the lever for unstoppable growth, and then breaks the lever.

But it's all right. This copy of *ras* may be corrupted, but the cell has a failsafe mechanism built into the shape of the DNA molecules. The helix is a double helix. On the other side of the double corkscrew there runs another strand of Gs, Ts, Cs and As which carries all the information of the genome, only in reverse, like the negative of a photograph or the mould a jelly was turned out of; and the cell, which is used to operating in an environment of small chemical accidents, operates a handy editorial enzyme that moves up and down the chromosomes checking that the two strands remain perfect opposites. The editorial enzyme doesn't find absolutely all of the changes the adducts gummed to Lebedev's DNA have made, but it finds most of them, the harmless and the harmful alike, methodically correcting each little mutation. It finds this one. The new C in the mutant version of RAS on one side clashes with the existing C on the reverse side. C against C isn't a legitimate opposite. A quick editorial snip, and there's the original G again. Lebedev's factory settings have been restored.

This has happened millions of times.

'Minister,' says Lebedev inside his head, 'I know that the decision has already been taken, but I must draw your attention – I must ask you to consider – I must question the wisdom – I must – I must –'

What's this? A bulky middle-aged man is strolling up the corridor towards them, brush-cut black hair gleaming in the lamplight, hands the size of hams playing little tunes on the air, equable smile on his face. For a moment Lebedev thinks the General Secretary himself is upon them, but it isn't; it's one of the regional Party bosses, he forgets the man's name, who thanks to the magical osmosis of power all tend to look faintly Brezhnev-ish these days, just as the littler bosses used to resemble Khrushchev, as far as they could, and before that Stalin. The cheery gaze passes over Lebedev as if the air were empty where he sits on the bench, and settles on the doorkeeper. Mr Belorussia, or is it Mr Moldavia, winks. She blushes and reaches a hand up to her meringue-hard hair.

'Hello, Frenchie,' he says. 'Is Himself available?'

Immediately she wiggles out from behind the desk and click-clacks across in her heels to open the big door for him. She is not thin and she fills the whole of her knee-length skirt. As Mr Kiev (or is it Mr Volodyavostok) steps deftly through the slot of daylight she's summoned, he whispers something that makes her giggle and drops a casually proprietorial hand onto her round behind. The simper hasn't quite left her face as she pulls the door to again, but it vanishes when she sees the direction of Lebedev's haggard gaze. Though as gazes go, this one is virtually abstract, there being so little left in him to respond to such things.

'Hmph,' she says. *Not for you.*

'Are you French, then?' asks Lebedev. She only glowers.

Another lung cell. There is a way for a blob of goo to cause a *ras* mutation that persists. The gummy electron-seeking missile has to arrive, and glue G into C in the exact right place, at the exact right moment in the life of the cell when for once the enzyme cannot compare *ras* to its negative. That is, when the lung cell is already busy dividing into two lung cells. The goo floats in, and finds inside the nucleus a double helix which has been unzipped into two separate strands, each of which is going to grow back into a complete copy of the genome. Of all the random blobs of goo in the random rainstorm, here comes the blob that suckers onto Chromosome 11 in the position to create the always-on version of *ras*, just as the unzipped halves of Chromosome 11 are waving loose. It's too late for the editorial enzyme: there's nothing to correct the mutant C against. Along the strand instead travels a polymerase, a construction enzyme, steadily building out the other half of a new double helix. And when it reaches the C, it obligingly supplies a new counterpart for the other side which is a match, which is a perfect opposite. The corrupted code has reproduced itself. After a while, there are two sets of completed chromosome pairs in the nucleus. They pull away from each other. The nucleus stretches, puckers out like dumb-bells, splits into two as well. Last the outside wall of the cell repeats the split, stretching and pulling and puckering back into a pair of separate fatty spheres. One contains *ras* in its original uncorrupted form, but beside it Lebedev now has a new lung cell with *ras* switched on in it forever. And immediately *ras* takes charge of the cellular machinery and starts the build-up to superfast cell multiplication. A cell running *ras* full-time won't co-operate with nearby cells in any other task. It isn't interested, for example, in being part of a lung. Binary at last, it only wants to become two cells, four cells, eight sixteen thirty-two –

But it's all right. The body is used to occasional runaway accidents with *ras*. It has one last defence mechanism. As *ras* goes crazy, another gene, away over on Chromosome 17, detects the molecular signature of the build-up and neatly, swiftly, initiates cell suicide. The cell dies. With it goes the mutant *ras*.

This has happened thousands of times.

What is the tactful, the effective way of announcing that your life's work has been wasted?

On 18 December last year Lebedev sat in a meeting at Minradioprom, the Ministry of Radio Production, and heard the assembled bigwigs of government and the Academy talk themselves into destroying the Soviet computer industry. That wasn't quite how they put it, of course. The question was what model of machine to develop for the Unified System which was supposed to manage the economy in the 1970s. On the one side lay the possibility of designing their own standardised range of next-generation mainframes. On the other was a proposal to copy the family of machines which were the standard commercial solution in the West, the IBM 360 series. Everyone at the meeting paid compliments to homegrown Soviet technology, but they had talked about it, most of them, as the risky option. They were charmed by the safety of choosing an existing product with existing, well-established software. And so they had gone with safe, despite all he could do.

But safe was an illusion. He had tried and tried and yet somehow failed to convey the simple truth that, if they chose IBM, they would not, in fact, get IBM machines. They would not get IBM software. They would not get IBM reliability. These things were not available for delivery to the Soviet Union. They would be committing themselves, instead, to reverse-engineering the IBM 360 in the dark, with limited documentation and no original model of a 360 to dismantle. It would take years. And the 360 had been introduced in 1965! It was half a decade old before the effort to copy it even began. So they would be condemning themselves not just to imitation, but to perpetual obsolescence as well. They'd be forever chasing the prospect of doing what the Americans had already done, years and years before. Oh, there would still be the special military machines to build, to guide the smashing of atoms and the launching of cosmonauts, but there'd be no general flowering. There'd be no more of the contest between the design bureaus which had kept the Institute for Precision Mechanics racing for processing speed against the Institute of Electronic Control Machines and the Institute of Cybernetics and SKB-245. There'd be no more glorious eccentricities, like Brusentsov's trinary processor at the University of Moscow, the only one in the world to explore three-state electronics. There'd be no pushing outward at the frontier of the achievable. There'd be no design any more, properly considered; just slow, disconsolate copying.

Only a fool would choose safety on these terms. Surely Kosygin can be brought to see it? Tactfully. Effectively. 'Minister –' But Lebedev has begun to sag. He peers at his watch in the gloom. It's hours, now, that he's been waiting here in the labyrinth. Bone ache is being joined by a fever that rises up through his emaciated body like hot mist. There's a film of damp on his forehead and things inside his mind are losing their clarity and starting to melt into each other.

Another lung cell. Chance upon chance upon chance upon chance. Of all the billions of cells in Lebedev's lungs, there will be some millions where the diol epoxide gum from his cigarettes stuck itself, not to *ras*, but to the gene on Chromosome 17 that initiates emergency cell suicide; and of those millions there will be some thousands where the crucial blob blew in just in time to land on a strand of DNA in the midst of cell division, and got itself copied. So, scattered here and there through the billions of cells whose little bulging windows of fat face the channels of the lung, there are some thousands, randomly distributed, where the suicide gene on Chromosome 17, later to be called P53, isn't working. Here's one of them. And into it, after fifty years of delicious Kazbek smoke, there flies one more random molecule of goo, and it travels straight to *ras* to scramble the vital G into C, and it arrives just in time, too, to evade the editorial enzyme and get copied into a new cell.

And it's not all right. The new cell with mutant *ras* in charge of it is a tumour unbound, freed from the body's safety systems to multiply and multiply, unstoppably, selfishly, altogether indifferent to its effect on Lebedev's lung, and on Lebedev.

This only has to happen once.

Lebedev starts to cough again and this time he can't stop. There's no far side to it, no end to it; it's like putting out an arm to balance yourself and finding there's no wall to lean on any more.

He tumbles down and down into the cough. It's all mucus in there, no air, no air, and he can't bring up the lump of noxious matter that's blocked his passages and he can't get out of the struggle to shift it either. He's choking. His ears roar. His vision pocks with little breeding asterisks of light, coagulated across the dim sfumato of the corridor. His head drops between his knees. Hack. Hack. Hack. Panic, and beyond panic to the threshold of a dizzy indifference. Then the obstruction comes free, drops out as a vile, metallic mouthful. Shaky-handed wiping; spitting; wiping.

'Comrade?'

His vision clears to darkness. She's standing over him, holding out her water glass, glaring at him with reluctant pity.

'You should go home,' she says.

'I'll wait,' he says. 'It doesn't matter how long.'

'No,' she says, 'you should go home. Don't you understand?'

The effects of carcinoma in a major airway include shortness of breath, weight loss, bone pain, chest and abdominal pain, hoarseness, difficulty swallowing and chronic coughing. Metastasis to spine, liver and brain is common: further symptoms may then include muscle weakness, impotence, slurred speech, difficulty walking, loss of fine motor co-ordination, dementia and seizures. Radiotherapy is of limited effectiveness. Fluid build-up behind the lung obstruction eventually leads to pneumonia and death.

This, unfortunately, is certain.

2.

Police in the Forest, 1968

'Mama? Listen to this,' said Max, whose book was propped against the jar of rowanberry preserve on his side of the breakfast table. Max was only normally clever at algebra; he was not especially good at playing chess; he did not crave the use of telescopes or gaze hungrily at the Computer Centre, like some of Akademgorodok's children. What Max liked was to read, and read, and read, anything he could get his hands on, from nonsense poetry to adventure stories, but particularly anything that was dense and spiky and gave him something to chew over. You could never give him a better present than a book. He laughed at adult jokes she didn't think he ought to be able to see just yet, sudden deep chuckles that seemed to conjure up close – too close, too sudden – the man he'd be, a man who, if he was going to be extremely good at anything, was going to be extremely good at words. It was a worry. This was a wonderful place to grow up if you were a budding physicist, but where was a good place for a budding poet? Were there any? He might at least be better off back in Leningrad. There was a thought to hold onto: something he might conceivably gain, her little hostage, dragged around by her decisions, if today went as she expected it would.

'Mama?'

'What?'

'I'm just getting to the end of this science-fiction book, and they're at a kind of place that gives wishes, like a genie, only it's alien technology, and it's very dangerous? And there's a silly man and a tough man, and the silly man rushes forward, and he makes this kind of enormous wish for everybody in the whole world to be happy, but the alien thing squishes him instead. And I was wondering, if it's supposed to be a kind of a – a kind of a –'

`'A metaphor?'

'Yes? I mean a sort of a sideways picture. You know. Of here.'

'Show me.' Zoya licked her fingers, and Max passed her the book over the black bread and the yoghurt. *Happiness for everybody*, she read where Max's finger was pointing. *Free! As much as you want! Nobody will leave unsatisfied! And then he was suddenly silent, as though a huge fist had punched him in the mouth.* She flipped it over to look at the spine. *Roadside Picnic.* Well, well.

'Maybe it's a coincidence,' said Max.

'No it isn't,' she said. 'It's the author being clever, like you. Right; come on, then, Mr Literature. Hop skip. Time for us to get moving.'

By the front door of the flat Max gave his usual, resigned demonstration that his satchel contained homework workbook textbook pencils. At ten he mislaid objects with such spectacular facility that it was as if all bags and pockets he had anything to do with connected to secret exits from the workaday cosmos; he had taken to spreading his hands and raising his eyebrows when things vanished, acting out the bemused shtick of a stage magician, and she doubted that his class teacher found it very charming. She pulled her coat on over her labcoat and they wrapped themselves up in scarves and gloves and woolly hats. It was the end of winter, but still around fifteen below zero outside, dry Siberian cold.

Tereshkova Street was churned to a hard black chaos like the surface of a filthy sea. Better to take the route to Max's school behind and between the apartment buildings, on the snowy paths under the trees. It was old snow now, creaking and snapping underfoot as they stepped through its crust. The sky was slaty-dark. From the block ahead and to the left, a column of white was still rising from the window of the apartment where a desperate tenant had cracked open the communal steam-pipe to get some heat. Their breaths rose in smaller columns. Max's nose sharpened to a bright pink point. A flight of computer programmers went by on cross-country skis, flick flick, flick flick, between the black uprights of the pines. Across the crunching expanse of Morskoi Prospekt, where the next grade up of apartment buildings glowed oxblood and ochre in the gloom, and the boxed-in wooden balconies twinkled with lights like harem windows in the Arabian Nights. Uphill towards the Presidium a blood-orange of a sun was just hoisting itself above the horizon: downhill, in the direction of the Ob Sea, you could hardly see anything in the darkness. The beach was for skating in winter, if you were hardy enough, and for hooking river-fish through holes sawed in the ice.

School 21 lay in the town's grandest zone, among the Academicians' houses. Here the sidewalks were swept, and they joined a steadily increasing traffic of other kids with satchels, trudging along. She was the only parent, so far as she could see. Max too had been taking himself to school these last couple of years, but on this particular day she wanted to walk him right to the gate, and actually watch him go in, under the wretched centennnial banner of Lenin blessing the children.

'Max –' she said.

'Hey, that professor you used to dance with is waving to you.'

She looked across the street and there, to be sure, was Leonid Vitalevich, climbing out of his green Volga and flapping an affable hand. In anyone else, this would represent a very public declaration of solidarity, under the circumstances, but with Leonid Vitalevich, you could never tell what he had noticed, or chosen to notice. This was the man who, they said, had tried to pose a mathematical problem to each of the candidates when his institute was deciding who to nominate to the Academy; genuinely not realising, so they said, that the fix was in from the outset. He had always been very pleasant to Zoya, though it was

343

a while now since there had been one of the old interdisciplinary seminars. Cybernetics was not the meeting ground it used to be. She smiled and waved back; but Leonid Vitalevich must have put his foot on a slippery patch because, ba-boomp, down he went into a heap of black coat and splayed legs. A crumpled old crow, with its feathers on end. His driver hurried round to pick him up and helped him away up the path to the Academicians' club.

One of a pair of older boys snickered. His friend punched him cheerfully on the shoulder.

'Move along, move along, nothing to see,' he said. 'Just another fat little *zhid* falling on his arse.'

Zoya glared, and would have said something, but Max gave her a very adult look. He was probably right. It was everywhere, now; not just spewing out of the mouths of teenagers, but from their parents in the institutes, and from students at the university. There'd been a case last winter when some of the Russian kids in a dorm decided it would be a good joke to lock the Jews out in the cold overnight. They'd put up a hand-painted sign saying A CHICKEN ISN'T A BIRD AND A JEW ISN'T A MAN.

'What were you going to say, Mama?' asked Max. 'The bell's going. I'll be late.'

'Just – not to be surprised if things are a bit . . . unpleasant today. If you get told some bad stuff about me.'

'Don't worry,' said Max. 'I'll keep my cool. Kostya told me what to do. Bye –' and he was off, running for the gate, before she could embarrass him by kissing him.

The sun was fully up as she recrossed Morskoi, spilling a brightening orange wash across the ground and weaving a confusion of shadows round the trees on the far side. Her lips burned with the cold, and she could taste the sluggish gasoline vapours left in the air by the passing buses. It was going to be fine, though: blue as the eye in a peacock's feather, overhead. Her spirits lifted despite herself. She had always loved the forest best, about living here; and the forest was still there to be delighted in, on the walk to work, even when the other pleasures of Akademgorodok had closed down, when people no longer trusted in the trustworthiness of strangers, when you could no longer hear a thousand conversations about people's work, nuclear fusion in the post office queue, ecology in the cinema, sociology at the laundry. The forest remained.

In winter the canopy of the silver birches turned to a leafless tracery, with dark little seed-balls among the slender twigs: nodes in a network too complex to be grasped by the eye and moving, moving, as a bitter breeze stirred through the treetops. The pines kept their needles, greenish-black under their outlining of frost. You would think it was too cold for the receptors in the human nose to work, but somehow the resinous smell still penetrated, cold and slow, thick as cough medicine. She stepped across the crackling whiteness between the pale trunks and the red. Other figures were in migration through the wood around her, but solitary, out of range of each other. She was not especially pleased when she rounded a corner in the path and found Valentin waiting under a tree for her, hugging his shoulders and puffing out clouds.

'Good morning,' he said. Since he went to Prague the year before, he had grown his blond hair out longer and developed a ridiculous moustache which continued down from the corners of his mouth to the bottom of his chin in straggly lines. Very Czech, very young, no doubt; but he had a little belly these days under his suede coat, and two toddlers at home. Past your prime, my boy, she thought.

'Yes?'

'I've got the next instalment of your research money.' No need to ask why he was handing her an envelope in a wood, when so far as she knew the grants from the Fakel collective were entirely legal and above board. The money wasn't the problem. It was being seen with her.

'I'm not sure there's much point,' she said.

'I don't think there's any point in us hanging onto it,' he said. 'We don't know how much longer we'll be going.' Fakel had been a roaring, and then an embarrassing, success. It did contract programming work for enterprises all over Siberia, and the money had poured in so fast that at one point, so they said, the Akademgorodok Komsomol had had two million roubles in its bank account. They had been hastily spending it on good works ever since: research grants, sports events, the Festival of Bards scheduled for tonight.

'Really?'

'Haven't you heard? They're closing all the social clubs. "Under the Integral", the Cybernetics Kaffee-klatch, the lot. Our bet is we'll be gone in a fortnight.'

'I'm sorry,' she said awkwardly.

'Yes; well. So you might as well take it. Go on. It might, you know, be useful.'

She put the envelope in her pocket, and cast around for some friendly response.

'I saw your genius just now,' she offered.

'Leonid Vitalevich? Not really my genius any more, you know? I haven't really done much at the Institute since the Fakel stuff began.'

'They say he's saving the steel-tube industry now, since they wouldn't let him save the world?'

'Mm,' said Valentin.

'Weren't you tempted?' she teased. 'I'm sure it's important work . . .'

Mistake. Valentin didn't smile; he rounded on her, red in his cheeks and misery in his eyes.

'Did you ever think', he hissed, 'that if you weren't so fond of laughing at people, you might not be in this mess? I don't understand you. I don't understand you at all. How can you be so irresponsible? How can you be so selfish? It's as if you think you're the only person in the world. The rest of us pay too, you know. God! If I were you I'd be shitting myself! Don't you even care what happens to your son?'

'Fuck off, Valentin,' she said, and walked away. She thought the conversation was over, but after fifty metres or so, with her hand pressed to her mouth, she heard the quick crunch-crunch of his feet running after her.

'Zoya, wait,' he said.

'What?'

'I meant to say – are you still seeing Kostya?'

'*What?*'

'Are you and he still – you know – ?'

'That's really none of your business, is it? It never bloody has been.'

Incredibly, he put his hand on her arm. She shook it off.

'Zoya, I just need –'

'For God's sake,' she said. 'Leave me to my irresponsibility, eh?'

This time he didn't follow. 'Are you all right?' he said to her departing back.

'I'm fine,' she said. 'I'm fine.'

So much for the peace of the forest. The rest of the way to the institute, she thought about Kostya. They were not, as it happened, seeing each other in the sense that Valentin had meant, and they hadn't been for some time. It was her doing. She had enjoyed the cradle-snatching aspect of the affair, to be honest; but she had not wanted it to grow into a decisive factor in her life. She had been married once and that was enough. She had liked smuggling him in and out of the apartment at times when Max would not have to meet him – snatching the two hours of Saturday afternoon when Max was at the Young Inventors' Club, and then going to pick him up, secretly alive and awakened in her clothes, her lips a little puffy with kissing, the taste of Kostya still in her mouth. He was not a braggart or an oaf, and he had let her be gently educational. But they were at different stages in their lives. He had wanted more than her spare afternoons, he had wanted to be in love and to be loved back and for what was happening between them to be the thing that set the story of his life, or at least the story of that part of his life. It was understandable. He was in his mid-twenties. He expected things to be cumulative, to make sense. He expected events to cut an intelligible figure in the air as they went by. And so she brought things quietly to an end, so that he could go off and fall in love elsewhere; have, with someone else, a passion with a narrative to it. After which, she could finally introduce him to Max, and make of him a family friend. They got along: Kostya could offer advice on negotiating the worlds of boys and men. And it was for her to cope, quietly, with the jealousies that assailed her, quite irrationally, when she saw him walking with some postgraduate slut.

'Pass please, Dr Vaynshteyn,' said the guard in the glass box, at the doorway to Cytology and Genetics.

'Come on, Tyoma, you know who I am.'

'Sorry, can't let you in without showing your pass. New rule. Gotta see everyone's pass.'

'What, you think I'm an impostor? You've been letting me in for six years.'

'From today, gotta see everybody's pass.'

'I don't have it with me.'

'Better go home and get it.'

'This is ridiculous . . .'

But the Director was coming in, overcoat flapping, smoothing his coiffure. He was clearly planning to sweep by without acknowledging her. She blocked his path with sour pleasure.

'Director, won't you explain to Tyoma here that you need me in the building today, pass or no pass?'

'Exempt from the rules as usual, my dear?'

She smiled at him with lots of teeth.

'You can't have your show trial without the accused,' she said. Pause. 'Sign her in.'

'That was characteristically tactful,' he said, when they were standing by the lift. The lift came. He got in. 'The academic council will be expecting you at one o'clock,' he said. 'Don't be late.' The doors closed.

Her four juniors were all waiting when she came into the lab. Literally waiting: over by the window in a huddle, not doing anything, not saying anything.

'Don't just stand there,' she said. 'This isn't a holiday. Tabulate!'

She hung up her coat and tried to concentrate. Thank heavens, another enormous pile of polyclinic data had been delivered and she could sink into the mechanical business of analysis. Tick the boxes, write the numbers on the cyclostyled returns, lose yourself in the soothing minutiae of the experiment, for just a little longer. Spina bifida, cystic fibrosis, mongolism – nine notifiable birth defects. Tick, tick, tick. This load came from a medical centre in Perm, within the ecological shadow of the heavy-metal complex there, and as she had expected with a local environment like that, the data showed a steadily elevated baseline level of mutations over time, with some particular spikes at dates that clearly corresponded to local events. But the two big spikes they had grown used to seeing were in place as usual, growing ever higher as the numbers mounted up: one for the late 1930s, one for the late 1950s. Two sudden peaks in the level of birth mutations in the human population, equally present in the medical record wherever around the Soviet Union they had looked so far. The key to interpreting them was to remember that these unfortunate babies were manifesting their parents' mutated genes. Therefore, the spikes corresponded to periods one generation earlier than each maximum of birth defects, when for some reason there had been a greater prevalence of mutated genes in the population; or, to put it in good Darwinian terms, a definite differential advantage in possessing those mutated genes. From her work on fruit-flies, she knew that an active tendency to mutation was often associated with the adaptability of the creature, when some serious environmental challenge came along. But for a tendency toward mutation to confer a survival advantage in the human population, there must, by implication, have been a squeeze on, in the human population, of the same sort of order of severity as the die-offs afflicting fruit flies when a virus swept through that they had no immunity to. Only a demographic disaster would have this kind of effect. Now, it was easy to guess what had been going on twenty-odd years before the first peak. Late thirties, less twenty years, took you back to the disaster years of the First War, the Revolution, the Civil War: an acknowledged era when the Four Horsemen stomped recumbent Russia. But the later spike was interesting. Late fifties, less twenty years, took you back to the late thirties, before the acknowledged disaster of the German invasion. Which strongly suggested that the dying had begun, on a momentous and huge and demographically significant scale, before the acknowledged evil of fascism could be blamed for it. She had pointed out none of this in the lab – but they were in effect studying history, she and her junior staff, recorded not in documents or archives or even in human memories, but in what no one expected was keeping a record, in human bodies themselves. Nothing could have made more sense, if you thought about it: where would the past endure, if it endured at all, but in the irrefutable, ineditable archive of the genes? The trick would be to find a way to publish the results.

Well; would have been. She looked at her watch. Quarter to one. Reluctantly, she disengaged her mind from the purities of reason, and picked up her coat.

'Thank you all,' she said, by the door. 'We've done good work.' She remembered the packet of money. 'Would you send this out to the polyclinics? It's their next payment. Goodbye.'

The Academic Council of the Institute of Cytology and Genetics was twenty of the most senior members of the staff, heads of department and so on: people she had known for years. Some were mere mediocrities, Party hacks for whom she had never concealed her dislike, but many of the rest she had laughed with and schemed with, and a few she had considered friends. One or two she had slept with, since Kostya. Almost all of them had once been allies in the silent battle to save real genetics from Lysenko.

'We have just one unpleasant item on the agenda today,' said the Director. 'A letter protesting against the conduct of a certain court case in Moscow, signed by forty-six employees of the Siberian Branch here in Akademgorodok, which was first printed in the American newspaper the *New York Times* and then read out, with the names of all its signatories, on the American propaganda radio-service the Voice of America. These signatories, I am sorry to say, include our own Dr Vaynshteyn, who we have asked here today to account for this extraordinary and destructive action. Now, I will just say this, before throwing the meeting open. This is not a court of law. It is a forum for comradely discussion. We are not here to inflict penalties, so nobody should feel a misplaced sense of anxiety, or mistake these proceedings for anything they are not.'

Snake, thought Zoya.

'Who'll begin?' asked the Director.

'I'd like to know why Dr Vaynshteyn concerned herself with this court case at all,' someone said. 'What did it have to do with her? Couldn't she mind her own business? She's not a legal expert.'

'I know the people in question slightly,' said Zoya.

'Of course you do. You've got an address book full of trouble-makers and undesirables. You don't make any secret of it.'

'I'd like to know', said someone else, 'why, if she had to meddle, she didn't address herself to the appropriate authorities. Why defame Soviet justice before the whole world? Why go tattling to the enemy, and drag the institute through the mud?'

'We didn't. We sent registered letters to the prosecutor, to the Supreme Court, to the Central Committee and to the General Secretary. No one else. I have receipts.'

'Then how do you explain the *New York Times* and the Voice of America?'

'I can't. Ask the people we sent the letters to.'

'Now you're accusing the Soviet government?'

'I don't see', said one of the ones around the table she had classed as a friend, 'that it matters very much how the letter reached the enemy. What matters is that the enemy knew where to look to find this sort of material. They knew where to look for disloyalty. For cynicism. For a willingness to betray colleagues.'

'Under the constitution, any citizen may petition any official on any subject,' she said.

'Yes, true,' said someone else, 'but that doesn't relieve you of the obligation to think before you open your mouth.'

'Can't you see how this plays into the hands of those who would like to drag us back to the past? Don't you value the freedoms we enjoy here?'

'So,' she said, 'you want me to serve freedom by shutting up.'

'If you can!'

'There's speech and there's speech, Dr Vaynshteyn. Are you a child, that you don't know that?'

'A dangerous child, Zoya.'

'Dr Vaynshteyn, you don't seem to be aware of how much we're resented.'

'The workers of Novosibirsk', said the rep from the labour union, 'do not resent the hard-working scientists of

Akademgorodok, who are preparing a better life for all by their heroic efforts. This is a slander. But the workers demand that the traitor Vaynshteyn, who is not fit to be called a scientist, should be expelled and face the full rigour of the law for her criminal anti-Soviet activity.'

'Well,' said the Director, 'we should all note the strength of feeling expressed there by the institute's workers, but I don't think there's any need at present to be talking in terms of punishment. Let's simply express our own feeling. I think we're ready to move towards a vote.'

A babble of voices.

'Just a vote of censure,' he said soothingly. 'No binding force. Hands please? Unanimous? Good. Dr Vaynshteyn, I'll show you out.'

In the corridor he said: 'Do you remember? You promised me to be a good comrade.' He said: 'Your residence permit is being revoked. I'll expect your resignation next week.'

'Fired,' she said in the House of Science that evening. 'You?'

'Fired,' agreed sarcastic Mo.

She scanned the crowd for Kostya. They were standing at the back of the audience for the Festival of Bards, which had looked likely to be cancelled as part of the crackdown but had gone ahead anyway, perhaps because all the performers had already arrived. The Fakel collective's money had paid for a collection of poets, balladeers and singers to converge on the town, and they were filing one by one across the little stage in the hot box of the House of Science's atrium, singing sings about booze and heartbreak, with occasional pleas for the end of the imperialist war in Vietnam. Max was at home in bed, having survived a day with less finger-pointing in it than she had feared. They had had the conversation that broached the imminent prospect of them going back to live in Leningrad with Grandma, and he had said he was all right with that. The student who was babysitting was curled up with Zoya's copy of *Zhivago*. Between the tight-packed crowd and the winter dark, green ferns and bamboos grew in the glass walls of the House of Science. They were in a little lighted vivarium, a flask sealed against the cold outside. Everything seemed to be happening for the last time; to be touched with sadness. She was in a mood of elegy.

The current bard finished, and a new one stepped up, a man in late middle age, gone shaggy and jowly, but with bright eyes. He had a moustache which might once have been dapper, but had escaped. He didn't look bad.

'Who's this?'

'Film-music composer, I think. Jingle-writer. Or something.'

'Hello,' said the bard. 'Let me just tune this a little.' He fiddled with his guitar. He was nervous. 'Now, all right. This is something called "The Gold-Miner's Waltz".'

And he began to strum in waltz time, just a basic strum-strum-strum, with his voice doing all the work over the top. And he sang:

> *We've called ourselves adults for ages*
> *We don't try to pretend we're still young*
> *We've given up digging for treasure*
> *Far away in the storybook sun.*
> *We don't strike out for the Equator,*
> *Or get the hell off, out of sight;*
> *It's silence not treasure that's golden,*
> *And that's what we dig for, all right.*

Aptly the room had grown very quiet indeed: uncannily hushed, to the extent that it was hard to believe there were a couple of hundred breathing humans in it. Perhaps they were holding their breath. The bard sang:

Hold your tongue. Hold your tongue.
Hold your tongue, and you'll make a ton.
Hold your tongue, hold your tongue, hold your tongue!

Strum-strum-strum, strum-strum-strum. There was more. She craned forward.

For ages we kept our hearts hardened
It was wiser to keep our eyes low
Many times we took refuge in silence
But our silence meant yes and not no

– and to her intense irritation a suave presence beside her was demanding attention. It was Shaidullin, no doubt fresh from concluding his own purge at the Institute of Economics. His shaved head gleamed. Oh, not now. Not another bout of ceremonial attack.

'A word in your ear, doctor,' he whispered. 'You should know that our Kostya is knocking.'

'What?'

'He's knocking on the Fifth Department's door. He's talking to them. I'm sorry.' He was gone.

. . . because, you know, silence is gold.
Hold your tongue, hold your tongue.
Hold your tongue and you'll be number one.
Hold your tongue, hold your tongue, hold your tongue!

Oh Kostya, she though, oh Kostya; and there, of course, he was, with the malign inevitability of nightmare, making his way towards her through the crowd and smiling, smiling. She closed her face and held her hand up by her chest, stop, and shook her head at him slowly, definitively. His face began to change but she looked away, back toward the bard. To be thought of later. To be wondered at, wept over, later.

And now we've survived to see better
Everyone talks such a lot
But behind the bright sparkling speeches
The dumbness spreads out like a blot.
Someone else can weep over the bodies,
For the insults and hunger untold.
We know there's more profit in silence.
Yes we know that silence is gold.

Oh, they'll close up everything here that can be closed, after this, she thought. And look what you're doing to yourself, my friend.

It's so easy, making a ton!
It's so easy, to be number one!
Or to have someone shot for a song!
Hold your tongue, hold your tongue, hold your tongue!

The end. The room was still rapt, stunned. She put her hands together and began to clap in the silence, till other people joined in, and others, and still others, till a good three-quarters of the audience were applauding. Not all of them. Some were staring appalled, and some looked as if they were taking notes. Shaidullin, back on the far side of room, was as impassive as an iron post. Poor man, she thought, you think it can still be mended, don't you?

But Sasha Galich, on stage, was laughing like a man released from an ancient burden.

3.

The Pensioner, 1968

There was a bench by the wall at the end of the dacha's grounds, overlooking a wheat field. Sometimes tourists came walking along the fieldpath, and wanted to have their photos taken with him, when they found the former First Secretary sitting there. Nobody was on the path today. There was just the grey heat of August, and himself sitting in his shirt and his hat, with his shortwave radio and the tape recorder his son had given him to record his memoirs. Kava the rook was scratching at the ground by his feet. He had expected, when they first sacked him from the Presidium, that he would at least be allowed to help with Party work at the lowest level, back in the most local of cells, or committees, or whatever they were called nowadays. He ought to know the name but the org chart had changed so many times while he was living up in the high, fruit-bearing canopy of the Party. He had just had a nostalgic memory of the way the meetings had been, at the beginning, in some raw-built concrete room under a bare bulb, with a newly-literate secretary stumbling proudly through the big words of the agenda; and he had hoped that he'd find something like that again, if they let him join in once more with the donkey work of painting May Day banners, and giving speeches in lunchrooms, and visiting kindergartens, and expounding *Pravda* editorials to workers at shift-end. (Make them laugh, that was the secret.) But none of that had happened. The word had gone out: he was untouchable. Nobody was to go near. Nobody was to speak to him, write to him, phone him; and though now and again it would be made distantly clear that his former colleagues were still thinking about him, still including him in their calculations, he never learned about it directly.

The consequences would filter down, in some little change of the regimen he lived under, or in a favour done for his son.

So the days stretched out, extraordinarily long and extraordinarily empty. He had gardened like crazy at first, laying out long ambitious vegetable beds, pruning and composting from dawn till dusk, except when Nina Petrovna called him in to meals – but it grew old, after a while. And you couldn't fill a mind with such things. Before, whenever he doubted, he had worked. Whenever he had been troubled by a memory, he had worked, telling himself that the best answer to any defect in the past must be a remedy in the future. The future had been his private solution as well as a public promise. Working for the future made the past tolerable, and therefore the present. But now no one wanted his promises. The hours gaped. There was too much time to think, and no means to lose the thoughts again in action. He couldn't rid himself of what he thought now. Little by little, in the most undisciplined way, things he had never wanted to remember drifted up from the depths; foul stuff, past hours and minutes it did nobody any good to recall, leaving their proper places in oblivion and rising up into the mind, like muck stirred up from the bottom of a pond to stain the clean water above. He did his best to keep his thoughts in order, for self-pity would be disgusting, and he had the example of Nina Petrovna's Bolshevik calm always before him. If she could manage the change in their lives, the change in her duties, without ever once complaining, so could he, surely. He could repair his mental filters and get through each day. But he understood now why, according to the rumour, that foul-mouthed block of beef Frol Kozlov should have ended up, on his deathbed, calling for a priest. God forbid that he himself should ever be so weak: but he could see now the appeal of the idea of being purged of it all, of it all somehow being taken magically away, so you could leave this life as innocent as you had entered it. It was this damnable idleness, that was what it was. Kozlov too must have lain in bed in the months after his stroke, with nothing to do but think. Perhaps he should have visited him. Too late for that; too late for anything but to haul himself onward through the days. Sometimes the stuggle in his head seemed so disconnected from the eventless world around him that it felt as if the whole thing, the whole bloody history, the whole of the vast country out there beyond the wheatfield, might have been a dream of his, one of those particularly intricate and oppressive fever dreams whose parts you struggle over and over to try to put into order, yet never can; as if there might never have been a Soviet Union at all, except in his head, only this field of Russian wheat.

It was worst if he was stupid enough ever to watch a war film on the giant television receiver in the living room, still with the engraved plate under the screen declaring that it was a birthday gift 'from your colleagues in the Central Committee and the Council of Ministers'. Knowing what they did to him, he never meant to look; yet somehow the tidy heroics drew him in, seeming to offer a sort of ease, a chance to be as comfortably proud of the past as the film. And there *were* things to be proud of, after all, about the war. All those brave boys they had bludgeoned on towards the enemy – well, the bravery had been as real as the bludgeoning; real enough to make you weep. And they had rid the world of a great evil. That was true. While he was actually watching, he felt only a veteran's mild, containable annoyance at the things the director got wrong. It was later that it would all turn poisonous: in the night, in the still solitary centre of the night. He would dream all the vile detail of war that the film had left out, and when he awoke, beside the steady breathing of Nina Petrovna, he would find the images he had dreamed of still equally vivid in his mind's eye; and hoisting up unstoppably behind them, lifted from the murk as if on hooks, out would come the other memories. Behind the picture of the piece of human gut frozen into the path to the forward bunker in Stalingrad, like mottled brown piping, the groaning trees in the

Western Ukraine in '45, when the NKVD hangmen had been at work, and the sight through an incautiously opened door in '37 where an interrogator had been demonstrating the possibilities of a simple steel ruler, and the starveling child vomiting grass during collectivisation. And more; and worse.

So much blood, and only one justification for it. Only one reason it could have been all right to have done such things, and aided their doing: if it had been all prologue, all only the last spasms in the death of the old, cruel world, and the birth of the kind new one. But without the work it was so much harder to believe. Without the work the future had no heft to keep the past at bay. And the world went on the same, so it seemed, unchanged, unredeemed, untransfigured. The same things went on happening, the same old necessities bit just as hard. The garden came no closer, where the lion would lie down with the lamb and all could play at criticism after dinner, if they had a mind to. Today the radio was reporting that Budapest had come around again, just like the time he sent the tanks in; only this time it was Prague, this time it was the Czechs who needed the fraternal arm across the throat to keep them in line. Cheering on the streets, said the radio. Everywhere the workers welcoming the soldiers. Oh yes. Before Prague, Budapest; before Budapest, East Berlin. It all happened over and over again. Over and over and over, with the garden at history's end scooting ahead, forever out of reach, as much of a justification as it had ever been, and as little of one. He fumbled with the tape machine, and found the RECORD key his son had shown him.

'Paradise', he told the wheatfield in baffled fury, 'is a place where people want to end up, not a place they run from. What kind of socialism is that? What kind of shit is that, when you have to keep people in chains? What kind of social order? What kind of paradise?'

He pressed STOP. Covered his mouth with his hand. And then, since he was tired of fear, of feeling it and of causing it, the retired monster sat very still on the bench by the field, and waited until Kava the rook hopped up onto his knee. A little wind came arrowing across the wheat and swayed the birches over his head. And the leaves of the trees said: can it be otherwise?

Three thousand kilometres east it is already night, but the same wind is blowing, stirring the dark branches of the pines around the upstairs window where Leonid Vitalevich is sitting by himself, optimising the manufacture of steel tubes. Five hundred producers. Sixty thousand consumers. Eight hundred thousand allocation orders to be issued per year. But it would all work out if he could persuade them to measure the output in the correct units. The hard light of creation burns within the fallible flesh; outshines it, outshines the disappointing world, the world of accident and tyranny and unreason; brighter and brighter, glaring stronger and stronger till the short man with square spectacles can no longer be seen, only the blue-white radiance that fills the room. And when the light fades the flesh is gone, the room is empty. Years pass. The Soviet Union falls. The dance of commodities resumes. And the wind in the trees of Akademgorodok says: can it be otherwise? Can it be, can it be, can it ever be otherwise?

The labourer awoke and saw that the princess, the flying carpet, and the magic tablecloth were gone. Only his walking boots remained.

Acknowledgements

More of a confession than an acknowledgement: I wrote this book without being able to speak or read Russian. I have therefore been able to draw on only a fraction of the available material, and readers should be aware that what they find here reflects the limited universe of sources that happen to have been translated into English; often, translated into English during the Cold War, as part of the West's anxious guesswork about Soviet developments. This has meant that, not being able to look in archives for myself or go to original documents (except in a very few cases where material was kindly translated for me), I have been unusually dependent on a particular few books which have served me as fundamental gateways to the place and era I was trying to understand, or pathfinders within it. They come up over and over again in the notes, but I would wish to express a specific debt of gratitude to them here as well: Sheila Fitzpatrick's *Everyday Stalinism*, William Taubman's monumental biography *Khrushchev: The Man and His Era*, and Michael Ellman's *Planning Problems in the USSR*. Needless to say, none of the errors, misunderstandings, falsehoods, naiveties, glaring omissions and plain old stupidities that are sure to be present here are the responsibility of these authors. But since this book is teetering on a pyramid of other people's expertise, it seems necessary to acknowledge whose work I'm standing on top of. I also couldn't have written it without the help of the two people who interpreted for me while I was in Russia, Josephine von Zitzewitz in St Petersburg, and Simmi Gill in Akademgorodok and Moscow. Ms Gill translated the key sections of *L. V. Kantorovich: Chelovek i Uchenii* for me, pointed me towards

Kolakowski, and provided high-quality irony on all occasions. For hospitality and encouragement, I am very grateful to Irene and Joseph Romanovsky, Kantorovich's daughter and son-in-law, and to Professor Yakov Fet of Akademgorodok and his wife, who patiently answered questions from what must have seemed to be a puzzlingly innumerate Englishman. Professor G. Khanin also kindly made time to talk to me. These people gave their hospitality and encouragement when I thought I was engaged in producing a much more conventional piece of non-fiction than this has turned out to be, and they may very well not like what I have done with the memory of Kantorovich. But I hope they may nevertheless recognise my essentially celebratory intentions. While I was writing the book, I benefited from conversations with Michael Ellman, Alena Ledeneva of the School of Slavic and Eastern European Studies at the University of London, and Djurdja Bartlett of the London College of Fashion; again, I was usually stumbling about in these conversations, trying to form my first sense of the subject-matter, so Drs Ellman, Ledeneva and Bartlett may have felt their generosity with their time was being wasted. It wasn't. Then, for reading and commenting from various different expert viewpoints on the draft of the book, I want to thank Emma Widdis, Margaret Bray, Gerald Stanton Smith, Oliver Morton, Andrew Brown, Claerwen James, Jonathan Grove, Jenny Turner, Kim Stanley Robinson, Peter Spufford, and David and Bernice Martin. Jessica Martin, meanwhile, had read it chapter by chapter, paragraph by paragraph, and sometimes in times of need sentence by sentence. My students at Goldsmiths were a pleasure to teach. My colleagues at Goldsmiths were a pleasure to be colleagues with. My editor Julian Loose waited and waited and waited for the book, only to receive something very different from what we had originally planned. My agent Clare Alexander dealt gracefully with the consequences. Lastly: my mother, the historian Margaret Spufford, has always been hearteningly sure that I should take risks as a writer. Without her encouragement I might not have been brave enough to move to this halfway house on the borders of fiction. Hence the dedication, though I know she didn't have anything so shockingly unscholarly in mind.

I did the reading for this book in Cambridge University Library, in the University Medical Library and Marshall Economics Library in Cambridge, in the British Library, and in the library of the Society for Co-operation in Russian and Soviet Studies in Brixton. Librarians are the unsung heroes of the world. And indispensable in any project as perverse as this one. St Deiniol's Library in Flintshire provided a wonderfully benign setting in which to write the last chapter. Throughout, the panther-footed Mr Google laid stack upon stack of documents at my elbow. I cannot imagine being able to have written this story in the world before the internet – in the world, in fact, of the story itself.

Notes

Part I

Introduction

4   **A bridge of white hazelwood**: this, and every quotation from a fairytale, comes from Aleksandr Afanas'ev [Afanaseyev], *Russian Fairy Tales*, translated by Norbert Guterman (New York: Pantheon, 1945), in some cases slightly adapted. For formal and anthropological analysis, see Maria Kravchenko, *The World of the Russian Fairy Tale* (Berne, 1987).

4   **Russians stopped telling *skazki***: for the deliberate attempt to manufacture a continuing Soviet 'folk' tradition, with Stalin cast as mythic champion or good tsar, see Frank J. Miller, *Folklore for Stalin: Russian Folklore and Pseudo-folklore of the Stalin Era* (Armonk: M. E. Sharpe, Inc., 1990); and also John McClure and Michael Urban, 'The Folklore of State Socialism', *Soviet Studies* vol. 35 no. 4 (1983), pp. 471–86; Felix J. Oinas, 'Folklore and Politics in the Soviet Union', *Slavic Review* 32 (1973), pp. 45–58; and Rachel Goff, 'The Role of Traditional Russian Folklore in Soviet Propaganda', *Perspectives: Student Journal of Germanic and Slavic Studies* (Brigham Young University), vol. 12, Winter 2004, at: http://germslav.byu.edu/perspectives/w2004contents.html. For an exploitation in contemporary fantasy of Russian folklore and the Soviet/post-Soviet setting, see Liz Williams, *Nine Layers of Sky* (New York: Bantam Spectra, 2003).

4   **The stories' name for a magic carpet**: see Kravchenko, *The World of the Russian Fairy Tale*.

4   **'In our day,' Nikita Khrushchev told a crowd**: see *Khrushchev in America: Full Texts of the Speeches Made by N. S. Khrushchev on His Tour of the United States, September 15–27, 1959* (New York: Crosscurrents Press, 1960), which includes this speech, made in Moscow on his return.

5   **All Russia was (in Lenin's words) 'one office, one factory'**: technically, in fact, a prediction by him about the working of post-revolutionary society, made just before the Bolshevik putsch, and published just after it, in *The State and Revolution* (1918), ch. 5. 'The whole of society will have become one office and one factory with equal work and equal pay.' There are many, many editions, but see, for example, V. I. Lenin, *Selected Works* vol. 2 (Moscow: Progress Publishers, 1970).

I.1 The Prodigy, 1938

8   **Without thinking about it, Leonid Vitalevich**: Leonid Vitalevich
     Kantorovich (1912–86), mathematician and economist, nearest Soviet
     equivalent to John von Neumann, later (1975) to be the only Soviet
     winner of the Nobel Prize for Economics (shared with Tjalling
     Koopmans). Calling someone by first name and patronymic expresses
     formal esteem, in Russian; he is mostly referred to that way here, to
     suggest that he is being viewed with respectful acquaintance but not
     intimacy. With fictional elaboration, this scene on the tram is true to his
     history, for which see his Nobel Prize autobiography, in Assar Lindbeck,
     ed., *Nobel Lectures, Economics 1969–1980* (Singapore: World Scientific
     Publishing Co., 1992); and the collection of his letters and articles, with
     colleagues' memoirs, in V. L. Kantorovich, S. S. Kutateladze and Ya. I.
     Fet, eds., *Leonid Vitalevich Kantorovich: Chelovek i Uchenii* ('Man and
     Scientist') (Novosibirsk: Siberian Branch of the Russian Academy of
     Sciences, vol. 1 2002, vol. 2 2004); and S. S. Kutateladze, 'The Path and
     Space of Kantorovich', talk at the international Kantorovich memorial
     conference, Euler International Mathematical Institute, St Petersburg,
     8–13 January 2004.

10   **Gangs worked the trams**: for 1930s crime and 1930s streetcars, see Sheila
     Fitzpatrick, *Everyday Stalinism: Ordinary Life in Extraordinary Times*
     (OUP, Oxford 2000), pp. 52–3.

11   **The slogan advertised Soviet Champagne**: it had begun as a comment
     by Stalin (naturally) to a meeting of combine-harvester drivers on 1
     December 1935 – 'Everybody now says that the material situation of
     the toilers has considerably improved, that life has become better,
     more cheerful' – and then been pressed into service in songs, speeches,
     posters, newspaper banner headlines. See Fitzpatrick, *Everyday Stalinism*,
     p. 90 and note; for Soviet Champagne, see Jukka Gronow, *Caviar with
     Champagne: Common Luxury and the Ideals of the Good Life in Stalin's
     Russia* (Oxford: Berg, 2003).

12   **On his professor suit would have been a cotton star**: for Jewish
     experiences of the USSR in the 1930s, and Jewish perceptions of it as a
     place of philosemitic enlightenment and opportunity, see Yuri Slezkine,
     The Jewish Century (Princeton NJ: Princeton University Press, 2004).

12   **A request from the Plywood Trust of Leningrad**: I have imagined
     the details of the approach to Kantorovich, but the origin of his
     mathematics of optimisation in the Plywood Trust's commission is
     absolutely authentic. When Kantorovich was celebrating his seventieth
     birthday in 1982, he was presented with a piece of plywood on which
     was inscribed 'I am a simple plank, but I too am rejoicing, because
     it all began with me'. The first publication of his method, proving
     his priority as discoverer, was in a sixty-eight-page pamphlet of 1939,
     Matematicheskie metody organizatsii i planirovaniya proizvodstva

('Mathematical methods of production management and planning'), and his university also organised a small conference; but very little notice was taken officially, which was probably the safest outcome for him, and it is not even clear whether the Plywood Trust used what he had presented to them: quite possibly not. The method was then independently reinvented in the United States by Tjalling Koopmans and by George Danzig, who while working on transport and allocation problems for the US Airforce during the war coined the phrase 'linear programming'. Koopmans' formulation had one difference from Kantorovich's: it assumed that any maximised selection of outputs would count as efficient, whereas for Kantorovich the selection was a given. It came from the planners, and there was only one of it to maximise. See Michael Ellman, *Planning Problems in the USSR: The Contribution of Mathematical Economics to Their Solution* 1960–1971 (Cambridge: CUP, 1973).

14　**He had seen a method which could do what the detective work of conventional algebra could not**: the Plywood Trust had in effect presented him with a group of equations to solve of the form $3a + 2b + 4c + 6d = 17$, where the unknown variables a, b, c, d stood for the unknown assignments of work between different machines – only with many, many more variables than just these four. These are known as 'linear' equations, because if graphed they produce straight lines, and it is a property of linear equations that you can only solve them if you have as many equations to work with as there are variables. Otherwise, they are 'undetermined' – there are an infinite number of possible solutions, and no way to decide between them. The Plywood Trust's equations were undetermined, since there were fewer of them than the immense number of variables they wanted to know. Kantorovich's first step was to realise that he had a criterion for choosing between the infinite solutions, in the knowledge that $a + b + c + d$, the total amount of work done by the machines, was to be *minimised* for the production of the target output of plywood in the Plywood Trust's plan. Or you could turn the problem around, and see yourself as maximising the output target. For a textbook explanation of linear programming, adapted to American business-school students, see Saul I. Gass, *Linear Programming: Methods and Applications* (New York: McGraw-Hill, 4th edn, 1975).

15　**Skyscrapers in Manhattan, and the promise of more in Moscow**: for the promise of the Stalinist future, see Lev Kopelev, *The Education of a True Believer* (New York, 1980), quoted in Fitzpatrick, *Everyday Stalinism*, p. 18; for specifically architectural visions of the future, see the website Unrealised Moscow, www.muar.ru/ve/2003/moscow/index_e. htm, a gathering of the kind of images whose hypnagogic power, taken collectively, is horribly well realised in Jack Womack, *Let's Put the Future Behind Us* (New York: Atlantic Monthly Press, 1996).

16 **An extra 3% year after year, compounded**: in an economy that consumed all the goods it produced, the 3% of extra output Kantorovich anticipates here would only have contributed a simple boost to production, not a compounding addition to the growth rate. But in an economy that partially re-invested its productive output in further productive capacity, the 3% extra growth would indeed have compounded – and the Soviet economy of the 1930s was exceptional in the degree to which it reinvested, rather than consuming, its production.

I.2 Mr Chairman, 1959

19 **Along the aisle the lads from the Tupolev bureau**: for the story of Tupolev junior's non-hostage hostagehood, see William Taubman, *Khrushchev: The Man and His Era* (New York: W. W. Norton, 2003), p. 422. The situation was particularly delicate because Tupolev senior had indeed been arrested for an imaginary political crime in the middle of the Second World War – and then continued to work on aircraft design as a prisoner in the 'first circle' of the Gulag.

22 **Everyone was wearing fine new outfits**: for the visible Soviet prosperity of the 1950s, see Abel Aganbegyan, *Moving the Mountain: Inside the Perestroika Revolution*, trans. Helen Szamuely (London: Bantam, 1989) and G. I. Khanin, '1950s: The Triumph of the Soviet Economy', *Europe–Asia Studies* vol. 55 no. 8 (December 2003), pp. 1187–1212; for the way in which the 1950s and 1960s saw the successful fulfilment of promises made in the 1930s, see Fitzpatrick, *Everyday Stalinism*, pp. 67–114.

22 **The Soviet economy had grown at 6%, 7%, 8%**: for the vexed question of Soviet growth rates, see below, introduction to part II. I have chosen here for Khrushchev, as seems likely, to believe the official Soviet figures, which naturally gave the highest rate.

24 **Let's compete on the merits of our washing machines**: this is the famous 'kitchen debate'. See Taubman, *Khrushchev*, pp. 417–18; and the coverage in the *New York Times*, vol. CVIII no. 37,072, 25 July 1959, pp. 1–4.

24 **Without me, they'll drown you like kittens**: for this prophecy of Stalin's, see Taubman, *Khrushchev*, p. 331. For the pipe-emptying and forehead-tapping episodes, see pp. 167–8 and 230.

26 **For the time being, you are richer than us**: see Taubman, *Khrushchev*, p. 427.

27 **If I'd known there would be pictures like these**: see Taubman, *Khrushchev*, p. 426.

27 **Were you in the war, Mr Lodge?**: see Nikita Khrushchev, *Khrushchev Remembers* (Little Brown, Boston 1970).

28   **He knew from reading Ilf and Petrov**: Ilya Ilf and Evgeny Petrov,
      famous authors of *The Twelve Chairs* (a satire of Soviet life under the
      New Economic Policy of the 1920s), drove across the USA in 1936–7.
      Their *Odenoetazhnaya Amerika* ('One-storey America'), complete with
      descriptions of the Ford production line and a striptease show, was
      the primary source for Khrushchev's generation's mental picture of the
      United States. Perhaps fortunately for them from the political point of
      view, both Ilf and Petrov died during the Second World War.

29   **What is that *ooo-ooo* sound**: despite forty years in politics, Khrushchev
      had genuinely never heard booing till he encountered it abroad. But I
      have relocated his first encounter with 'the ooo-ooo noise' to New York
      in 1959 from London in 1956. See Taubman, *Khrushchev*, p. 357.

29   **We had this in Moscow and Leningrad before the war**: for the 1930s
      Soviet experiment with fast food, see Gronow, *Caviar with Champagne*.

30   **Of course he admired the Americans**: for an overview of the Soviet
      infatuation with American industry, see Stephen Kotkin, *Magnetic
      Mountain: Stalinism as a Civilization* (University of California Press,
      1995) and *Steeltown, USSR: Soviet Society in the Gorbachev Era* (Berkeley
      CA: University of California Press, 1991); with American management
      techniques, see Mark R. Beissinger, *Scientific Management, Socialist
      Discipline and Soviet Power* (Cambridge MA: Harvard University Press,
      1988); for American mass culture, and especially jazz, see Frederick
      S. Starr, *Red and Hot: The Fate of Jazz in the Soviet Union, 1917–1980*
      (New York: OUP, 1983). Before the Second World War, this was an
      enthusiasm for a capitalist culture perceived as being removed from,
      even neutral in, the USSR's rivalry with the old imperial powers of
      Europe. After 1945, it became a much more problematic perception of
      a resemblance to an avowed enemy.

32   **Do you have a gadget that puts the food in your mouth**: see *New York
      Times*, vol. CVIII no. 37,072, 25 July 1959, pp. 1–4.

32   **He opened his reply with a few jokes**: the official texts of Khrushchev's
      speeches in America, shorn of heckles and improvisations, but not
      of jokes, are in *Khrushchev in America* and *Let Us Live in Peace and
      Friendship: The Visit of N S Khrushchov [sic] to the USA, Sept* 15–27, 1959
      (Moscow: Foreign Languages Publishing House, 1959); for accounts of
      the speeches in their disorderly contexts, see Taubman, *Khrushchev*, pp.
      424–39, and Gary John Tocchet, 'September Thaw: Khrushchev's Visit
      to America, 1959', PhD thesis, Stanford 1995, and Peter Carlson, *K Blows
      Top: A Cold War Comic Interlude Starring Nikita Khrushchev, America's
      Most Unlikely Tourist* (New York: Public Affairs, 2009).

33   **Painted by a donkey with a brush tied to its tail**: not a judgement
      Khrushchev is on record of making of Picasso, but characteristic of
      his reactions to art that was in any way abstract or non-figurative. See
      Taubman, *Khrushchev*, pp. 589–90.

33 **Their cheeks were not notably bloated**: it was a source of amazed comment to Khrushchev, on his international visits, that the rich and powerful in the West did not resemble the Soviet caricatures of them. For capitalists' lack of top hats and snouts, see Taubman, *Khrushchev*, pp. 351 and 428; for the surprising failure of the King of Norway and the Queen of England to be sinister and degenerate, see pp. 612 and 357. It's possible that one reason for his hostility to the British Prime Minister Harold Macmillan was that, in Macmillan, he had for once met someone who did look a little like a Soviet stereotype of an aristocrat. 'I want him to rush here, so that I can see him with omelette all over his dinner jacket': Taubman, *Khrushchev*, p. 467.

34 **He knew how it was to handle a workforce**: Khrushchev found it relatively easy, though psychologically alarming, to identify with businessmen, whom he tended to interpret as direct Western counterparts to Soviet manager-politicians such as himself.

34 **Bring on your questions, I'm not tired yet**: Khrushchev's dialogues with the billionaires at Harriman's townhouse are as recorded by J. K. Galbraith's amused ear, in 'The Day Khrushchev Visited the Establishment', *Harper's Magazine* vol. 242 no. 1,449 (February 1971), pp. 72–5.

39 **I am an old sparrow**: see Taubman, *Khrushchev*, p. 429.

I.3 Little Plastic Beakers, 1959

42 **'Now remember,' Khristolyubov went on**: this one-eared Party official is fictional, but the campaign to guide the reaction of Soviet visitors to the American exhibition by sending in pairs of Komsomol hecklers was quite real. See Walter Hixson, *Parting the Curtain: Propaganda, Culture, and the Cold War, 1945–1961* (New York: St Martin's Press, 1997).

42 **American girls in polkadotted knee-length dresses**: for photographs of the American exhibition in Sokolniki Park, and of the Muscovite visitors to it, see *Life Magazine*, vol. 47 no. 6, 10 August 1959, pp. 28–35, with little plastic beakers on p. 31; for descriptions of the exhibits, see Walter Hixson, *Parting the Curtain*; for a reading of the design politics of Buckminster Fuller's dome, see Alex Soojung-Kim Pang, 'Dome Days: Buckminster Fuller in the Cold War' in Jenny Uglow and Francis Spufford, eds, *Cultural Babbage: Technology, Time and Invention* (London: Faber & Faber, 1996), pp. 167–92; for press reaction in the US, see *New York Times*, vol. CVIII no. 37,072, 25 July 1959, pp. 1–4.

43 **She had added a green leather belt bought at the flea market**: that is to say, at one of the legal bazaars or car-boot sales (without car boots) where Soviet citizens could sell their possessions second-hand. You could dispose of bric-a-brac and you could put your own handicrafts up for sale, like paintings or carved wooden spoons, but you couldn't

manufacture anything without falling foul of Article 162 of the Criminal Code, dealing with 'the exercise of forbidden professions', or resell things bought from state stores, because that contravened Article 154, forbidding 'speculation'. For the intricacies of the Soviet rules governing personal property, see P. Charles Hachten, 'Property Relations and the Economic Organization of Soviet Russia, 1941 to 1948: Volume One', PhD thesis, University of Chicago 2005.

44 **On all seven screens, the night sky bloomed**: for descriptions of Charles and Ray Eames's deliberately overwhelming audio-visual presentation for the exhibition, and stills, see Beatriz Colomina, 'Information obsession: the Eameses' multiscreen architecture', *The Journal of Architecture* vol. 6 (Autumn 2001), pp. 205–23, and Craig D'Ooge, '"Kazam!" Major Exhibition of the Work of American Designers Charles and Ray Eames Opens', *Library of Congress Information Bulletin*, May 1999.

47 **The fact that Roger Taylor, unexpectedly, was a Negro**: though Roger Taylor himself is an invention, there were a small number of African-Americans among the Russian-language students recruited to be exhibition guides, a controversial decision back in the US, and a source of exactly the kind of difficulty represented here to Komsomol hecklers equipped with talking-points about American racism. See Hixson, *Parting the Curtain*.

48 **Is this the national exhibition of a powerful and important country**: Galina and Fyodor's objections during the tour are modelled on contemporary Soviet press reaction, as recorded in *Current Digest of the Soviet Press* (Ann Arbor MI: Joint Committee on Slavic Studies), vol. XI no. 30, pp. 3–4, 7–12; vol. XI no. 31, pp. 10–13.

53 **The Soviet car-make which came closest in terms of lip-licking appeal**: I've followed the male conversation at the beginning of Boris and Arkady Strugatsky's *Monday Begins on Saturday* in nominating the Gaz Chaika. For further Soviet automobiliana, see www.autosoviet.com, and below, part V chapter 1.

I.4 White Dust, 1953

59 **For him the beginning was the day he walked to the village**: Emil Shaidullin's walk to his in-laws in 1953 is a fictional embroidery on the similar journey taken by Abel Aganbegyan, and described in his *Moving the Mountain*. The events of Emil's walk should not be read back to Professor Aganbegyan's, any more than Emil's character, throughout this book, should be taken as a portrait of Professor Aganbegyan.

64 **Stalin's little book**: J. V. Stalin, *Economic Problems of Socialism in the USSR*, English edition (Moscow: Foreign Languages Publishing House, 1952).

65   **And while Marx didn't say much about economics after the revolution**:
       for most of what he did say about it, see Robert Freedman, ed., *Marx on*
       Economics (New York: Harcourt Brace, 1961), pp. 229–41.

65   **Here and there, economists were starting to talk to biologists and**
       mathematicians: for this first, semi-clandestine stage in the conversation
       of the disciplines which would produce Soviet cybernetics, which was
       not quite the same thing as Western cybernetics, see Slava Gerovitch,
       From Newspeak to Cyberspeak: A History of Soviet Cybernetics (Boston:
       MIT Press, 2002).

66   **For economics, after all, was a theory of everything**: for a readable
       narrative history of the discipline's history and universal ambitions,
       see Robert L. Heilbroner, *The Worldly Philosophers: The Lives, Times*
       and Ideas of the Great Economic Thinkers, 4th edn (New York: Simon
       and Schuster, 1971). For a much more intricate and specific (but
       still narrative) study of the ambitions that seemed to be enabled by
       economics' encounter with information technology in the post-war
       twentieth century, see Philip Mirowski, *Machine Dreams: Economics*
       Becomes a Cyborg Science (Cambridge: CUP, 2002).

66   **Value shone in material things once labour had made them useful**:
       the 'labour theory of value', as originated by Adam Smith and passed
       via David Ricardo to Marx. Soviet economists tended to be aware
       of pre-Marxian classical economics, at least in the form of citations
       and summaries, but not the post-Marxian development of it. The
       'marginalist revolution' of the late nineteenth century was little
       known, and with it the characteristic mathematical formalisations of
       Western economics. Those who were well-enough informed to know
       about the 'socialist calculation debate' (see below, introduction to part
       II) were conscious that their proposals for optimal asset allocation
       presupposed a Walrasian model of general equilibrium, but Pareto
       was reputed only as a quasi-fascist, and Keynes as one more 'bourgeois
       apologist', whose fancy footwork could not disguise the unchanging
       operations of capital, as diagnosed once and for ever by Marx. For
       Marx's formulation of the labour theory, see Freedman, ed., *Marx on*
       Economics, pp. 27–63; Leszek Kolakowski, *Main Currents of Marxism:*
       The Founders, the Golden Age, the Breakdown, translated from the
       Polish by P. S. Falla, one-volume edition (New York: W. W. Norton,
       2005), pp. 219–26. For the question of what Soviet economists knew,
       see Aganbegyan, *Moving the Mountain*; Joseph Berliner, 'Economic
       Reform in the USSR' in John W. Strong, ed., *The Soviet Union under*
       Brezhnev and Kosygin (New York: Van Nostrand Reinhold, 1971), pp.
       50–60; Aron Katsenelinboigen, *Soviet Economic Thought and Political*
       Power in the USSR (New York: Pergamon, 1980); Alex Simirenko, ed.,
       Soviet Sociology (London: RKP, 1967). For a general exploration of
       what Soviet intellectuals under Khrushchev knew about the world, see

Robert English, *Russia and the Idea of the West: Gorbachev, Intellectuals, and the End of the Cold War* (New York: Columbia University Press, 2000).

66 **But Marx had drawn a nightmare picture**: for Marx's vision of the alienated dance of the commodities, and its philosophical roots and imaginative implications, see Edmund Wilson, *To the Finland Station: A Study in the Writing and Acting of History* (New York, 1940), ch. 15, and Kolakowski, *Main Currents of Marxism*, pp. 226–74.

68 **Machine-Tractor Station**: the rural depots, with their own specialised workforce, where the equipment for mechanised farming was kept (until Khrushchev disastrously sold the machinery to the collective farms, which had no budget to maintain it). For the sorry history of Soviet agriculture, see Alec Nove, *Economic History of the USSR, 1917–1991*, final edition (London, 1992).

69 **It looked like the set for some Chekhov story**: specifically, 'Peasants', in Anton Chekhov, *The Lady with the Little Dog and Other Stories, 1896–1904*, translated by Ronald Wilks (London: Penguin, 2004) – though Emil appears to be thinking of 'Gooseberries' in the same collection. See also Janet Malcolm, *Reading Chekhov: A Critical Journey* (New York: Random House, 2001). A portrait of Soviet peasant life more contemporary with Emil's walk (but no less depressing) is Solzhenitsyn's 'Matryona's House', in *Matryona's House and Other Stories*, translated by Michael Glenny (London: Penguin, 1975).

73 **A good Kazan Muslim**: the implication here is that, at least on his father's side, Emil Arslanovich is a Tatar. Though in Russian stereotype a Tatar has the facial features of Genghis Khan, the Mongol contribution to the Tatar gene pool was rather small, and blond Tatars are not at all unusual: as a group, they largely resemble Bulgarians, with whom they share an ancestry. Kazan had possessed a Muslim intelligentsia for centuries, but Tatars were not one of the minorities famous in the USSR for educational mobility, like Jews and Armenians, and they were not very strongly represented in twentieth-century Soviet intellectual life, with exceptions such as the computer designer Bashir Rameev. Presumably, Emil's reasonably comfortable family experience under Stalin means that his parents (at least Party middle-rankers, judging by his own sharply upward career trajectory) successfully negotiated the sudden reversal of Soviet 'nationalities' policy during the later thirties. For this, see Terry Dean Martin, *The Affirmative Action Empire: Nations and Nationalism in the Soviet Union, 1929–1939* (Ithaca NY: Cornell University Press, 2001). For a fabulously dismal description of post-Soviet Kazan, see Daniel Kalder, *Lost Cosmonaut: Travels to the Republics That Tourism Forgot* (London: Faber, 2006).

75 **The title song from the old musical, 'The Happy-Go-Lucky Guys'**: see James von Geldern and Richard Stites, eds, *Mass Culture in*

Soviet Russia. Tales, Poems, Songs, Movies, Plays and Folklore 1917–1953 (Bloomington IN: Slavica, 1995).

75 **'Did something bad happen here?'**: see Robert Conquest, *Harvest of Sorrow: Soviet Collectivisation and the Terror-Famine* (London: Pimlico, 2002). Throughout this book, it is necessary to remember that, on certain crucial points, most people in the Soviet Union will have known less about its history than does an averagely-informed Westerner in the twenty-first century.

Part II

Introduction

81 **Socialism would come, not in backward agricultural Russia**: at the very end of his life, disappointed by the slow pace of revolution in England and Germany and the USA, Marx reassessed Russia's political potential. But he did not alter his analysis of the economic prerequisites of socialism. See Teodor Shanin, ed., *Late Marx and the Russian Road: Marx and 'the peripheries of capitalism'* (London: Routledge and Kegan Paul, 1983).

81 **But it also created progress**: see, to take the most famous of many passages, the paean to the 'most progressive part' played by the bourgeoisie, for which read capitalism, in *The Communist Manifesto* (1848).

81 **It would be a world of wonderful machines and ragged humans**: as portrayed, for instance, in Marx-influenced turn-of-the-twentieth-century fictions of the future such as H. G. Wells's *When the Sleeper Wakes* and Edward Bellamy's *Looking Backwards*.

82 **All the 'springs of co-operative wealth' would flow abundantly**: 'and on its banners society would inscribe at last . . . according to their needs.' Marx, 'Critique of the Gotha Programme', 1875.

82 **It was going to be an idyll**: Marx's own hunting and fishing and criticising version is from *The German Ideology* (1845–6). For a late nineteenth-century elaboration of the idyll into a full utopia, see William Morris, *News from Nowhere*; for late twentieth-century Marxian idylls, try Ken Macleod's *The Cassini Division* (London: Legend, 1998), and any of Iain M. Banks's 'Culture' novels, especially *Look to Windward* (London: Orbit, 2000).

82 **A tiny, freakish cult**: the membership of the Bolshevik faction of the Russian Social-Democratic Labour Party was 'several thousand' in 1903, swelled in the aftermath of the failed 1905 revolution to a maximum of maybe seventy-five thousand by 1907 (but this was while temporarily re-unified with the Mensheviks), and then (separate again) plunged during the period of disillusionment and police repression that followed, until

by 1910 no Bolshevik branch anywhere in the country had more than 'tens of members', and from his exile Lenin could contact no more than thirty to forty reliable people. See Alan Woods, *Bolshevism – The Road to Revolution: A History of the Bolshevik Party* (London: Well Red, 1999). In 1912, when the Bolsheviks held a separate party congress in Prague, the membership was around five hundred, and according to the delegate from St Petersburg, Lenin could count on 109 supporters in the city. See R. B. McKean, *St Petersburg Between the Revolutions: Workers and Revolutionaries* (New Haven CT: Yale University Press, 1990). That was the nadir, and membership was higher by 1914; but it was the First World War that really changed things.

83   **There was in fact an international debate in the 1920s:** useful summaries of, and commentaries on, the socialist calculation debate can be found in Mirowski, *Machine Dreams*, Joseph E. Stiglitz, *Whither Socialism?* (Cambridge MA: MIT Press, 1994) and Geoffrey M. Hodgson, *Economics and Utopia: Why the learning economy is not the end of history* (London: Routledge, 1999), especially 'Socialism and the Limits to Innovation', pp. 15–61. Von Mises' opening criticisms are to be found in Ludwig von Mises, *Socialism*, 1922, translated by J. Kahane (Indianapolis: Liberty Fund, 1981). For Hayek's initially ignored but deeply influential contribution, see F. A. Hayek, 'The Use of Knowledge in Society', *The American Economic Review* vol. 35 issue 4 (September 1945), pp. 519–30. For late rejoinders by two Western socialists, see W. Paul Cockshott and Allin F. Cottrell, 'Calculation, Complexity and Planning: The Socialist Calculation Debate Once Again', *Review of Political Economy* vol. 5 no. 1, July 1993, pp. 73–112; and Cockshott and Cottrell, 'Information and Economics: A Critique of Hayek', *Research in Political Economy* vol. 16, 1997, pp. 177–202.

85   **Investment for industry, therefore, had to come the slow way:** a policy particularly associated with Nikolai Bukharin, 'Rightist' Bolshevik and theorist of the NEP. See Moshe Lewin, *Political Undercurrents in Soviet Economic Debates: From Bukharin to the Modern Reformers* (Princeton NJ: Princeton University Press, 1974).

86   **Slave labour was a tremendous bargain:** see Anne Applebaum, *Gulag: A History of the Soviet Camps* (New York: Random House, 2003).

86   **Ever to leave the kolkhoz:** the collective farm, in theory an independent co-operative selling food to the state, in practice a mechanism of forced labour under an appointed director.

86   **A society in a state of very high mobility:** see Sheila Fitzpatrick, *Education and Social Mobility in the USSR* 1921–1934 (Cambridge: CUP, 1979); Fitzpatrick, *Everyday Stalinism*, pp. 85–8.

86   **Then a middle-class life beckoned in short order:** for the new respectability of the Stalinist bougeoisie, see Vera S. Dunham, *In Stalin's Time: Middleclass Values in Soviet Fiction* (Cambridge: CUP, 1976), and

T. L. Thompson and R. Sheldon, eds, *Soviet Society and Culture: Essays in Honour of Vera S. Dunham* (Boulder CO: Westview Press, 1988); Fitzpatrick again.

87 **And a fur coat for Mrs Red Plenty to wear**: for the wearable dimension of the Stalinist good life, see Djurdja Bartlett, 'The Authentic Soviet Glamour of Stalinist High Fashion', *Revista de Occidente* no. 317, November 2007; and ibid., 'Let Them Wear Beige: The Petit-Bourgeois World of Official Socialist Dress', *Fashion Theory* vol. 8 issue 2, pp. 127–64, June 2004

87 **And it did grow. It was designed to**: a point made in Mark Harrison, 'Post-war Russian Economic Growth: Not a Riddle', *Europe–Asia Studies* vol. 55 no. 8 (2003), pp. 1,323–9. For a consideration of the specific window of opportunity that was open to a command economy in the middle of the twentieth century, see Stephen Broadberry and Sayantan Ghosal, 'Technology, organisation and productivity performance in services: lessons from Britain and the United States since 1870', *Structural Change and Economic Dynamics* vol. 16 issue 4 (December 2005), pp. 437–66.

87 **Indeed, there was a philosophical issue here**: for the planners' philosophical fidelity to Marx, despite everything, see Paul Craig Roberts, *Alienation and the Soviet Economy* (Albuquerque: University of New Mexico Press, 2002).

88 **This made it difficult to compare Soviet growth**: there is a whole specialised literature, spread over fifty years, on the difficulty of assessing the USSR's growth rate. For an accessible way in, see Alec Nove, *Economic History of the USSR*, and Paul R. Gregory and Robert C. Stuart, *Russian and Soviet Economic Performance and Structure*, 6th edn. (Reading MA: Addison-Wesley, 1998). For Western calculations during the Cold War, see Abram Bergson and Simon Kuznets, eds, *Economic Trends in the Soviet Union* (Cambridge MA: Harvard University Press, 1963); Janet G. Chapman, *Real Wages in Soviet Russia Since 1928*, RAND Corporation report R-371-PR (Santa Monica CA, October 1963); Franklyn D. Holzman, ed., *Readings on the Soviet Economy* (Chicago: Rand-McNally, 1962). As a useful retrospective, see Angus Maddison, 'Measuring the Performance of a Communist Command Economy: An Assessment of the CIA Estimates for the USSR', *Review of Income and Wealth* vol. 44 no. 3 (September 1998), pp. 307–23. For Soviet reassessments of the historic growth record during perestroika, see Tatyana Zaslavskaya, 'The Novosibirsk Report', English translation by Teresa Cherfas, *Survey* 1 (1984), pp. 88–108; Abel Aganbegyan, *Challenge: The Economics of Perestroika*, translated by Michael Barratt Brown (London: I. B. Tauris, 1988); and most pessimistic of all, G. I. Khanin's calculations, as described in Mark Harrison, 'Soviet economic growth since 1928: The alternative statistics of G. I. Khanin', *Europe–Asia*

Studies vol. 45 no. 1 (1993), pp. 141–67. Then, for Khanin's response to the Western studies, see G. I. Khanin, *Sovetskii ekonomicheskii rost: analiz zapadnykh otsenok* ('Soviet economic growth: an analysis of western evaluations') (Novosibirsk: EKOR, 1993). And finally, for Khanin's revisionist reappraisal of his own previous pessimism, see Khanin, '1950s – The Triumph of the Soviet Economy', which proposes a completely new growth metric based on fuel consumption.

88   **People in the West felt the same mesmerised disquiet:** for the analogy between Western reactions to Soviet growth and to the growth of Japan/China/India, see Paul Krugman, 'The Myth of Asia's Miracle: A Cautionary Fable', *Foreign Affairs* vol. 73 no. 6 (November/December 1994), pp. 62–78.

89   **Set about civilising their savage growth machine:** see Nove, *Economic History of the USSR.*

90   **There was a devil in the detail:** the figures in the discussion that follows come from Gregory and Stuart, *Russian and Soviet Economic Performance and Structure.*

II.1 Shadow Prices, 1960

93   **'Is this heresy?' said Leonid Vitalevich:** the speech I have given him here is a patchwork of elements, heavily edited and simplified, from his real speeches to the conference on mathematics and economics really held by the Russian Academy of Sciences in April 1960. Texts from Kantorovich, Kutateladze and Fet, eds, *L. V. Kantorovich: Chelovek i Uchenii*, pp. 117–26. For coverage of the conference, see P. Zhelezniak, 'Scientific Conference on the Application of Mathematical Methods in Economic Studies and Planning', *Problems of Economics* (translated digest of articles from Soviet economic journals, International Arts & Sciences Press, NY) vol. 3 no. 7, November 1960, pp. 3–6; originally in *Planovoe Khozyaistvo* no. 5, 1960.

93   **Thought Academician Nemchinov, watching from the back of the seminar room:** Vasily Sergeyevich Nemchinov (1894–1964), geneticist turned economist, Academician-Secretary of the Department of Economic, Philosophical and Legal Sciences in the Academy of Sciences, patron and institutional godfather of the mathematical revival of Soviet economics. I have slightly exaggerated the extent to which the conference was his idea: it actually originated with an initiative by Kantorovich himself. For a sample of his adroit political footwork during the transition to a mathematical economics, see V. S. Nemchinov, 'Value and Price Under Socialism', *Problems of Economics* (International Arts & Sciences Press, NY) vol. 4 no. 3, July 1961, pp. 3–17; originally in *Voprosy Ekonomiki* no. 12, 1960. For a gathering of the scientists to whom he acted as co-ordinator, see V. S. Nemchinov, ed., *The Use of Mathematics in Economics*, edited in English by Alec

Nove (Edinburgh: Oliver & Boyd, 1964). One of the most important
names to be found there is completely missing in this narrative: V. V.
Novozhilov, Leningrad economist and close intellectual ally of Leonid
Kantorovich, whose work on the relative efficiency of investments
found a more-or-less politically acceptable way of reintroducing the
idea of capital's productivity, and who provided a vital connection to
the pre-revolutionary tradition of Russian economics. He is missing
here for storytelling reasons. But see V. V. Novozhilov, 'On Choosing
Between Investment Projects', translated by B. Ward, *International
Economic Papers* 6 (1956), pp. 66–87, and V. V. Novozhilov, 'Calculation
of Outlays in a Socialist Economy', *Problems of Economics* (International
Arts & Sciences Press, NY) vol. 4 no. 8, December 1961, pp. 18–28;
originally in *Voprosy Ekonomiki* no. 2, 1961; and V. V. Novozhilov,
Problems of Cost-Benefit Analysis in Optimal Planning, translated by
H. McQuiston (White Plains NY, 1970). For a contemporary Western
appraisal of what the alliance of Kantorovich and Novozhilov might
mean, see R. Campbell, 'Marx, Kantorovich and Novozhilov: *Stoimost'*
versus Reality', *Slavic Review* 40 (October 1961), pp. 402–18.

93 **Telling when the party line in their subject was about to change**: for
discussions of academic politics in Stalinist and post-Stalinist Russia, see
Loren R. Graham, *Science and Philosophy in the Soviet Union* (New York:
Alfred A. Knopf, 1972), and Gerovitch, *From Newspeak to Cyberspeak*.
For a fictional reflection, see the experiences of the particle physicist
Viktor Shtrum in Vasily Grossman's moral monument of a novel, *Life
and Fate*, translated by Robert R. Chandler (London: Harvill, 1995).

94 **A letter of terrifying frankness to the most powerful person he could
think of**: according to his daughter, in conversation with the author in
St Petersburg in 2004, he wrote to every Soviet leader from Stalin to
Andropov.

95 **A hand had gone up**: though this confrontation is a device to dramatise
the ideological conflict over Kantorovich's 'heresy', the conference
really was marked by sharp antagonism between him and Boyarskii,
who had published a very hostile review of his *Best Use of Economic
Resources* in the journal *Planovoe Khozyaistvo* ('Planned Economy') the
year before. The intervention I have given Boyarskii here, however, is
based on an equally hostile article of his from 1961. See A. Boyarskii,
'On the Application of Mathematics in Economics', *Problems of
Economics* (translated digest of articles from Soviet economic journals,
International Arts & Sciences Press, NY) vol. 4 no. 9, January 1962,
pp. 12–24; originally in *Voprosy Ekonomiki* no. 2, 1961. Whatever form
the real exchange between Kantorovich and Boyarskii took, it is clear
that Kantorovich won it. 'This is not the first such review on Comrade
Boyarskii's conscience but following my reply and judging by the
audience's reaction and that of Boyarskii himself, I have a feeling he

won't be writing any more reviews of this sort in future': Kantorovich, in his speech to the Presidium of the Academy, 20 May 1960, in *Leonid Vitalevich Kantorovich: Chelovek i Uchenii*, vol. 1. Or, for another hostile commentary on the book, see A. Kats, 'Concerning a Fallacious Concept of Economic Calculation', *Problems of Economics* vol. 3 no. 7, November 1960, pp. 42–52; originally published in *Voprosy Ekonomiki* no. 5, 1960.

97 **Shadow prices**: the multipliers on which Kantorovich's solution to optimisation problems depended. Essentially, they were opportunity costs: they represented the cost of choosing one particular arrangement of production in terms of the amount of production forgone by choosing it. Their ideological significance lay in the way that, without making any reference to demand or to markets, Kantorovich had discovered a demand-like logic in the structure of production itself. In his scheme, it was the volume of planned output that was to be maximised, not the customer's satisfaction, but he had still introduced the idea that the utility of the output to somebody should be the guide to how production was configured.

97 **Any increase in the requirements of some article**: see L. V. Kantorovich, *The Best Use of Economic Resources*, translated by P. F. Knightsfield (Oxford: Pergamon Press, 1965).

98 **'For example! Do you see my tie?'**: the parable of the necktie is completely invented. Kantorovich's habit of seeming to wander off during lectures, however, is genuine. A witness in Akademgorodok in 2006 described to me the disconnected fragments he would appear to be uttering, and the perfect sense they would turn out to make when you studied your notes afterwards.

100 **'It's true that there is a formal resemblance', said Leonid Vitalevich**: his next point is, again, a slightly modified quotation from *The Best Use of Economic Resources*. It is worth noting that there is no way at all of telling how sincere the real Kantorovich was being when he asserted that his shadow prices had a 'meaning' completely different from market prices. As was pointed out to me in conversation in Akademgorodok, he was notable for the care with which he confined himself in writing to the practical and mathematical aspects of his work, and never even hinted at what he considered to be its social or ideological implications. The same witness gave as *his* opinion that Kantorovich, as a brilliantly intelligent man, must have been wholly sceptical from the beginning about Soviet socialism – but there seemed to me to be a danger of anachronism in the judgement, and Kantorovich's tenacity as a system-builder argued for the rather different interpretation of him which I have made here.

102 **'Coat, winter, men's, part-silk lining, wool worsted tricot, cloth group 29–32':** there was a Ministry of Trade retail handbook, and it will have had a listing for better-quality men's overcoats very like this, but my source – Chapman, *Real Wages in Soviet Russia Since* 1928 – happens to track the prices only of better-quality's women's overcoats among its basket of consumer goods, so I have confabulated the men's coat's entry from that.

102 **Granite giants holding up the Academy's facade:** so far as I know, there are no muscle-bound stone Atlantids straining to support the Academy of Sciences in Moscow. Those are all in Leningrad/St Petersburg. But the symbolism is too good to miss; and if a fairytale would be improved by giants, it gets giants.

103 **And his manuscript goes up and down in the world, round and round:** the story of the manuscript's alarming adventures at Gosplan can be found in Abel Aganbegyan, *Moving the Mountain*. It should be noted that it was the head of Gosplan's prices department himself, when he later became Aganbegyan's doctoral supervisor, who told him the story, which suggests that the reaction to the book at Gosplan (at least in the prices department) was, though just as uncomprehending, significantly less thuggish in reality than in this burlesqued version.

104 **Popped them out into a fist-sized mushroom cloud:** Kantorovich was part of the mathematical team under Academician Sobolev on the Soviet A-bomb project.

106 **'Quite a nice package,' said Nemchinov:** see Paul R. Josephson, *New Atlantis Revisited: Akademgorodok, the Siberian City of Science* (Princeton NJ: Princeton University Press, 1997) .

II.2 From the Photograph, 1961

110 **But the BESM-2 is hard at work; and so is its designer:** for the histories of the BESM and of Sergei Alexeevich Lebedev, see Boris Nikolaevich Malinovsky, *Pioneers of Soviet Computing*, ed. Anne Fitzpatrick, trans. Emmanuel Aronie, pp. 1–22. Available at http://web. archive.org/web/20070121053156/http://sovietcomputing.com/. See also D. A. Pospelov & Ya. Fet, *Essays on the History of Computer Science in Russia* (Novosibirsk: Scientific Publication Centre of the RAS, 1998), and the chapter about Lebedev and the very first Soviet computer in Mike Hally, *Electronic Brains: Stories from the Dawn of the Computer Age* (London: Granta, 2005), pp. 137–60.

112 **And, more secretly still, an M-40 exists, and an M-50 too:** for Lebedev's computers for the Soviet missile-defence project, and the imaginary Moscow in the Kazakh desert, see Malinovsky, *Pioneers of Soviet Computing*, pp. 101–3. For 'military cybernetics' in general, see Gerovitch, *From Newspeak to Cyberspeak*.

112 'We can shoot down a fly in outer space, you know': Malinovsky,
     Pioneers of Soviet Computing, p. 103

114 **Remembering the story his rival Izaak Bruk told him**: see Malinovsky,
     Pioneers of Soviet Computing, p. 70, which does not however specify
     the codename flower the vacuum tube buyer had to mention. As well
     as supplying tulips, my rendition of the story has also simplified the
     bureaucratic level at which the polite people opposite the knitwear shop
     (real) operated. They actually told the student, 'We only act at the level
     of raikom third secretary.'

115 **The BESM. A picture of what? Of potatoes**: the potato-optimising
     programme for the Moscow Regional Planning Agency was absolutely
     real, but was not written until 1966, and therefore probably ran on
     a BESM-6 or an M-20 rather than a BESM-2. It belongs, truthfully,
     to the period of slightly chastened moderate-sized implementations
     of 'optimal planning', rather than to the early period of grand
     expectations. I have cheated, and brought it forward in time, in
     order to give the optimism of 1961 some definite narrative substance.
     Altogether, in fact, this fairytale version of the history of mathematical
     economics needs to confess to tidying and foreshortening the
     movement from hope to despair it chronicles. The numbers of
     delivering and consuming organisations are authentic, and the variables
     and constraints; the dwindling kilometre-numbers are made up
     from thin air. For this and other 1960s experiments in mathematical
     planning, see Michael Ellman, *Soviet Planning Today: Proposals for
     an Optimally Functioning Economic System* (Cambridge: CUP, 1971),
     and *Planning Problems in the USSR*. Other sources, without Ellman's
     bite and analytical clarity, are John Pearce Hardt, ed., *Mathematics
     and Computers in Soviet Economic Planning* (New Haven CT: Yale
     University Press, 1967), and Martin Cave, *Computers and Economic
     Planning: The Soviet Experience* (Cambridge: CUP, 1980).

116 **The recording clerks sally out from the Ministry of Trade's little
     booths**: among other things, as an information-gathering exercise, to
     collect a set of market-clearing prices which could then be used to help
     establish the price level for the bulk of food trade, in state stores. The
     state price was always cheaper, guaranteeing that food at the state price
     would always be in shortage relative to the money available to pay for it,
     but how much cheaper it was varied, depending both on the irregular
     jumps of the official prices and the more continuous adjustment of the
     market prices. See Chapman, *Real Wages in Soviet Russia Since 1928*;
     as Chapman points out, the premium that could be charged at the
     kolkhoz market gives a measure of how difficult food was to find at the
     state price. In relatively good times for official Soviet agriculture, the
     prices ran relatively close together; in bad times, they diverged wildly.
     According to the *Narkhoz* statistical almanac for 1968, between 1960 and

1968 kolkhoz market prices rose 28%: see Ellman, *Planning Problems in the USSR.*

116 **No wonder that Oskar Lange over in Warsaw gleefully calls the marketplace a 'primitive pre-electronic calculator'**: not in print he didn't, in fact, until 1967. See Oskar Lange, 'The Computer and the Market' in C. Feinstein, ed., *Capitalism, Socialism and Economic Growth: Essays Presented to Maurice Dobb* (Cambridge: CUP, 1967), pp. 158–61. But the idea that the computer had conclusively resolved the socialist calculation debate in socialism's favour was very much a commonplace of the early sixties.

117 **'Sorcery!' he said, and winked**: see Hally, *Electronic Brains.*

117 **Universally caressed and endorsed, very nearly the official solution to every Soviet problem**: see Gerovitch, *From Newspeak to Cyberspeak.* Cybernetics did appear in the Party Programme: see the complete text of the programme, and commentaries, in Leonard Schapiro, ed., *The USSR and the Future: An Analysis of the New Program of the CPSU* (New York: Institute for the Study of the USSR/Frederick A. Praeger Inc., 1963). First had come the oppositional stage, during which cybernetics was officially condemned and seemed to scientists to represent a language of de-ideologised honesty. Then came this period of official acceptance, and excited claims for cybernetics' reforming powers. Later would come a period of decay, in which Soviet cyberspeak became one more variety of officially sanctioned vacuity, as satirised (for example) in Aleksandr Zinoviev's *The Yawning Heights*, translated by Gordon Clough (New York: Random House, 1978).

118 *Ot zadachi,* 'from the problem', and *ot fotografii,* 'from the photograph': the distinction is discussed in Ellman, *Planning Problems in the USSR.* Both conservative criticism of mathematical economics, for instance from within Gosplan, and criticism by more radically sceptical economists, like Janos Kornai of Hungary, often focused on the obvious weakness involved in working 'from the photograph'. See Kornai, *Anti-Equilibrium* (Amsterdam, 1971); for a Gosplan critique of reforming impracticality, twenty years later but directed at much the same target, see Michael Ellman and Volodyamir Kontorovich, *The Destruction of the Soviet Economic System: An Insiders' History* (Armonk NY: M. E. Sharpe, 1998). To some extent the distance from the system at which the optimisers were working had to do with their status as un-trusted academic outsiders to the real operation of industry. It also followed from the powerfully abstracting nature of Kantorovich's models, which could reduce a whole technology to the letter 't' in an equation. But the optimisers of course saw and understood the difficulty: it was one reason for their increasing interest in systems of indirect control which did not require complete information at the centre.

II.3 Stormy Applause, 1961

120 **Lucky Sasha Galich**: for my portrayal here of the songwriter, screenwriter, playwright and poet Alexander Galich (1919–77) I have drawn heavily on the biographical introduction, 'Silence is Connivance: Alexander Galich', to Alexander Galich, *Songs and Poems*, edited and translated by Gerald Stanton Smith (Ann Arbor MI: Ardis, 1983), pp. 13–54. See also Alexander Galich, *Dress Rehearsal: A Story in Four Acts and Five Chapters*, translated by Maria R. Bloshteyn (Bloomington IN: Slavica, 2007).

121 **'I loved *Moscow Does Not Believe in Tears*', she said**: not the award-winning film of 1980, or Ilya Ehrenburg's novel of the 1930s, but the middle one of the three artefacts to bear the name *Moskva ne slezam verit*, a play on which Galich collaborated in 1949. I have not been able to find out its content, and it is quite possible that I am mistaken in guessing that it shows a sensitivity to the struggles of women which Marfa Timofeyevna the Glavlit rep would admire. But then Marfa Timofeyevna is herself pure fiction, no more substantial than the clouds over Moscow.

122 **The address that Khrushchev was due to give to the Party Congress today**: for the real text of it, complete with italicised rapture, see *Current Digest of the Soviet Press* (Ann Arbor MI: Joint Committee on Slavic Studies), vol. 13 no. 45, p. 25.

123 **Letters; letters from readers across the whole double-page spread**: the correspondence from the Soviet public on the Draft of the 1961 Party Programme was just as copious as I've represented it being here, and genuinely covered all the subjects listed here from peas to television parlours. See Wolfgang Leonhard, 'Adoption of the New Programme', in Schapiro, ed., *The USSR and the Future*, pp. 8–15. However, the particular letter about taxis in the imaginary Morin's imaginary newspaper which Galich looks at here comes in fact from the postbag of the Party's journal *Kommunist*. See *Current Digest of the Soviet Press* (Ann Arbor MI: Joint Committee on Slavic Studies), vol. 13 no. 42, pp. 13–17; vol. 13 no. 43, pp. 18–23.

124 **'Of considerably higher quality than the best products of capitalism'**: again, see the text of the Programme in Schapiro, ed., *The USSR and the Future*.

126 **The censor turned to him and said: 'Oh, so the Jews won the war for us now, did they?'**: for dramatic simplicity I've conflated the dress rehearsal with the meeting next day when a version of these words was really said to Galich. See Galich, *Dress Rehearsal*.

127 **It's bachelor freedom all the way with you, isn't it?**: Alexander Galich was married twice, in 1941 to Valentina Arkhangelskaya, from whom he separated in 1944, and from 1945 to his death to Angelina Nikolaevna Shekrot, who followed him into exile from Russia in the 1970s, but 'did

not demand fidelity . . . and took a rather ironic view of her husband's romantic affairs', according to www.galichclub.narod.ru/biog.htm.

130   **To sign a petition protesting some new slander broadcast by Radio Free Europe:** a regular duty of trusted writers like Galich. The lunch with the fictional Morin, the episode of the French journalists, the tactlessly visible ground-floor restaurant of the Writers' Union – all cloud-moulded, all untrue; but Galich's status as the insider's insider is entirely factual.

131   **'The Universal Abundance of Products', read Galich:** the quotations that follow are not from a newspaper feature on 'Life in 1980', but a learned article by I. Anchishkin of the Institute of Economics of the Academy of Sciences. See I. Anchishkin, 'The Problem of Abundance and the Transition to Communist Distribution', in Harry G. Shaffer, ed., *The Soviet Economy: A Collection of Western and Soviet Views* (New York: Appleton-Century-Crofts, 1963), pp. 133–8; originally published in *Voprosy Ekonomiki* no. 1, 1962.

133   **On the island opposite Christ the Saviour:** at this time, the riverside site of the Cathedral of Christ the Saviour was occupied by a popular open-air swimming pool, which had filled in the hole intended to accommodate the foundations for a gargantuan Palace of Soviets. As of the present day, all of the twentieth-century changes to the site have been reversed, and the Cathedral of Christ the Saviour stands there again, as it did in 1900.

133   **The soundtrack it would have, if it were filmed on a day like today:** to make a movie such as 1964's *Ya shagayu po Moskve*, 'I Walk around Moscow', directed by Georgii Daniela; or *Zastava Ilicha*, 'Ilich's Gate', directed by Marlen Khutsiev, which was made in 1961, but not released till 1965, under the title *Mne Dvadtsat' Let*, 'I Am Twenty'.

133   **He remembered a joke. What is a question mark? An exclamation mark in middle age:** authentic, and taken, as are all the Soviet jokes in this book, from Seth Benedict Graham, 'A Cultural Analysis of the Russo-Soviet *Anekdot*', PhD thesis, University of Pittsburgh 2003

134   **He had had one of the happy childhoods Stalin had promised would someday be universal:** here I have taken the data about Galich's childhood in the biographical essay prefacing Galich, *Songs and Poems*, and amplified it with some of the sights and sounds of happy (Jewish) Soviet childhoods of the 1930s evoked in Slezkine, *The Jewish Century*, pp. 256–7.

135   **Surly boys cracking into smiles at his teasing *chastushki*:** *chastushki* are improvised satirical verses, designed to provoke good-humoured, only very slightly rueful laughter in the person they describe. Inventing inoffensively Stalinist *chastushki* which were still funny must have posed problems of tone, which the young Galich, who really did go off to entertain the troops like this, was presumably good at solving. The songs mentioned are real hits of the Great Patriotic War; 'Goodbye Mama, Don't Be Sad' is a real tear-jerking number by the young Galich.

135 **Wandering on a vague impulse of solidarity into a meeting of the Writers' Union Yiddish section:** event real, dialogue invented. This was one of the indicative moments of the turn to undisguised anti-Semitism in the late Stalinist period. The position of Soviet Jews had been worsening since the Nazi–Soviet pact of 1938, but things took a sudden downward turn after the foundation of the State of Israel in 1948, which effectively reclassified all Jews in Stalin's eyes as people of potentially divided loyalties. All explicitly Jewish Soviet organisations were closed, including the Yiddish Section of the Writers' Union, the Yiddish-language theatre, and the Jewish Anti-Fascist Committee, which had raised support for the Soviet war effort among the western diaspora. As a result of these moves, a number of Soviet citizens who had thought of their Jewishness as one of the least important facts about themselves began to feel differently.

135 **Quiet conversations with a returned choreographer:** all the details here of how he came to see the monsters in the wood are made up, though he was certainly *svoi* in the sense that the concocted uncle's friend means, and the real horrors of the famous year 1937 did indeed include (for secret policemen) the problems of disposing of a very large number of bodies, very fast. Whoever Galich had conversations with, they were of a kind to get him writing, eventually, songs that were mistaken for the work of a genuine ex-Gulag prisoner.

137 **The words he was supposed to have said, back in April, when they lit the rocket beneath him:** see *The First Man in Space. Soviet Radio and Newspaper Reports on the Flight of the Spaceship Vostok*, compiled and translated by Joseph L. Ziegelbaum, Jet Propulsion Laboratory/ Astronautics Information Translation 22, 1 May 1961 (JPL, California Institute of Techology).

Part III

Introduction

141 **In 1930 the Bolsheviks abolished universities:** for the reconfiguration of Soviet education in the 1930s, Stalin's call for a 'productive-technical intelligentsia', the rise of the 'promotees', and the 'eight small benches' inherited by the Poultry Institute of Voronezh, see Fitzpatrick, *Education and Social Mobility in the USSR*.

141 **Pre-revolutionary Russian intellectuals felt a sense of public obligation:** the classical discussion of the Russian intellectual tradition is Isaiah Berlin, *Russian Thinkers*, ed. Henry Hardy and Aileen Kelly (London: Hogarth Press, 1978).

144 *Kulturny*, a term which stretched from brushing your teeth regularly to reading Pushkin and Tolstoy: see Fitzpatrick, *Everyday Stalinism*, pp. 79–83.

145 By definition, friends of truth, friends of thought and reason and humanity and beauty, were . . . friends of Stalin: for Stalinism as an eagerly-adopted way of being modern and enlightened, see Jochen Hellbeck, *Revolution on My Mind: Writing a Diary Under Stalin* (Cambridge MA: Harvard University Press, 2006).

146 From being one of the most illiterate places on the planet to being, by some measures, one of the best educated: for the Soviet university system of the 1960s and its social functioning, see L. G. Churchward, *The Soviet Intelligentsia: An Essay on the Social Structure and Roles of Soviet Intellectuals During the 1960s* (London: RKP, 1973).

147 Mikhail Romm's 1962 hit film: *Devyat' dnei odnogo goda* ('Nine Days in One Year'), 1962.

147 The gentle satire of the Strugatsky brothers' 1965 novel: Arkady and Boris Strugatsky, *Ponedelnik nachinaetsya v subbotu*, translated as *Monday Begins on Saturday* by Leonid Renen (New York: DAW, 1977); translated as *Monday Starts on Saturday* by Andrew Bromfield (London: Seagull Publishing, 2005).

148 Groups of intellectuals were gathered together to be shouted at: see Taubman, *Khrushchev*, pp. 306–10, 383–7, 589–96, 599–602; and Fedor Burlatsky, *Khrushchev and the First Russian Spring*, translated by Daphne Skillen (London: Weidenfeld & Nicolson, 1991), pp. 140–3.

148 'I can't deny, Nikita Sergeyevich, that I did find some errors': see Graham, *A Cultural Analysis of the Russo-Soviet* Anekdot.

148 Seen in absolute terms, more Jews than ever before: for the breakdown of employment in the sciences in the USSR by 'nationality', from which these figures come, see Churchward, *The Soviet Intelligentsia*.

149 Khrushchev's red-faced rage over the Academy rejecting one of Lysenko's stooges: in an extremely rare example of out-and-out electoral rebellion in a Soviet institution, the Academicians used their secret ballot in 1964 to disbar Lysenko's candidate. See Taubman, *Khrushchev*, p. 617.

III.1 *Midsummer Night, 1962*

151 A dust-up between institutes over rights in the next blocks to be completed: this particular dispute is invented, but the first few years of the Academy's new science town outside Novosibirsk, founded in 1958, were indeed marked by fierce, sometimes unruly arguments between the disciplines over who got which new buildings. Cytology and Genetics itself obtained its premises by seizing, one weekend, a facility promised to the Computer Centre, and the Computer Centre nearly lost its next

earmarked site as well, to an opportunistic grab by a group researching transplant surgery. For the history of Akademgorodok, I have depended heavily throughout this chapter on Josephson, *New Atlantis Revisited*; and for the look and the atmosphere of the place also on my own visit in 2006, corrected for anachronisms (I hope) by the photographs in the museum of the Siberian Branch of the Russian Academy of Sciences. But see also Jessica Smith, 'Siberian Science City', *New World Review*, third quarter 1969, pp. 86–101, and the section on Akademgorodok in Manuel Castells and Peter Hall, *Technopoles of the World: The Making of 21st Century Industrial Complexes* (London: Routledge, 1994). The pictures in 'Star City', *Colors* 45, August–September 2001, offer an evocative parallel portrait of the Soviet science town devoted to space technology. Colin Thubron's *In Siberia* (London: Chatto and Windus, 1999), pp. 63–78, draws a desolate, superstition-ridden portrait of Akademgorodok's post-Soviet condition, but my sense was that the ambivalent, half-delivered promise of the place still lingered. As someone I spoke to joked, 'There was a lot of freedom here. Oh, I'm sorry, I made a mistake in my English. I meant, there was a *bit* of freedom here.'

151 **In the kitchen, predictably, only the cold tap worked**: other defects complained of by the Academy to the town's builders, Sibakademstroi, included poorly fitted concrete panels, and hallways so damp they grew more than thirty varieties of mushroom. But Zoya's apartment is nevertheless luxurious by all ordinary Soviet standards. It comes about halfway down a ladder of accommodation exactly matched to the hierarchy of academic status. As a senior researcher and lab head, she gets a living space smaller than the houses and half-houses reserved for Academicians and Corresponding Members of the Academy, and the very best flats, which are reserved for holders of the Candidate of Science degree, but bigger and better than the sequentially dwindling flats for ordinary researchers and technical staff and the dormitories for grad students. Envy of the town's material privileges was a factor in the unhelpfulness of the city government of Novosibirk over such issues as the water supply. At one point, the city stole an entire trainload of supplies earmarked for Akademgorodok, and Academician Lavrentiev, the de facto mayor, had to ring Khrushchev personally to get it back. See Josephson, *New Atlantis Revisited*.

155 *Progulka*, **going for a wander**: see the chapter on recreations and leisure in Thompson and Sheldon, eds, *Soviet Society and Culture*.

158 **Both members of a seminar intended to train up the economic and the mathematical alike into cyberneticians**: while Kostya and Valentin are both fictional, the seminar wasn't. Kantorovich and Aganbegyan, who ran it in the non-fairytale USSR, were deliberately creating a pool of expertise which crossed disciplinary boundaries. See 'The Siberian Algorithm' in Josephson, *New Atlantis Revisited*.

159 **Listening to the jazz programmes on Radio Iran**: at this point, sixteen
years before the revolution against the Shah, a potent source of current
western music for Soviet jazz fiends, and well within broadcast range of
western Siberia, too. See Starr, *Red and Hot*.

159 **'Mutagenesis,' she said**: Zoya Vaynshteyn, fictional from head to
toe in her green dress out of Italian *Vogue*, is sharing here in the real
research of the geneticist Raissa Berg (1913–2006), who really arrived in
Akademgorodok at about this date, and really departed from it under
very similar circumstances (see part VI, chapter 2), but who was not
thirty-one and did not have a child of four. See her autobiography:
Raissa L. Berg, *Acquired Traits: Memoirs of a Geneticist from the Soviet
Union*, trans. David Lowe (New York: Viking Penguin, 1988), and the
biographical article about her by Elena Aronova in the online Jewish
Women's Archive: http://jwa.org/encyclopedia/article/berg-raissa-lvovna.

160 **The party, it seemed, was being held in the restaurant of the hotel**:
an eight-storey building which had originally been scheduled to have
twelve storeys. Khrushchev, taking a personal interest in the new town
he had backed, found the height extravagant. 'That's what I think of
your skyscraper,' he said, making snipping movements with two fingers.
See Josephson, *New Atlantic Revisited*.

161 **The green dress, she was glad to confirm from a rapid eye-gulp at the
room, more than held up**: the Soviet Union produced a small amount
of little-worn 'high fashion', and weirdly enough a vestigial tradition of
couture survived in the satellite countries which party wives of sufficient
status could patronise. See Bartlett, 'The Authentic Soviet Glamour
of Stalinist High Fashion'. But for all practical purposes, anyone who
wanted to wear anything different from the unsurprising stock in the
department stores would need to rely, like Zoya and her friends here, on
their own skill with a needle, and the luck of access to pictures that could
serve as patterns. For an English-language review of a special issue of the
Russian journal *Fashion Theory* devoted to Soviet dress, see Anna Malpas,
'Style for Socialists', *Moscow Times*, 27 April 2007.

162 **When Eddie Rosner's big band was serenading the Red Army**: in 1939
the jazz musician Eddie Rosner, finding himself stuck in Warsaw during
the German invasion, presented himself to the Gestapo and demanded
assistance as a German citizen, omitting to mention that he was a Jewish
German citizen. They lent him a car, and he had himself driven straight
to the Soviet forces who had seized the other half of Poland under
the terms of the Nazi–Soviet pact. He crossed over, and next turned
up in Minsk, where he put together a band under the patronage of a
Byelorussian Party bigwig; then, with his reputation travelling ahead
of him, he moved on to Moscow, where he was housed in the grandest
of hotel suites overlooking Red Square. Throughout the war, and up
until the Zhdanov-led repression of everything that had been allowed to

loosen in Soviet culture during the war years', he rode high, immensely popular with the public. Your mental picture of the Red Army's advance into Nazi-occupied Europe is not complete if it does not include, alongside the mass rapes and the dromedaries pulling baggage wagons, the sight of Eddie Rosner and his band playing 'The Chattanooga Choo-Choo' among the ruins of cities. See Starr, *Red and Hot*. All the songs the scratch combo of scientists in the Akademgorodok hotel play at the party are real numbers from different eras of Soviet jazz.

165 **In fact Academician Glushkov . . . has proposed a rival system:** see Gerovitch, *From Newspeak to Cyberspeak*, pp. 271–4.

165 **It turns out that the mathematics is indifferent to whether the optimal level of production is organised hierarchically:** I'm being a little anachronistic here. In a paper published in America in 1961, George Danzig (the mathematician who had independently rediscovered Kantorovich's Plywood Trust breakthrough while working for the USAF during the war) showed with P. Wolfe that some linear programmes could be split into almost independent sub-programmes; in 1963, another American paper, by C. Almon, showed that this could be interpreted as central planning without complete information. Formal Soviet response to the idea didn't arrive until a paper of 1969 by Katsenelinboigen, Ovsienko and Faerman, but it must have been an influence much sooner. See Ellman, *Planning Problems in the USSR*.

167 **'A programmer . . . must combine the accuracy of a bank clerk with the acumen of an Indian tracker':** see A. P. Ershov, *The British Lectures* (Heyden: The British Computer Society, 1980). Ershov (1931–88) was a heroic figure in the thwarted attempt to get computers out of the exclusive grip of academia, industry and the military, and into the hands of Soviet citizens.

169 **One of Timofeev-Ressovsky's famous genetics summer schools:** true, including the lake. See Gerovitch, *From Newspeak to Cyberspeak*, and Berg, *Acquired Traits*.

176 **Small cuts on rayon and sugar, 25% rise on butter, 30% rise on meat:** the price rise went into effect on 1 June 1962. For the politicking leading up to it, see Taubman, *Khrushchev*, pp. 518–19. For the general economic context, see Nove, *Economic History of the USSR*.

178 **It costs eighty-eight roubles to produce a hundred kilos of usable meat:** figures taken from A. Komin, 'Economic Substantiation of Purchase Prices of Agricultural Products', *Problems of Economics* (translated digest of articles from Soviet economic journals, International Arts & Sciences Press, NY) vol. 5 no. 9, January 1963, pp. 29–36, originally in *Planovoe Khosyaistvo* no. 7, 1962; and S. Stoliarov and Z. Smirnova, 'Analysis of Price Structure', *Problems of Economics* vol. 6 no. 9, January 1964, pp. 11–21, originally in *Vestnik Statistiki* no. 1, 1963.

179 **Cheap meat, cheap butter, cheap eggs, and cans of salmon on public holidays**: perks also determined strictly by seniority. See Berg, *Acquired Traits*, pp. 346–50; Josephson, *New Atlantis Revisited*.

182 **'"Blue in Green",' he announced, 'by Mr Miles Davis'**: of course, from *Kind of Blue*, 1959. Bebop had its Soviet followers, but it was at the avant-garde, ideologically risky edge of jazz in this relatively jazz-friendly period. See Starr, *Red and Hot*. Kostya will presumably have been getting his Miles Davis from Radio Iran.

183 **I've heard things said tonight in public that I thought were strictly whispers for the kitchen**: I have exaggerated the town's freedom of speech to make it audible, and the excitement about it therefore comprehensible, for Western readers. Imagine a degree of ordinary constraint that corresponds to nothing in your (our) experience, and then imagine that constraint loosened into a state that we would still find stiff and cautious and calculating, but which struck those experiencing it as (relatively speaking) a jubilant holiday from caution.

184 **Dusted off the whole area with DDT, using a jet engine as a fan**: an insecticidal assault carried out in the spring of 1959. See Josephson, *New Atlantis Revisited*.

186 **'It's the Ob Sea, thank you very much,' said Kostya**: all quite true. The Ob Sea can be found on Google Maps, just south-south-west of Novosibirsk. For the ideological background to moulding nature like putty, see Kolakowski, *Main Currents of Marxism*, on Engels's *Dialectics of Nature*, pp. 308–26, and on the 'Promethean motif' in the thought of Marx, pp. 337–9. The Ob Sea itself dates from the mid-1950s, the beach from the aftermath of a cyclone in October 1959, when it was decided to stabilise the shoreline with three miles of sand.

III.2 The Price of Meat, 1962

187 **Volodya stood by the parapet at the edge of the flat roof of the city procuracy**: although Volodya himself is invented, along with Basov the regional first secretary, and the situation that Volodya finds himself in with his seniors disgraced, the Novocherkassk massacre of 3 June 1962 was all too real. My main source was Samuel H. Baron, *Bloody Saturday in the Soviet Union: Novocherkassk 1962* (Stanford CA: Stanford University Press, 2001). Aleksandr Solzhenitsyn, *The Gulag Archipelago 3, 1918–1956, An Experiment in Literary Investigation V–VII*, translated by H. T. Willetts (London: Collins/Harvill, 1978), pp. 506–14, contains a passionate and horrified account of the massacre, but it was compiled in the rumour-chamber of samizdat, and is not reliable in detail. For an eye-witness account, drawn on by Baron, see Piotr Siuda, 'The Novocherkassk Tragedy, June 1–3 1962', *Russian Labour Review* 2, 1993.

187 **Red flags flying, portraits of Lenin held high:** Samuel Baron
conjectures that the strikers, having no model for the act of going
on strike that was ordinary and moderate and civic, may have found
themselves imitating revolutionary behaviour as they had seen it in
Soviet film and drama, because it was the only model of mass action
that was available to them.

187 **The grey pea soup and gristle served in their canteen:** all the details of
food are authentic.

188 **Only to see the visitors from Moscow pouring out of the building:**
the panicky retreat from the Party office on the square to the barracks is
factual, but I have confabulated the convoy of Chaikas.

188 **The special forces squad had rescued them at dawn:** true, but the idea
of the local apparatchiks being carried around as an object-lesson in
blame is my invention.

190 **Putting in his footsoldier-time at some convenient raikom or gorkom
in the Moscow region:** a 'raikom' was a Party committee for a county,
and a 'gorkom' was the same thing for a town, while an 'obkom', one
step further up the ladder, was a committee for a whole region.

190 **Even with his spets for the party store:** a 'spets' was the document that
gave you access to a *spetsraspredelitel'*, a closed distribution system for
goods. See Fitzpatrick, *Everyday Stalinism*, for the 1930s beginning of
such arrangements; Alena Ledeneva, *Russia's Economy of Favours: Blat,
Networking and Informal Exchange* (Cambridge: CUP, 1998), for their
later growth and elaboration.

191 **But Kurochkin, to his horror, had followed him:** the scene in the
conference room is all confabulation, from the humiliation of Kurochkin
(the real, historical director of the Budenny Electric Locomotive Factory
in Novocherkassk) to the means by which Kozlov and Mikoyan reached
their decision, though it appears to be true that Kozlov was pushing for
the military option and Mikoyan was reluctant.

192 **It had been a little after eight o'clock yesterday morning:** Volodya's
memory of Kurochkin's disastrous performance in front of the crowd is
faithful to fact, including the 'let them eat liver pies' moment. I am not
aware that anyone at the time noticed the Marie Antoinette parallel.

195 **From the receiver, Volodya could hear the thready murmur of a voice
familiar from newsreels:** for Khrushchev's part in events, see Taubman,
Khrushchev, pp. 519–23.

195 **Shots have been fired at the central police station:** I have compressed
the timeline, but this was the report that triggered the decision to suppress
the strike by force. It is not clear whether a genuine violent attack was
underway, or whether this was another piece of naively insurrectionary
behaviour by people who were unpractised at protest.

196 'And get me some real grub,' he was saying. 'This place is such a
fucking hole . . .': relocated to this moment, but an authentic remark by
Kozlov in Novocherkassk. See Taubman, *Khrushchev*, p. 522.

197 'All soldiers out of the crowd,' he squawked: the sequence of what the
officer on the gorkom steps said to the crowd is genuine, although I
have confabulated direct speech out of reports of subject matter. The
slogans of the crowd are real, and so is the strikers' tenacious refusal to
believe they could be under real threat.

199 'Are you out of your mind? In our time?': authentic incredulity. Samuel
Baron suggests that the main reference in the strikers' memories for a
demonstration that *was* fired upon will have been 'Bloody Saturday' in
1905, when workers loyally carrying pictures of the Tsar were attacked
by Cossacks. But that was part of the official iconography of Tsarist
iniquity. The speaker here seems to have been taking it for granted that
nothing of the sort could happen in the modern, enlightened country
where he lived.

199 It was the crew on Volodya's rooftop who were doing it: at this point,
the narrative becomes contentious. It is not clearly established who
did the actual shooting at Novocherkassk – the regular soldiers on the
gorkom steps, the Interior Ministry troops who had been drafted into
the town, or some other group brought in by the security services.
Nor is it clear where they were shooting *from*. Baron's *Bloody Saturday*
outlines several possible scenarios, and I have chosen one.

199 The far side blew out in a geyser of red and grey: the details of the
massacre are mixture of real and imaginary. The grey-bearded drinker
shot in the head is imaginary; the nursing mother sprayed with blood
and brains is not, and neither is the hairdresser ceasing to be in the salon
up the street. Baron has a complete list of the dead.

Part IV

Introduction

205 Khrushchev gave a speech to an audience of Soviet and Cuban
teenagers: see Taubman, *Khrushchev*, p. 523.

205 Fire hoses were used to wash the blood off the ground: see Baron,
Bloody Saturday in the Soviet Union.

206 Till he had a stroke the following April: see Taubman, *Khrushchev*, pp.
613–14.

206 Contemporary joke: What do you call Khrushchev's hairdo?: see
Graham, 'A Cultural Analysis of the Russo-Soviet *Anekdot*'.

206 New cybernetics institutes and departments had sprung up: see
Gerovitch, *From Newspeak to Cyberspeak*.

206 But Nemchinov himself was no longer in charge: for a sharp-tongued

account of his sudden loss of standing, and the appointment of Academician Fedorenko to TSEMI instead, see Katsenelinboigen, *Soviet Economic Thought and Political Power in the USSR.* Trying to read the situation from California eight years later, Simon Kassel, *Soviet Cybernetics Research: A Preliminary Study of Organisations and Personalities*, RAND Corporation report R-909-ARPA (Santa Monica CA, December 1971), pp. 86–7, remarked that Fedorenko seemed to be 'without observable experience in computer technology or automation', and wondered whether this was why TSEMI 'appears to have gradually changed from an economics laboratory, engaged in the realization of a preconceived theoretical system of ideas, into an operational support agency for the Gosplan'. The banner saying 'Comrades, Let's Optimise!' was seen by Michael Ellman on a research visit to Moscow in the mid-sixties: Ellman, *Soviet Planning Today.*

207 **'The main task,' he had told a new conference at Akademgorodok:** see V. Kossov, Yu. Finkelstein, A. Modin, 'Mathematical Methods and Electronic Computers in Economics and Planning' [report of Novosibirsk conferences, October and December 1962], *Problems of Economics* (International Arts & Sciences Press, NY) vol. 6 no. 7, November 1963; originally in *Planovoe Khozyaistvo* no. 2, 1963.

207 **Academician Glushkov's group down in Kiev:** see, again, Gerovitch, *From Newspeak to Cyberspeak*, pp. 271–4, and for Glushkov's life history and the story of his negotiations with government, Malinovsky, *Pioneers of Soviet Computing*, pp. 29–59.

207 **An economist from Kharkov by the name of Evsei Liberman:** see E. G. Liberman, 'Planning Production and Standards of Long-Term Operation', *Problems of Economics* (International Arts & Sciences Press, NY) vol. 5 no. 8, December 1962, pp. 16–22; originally in *Voprosy Ekonomiki* no. 8, 1962. Liberman was interpreted outside the Soviet Union as being the leader of economic reform in general, as in V. G. Tremi, 'The Politics of Libermanism', *Soviet Studies* 19 (1968), pp. 567–72. He was put on the cover of *Time* – 'Borrowing from the Capitalists', *Time Magazine*, 12 February 1965 – and an answer appeared under his name in the magazine *Soviet Life* in July 1965, for which see E. G. Liberman, 'Are We Flirting With Capitalism? Profits and "Profits"', *Problems of Economics* (International Arts & Sciences Press, NY) vol. 8 no. 4, August 1965, pp. 36–41.

207 **Every enterprise in the Soviet Union had to agree a *tekhpromfinplan*:** for the *tekhpromfinplan* system, and a mercilessly lucid demonstration of why it could not produce a plan that was either complete or consistent, see Ellman, *Planning Problems in the USSR.* For the *zaiavki* (indents) see Herbert S. Levine, 'The Centralized Planning of Supply in Soviet Industry', in Franklyn Z. Holzman, ed., *Readings on the Soviet Economy* (Chicago: Rand McNally, 1962).

208 **But at the time we are talking about, the intermediary was a** *sovnarkhoz*: see, again in Holzman, ed., *Readings on the Soviet Economy*, David Granick, 'An Organizational Model of Soviet Industrial Planning', and Oleg Hoeffding, 'The Soviet Industrial Reorganization of 1957'. For an assessment of the effects of Khrushchev's experiment with the *sovmarkhozy*, and the planning of production by region rather than 'branch', see Nove, *Economic History of the USSR*.

208 **Every spring, as the Soviet Union's rivers broke up into granitas of wet ice**: for the detailed chronology of the planning year, in pristine theory and imperfect practice, see Levine, 'The Centralized Planning of Supply in Soviet Industry'.

210 **All clear so far?**: a phrase shamelessly borrowed from the explanation of mid-twenty-first-century US military procurement in Kim Stanley Robinson, *The Gold Coast* (New York: Tor, 1988).

IV.1 The Method of Balances, 1963

212 **Maksim Maksimovich Mokhov was a very kind man**: but an entirely fictional one. Deputy Director of the Sector of Chemical and Rubber Goods was a real job, but the relationship I have suggested between professional-bureaucrat deputies and political-appointee sector directors is conjectural, and I have no knowledge of anyone being called up from the middle ranks to serve in a 'kitchen cabinet' for the Minister, as Mokhov does here. He is acting in this book as a confabulated embodiment of the institution. His tone of voice draws on the exasperated Gosplan witness in Ellman and VolodyaKontorovich, eds, *The Destruction of the Soviet Economic System*, and on the Gosplan official interviewed in Adam Curtis's TV documentary 'The Engineers' Plot', programme 1 of *Pandora's Box*, BBC TV 1992; but also, and especially on his return in part V chapter 2, on Dostoevsky's Grand Inquisitor in *The Brothers Karamazov*. There's also useful material on official attitudes (at different levels) to property, in Hachten, *Property Relations*.

213 **When he handed out the traditional bouquets on Women's Day**: International Women's Day was celebrated (and still is in present-day Russia) on 8 March, with this flower-giving tradition by men as a kind of courtly grave-marker for the early Soviet Union's feminism.

214 **For chemicals were a vital sector at present**: for the rapid build-up of the chemical industry, see Theodore Shabad, *Basic Industrial Resources of the USSR* (New York: Columbia University Press, 1969).

214 **'Suppressed inflation' or a 'permanent sellers' market'**: two linked phenomena, though the first chiefly affected the Soviet Union's perpetually low-priority consumer sector, and the second was true of the cherished industrial sector too. The USSR had 'suppressed inflation' in the sense that it had the classic conditions for runaway inflation in a

market economy, with far too much money chasing far too few goods to buy – but insisted on fixed prices for the scarce goods, thus pushing competition for them into non-money forms. The 'permanent seller's market' was the situation in which both individual consumers, and more significantly whole enterprises, were so desperate to be able to buy that they would accept whatever the seller gave them, almost irrespective of quality or convenience.

215 **Across the herringbone parquet of the eighteenth floor**: my visual sense of the Gosplan building comes from Curtis, 'The Engineer's Plot', but I have no real information about its internal geography.

215 **He had brought it back himself, by train from Berlin**: a little later he could, if he were very lucky, have bought it from a popular Moscow showroom for East German goods. Under communism, East Germany continued to manufacture office furniture to 1920s and 1930s designs, some of them rather stylish; and it was unusual too, for an Eastern Bloc country, in having a substantial industry producing plastic homewares, which were held up as a sign of socialist rationality. See Eli Rubin, *Synthetic Socialism: Plastics and Dictatorship in the German Democratic Republic* (Chapel Hill NC: University of North Carolina Press, 2009). An equivalent to Galina in the GDR would not have been so impressed by the little beakers in Sokolniki Park.

215 **Chemical-industry input coefficients**: a planner's tool giving standardised proportions of the inputs required to produce a unit of a given output, the idea being that all enterprises could be kept up to a set level of efficiency by supplying them only with the appropriate level of materials. Also known as input norms. For the pitfalls of this system, and the tendency for the norms to proliferate into a mass of exceptions, and rules applying to one factory only, see Ellman, *Planning Problems in the USSR*.

215 **'That's how the steel was tempered,' he said**: Mokhov is alluding to the title of Nikolai Ostrovsky's famous socialist-realist novel *How the Steel Was Tempered* (1936), which had become a common catchphrase. Computer programmers at Akademgorodok shouted it in August 1960 as they fought with the construction workers who kept turning off their power supply. See Josephson, *New Atlantis Revisited*.

215 **The balances were kept in a long, library-like room lined with filing cabinets**: the individual balances looked as I describe them here, and as a paper system they worked in the way I describe, and they must certainly have been kept in filing cabinets in *a* room (or rooms) in Gosplan, but this particular room I have invented. The Soviet gorgon with hair the colour of dried blood is a generic gorgon, from Central Casting.

215 **A workspace where there was a convenient spare abacus**: the most common calculating device throughout the history of Soviet Russia, and

slightly different in construction from a Chinese abacus. See Wikipedia
for description and photograph.

215 **373 folders, each holding work-in-progress on the balance for a
commodity**: the number of these most strategic commodities, also
known as 'funded commodities', was diminishing in an attempt to
make the system more manageable. There'd been 892 of them in 1957,
and 2,390 in 1953 – but the deleted ones were presumably reappearing
in the wider category of 'planned commodities', which didn't need
their balances signed off by the Council of Ministers but still had to be
calculated by Gosplan. When these were included, Gosplan's annual
output of commodity allocations went up from *c.*4,000 typescript pages
in twenty-two volumes to *c.*11,500 pages in seventy volumes. Figures all
from Gertrude E. Schroeder, 'The "Reform" of the Supply System in
Soviet Industry', *Soviet Studies*, vol. 24 no. 1, July 1972, pp. 97–119.

217 **A little problem with Solkemfib, the viscose plant at Solovets**:
Solkemfib is an invented addition to the genuine portfolio of new-
generation chemical fibre plants that were opening in the Soviet
Union in the early 1960s. I've picked up details for Solkemfib from
Ye. Zhukovskii, 'Building the Svetlogorsk Artifical Fiber Plant',
Sovetskaya Belorussya, 2 December 1962; translated in *USSR Economic
Development, No. 58: Soviet Chemical Industry*, US Dept of Commerce
Joint Publications Research Service report 18,411, 28 March 1963, pp.
17–20. The town of Solovets, on the other hand, is allusive rather
than just illusory. There was a real place of that name, an island in the
White Sea where some of the nastiest atrocities in the early history of
the Gulag took place. The name was borrowed by Arkady and Boris
Strugatsky in the 1965 novel *Monday Begins on Saturday*, to give a little
unacknowledgeable satirical edge to the town off in the northern forests
somewhere where the institute for studying magic stands. And I've
borrowed it in turn, to give my viscose factory a fantastical (and slightly
sinister) frame.

217 **Really, it was only salt, sulphur and coal in, viscose out**: exhaustive
descriptions of the viscose production process can be found on
Wikipedia. Wood (pine/fir/larch/aspen) is boiled up with sodium
bisulphite in digesters to give a special grade of cellulose called
'dissolving pulp', which is then steeped in sodium hydroxide (lye),
squeezed out, crumbled, and aged in the oxygen of the air, before being
churned with the industrial solvent carbon disulphide. This gives you
cellulose xanthate, which is chemically viscose, but not yet in usable
form; so you dissolve it again in more sodium hydroxide, and squirt it
through spinnerets into a 'spin bath' of sulphuric acid, where the viscose
liquid becomes filaments which can be stretched, wound, washed,
bleached, rewashed and dried as viscose yarn. This is the form of viscose
that can be woven as 'rayon' or 'art silk', as in Leonid Vitalevich's necktie

in part II chapter 1. Squirted through different spinnerets, however, the liquid can become viscose tyre cord or even cellophane. Solkemfib is not in the cellophane business. It clearly has one line set up for fabric and the other for cord. Of the three basic inputs Mokhov mentions, you need the salt to make the lye and the sodium bisulphite, the sulphur to make the sodium bisulphite, the carbon disulphide and the sulphuric acid, and the coal to make the carbon disulphide. Simple though these inputs are, they will still have put the Soviet viscose industry in competition for raw materials with soap-making, rubber-vulcanising, glue-manufacturing, ore-processing, petroleum-refining, steel-galvanising, brass-founding, metal-casting and fertiliser-producing. For an outline of the different industries' interconnecting needs, see Shabad, *Basic Industrial Resources of the USSR*.

219 **The original shortfall leaping from commodity to commodity**: for the classic analysis of the reasons for inevitable, permanent shortage in 'unreformed' planned economies, see Janos Kornai, *Economics of Shortage*, vol. A (Amsterdam/Oxford/New York, 1980). Kornai points out that, as well as the 'vegetative process' by which in such a system every actor sensibly overstates their needs, the system's own insistence on perpetual growth ensures that any given supply of a material is going to be too little for what its users would want to do with it.

219 **In theory . . . you would need to revise all the balances a minimum of six times over, and a maximum of thirteen times**: see the very clear exposition of the theory, and the pragmatic Soviet ways around it, in Ellman, *Planning Problems in the USSR*.

219 **It was the basis for Emil Shaidullin's entertaining prediction**: really a prediction by Abel Aganbegyan, made in 1964.

222 **The PNSh-180-14s continuous-action engine for viscose**: a real machine, referred to in 'Results of the Work of the Chemical Fibres Industry for 1968', *Fibre Chemistry* vol. 1 no. 2, March–April 1969, pp. 117–20; translation of *Khimicheskie Volokna* no. 2, March–April 1969, pp. 1–3. But I have no evidence that it was yet in production in 1963, and the technical upgrade, the figure of 17 for the annual output, the nomination of the Uralmash machine-building combine as its manufacturer, the description of it as a metal porcupine as big as a subway hall and the idea that it had its own balance at Gosplan all, all come straight out of the conjurer's hat of invention.

222 **The page in front of him was simplicity itself**: taken from the model of a balance-page illustrated in Levine, 'The Centralised Planning of Supply in Soviet Industry'.

223 **He was supposed to get chemical-fibre production up to 400,000 tonnes per annum by 1965**: target taken from Shabad, *Basic Industrial Resources of the USSR*.

Notes

IV.2 Prisoner's Dilemma, 1963

224 **They were off to the fleshpots together for the annual jamboree:** the festive jaunt to Moscow to deliver the plan, and a lot of the rest of the behaviour of Solkemfib's management, comes from Joseph Berliner, *Factory and Manager in the USSR* (Cambridge MA: Harvard University Press, 1957). See also, by the same author, 'Informal Organization of the Soviet Firm', *Quarterly Journal of Economics*, August 1952, pp. 342–65; *The Innovation Decision in Soviet Industry* (Boston: MIT Press, 1976); and *Soviet Industry from Stalin to Gorbachev: Essays on Management and Innovation* (Ithaca NY: Cornell University Press, 1988). An archetypal Soviet manager is among the semi-fictional 'portraits' in Raymond A. Bauer, *Nine Soviet Portraits* (Boston: MIT Press, 1965).

225 **The hotel Icebound Sea faced across the town square:** from the hotel to the fisheries-trust teashop, all details faithfully reflect the Strugatskys' version of the town of Solovets.

227 **They'd hit the gross target for the year 1962 dead on, 100% delivered of the 14,100 tonnes of viscose planned:** a target figure for Solkemfib concocted by calculating the average planned output for a real Soviet viscose plant in 1962 from Shabad, *Basic Industrial Resources of the USSR.*

229 **All seeing the possibilities, all liking what they saw:** I am probably anticipating the shamelessness of managerial behaviour in the later 1970s and 1980s by making Arkhipov, Mitrenko and Kosoy be willing to countenance an actual act of sabotage. It probably took longer than this for the fearful restraint of the Stalin time to come apart. But this was the direction in which things were going, so again, a real process has been foreshortened here. For an illuminating discussion of late-Soviet managerial gamesmanship, see Yevgeny Kuznetsov, 'Learning in Networks: Enterprise Behaviour in the Former Soviet Union and Contemporary Russia', in Joan M. Nelson, Charles Tilley and Lee Walker, eds, *Transforming Post-Communist Political Economies* (Washington DC: National Academy Press, 1997).

229 **Let alone to tolerate the signature stink of the viscose process:** caused by the breakdown of dense quantities of carbon disulphide in the plants' air, into even fouller-smelling carbonyl sulphide. Rotting cabbage was the usual comparison.

230 **He had been imprisoned, but was now released:** for the situation of ex-political prisoners, see Solzhenitsyn, *Gulag Archipelago* vol. 3 part VI, 'Exile', pp. 335–468. Having the decree of exile lifted did not automatically restore one's original residence rights. For a treatment in fiction of a prisoner's unsettling reappearance among the comfortable and prosperous, see Vasily Grossman, *Forever Flowing*, translated by Thomas P. Whitney (New York: Harper & Row, 1972).

IV.3 Favours, 1964

234 **Over the ridge where the floor heaved up they danced**: I have no
knowledge of any bulge in the dancefloor of the Sverdlovsk Palace of
Culture. But the Novosibirsk Palace of Culture has one.

234 **A real Spaniard marooned here, in a crude cold steel town**: and there
were real Spaniards scattered around the Soviet Union, in just Senora
Lopez's position.

234 **It was his business to do so, he made his living snapping up these
trifles**: Chekuskin's methods of operation in this chapter are elaborated
from Joseph Berliner's description of the work of the *tolkach* or 'pusher'
in *Factory and Manager in the USSR*, with his capacity for instant
friendship, and his memory for birthdays and children's names, and
his plausible entrée to every office in town. (The stereotypical traits
of the successful salesman, in fact, here inverted for a situation in
which buying rather than selling is the art that requires persuasion.)
Berliner drew his information from post-war interviews with
Displaced Persons, so the *tolkach* as he describes him is a creature of
the 1930s: but the institutions of the Soviet economy that made the
tolkach necessary remained essentially unchanged all the way from
the Stalinist industrialisation to the fall of the state in 1991, and there
were indignant newspaper reports and anti-*tolkach* cleanup campaigns
every few years throughout the 1950s, 1960s and 1970s, which suggests
a basic continuity. Given Chekuskin's continual use of individual
favour-trading to oil the wheels of his industrial negotiations, another
important source was Ledeneva, *Russia's Economy of Favours*. I've made
Chekuskin extremely *blatnoi*, rich in connections, but he isn't quite a
blatmeister, a maestro of individual deal-making about flats and schools
and telephones and doctors and Black Sea holidays, because – to use
Ledeneva's elegant analysis of the psychology of *blat* – a *blatmeister*
co-ordinated the mutual backscratching of many overlapping circles
of friends, and could only thrive if perceived as a real friend, whereas
Chekuskin is fundamentally a commercial figure, who leans across the
boundary into the world of *blat*, just as he also does into the world of
the black market. Ledeneva is invaluable on the distinctions of feeling
involved, the crucial one of which is the extent to which, in each of
these three adjacent worlds of illicit behaviour, the actors let themselves
see clearly what they were doing. *Blat* transactions were thoroughly
mystified; they were conceptualised as part of the warmth of friendship,
and could never be explicitly paid for by a return favour, though anyone
who didn't tend his or her end of a *blat* relationship would soon find the
supply of friendly help drying up. The *tolkach* business knew it was a
business; but it was one in which, as Chekuskin says below, Everything
is Personal. The money was there, the price of a transaction had to be

paid, but the object was to find non-money reasons for the transaction to take place. And at the other end of the scale, the black market *was* a market, of a rudimentary kind, where goods (for instance, stolen petrol) were sold to relative strangers in order to obtain cash. It was the limited utility of cash that limited the size of the black market.

238 **A flying saucer swoops down over the earth and grabs a Russian, a German and a Frenchman**: authentic joke, in the subgenre of comfortable self-insults to the Russian character, from Graham, 'A Cultural Analysis of the Russo-Soviet *Anekdot*'. The aliens give all three abductees a pair of shining steel spheres and lock them in tiny compartments aboard the spaceship. They'll release the one who can think of the most amazing thing to do with the spheres, they say. The German juggles with his spheres: not bad. But the Frenchman juggles with them while standing on his head and singing a beautiful love song. Surely he must be the winner – 'but we'll just check what the Russian can do,' say the aliens. In a moment, they're back. 'Sorry, but the Russian wins.' 'In God's name, how?' says the Frenchman. 'What else could he possibly have come up with?' 'Well,' say the aliens in awe, 'he broke one, and lost the other . . .'

241 **Over the intersection to the big portico of the Central Hotel**: Sverdlovsk here has a generic Soviet geography, not the actual geographical detail of the actual city (now Ekaterinburg again).

241 **Feeling a certain wavering in his legs, as if they were anticipating a sudden need to flee**: because Chekuskin's activities are technically, of course, all illegal under Article 153 of the Soviet Criminal Code, prohibiting commercial middlemen.

244 **A gentleman named Gersh, who did pickled herrings in jars**: or Hersch, as he would have been in other countries. Russian has no 'h', and renders the 'h' sound as 'g' rather than as (the other option) 'kh'. The USSR was invaded in 1941 by a German dictator called Gitler. Mr Gersh's pickled herring business, on the other hand, clearly operated during the New Economic Policy of the mid-1920s.

246 **A brown hundred on the outside**: for contemporary banknotes, see http://commons.wikipedia.org/wiki/Category:Banknotes_of_the_Soviet_Union,_1961.

248 **No one would have printed on a cup or a bowl what these citizens had imprinted on themselves**: all of the tattoo designs here are authentic, and can be found in Danzig Baldaev et al., *Russian Criminal Tattoo Encyclopedia* (Gottingen: Steidl, 2004).

249 **He had heard about the thieves' marathon card sessions**: for thieves and their card games in the Gulag, see Aleksandr Solzhenitsyn, *The Gulag Archipelago 2, 1918–1956, Parts III–IV*, translated by Thomas P. Whitney (London: Collins/Harvill, 1975), pp. 410–30. For a fictional representation, drawing on the Siberian experience of the imprisoned

Yugoslav Karlo Stajner, see Danilo Kis, 'The Magic Card Dealing' (story), in *A Tomb for Boris Davidovich*, translated anonymously from the Serbian (New York: Harcourt Brace Jovanovich, 1978).

258 **Couple of *stilyagi*. Really stomped me, the little bastards**: quiffed, music-loving members of the Soviet Union's first distinctive teenage tribe. Associated with delinquency, and therefore conveniently blamable for all ills, and not just by Russians; Anthony Burgess claimed that it was a violent encounter with *stilyagi* outside a Leningrad nightclub that inspired him to create Alex and his droogs in *A Clockwork Orange*.

262 **This is a *budget* problem? Nobody cares about those**: I have cheated here slightly, and given Uralmash a problem with money which, strictly speaking, would not have existed in this form until after the 1965 reform, which changed the measure of plan fulfilment from physical volume of output to profit made. Hence the need here for the additional factor of special scrutiny by Gosplan. Otherwise, in 1963, the chemical fibre equipment division of Uralmash really would have worried about the number of machines produced, and little else. By having Solkemfib's problem with getting their upgrade turn, anachronistically, on price irrationality, I'm dramatising in advance the consequences of a price-irrational reform when it comes in the next chapter.

263 **Pricing of equipment in the chemical industry is calculated chiefly by weight**: a genuine statement, but actually made, later, to a plant manufacturing car-tyre-moulding machines in Tambov. See Ellman, *Planning Problems in the Soviet Union*.

Part V

Introduction

269 **The same bet that Plato had twenty-five centuries earlier**: see Plato, *The Republic*, 473d. As Benjamin Jowett's 1871 translation puts it, 'Until philosophers are kings, or the kings and princes of this world have the spirit and power of philosophy, and political greatness and wisdom meet in one, and those commoner natures who pursue either to the exclusion of the other are compelled to stand aside, cities will never have rest from their evils, – nor the human race, as I believe . . .' The classic twentieth-century philosophical rejoinder to Plato is Karl Popper, *The Open Society and Its Enemies* (1945).

269 **The Party existed, its hierarchy shadowing all other hierarchies**: for the Leninist justification for cadres' unlimited authority, see Kolakowski, *Main Currents of Marxism*, pp. 664–74, 754–63. For the way the dual structure of power left the Soviet state 'booby-trapped with idealism', and the role it eventually played in the downfall of the USSR, see Stephen Kotkin, *Armageddon Averted: The Soviet Collapse*,

1970–2000 (Oxford: OUP, 2001). Conversely, for an argument that the philosophical kingship of the USSR only continued a traditional local approach to modernisation, see Marshall T. Poe, *The Russian Moment in World History* (Princeton NJ: Princeton University Press, 2003).

270 **They were the agents of humanity's future**: or, in Stalin's famous phrase, 'the engineers of human souls'.

270 **They acted as progress-chasers, fixers, censors, seducers**: but not, by design, as bureaucrats, in one very specific sense of the word. The Soviet Union had regular campaigns against 'bureaucracy', hard though this is for an outsider to make immediate sense of in a system where every employee was a state employee. 'Bureaucracy' as a Soviet pejorative implied coldness, impersonality, slowness, trivial rule-following. Apparatchiks were supposed, by contrast, to be quick, 'conscious', lively, free to engage in brilliant improvisation to get the job done by any means necessary. See Fitzpatrick, *Everyday Stalinism*, pp. 28–35. And there was some support for this model of power at the receiving end: it was the aim of anyone dealing with an official to try and get themselves treated *po-chelovecheski*, 'like a human being', on the basis of an emotional recognition rather than some cold rule. See Ledeneva, *Russia's Economy of Favours*. The result was that Soviet bureaucracy, while pervasive, did not exhibit some of the classic features of bureaucracy elsewhere. It was not predictable and rule-governed; thus, by a neat circle of cause and effect, you *had* to approach it personally, emotionally, looking for the individual with whom to make a relationship.

271 **Not exactly virtue, but a sort of intentionally post-ethical counterpart to it**: see Charles Taylor's characterisation of 'the Bolshevik stance' as a version of disengaged liberal benevolence in which one's identity as a good person has been entirely invested in a 'titanic control over history'. Charles Taylor, *A Secular Age* (Cambridge MA: Belknap Press of Harvard University Press, 2007), pp. 682–3.

272 **High-level Party meetings became extravagantly foul-mouthed from the 1930s on**: see Aganbegyan, *Moving the Mountain*.

272 **'When I was a miner,' he snapped**: see Taubman, *Khrushchev*, p. 590.

273 **In 1964, Khrushchev was entirely surrounded by people he had appointed himself**: for the political history of the last frantic months of Khrushchev's leadership, see Taubman, *Khrushchev*, pp. 3–17, 620–45. For the warning signs of the approaching putsch, which Sergei Khrushchev tried to get his father to notice, see the first two chapters of Sergei Khrushchev, *Khrushchev on Khrushchev: An Inside Account of the Man and His Era*, edited and translated by William Taubman (Boston MA: Little Brown, 1990). For the shifting mood in the Presidium among Khrushchev-made figures such as Andropov, see Burlatsky, *Khrushchev and the First Russian Spring*, pp. 196-203.

274 'You'd think as first secretary I could change anything in this country':
see Taubman, *Khrushchev*, p. 598.

V.1 Trading Down, 1964

276 **The Zil had disappeared in the night**: though the chauffeur himself is
fictional, the sequence of appearing and disappearing cars on the day
after Khrushchev's fall from power is entirely factual. For a description
of that day on which this chapter draws heavily, see Sergei Khrushchev,
Khrushchev on Khrushchev, pp. 165–9. See also Taubman, *Khrushchev*,
pp. 620–1.

276 **It was a copy of the Cadillac Eldorado**: the American originals for the
Zil, Chaika and Volga are all authentic. The Soviet car industry had
been founded in the 1930s with the import of a complete Buick/Ford
production line, including American engineers to act as consultants,
and Soviet automobile design was still very imitative of American
models, though not always on a neat one-to-one basis. Some Soviet
cars copied several different American cars at once. Later, with the
establishment of the giant plant to build Fiats at Tolyatti on the Volga,
the American influence was diluted, and by the 1980s the Soviet
Union had a distinctive automotive style of its own, though without
anything approaching the idiosyncrasy of the Czech Tatra marque or the
cardboard-chassised Trabant in the GDR. But then, both East Germany
and Czechoslovakia had had indigenous motor industries of their own
before the Second World War. Middle-class consumers who cannot
afford German or Japanese imports continue to buy Volgas in present-
day Russia. For a roll-call of models, with photographs, see
www.autosoviet.com.

278 **It had come straight from the general-service pool**: I have no
knowledge of the Kremlin's carpool arrangements, and this is guesswork.

279 **But compared to the Zil it was a tin can**: the chauffeur is being snotty
in the extreme about the Gaz M-21 Volga, which most Soviet citizens
coveted, and which is now recalled by Russians in their fifties and sixties
with the kind of nostalgia that the chromed monsters of Detroit rouse
up in Americans of the same age. There are numerous M-21 fan sites on
the internet.

279 **Metamorphosed into a Moskvitch. Or a bicycle**: the Moskvich 400,
produced from 1946 to 1964 by MZMA, the Moscow Factory for Small
Displacement Automobiles, closely resembled the 1938 model of the
Opel Kadett. This was because it was manufactured with the tooling
for the 1938 Kadett, which the Red Army had captured intact during
the advance into Germany. But after 1964 it was redesigned with 'sleek
modern lines', and the Moskvich 412 even won a small export following
among budget-conscious Western motorists. Thanks to stern rules
limiting the value of the prizes that could be offered on television in

Britain, the star prize in the early 1970s on the British TV gameshow *Sale of the Century* was frequently a 412 in bright orange. See Andrew Roberts, 'Moscow Mule', *The Independent* Motoring Section p. 7, 11 October 2005.

279 **She had made canapés for the President of Finland:** this, the seventieth birthday party and the reception for the Chinese Foreign Minister were all real occasions, but the cook herself is imaginary.

280 **'Good morning, Nikita Sergeyevich,' he said:** the real words of the real Sergei Melnikov, from Sergei Khrushchev, *Khrushchev on Khrushchev*. Melnikov appears to have tried to treat the fallen leader with as much dignity as possible, and was fired a few years into Khrushchev's retirement for showing excessive sympathy. Khrushchev's reply is word-for-word accurate as well.

282 **'No one needs me now,' he said to the air straight in front of him:** a real utterance of Khrushchev's on that first stunned day, but addressed to 'no one in particular', not a chauffeur.

V.2 Ladies, Cover Your Ears! 1965

283 **Emil splashed his head with cold water:** the entire occasion described in this chapter is a confabulation, designed to dramatise the disappointment of the reform economists over the limits of the 'Kosygin reforms' of 1965. Kosygin did make a point of stopping off in Akademgorodok on his way back from a state visit to Vietnam, and while talking to Kantorovich and Aganbegyan there did utter the immortal sentences 'What have prices to do with it? What are you talking about?' – but most of the reformers' access to discussions over the design of the reform was through committees and reports of the Academy of Sciences, in which they struggled to make themselves heard clearly. The case against adopting Kantorovich's prices, though, which I have put into Kosygin's mouth and the mouth of the fictional Mokhov, is so far as I have been able to find out the probable one, compounded of shrewd realism as well as self-interest and incomprehension. And Kosygin's character as represented here is also authentic, down to the habit of continual contemptuous interruption. Abel Aganbegyan really did in fact lose his temper in the face of it, and snap '*I* don't understand?' back at him, with temporarily disastrous results, but not until ten years later, in the mid-1970s. See Aganbegyan, *Moving the Mountain*. For my understanding of the technical aspects of the reform, I have used the analysis in Ellman, *Planning Problems in the USSR*, and (by the same author) 'Seven Theses on Kosyginism' in *Collectivism, Convergence and Capitalism* (London: Harcourt Brace, 1984). There is an accessible account of the reform's aims in Berliner, 'Economic Reform in the USSR'. For a general sense of the economists as players in contemporary Soviet politics, see R. Judy, 'The Economists',

in G. Skilling and F. Griffith, eds, *Interest Groups in Soviet Politics* (Princeton NJ: Princeton University Press, 1971). For a much more fine-grained and bitchy account, see Katsenelinboigen, *Soviet Economic Thought and Political Power in the USSR*.

283 **Mr K. had slipped into real puce-faced spittle-streaked raving**: it had been in the interests of the Presidium majority who overthrew Khrushchev that his instability should be exaggerated, and Emil has clearly picked up some deliberately hyperbolic gossip. But the First Secretary's temper had been getting out of control, and there had been spur-of-the-moment threats to the Red Army (see Taubman, *Khrushchev*, pp. 585–6) and the Academy (Taubman, *Khrushchev*, p. 616).

284 **The new men exuded a deliberate, welcome calm**: for the mood-music of the transition, see Michel Tatu, *Power in the Kremlin: From Khrushchev's Decline to Collective Leadership*, translated from the French by Helen Katel (London: Collins, 1969), and Burlatsky, *Khrushchev and the First Russian Spring*.

284 **A peculiar and discordant piece had been published in *Ekonomicheskaya Gazeta***: see unsigned article, 'Economics and Politics', *Problems of Economics* (International Arts & Sciences Press, NY) vol. 7 no. 11, March 1965; originally in *Ekonomicheskaya Gazeta*, 11 November 1964.

285 **There came a reorganisation of the lacework of Party committees within all the institutes**: see Josephson, *New Atlantis Revisited*.

286 **An experiment in letting clothing stores determine the output of two textile factories**: for the experiment at the Bolshevichka and Mayak factories, see V. Sokolov, M. Nazarov and N. Kozlov, 'The Firm and the Customer', *Problems of Economics* (International Arts & Sciences Press, NY) vol. 8 no. 4, August 1965, pp. 3–14; originally in *Ekonomicheskaya Gazeta*, 6 Jan 1965.

286 **'We have to free ourselves completely,' he said**: this technocratic speech was given on 19 March 1965, published in Gosplan's journal *Planovoe Khozyaistvo* no. 4, April 1965, and reprinted in *Ekonomicheskaya Gazeta* on 21 April 1965. Quoted in English in Tatu, *Power in the Kremlin*, p. 447. Kosygin's report on the completed reform measure appeared in *Izvestiya*, 28 September 1965; see A. N. Kosygin, 'On Improving Industrial Management, Perfecting Planning, and Enhancing Economic Incentives in Industrial Production', *Problems of Economics* (International Arts & Sciences Press, NY) vol. 8 no. 6, October 1965, pp. 3–28.

286 **A beautiful paper at the end of last year had skewered Academician Glushkov's hypercentralised rival scheme**: see Vsevolod Pugachev, 'Voprosy optimal'nogo planirovaniia narodnogo khoziaistva s pomoshch'iu edinoi gosudarstvennoi seti vychistel'nykh tsentrov', *Voprosy Ekonomiki* (1964) no. 7, pp. 93–103. No English translation.

According to Katsenelinboigen, *Soviet Economic Thought*, Pugachev was a TSEMI economist deployed to Gosplan who had gone over to the planners' critique of mathematical reform.

287 **They had decided he'd better not, for obvious reasons**: I have once again exaggerated and coarsened Kantorovich's unworldliness. He was not a skilled politician, but in this case he served alongside Aganbegyan on the 'Commission of 18' tasked by the Academy to prepare its submission on the reform.

289 **An optimal plan is by definition a profitable plan**: from Kantorovich, *The Best Use of Economic Resources*.

289 **There was a report in January in *Ekonomicheskaya Gazeta***: Emil is referring to Sokolov, Nazarov and Kozlov, 'The Firm and the Customer', cited above.

292 **We should let a machine take over a job as sensitive as deciding prices?**: See the discussion in Ellman, *Planning Problems in the USSR*, of which elements were, and were not, usually adopted when an 'optimal plan' had been drawn up for some Soviet institution.

294 **'He liked to smash telephones,' said Emil**: true. See Fitzpatrick, *Everyday Stalinism*, for the uninhibited management styles of Stalin's industrial barons like Kaganovich and Ordzhonikidze. The Committee on Labour was Lazar Kaganovich's last major appointment. He was pushed out of the Presidium in disgrace by Khrushchev in 1957 as one of the 'anti-Party group', and sent to run the Urals Potash Works in Solikamsk, Perm Province. See Taubman, *Khrushchev*, p. 369.

295 **I specialise more in, uh, *organisation*, and, uh, *psychology***: an anecdote taken from Burlatsky, *Khrushchev and the First Russian Spring*, pp. 213–14. Apparently Brezhnev made little rotary hand movements in the air as he said it.

299 **'Do you know what my first job was, when I got back from the war?'**: the details of the rota, the delivery vans and the incinerator are all invented, but the postwar burning of the bonds is real. See Hachten, *Property Relations*. The currency reform of 1947, which converted old roubles to new roubles in savings accounts at the rate of 10:1 while keeping prices the same, was another deliberate move to abolish the state's liabilities. And Khrushchev did it again when, on 8 April 1957, he deferred the repayment of all outstanding bond issues 'for 20–25 years', and the 3% interest due on them too, which had been paid out as lottery prizes to bondholders. But in this last case, the gain to citizens' pay-packets in not having to buy any more new bonds outweighed the theoretical loss of all their previous subscriptions. See James R. Miller, 'History and Analysis of Soviet Domestic Bond Policy', *Soviet Studies* 27 no. 4 (1975), p. 601; and Franklyn D. Holzman, 'The Soviet Bond Hoax', *Problems of Communism* 6, no. 5 (1957), pp. 47–9.

RED PLENTY

V.3 Psychoprophylaxis, 1966

302 **He was registered with the All-Union Legal Correspondence Institute:**
founded in 1932, with more than forty thousand graduates by 1968.
Added together, students attending evening classes (652,000 in 1967–8)
and studying by correspondence (1.77 million in 1967–8) earned almost
half of the bachelor's degrees awarded in the USSR, and for law degrees
the proportion was even higher, 43,000 out of 65,000 in 1967–8.
A law degree was a tool of working-class social mobility, as in the
United States, appealing to those on the rise, like Fyodor, rather than
to those with established family traditions of education. Figures from
Churchward, *The Soviet Intelligentsia.*

302 **The thousand skirmishes of *communalka* life:** see Fitzpatrick, *Everyday
Stalinism*, pp. 47–9; and for the special political claustrophobia of
communal flats in times of purge and denunciation, see Orlando Figes, *The
Whisperers: Private Lives in Stalin's Russia* (London: Allen Lane, 2007), which
includes floor plans of the extraordinarily crammed places his witnesses
inhabited. For the surreal spectacle of Stalin himself picking his way
through a *communalka*, and looking with touristic interest at the writing on
the wall around the telephone, see Grossman, *Life and Fate.*

305 **Orange or lime-green orlon:** orlon being the Soviet brand-name
equivalent to Western nylon.

307 **The deputy director of a pig farm's on trial:** a famous case from 1969,
hoicked back in time for the usual unscrupulous reasons of dramatic
foreshortening. For the trial coverage, as presented for the outrage of
liberal-minded intellectuals, see *Literaturnaya Gazeta* (1969) no. 27, p. 10.

308 **One of the three Moscow maternity homes that specialised in
Rh-neg patients:** I get my details of hospital conditions for this chapter
from Katherine Bliss Eaton, *Daily Life in the Soviet Union* (Westport
CT: Greenwood Publishing Group, 2004), pp. 185–7, and Peter Osnos,
'Childbirth, Soviet Style: A Labor in Keeping With the Party Line',
Washington Post, 28 November 1976, pp. G13–G14. Some details of
Soviet medical procedure for childbirth come from Elizabeth Lee,
'Health Care in the Soviet Union. Two. Childbirth – Soviet Style',
Nursing Times (1984), 1–7 February; 80 (5): 44–5, which is a view of
a system by a British midwife, focused mainly on differences in goals
and intentions. All of these apply to periods ten to twenty years after
the date at which Galina is giving birth, so some of what happens
here is inevitably conjectural. But the system does not appear to have
changed fundamentally, and any allowance made for decaying facilities
and increasing cynicism as the Brezhnev years went on can be balanced
against the truth that the special Rhesus-negative maternity hospitals
were the sought-after best of the system. A different kind of allowance
needs to be made for my other major source on procedure. I. Velvovsky,
K. Platonov, V. Ploticher and E. Shugom, *Painless Childbirth Through*

Psychoprophylaxis: Lectures for Obstetricians, translated by David A.
Myshne (Foreign Languages Publishing House, Moscow 1960) is a
manual for export, offering an idealised version of psychoprophylactic
childbirth as it would have been if implemented in every Soviet hospital
with the care it was given in the one hospital where it was invented.
What Galina experiences is my best guess at psychoprophylaxis as
actually practised.

309 **And then he was backing, dwindling, absenting himself from the
scene**: husbands were forbidden to attend childbirths, or even to visit
during the mandatory ten-day stay in the hospital afterwards. Some
will have been sorrier than others about this, just as some women will
have been sorrier than others for the enforced rest from family life. See
Hedrick Smith, *The Russians* (London, 1976), for a description of the
gaggle of men crowded beneath the recovery-ward windows to see the
babies their wives were holding up, and to load eatables into the baskets
the women lowered on strings.

309 **A face beneath the white flowerpot that seemed to disapprove of
the world**: Inna Olegovna is entirely fictional, but my sketch of her
aunt-like self-righteousness borrows from my memory of the array of
censorious, reproving middle-aged men and women in the late-Soviet
documentary film *Is It Easy to Be Young?*

310 **Everything was white tiles, but not very clean ones**: see Eaton, *Daily Life
in the Soviet Union*, p. 186. Her witness reports 'sliminess'.

310 **She let the midwife take back the gown and put her under a sluggish
blood-warm shower**: the shower, the enema, the shaving and the
painting with disinfectant were all standard procedure. Having to walk
up flights of stairs while in labour was not standard procedure, but
happened frequently anyway.

311 **'Primipara,' she said to the Angry Aunt, standing by with a clipboard**:
medical vocabulary authentic, and taken from the sample case histories
given in Velvovsky et al., *Painless Childbirth Through Psychoprophylaxis*.

311 **'You didn't do the psychoprophylaxis classes?'**: expectant mothers
were in theory supposed to be led by patient stages through a
confrontation with their fears over birth pain, a reassuring explanation
of the physiology of childbirth and a demonstration of relaxation and
breathing techniques. In fact, in almost every case the classes were
taught by midwives or doctors who had not been specially trained,
and did indeed consist mainly of the 'stuff about taking lots of walks'
which Galina's neighbour reports to her on the labour ward, with the
specifics of what to expect and to do reduced to an unhelpful gabble at
the end. Not knowing that there was anything important to learn, most
women, like Galina, didn't bother to go. So the positive programme of
the psychoprophylactic method scarcely touched them, yet they were
still subject to the prohibition on drugs associated with it, and were still

likely to be judged as if difficulty with the pain represented a failure of virtue on their part.

312 **When the contractions come, breathe deeply**: if the few bits of psychoprophylactic advice Galina gets seem vaguely familiar, that's because they are. Psychoprophylaxis, in a melancholy irony, is the basis of the phenomenally successful Lamaze method for natural birth in the West. The Soviet ideas were carried back to Paris by the French doctor (and communist) Fernand Lamaze, and humanised there – partly by bringing in birth partners, and less passive positions for labour, and more sophisticated techniques of auto-suggestion, but most of all by being made voluntary. A woman 'doing Lamaze' can aim for a birth with minimal medical intervention while knowing that the pethidine and the gas and the epidurals are there if she needs them. Psychoprophylaxis may seem to Galina here to be just another form of compulsory pretence; but it would be equally just to see it as another piece of mangled Soviet idealism, another genuinely promising idea ruined by the magic combination of compulsion and neglect. Velvovsky and his colleagues were the century's pioneers in trying to see childbirth as something better than an illness to be endured.

313 **It was really only messages from the subcortex of the brain which you could turn off by stimulating the cortex**: one reason for the rapid promotion of psychoprophylaxis to orthodoxy in the USSR lay in its use of a Pavlovian framework that dovetailed with late-Stalinist ideological preferences. For the history and personalities involved here, and the role played by this association with soon-discredited science in later Soviet obstetricians' indifference to the technique they were supposed to be promoting, see John D. Bell, 'Giving Birth to the New Soviet Man: Politics and Obstetrics in the USSR', *Slavic Review* vol. 40 no. 1 (Spring 1981), pp. 1–16.

313 **It means they're not going to give us any painkillers**: in some hospitals, a single small injection of painkillers was allowed. See Eaton, *Daily Life in the Soviet Union*.

314 **She had only brought a bowl of water, and briskly wiped all the foreheads in the room with it**: the only thing a midwife was permitted to do for women at this stage of labour, apart from watching for complications which might require surgery.

317 **So pull yourself together and breathe right, or you'll kill the baby**: an encouraging remark passed on to the American journalist Peter Osnos by the woman who had it said to her. See Osnos, 'Childbirth, Soviet Style'.

317 **They were all mashed flies, swatted and left to fester**: attested in Eaton, *Daily Life in the Soviet Union*.

318 **Baby already papoosed up and whisked away**: immediately after birth, the newborn was swaddled in a tight roll of white cloth, held up for the

mother to see, and then carried off to a nursery for twenty-four hours –
apparently to reduce mother–baby transmission of infections, although
it is hard to see how this can have worked. After that, the baby would
be returned for breastfeeding, the Soviet Union being, in one more
authoritarian commitment to naturalness, partly caused by the faulty
supply of powdered milk, an entirely pro-breast society. See Eaton,
Daily Life in the Soviet Union, and Lee, 'Health Care in the Soviet
Union'.

Part VI

Introduction

323 **The 'Kosygin reforms' of 1965 put a lot more money in factory
managers' pockets**: see Ellman, *Planning Problems in the Soviet Union*.
The reforms created, as well as the cash bonus fund for managers (still
tied to the overfulfilment of the plan), three 'incentive funds' indexed
to enterprises' sales growth. These were supposed to stimulate local
initiatives, and received about 14% of profits by 1968; their distribution
was strongly skewed towards management and 'engineering-technical
personnel', with the result that they reversed the very egalitarian
income policy of Khrushchev's time, under which in some places
foremen had received less than workers and workers had earned more
than all white-collar staff *without* technical qualifications. It is also
worth remembering that management had very considerable discretion
about how the two non-cash incentive funds (for local investment and
workers' facilities) were actually spent, so long as the books looked all
right.

323 **There was only a 0.5% upward blip in growth**: see above, note to
the introduction to part II, for the full panoply of sources on Soviet
growth. Figures here from Gregory and Stuart, *Russian and Soviet
Economic Performance and Structure*.

323 **In 1961 the first oilfield had been discovered in western Siberia**: for the
transforming effects of the Soviet oilstrikes, and their fortuitous timing,
see Tony Judt, *Postwar: A History of Europe Since 1945* (London: William
Heinemann, 2005); also Nove, *Economic History of the USSR*, and
Shabad, *Basic Industrial Resources of the USSR*.

324 **There were thirty million TV sets in Soviet homes in 1968**: figures here
from Nove, *Economic History of the USSR*.

324 **A heavy-industrial sector which had once been intended to exist as
a springboard for something else, but which had now become its
own justification**: as seen as early as the mid-1960s, with oblique but
inescapable intellectual force, in the 'variant calculation' performed
by the Gosplan Research Institute for the 1966–70 Five-Year Plan.

Gosplan's figures showed that increasing the rate of investment in the economy would increase output growth in industry but give only minimal extra growth in consumption – 0.3% extra consumption growth for nearly 6% more investment. Industrial growth in the USSR did not carry over into general prosperity. The linkages were missing. See Ellman, *Planning Problems in the USSR*.

324 **More of the total effort of the economy that hosted it than heavy industry has ever done anywhere else:** far more, for instance, than Britain, France or the United States in the most frenzied stages in the history of their industrial revolutions, or India and China now. In this highly specialised and fetishised sense, the USSR had indeed overtaken and surpassed. See Nove, *Economic History of the USSR*.

325 **The control system for industry grew more and more erratic:** for the ever wilder game-playing by management, and ever more drastic surprise moves by planners, see Kuznetsov, 'Learning in Networks'.

325 **One economist has argued that, by the end, it was actively destroying value:** see Hodgson, *Economics and Utopia*. His example is the men's shirt so unwearably hideous that 'even Soviet citizens' would not touch it, woven from cotton that could have been sold on the world market for actual money.

325 **Indeed an emigré journal reported the rumour:** see Dora Sturman, 'Chernenko and Andropov: Ideological Perspectives', *Survey* 1 (1984), pp. 1–21.

325 **Brezhnev-era Soviet joke-telling:** for many, many real examples, see Graham, 'A Cultural Analysis of the Russo-Soviet *Anekdot*'. The Brezhnev joke had a characteristic tone of near-endearment about it, as if the stupidity of what was being mocked was ultimately comfortable. For instance: the General Secretary is entering the third hour of his speech to the Party Congress when the comrades from the organs of security suddenly swoop and arrest a group of American spies in the audience. 'Brilliant work!' says Brezhnev. 'But how did you pick them out?' 'Well,' say the KGB men modestly, 'as you yourself have observed, Comrade General Secretary, the enemy never sleeps . . .'

326 **Science . . . was to be 'administered' not 'supported':** a deliberate change of vocabulary after 1965 by Brezhnev's new Central Committee Secretary for Science, Trapeznikov. See Josephson, *New Atlantis Revisited*.

326 **The discreet little unmarked offices of the security service's Fifth Department:** see Churchward, *Soviet Intelligentsia*.

326 **A minute fraction of the intelligentsia gave up on the Soviet system altogether:** Churchward's taxonomy of Soviet intellectuals in the 1960s classes 75% of them as 'Careerist Professionals', with most of the remainder accounted for by the various wings of the 'Humanist Intelligentsia' of the arts establishment. Everyone in the

Akademgorodok sections of this book with the exception of Zoya Vaynshteyn and Mo would fall into the 'Loyal Oppositionist' subgroup of Churchward's Careerists.

326 **Several times in the late 1960s and 1970s there were strikes**: see Nove, *Economic History of the USSR*.

326 *Ty-mne, ya-tebe*, **'you to me and I to you'**: the Russian proverb equivalent to 'You scratch my back and I'll scratch yours', but with particular *blat* associations. For this and other phrases of the *blat* vocabulary of the 1960s–1980s, see Ledeneva, *Russia's Economy of Favours*.

326 **The vast majority of the Soviet population were, indeed, basically contented**: for the lack of pressure from below for change, and the origin instead within the Party of the system's collapse in the late 1980s, see Kotkin, *Armageddon Averted*. On the face of it, one of the great historical mysteries of the twentieth century should be the question of why the Soviet reformers of the 1980s didn't even consider following the pragmatic Chinese path, and dismantling the economic structure of state socialism while keeping its political framework intact. Instead, the Soviet government dismantled the Leninist political structure while trying with increasing desperation to make the planned economy work. But the mystery resolves rather easily if it is posited that Gorbachev and the intellectuals around him, all children of the 1930s and young adults under Khrushchev, might strange to say have been really and truly socialists, guarding a loyal glimmer of belief right through the Brezhnevite 'years of stagnation', and seizing the chance after two decades of delay to return to their generational project of making a socialism that was prosperous, humane, and intelligent. With disastrous results. This whole book is, in fact, a prehistory of perestroika.

326 **The environment was increasingly toxic**: as revealed not just in life-expectancy figures trending gently downwards again from the 1960s, but also in falling birth weights and other physical indicators. See Elizabeth Brainerd, 'Reassessing the Standard of Living in the Soviet Union: An Analysis Using Archival and Anthropometric Data', William Davidson Institute Working Paper no. 812 (January 2006). Available at SSRN: http://ssrn.com/abstract=906590.

327 **Time for *KVN, Klub veselykh i nakhodchivykh***: for the influence of humourous Soviet TV, see Graham, 'A Cultural Analysis of the Russo-Soviet *Anekdot*'.

327 **Brezhnev himself, for example, was very taken with denim jackets**: the story of the General Secretary's one-off jean jacket is in his tailor's memoir. See Aleksandr Igmand with Anastasia Yushkova, *Ya Odeval Brezhneva* ('I Dressed Brezhnev') (Moscow: NLO, 2008). I found it, however, in an English-language review of the book: Anna Malpas, 'Suits You, Ilyich', *Moscow Times*, 14 November 2008.

VI.1 The Unified System, 1970

329 **A cell. A lung cell:** the molecular biology of this chapter is accurate as
far as it goes, and I am assured that the dwindling probabilities of the
molecular events in it are at least of the right orders of magnitude. But
it should be remembered that the chapter only follows one possible
route by which one toxin in tobacco smoke can induce one variety
of lung cancer. There are many other routes, other toxins, and other
cancers, so a realistic path towards carcinogenesis would be much less
linear than the simple illustrative zoom I have selected here. It would
trace its way in massive parallel through a massively forking labyrinth of
probabilities. I drew heavily on – inhaled heavily from – Theodora R.
Devereux, Jack A. Taylor and J. Carl Barrett, 'Molecular Mechanisms
of Lung Cancer: Interaction of Environmental and Genetic Factors',
Chest 1996, 109; 14–19; and on Stephen S. Hecht, 'Tobacco carcinogens,
their biomarkers and tobacco-induced cancer', *Nature Reviews Cancer* 3,
October 2003, pp. 733–44. I am also indebted to Dr Claerwen James for
enlightenment via conversation and email.

330 **Lebedev has smoked sixty unfiltered Kazbek a day for fifty years:**
I'm making up the specific numbers, but he's known to have been a
persistently heavy smoker. See Malinovsky, *Pioneers of Soviet Computing*,
p. 26.

330 **Hero of Socialist Labour, Order of the Red Banner of Labour, two
Orders of Lenin:** Lebedev's authentic ironmongery. The Orders of
Lenin are the biggest deal. For the fringe benefits of the various Soviet
medals, see the Wikipedia entries for each.

330 **As the joke says, if a crocodile ate him:** authentic. See, again, Graham,
A Cultural Analysis of the Russo-Soviet Anekdot.

330 **'The Minister does know I'm waiting, doesn't he?' says Lebedev:** this
scene, up at the macro scale of the dark corridor in the Kremlin, is a
fantasia generated from the single true fact (for which see Malinovsky,
Pioneers of Soviet Computing, p. 26) that Lebedev did drag himself
to a meeting with Kosygin in 1970, when he had a 'life-threatening
pulmonary illness', to remonstrate about the decision in December
1969 to abandon independent Soviet computer design in favour of
trailing after IBM, years late; and Kosygin did refuse to see him. But in
life, the palming-off took the form of an unsatisfactory encounter with
one of Kosygin's deputies, not the complete stonewalling that happens
here, and no doubt it happened in bright daylight.

331 **And the ignorance is particularly bad in the Soviet Union:** for a
sense of what Soviet medicine did know, clinically, about cancer in the
mid-sixties, see the vivid descriptions of diagnosis and radiotherapy in
Aleksandr Solzhenitsyn's banned *Cancer Ward,* translated by Nicholas
Bethell and David Burg (London: Bodley Head, 1968).

337 **On 18 December last year Lebedev sat in a meeting at Minradioprom**:
Malinovsky has a partial transcript of the discussion at this crucial
meeting, which was complicated by political rivalries between different
bureaux which stood to lose or gain depending which way the decision
went, and by the fact that Lebedev and his allies' proposal to maintain
native Soviet design capability came with a secondary plan to co-
operate with ICL in Britain. See *Pioneers of Soviet Computing*, pp.
130–2. For the IBM-modelled 'Unified System' as it actually inched
into existence in the 1970s, late at every stage, see N. C. Davis and
S. E. Goodman, 'The Soviet Bloc's Unified System of Computers',
Computing Surveys vol. 10 no. 2 (June 1978), pp. 93–122.

338 **Brusentsov's trinary processor at the University of Moscow**: see
Malinovsky, *Pioneers of Soviet Computing*, pp. 134–8.

340 **Fluid build-up behind the lung obstruction eventually leads to
pneumonia and death**: despite the tone of clinical certainty here, I
do not know what kind of carcinoma Sergei Lebedev contracted, or
even for sure that his 'serious lung disease' *was* cancer, though it seems
overwhelmingly likely. But he did die of it, whatever it was, in July
1974; the fuzzy undesigned probabilistic machinery of his body did, in
one fashion or another, generate the deterministic process required to
shift him, conclusively, from 1 to 0.

VI.2 Police in the Forest, 1968

341 **Crave the use of telescopes, or gaze hungrily at the Computer Centre,
like some of Akademgorodok's children**: for whom the ingenious
Academician Lavrentiev, wanting to nurture future generations of
scientists, created the 'Club of Young Inventors'. There was also an
annual summer school at Akademgorodok to which teenagers from across
the USSR competed to come, to play mathematical games and have their
brains stretched by the great. See Josephson, *New Atlantis Revisited*.

341 **If today went as she expected it would**: in this chapter I've
telescoped together two adjacent but not simultaneous real events at
Akademgorodok, the disciplinary meetings called in the Institutes
to punish the forty-six signatories of the letter protesting the trial in
Moscow of the dissident Aleksandr Ginzburg (early April 1968) and the
Festival of Bards at which Sasha Galich gave the one and only public
performance in the USSR of his satirical songs (May 1968). Raissa
Berg, the real biologist in whose shoes the fictional Zoya Vaynshteyn
is standing, was indeed one of the signatories, did indeed get fired in
the same adroitly indirect manner as Zoya does, and did indeed have
difficulties with an unexpected informer among her family circle – but
Zoya's character, relationships and motives here are all invention.

342 **She flipped it over to look at the spine. *Roadside Picnic*. Well, well**:
another compression of the chronology. Arkady and Boris Strugatsky's

wonderful *Piknik na Obochine*, which Max is reading here, was in truth not published until 1972. The quotation is from the 1977 English translation by Antonina W. Bouis (London: Macmillan).

343 **Computer programmers went by on cross-country skis**: an ordinary method of Akademgorodok transportation, in winter. See Josephson, *New Atlantis Revisited*.

343 **Under the wretched centennial banner of Lenin blessing the children**: the hundredth anniversary of Lenin's birth in 1868, celebrated with outbreaks of unctuous Leninolatry in all artistic media. See Graham, 'A Cultural Analysis of the Russo-Soviet *Anekdot*', for the intriguing possibility that the security services may have deliberately seeded Soviet society in 1968 with several new tempting genres of *ankedoty*, in order to head off the possibility of a plague of Lenin jokes.

343 **The man who, they said, had tried to pose a problem to each of the candidates**: see Aganbegyan's memoir of Kantorovich in Kantorovich, Kutateladze and Fet, eds, *L. V. Kantorovich, Chelovek i Uchenii*.

344 **Cybernetics was not the meeting ground it used to be**: for the decline of cybernetic hopes, see Gerovitch, *From Newspeak to Cyberspeak*.

344 **Down he went into a heap**: as I was told in Akademgorodok, one of the legendary qualities of Kantorovich (alongside his fondness for dancing with tall women, and his wish to be driven everywhere by car if possible) was the ease with which he managed to have accidents.

344 **A good joke to lock the Jews out in the cold overnight**: for the depressing resumption of ordinary post-Stalin levels of anti-Semitism in what had been a relatively prejudice-free zone, see Josephson, *New Atlantis Revisited*. For the specific incident of the dormitory lockout, and the Jews/chickens sign, see Berg, *Acquired Traits*, p. 366.

345 **Nuclear fusion in the post office queue**: it was exactly this conversation, overheard in late 1962 while waiting for a stamp, which charmed the visiting sociologist Tatyana Zaslavskaia into moving to Akademgorodok. See Josephson, *New Atlantis Revisited*. The clampdown at Akademgorodok, beginning in 1965 but severely intensified after 1968, never quite eliminated the town's free-speaking ways, because it never eliminated the combustible and facinating mixture of people, but it removed the public venues for unguarded speech and restored something like a Soviet-normal degree of caution.

345 **The grants from the Fakel collective were entirely legal and above board**: Fakel, meaning 'torch', had been founded in June 1966 as a 'young people's scientific production association'. In effect, it was the nearest thing in Soviet history to a spun-out tech startup. By 1968, when it was indeed suppressed, it had fulfilled more than a hundred commissions for software and could call on the talents of eight hundred people, 250 of them undergraduates. See Josephson, *New Atlantis Revisited*.

346 **Under the Integral, the Cybernetics Kaffee-klatch, the lot:**
Akademgorodok had been remarkable for the profusion and freedom of
its social clubs, where you could find dancing, snacks, cards, improvised
art shows, and discussion, discussion, discussion. At the *Kofeinyi Klub
Kibernetiki* – jokily, the KKK – the rule was that anyone who spoke had
to address the listeners as 'respected non-empty set of thinking systems'.
But often there weren't any listeners, exactly. KKK meetings were
notorious for ending with everyone down at the front, all scribbling
excitably on the blackboard and trying to talk at once. See Josephson,
New Atlantis Revisited.

346 **'They say he's saving the steel-tube industry now, since they wouldn't
let him save the world?':** A sarcastic allusion to Kantorovich's important
role, throughout the second half of the 1960s, in a project to rationalise
production scheduling in the rolling mills controlled by Soyuzglavmetal,
'Union Metal Supply'. The team he led created the part of a vast
software ensemble that automated and optimised the traditional paper
files of *bronirovshchiki*, production schedulers. Kantorovich may well
have thought of the project as a very large-scale demonstration of the
viability of optimal planning. Needless to say, while the planners were
happy to let him use his shadow prices as an analytical tool for tuning
a mill's output, they declined to take up his larger scheme of using
them to automate and decentralise their own activities. It was claimed
that, by the second half of 1969, the optimised method was giving an
extra output of sixty thousand tonnes of steel tubes. Whatever the exact
truth, the irony remains that, in the 1970s, it was down Kantorovich's
optimised pipes that the oil flowed which Brezhnev's government used
as their free-money alternative to sorting out the economy. See Ellman,
Planning Problems in the USSR.

349 **Tick the boxes, write the numbers on the cyclostyled returns:** a
conjectural rendition, with invented details, of the real research project
pursued at Akademgorodok by Raissa Berg until she was fired for
signing the 1968 protest letter. The process of deduction here, from rates
of birth defect to concealed social history, is entirely authentic. See Berg,
Acquired Traits, pp. 356–9.

351 **'We have just one unpleasant item on the agenda today,' said the
Director:** much, but not quite all, of the dialogue that follows is a
greatly redacted and compressed version of real utterances recorded
by Raissa Berg from memory after her own equivalent hearing, and
triumphantly recorded in an appendix of her autobiography *Acquired
Traits*, pp. 453–68. I have selected to suppress a set of criss-cross
personality clashes too complex to convey, and to bring out the almost
universal exasperation with 'dissident' behaviour.

353 **They were filing one by one across the little stage in the hot box of
the House of Science's atrium:** in fact, the Festival of Bards was held in

the much larger auditorium of the House of Science, which held two thousand people, but I have moved it for the simple reason that, of the two, the atrium is the space I have seen and can describe. Even in the auditorium, the concert was as packed as I have represented it being here. And so many people were unable to get tickets at all, particularly among the students of Novosibirsk State University, which had a campus at Akademgorodok, that a deputation fetched Galich from the hotel at midnight and carried him off to play a complete second show at 2 a.m. in the eight-hundred-seater 'Moscow' cinema. Other performers at the first, official show included Volodyamir Vysotsky, Bulat Okudzhava and Iulii Kim. See Josephson, *New Atlantis Revisited*.

354 **'Who's this?' 'Film-music composer, I think'**: Zoya's ignorance of who Galich is, and her complete surprise at what he sings, are unrealistic here. Anyone with her sympathies and connections, even if they were wholly uninterested in music, would by 1968 have heard of his underground songs, which by now he had been composing – and singing to friends – for some years. Probably she would actually have listened to some of them. They circulated as *magnetizdat*, illicit tape recordings. So once again here, I have cheated for the sake of heightened drama, and in order to bring out more strongly the genuine shock and astonishment caused when Galich uttered *in public* thoughts that were only permissible in the most private of conversations. For Galich's *magnetizdat* reputation, and the impact of his performance on the Akademgorodok audience, see Berg, *Acquired Traits*, pp. 375–7; for the institutional consequences of the Festival of Bards, see Josephson, *New Atlantis Revisited*; for the consequences for Galich himself, including his expulsion from the Writers' Union, loss of all privileges and eventual exile from the USSR, see the biographical introduction to Galich, *Songs and Poems*.

354 **This is something called 'The Gold-Miner's Waltz'**: a real Galich song, with the translation by Gerald Stanton Smith slightly tweaked by the author for singability, but not one he is on record as performing that night. Instead he played 'Clouds', about an ex-prisoner of the Gulag getting drunk in a bar, 'The Ballad of Surplus Value', about a Soviet citizen who inherits a fortune, and 'Ode to Pasternak'. It was this last one that smashed all the taboos of appropriate speech and brought the house down gasping at Akademgorodok – but the 'Ode' is complicatedly allusive in its outrage, so I have substituted the more self-explanatory silence-breaking of 'The Gold-Miner's Waltz'. Besides, it has treasure islands in it.

354 **Just a basic strum-strum-strum, with his voice doing all the work over the top**: another calculated artificial naivety on Zoya's part, because this is pretty much what the whole Soviet genre of 'bard songs' sounds like. Think Jacques Brel.

357 **There was a bench by the wall at the end of the dacha's grounds**:
Khrushchev's retirement dacha had a bench, where he liked to sit with
his dog Arbat and his rook Kava, and it had a wall by a fieldpath,
where passing Soviet citizens in holiday mood did indeed shyly stop
and ask to have their photos taken with him. But the bench was not by
the wall. For the authentic melancholy of Khrushchev's last years, see
Taubman, *Khrushchev*, pp. 620–45, and Sergei Khrushchev, *Khrushchev
on Khrushchev*, pp. 165–332.

358 **Frol Kozlov . . . on his deathbed, calling for a priest**: recounted in
Burlatsky, *Khrushchev and the First Russian Spring*, p. 199.

359 **It was worst if he was stupid enough ever to watch a war film**:
Khrushchev's war movie-induced nightmares were described by
Sergei Khrushchev in 2008 in a lecture attended by the writer
Michael Swanwick. See Swanwick's blog entry on the event at http://
floggingbabel.blogspot.com/2008/02/khrushchev-isnt-he-russian-
novelist.html [*sic*].

359 **The giant television receiver in the living room**: presented on his
seventieth birthday, with many unctuous speeches, just before they
deposed him. See Taubman, *Khrushchev*, p. 614.

359 **Out would come the other memories**: which are my imaginings of
remembered horrors for him, not attested incidents. But when the
playwright Mikhail Shatrov asked him, late on in his retirement, what he
regretted, he said: 'Most of all the blood. My arms are up to the elbows in
blood.' See Taubman, *Khrushchev*, p. 639.

360 **'Paradise', he told the wheatfield in baffled fury**: not really said in
direct response to the Soviet invasion of Czechoslovakia in August 1968,
as here, but a real quotation from the tapes Khrushchev recorded in
retirement. This was among the passages held back from the transcribed
memoir his son had smuggled to the West for publication, with help
from sympathetic hands in the security service. So it's not in Nikita
Khrushchev, *Khrushchev Remembers* (Boston MA: Little Brown, 1970);
or in the first volume of supplementary material, *Khrushchev Remembers:
The Last Testament* (Boston MA: Little Brown, 1974). See instead
Nikita Khrushchev, *Khrushchev Remembers: The Glasnost Tapes*, ed. and
translated by Jerrold V. Schecter and Vyacheslav V. Luchkov (Boston
MA: Little Brown, 1990).

361 **Five hundred producers. Sixty thousand consumers. Eight hundred
thousand allocation orders**: figures from the account of the
Soyuzglavmetal project in Ellman, *Planning Problems in the USSR*.

Bibliography

Books

Abel Aganbegyan, *Challenge: The Economics of Perestroika*, translated by Michael Barratt Brown (London: I. B. Tauris, 1988)

—, *Moving the Mountain: Inside the Perestroika Revolution*, trans. Helen Szamuely (London: Bantam, 1989)

Aleksandr Afanas'ev [Afanaseyev], *Russian Fairy Tales*, translated by Norbert Guterman (New York: Pantheon, 1945)

Anne Applebaum, *Gulag: A History of the Soviet Camps* (New York: Random House, 2003)

Isaac Babel, *The Complete Works of Isaac Babel*, edited by Nathalie Babel, translated by Peter Constantine (New York: W. W. Norton, 2002)

Danzig Baldaev et al., *Russian Criminal Tattoo Encyclopedia* (Gottingen: Steidl, 2004)

Samuel H. Baron, *Bloody Saturday in the Soviet Union: Novocherkassk 1962* (Stanford CA: Stanford University Press, 2001)

Raymond A. Bauer, *Nine Soviet Portraits* (Boston: MIT Press, 1965)

Anthony Beevor and Luba Vinogradova, eds, *A Writer at War: Vasily Grossman with the Red Army 1941–1945* (London: Harvill, 2005)

Mark R. Beissinger, *Scientific Management, Socialist Discipline and Soviet Power* (Cambridge MA: Harvard University Press, 1988)

Raissa L. Berg, *Acquired Traits: Memoirs of a Geneticist from the Soviet Union*, trans. David Lowe (New York: Viking Penguin, 1988)

Abram Bergson and Simon Kuznets, eds, *Economic Trends in the Soviet Union* (Cambridge MA: Harvard University Press, 1963)

Abram Bergson, *Economics of Soviet Planning* (New Haven CT: Yale University Press, 1964)

—, *Planning and Productivity Under Soviet Socialism* (New York: Columbia University Press, 1968)

Isaiah Berlin, *Russian Thinkers*, ed. Henry Hardy and Aileen Kelly (London: Hogarth Press, 1978)

Joseph Berliner, *Factory and Manager in the USSR* (Cambridge MA: Harvard University Press, 1957)

—, *The Innovation Decision in Soviet Industry* (Boston: MIT Press, 1976)

—, *Soviet Industry from Stalin to Gorbachev: Essays on Management and Innovation* (Ithaca NY: Cornell University Press, 1988)

Fedor Burlatsky, *Khrushchev and the First Russian Spring*, translated by Daphne Skillen (London: Weidenfeld & Nicolson, 1991)

Peter Carlson, *K Blows Top: A Cold War Comic Interlude Starring Nikita Khrushchev, America's Most Unlikely Tourist* (New York: Public Affairs, 2009)

Manuel Castells and Peter Hall, *Technopoles of the World: The Making of 21st Century Industrial Complexes* (London: Routledge, 1994)

Manuel Castells and E. Kiselyova, *The Collapse of the Soviet Union: The View from the Information Society* (Berkeley CA: University of California Press, 1995)

Manuel Castells, *The Information Age: Volume III: End of Millennium* (Oxford: Blackwell, 1998)

Martin Cave, *Computers and Economic Planning: The Soviet Experience* (Cambridge: CUP, 1980)

Janet G. Chapman, *Real Wages in Soviet Russia Since 1928*, RAND Corporation report R-371-PR (Santa Monica CA, October 1963)

Anton Chekhov, *The Lady with the Little Dog and Other Stories, 1896–1904*, translated by Ronald Wilks (London: Penguin, 2004)

L. G. Churchward, *The Soviet Intelligentsia: An Essay on the Social Structure and Roles of Soviet Intellectuals During the 1960s* (London: RKP, 1973)

Robert Conquest, *Harvest of Sorrow: Soviet Collectivisation and the Terror-Famine* (London: Pimlico, 2002)

Fyodor Dostoevsky, *The Gambler*, translated by Hugh Aplin (London: Hesperus Press, 2006)

Vera S. Dunham, *In Stalin's Time: Middleclass Values in Soviet Fiction* (Cambridge: CUP, 1976)

Ilya Ehrenburg, *Ottepel* (1954), translated by Manya Harari as *The Thaw* (Chicago: Regnery, 1955)

Katherine Bliss Eaton, *Daily Life in the Soviet Union* (Westport CT: Greenwood Publishing Group, 2004)

Michael Ellman, *Soviet Planning Today: Proposals for an Optimally Functioning Economic System* (Cambridge: CUP, 1971)

—, *Planning Problems in the USSR: The Contribution of Mathematical Economics to Their Solution 1960–1971* (Cambridge: CUP, 1973)

—, 'Seven Theses on Kosyginism', in *Collectivism, Convergence and Capitalism* (London: Harcourt Brace, 1984)

Michael Ellman and Volodyamir Kontorovich, eds, *The Destruction of the Soviet Economic System: An Insiders' History* (Armonk NY: M. E. Sharpe, 1998)

Robert English, *Russia and the Idea of the West: Gorbachev, Intellectuals, and the End of the Cold War* (New York: Columbia University Press, 2000)

A. P. Ershov, *The British Lectures* (Heyden: The British Computer Society, 1980)

Orlando Figes, *Natasha's Dance: A Cultural History of Russia* (London: Allen Lane, 2002)

—, *The Whisperers: Private Lives in Stalin's Russia* (London: Allen Lane, 2007)

Sheila Fitzpatrick, *Tear Off the Masks! Identity and Imposture in Twentieth-Century Russia* (Princeton NJ: Princeton University Press, 2005)

—, *Everyday Stalinism: Ordinary Life in Extraordinary Times* (OUP, Oxford 2000)

—, *Education and Social Mobility in the USSR 1921–1934* (Cambridge: CUP, 1979)

Robert Freedman, ed., *Marx on Economics* (New York: Harcourt Brace, 1961; Harmondsworth: Pelican, 1962)

Alexander Galich, *Songs and Poems*, ed. and trans. Gerald Stanton Smith (Ann Arbor MI: Ardis, 1983); see especially the biographical introduction, 'Silence is Connivance: Alexander Galich', pp. 13–54

—, *Dress Rehearsal: A Story in Four Acts and Five Chapters*, translated by Maria R Bloshteyn (Bloomington IN: Slavica, 2007)

Saul I. Gass, *Linear Programming: Methods and Applications* (New York: McGraw-Hill, 4th edn, 1975)

James von Geldern and Richard Stites, eds, *Mass Culture in Soviet Russia. Tales, Poems, Songs, Movies, Plays and Folklore 1917–1953* (Bloomington IN: Slavica, 1995)

Slava Gerovitch, *From Newspeak to Cyberspeak: A History of Soviet Cybernetics* (Boston: MIT Press, 2002)

Nikolai Gogol, *Dead Souls*, translated by Richard Pevear and Larissa Volokhonsky (New York: Pantheon Books, 1996)

Loren R. Graham, *Science and Philosophy in the Soviet Union* (New York: Alfred A. Knopf, 1972)

Seth Benedict Graham, *A Cultural Analysis of the Russo-Soviet Anekdot*, PhD thesis, University of Pittsburgh 2003

Paul R. Gregory and Robert C. Stuart, *Russian and Soviet Economic Performance and Structure*, 6th edn (Reading MA: Addison-Wesley, 1998)

Jukka Gronow, *Caviar with Champagne: Common Luxury and the Ideals of the Good Life in Stalin's Russia* (Oxford: Berg, 2003)

Gregory Grossman, ed., *Value and Plan: Economic Calculation and Organization in Eastern Europe* (Berkeley CA: University of California Press, 1960)

Vasily Grossman, *Life and Fate*, translated by Robert Chandler (London: Harvill, 1995)

—, *Forever Flowing*, translated by Thomas P. Whitney (New York: Harper & Row, 1972)

P. Charles Hachten, 'Property Relations and the Economic Organization of Soviet Russia, 1941 to 1948: Volume One', PhD thesis, University of Chicago 2005

Mike Hally, *Electronic Brains: Stories from the Dawn of the Computer Age* (London: Granta, 2005)

John Pearce Hardt, ed., *Mathematics and Computers in Soviet Economic Planning* (New Haven CT: Yale University Press, 1967)

Robert L. Heilbroner, *The Worldly Philosophers: The Lives, Times and Ideas of the Great Economic Thinkers*, 4th edn (New York: Simon & Schuster, 1971)

Jochen Hellbeck, *Revolution on My Mind: Writing a Diary Under Stalin* (Cambridge MA: Harvard University Press, 2006)

Fiona Hill and Clifford Gaddy, *The Siberian Curse: How Communist Planners Left Russia Out in the Cold* (Washington DC: Brookings Institution Press, 2003)

Walter Hixson, *Parting the Curtain: Propaganda, Culture, and the Cold War, 1945–1961* (New York: St Martin's Press, 1997)

Geoffrey M. Hodgson, *Economics and Utopia: Why the learning economy is not the end of history* (London: Routledge, 1999)

Mark Holborn and Torsten Nystrom, eds, *Propaganda: Photographs From Soviet Archives* (Chichester: Bonnier Books, 2007)

Franklyn D. Holzman, ed., *Readings on the Soviet Economy* (Chicago: Rand-McNally, 1962)

Yvonne Howell, *Apocalyptic Realism: The Science Fiction of Arkady and Boris Strugatsky* (New York, 1994)

Aleksandr Igmand with Anastasia Yushkova, *Ya Odeval Brezhneva* ('I Dressed Brezhnev') (Moscow: NLO, 2008)

Ilya Ilf and Yevgeny Petrov, *The Twelve Chairs*, translated by John H. C. Richardson (Evanston IL: Northwestern University Press, 1997)

—, *Odenoetazhnaya Amerika* ('One-Storey America'), Moscow, 1937; *In Little Golden America*, translated by Charles Malamuth (New York: Farrar & Rinehart, 1937)

Paul R. Josephson, *New Atlantis Revisited: Akademgorodok, the Siberian City of Science* (Princeton NJ: Princeton University Press, 1997)

Tony Judt, *Postwar: A History of Europe Since 1945* (London: William Heinemann, 2005)

Daniel Kalder, *Lost Cosmonaut: Travels to the Republics That Tourism Forgot* (London: Faber, 2006)

L. V. Kantorovich, *The Best Use of Economic Resources*, translated by P. F. Knightsfield (Oxford: Pergamon Press, 1965)

—, 1975 Nobel Prize autobiography, in Assar Lindbeck, ed., *Nobel Lectures, Economics 1969–1980* (Singapore: World Scientific Publishing Co., 1992)

V. L. Kantorovich, S. S. Kutateladze and Ya. I. Fet, eds, *Leonid Vitalevich Kantorovich: Chelovek i Uchenii* ('Man and Scientist') (Novosibirsk: Siberian Branch of the Russian Academy of Sciences, vol. 1 2002, vol. 2 2004)

Simon Kassel, *Soviet Cybernetics Research: A Preliminary Study of Organisations and Personalities*, RAND Corporation report R-909-ARPA (Santa Monica CA, December 1971)

Volodyamir Katkoff, *Soviet Economy 1940–1965* (Baltimore MD: Dangary, 1961)

Aron Katsenelinboigen, *Soviet Economic Thought and Political Power in the USSR* (New York: Pergamon, 1980)

G. I. Khanin, *Sovetskii ekonomicheskii rost: analiz zapadnykh otsenok* ('Soviet economic growth: an analysis of western evaluations') (Novosibirsk: EKOR, 1993)

Catriona Kelly, *Refining Russia: Advice Literature, Polite Culture and Gender from Catherine to Yeltsin* (Oxford: OUP, 2001)

Nikita Khrushchev, *Khrushchev Remembers* (Little Brown, Boston 1970)

—, *Khrushchev Remembers: The Last Testament*, trans. and ed. Strobe Talbott (Little Brown, Boston 1974)

—, *Khrushchev Remembers: The Glasnost Tapes*, trans. and ed. Jerrold V. Schecter and Vyacheslav V. Luchkov (Little Brown, Boston 1990)

Sergei Khrushchev, *Khrushchev on Khrushchev: An Inside Account of the Man and His Era*, trans. and ed. William Taubman (Boston MA: Little Brown, 1990)

Khrushchev in America: Full Texts of the Speeches Made by N. S. Khrushchev on His Tour of the United States, September 15–27, 1959 (New York: Crosscurrents Press, 1960)

Danilo Kis, 'The Magic Card Dealing' (story) in *A Tomb for Boris Davidovich*, translated anonymously from the Serbian (New York: Harcourt Brace Jovanovich, 1978)

Leszek Kolakowski, *Main Currents of Marxism: The Founders, the Golden Age, the Breakdown*, translated from the Polish by P. S. Falla (London: OUP, 1978); one-volume edition (New York: W. W. Norton, 2005)

Janos Kornai, *Anti-Equilibrium* (Amsterdam, 1971)

—, *Economics of Shortage*, volume A (Amsterdam/Oxford/New York, 1980)

—, 'Preface to Second Hungarian Edition' in *Overcentralization in Economic Administration: A Critical Analysis Based on Experience in Hungarian Light Industry* (OUP, 1994), pp. xii–xxv

Stephen Kotkin, *Steeltown, USSR: Soviet Society in the Gorbachev Era* (Berkeley CA: University of California Press, 1991)

—, *Magnetic Mountain: Stalinism as a Civilization* (University of California Press, 1995)

—, *Armageddon Averted: The Soviet Collapse, 1970–2000* (Oxford: OUP, 2001)

Maria Kravchenko, *The World of the Russian Fairy Tale* (Berne, 1987)

lena Ledeneva, *Russia's Economy of Favours: Blat, Networking and Informal Exchange* (Cambridge: CUP, 1998)

Wassily Leontief, *Essays in Economics: Theories and Theorizing* (New York: OUP, 1966)

V. I. Lenin, *The State and Revolution*, in *Selected Works* vol. 2 (Moscow: Progress Publishers, 1970)

Let Us Live in Peace and Friendship: The Visit of N. S. Khrushchov [sic] *to the USA, Sept 15–27, 1959* (Moscow: Foreign Languages Publishing House, 1959)

Moshe Lewin, *Political Undercurrents in Soviet Economic Debates: From Bukharin to the Modern Reformers* (Princeton NJ: Princeton University Press, 1974)

—, *The Soviet Century* (London: Verso, 2005)

R. B. McKean, *St Petersburg Between the Revolutions: Workers and Revolutionaries* (New Haven CT: Yale University Press, 1990)

Ken Macleod, *The Cassini Division* (London: Legend, 1998)

Janet Malcolm, *Reading Chekhov: A Critical Journey* (New York: Random House, 2001)

Boris Nikolaevich Malinovsky, *Pioneers of Soviet Computing*, ed. Anne Fitzpatrick, trans. Emmanuel Aronie. Available at www.sovietcomputing.com

Terry Dean Martin, *The Affirmative Action Empire: Nations and Nationalism in the Soviet Union, 1923–1939* (Ithaca NY: Cornell University Press, 2001)

Frank J. Miller, *Folklore for Stalin: Russian Folklore and Pseudo-folklore of the Stalin Era* (Armonk: M. E. Sharpe, Inc., 1990)

Philip Mirowski, *Machine Dreams: Economics Becomes a Cyborg Science* (Cambridge: CUP, 2002)

Ludwig von Mises, *Socialism*, 1922; trans. from the German by J. Kahane (Indianapolis: Liberty Fund, 1981)

Nikolai Nekrasov ('Nicholas Nekrassov'), *Who Can Be Happy and Free in Russia?*, trans. Juliet M Soskice (London, 1917)

V. S. Nemchinov, ed., *The Use of Mathematics in Economics*, ed. in English by Alec Nove (Edinburgh: Oliver & Boyd, 1964)

Alec Nove, *The Soviet Economic System*, 3rd edn (London: Allen & Unwin, 1986)

—, *Economic History of the USSR*, 1917–1991, final edition (London, 1992)

V. V. Novozhilov, *Problems of Cost-Benefit Analysis in Optimal Planning*, trans. H. McQuiston (White Plains NY, 1970)

Marshall T. Poe, *The Russian Moment in World History* (Princeton NJ: Princeton University Press, 2003)

Karl Polanyi, *The Great Transformation: The Political and Economic Origins of Our Time* (Boston MA: Beacon Press, 2001)

I. A. Poletaev, *Signal* (Moscow: Sovetskoe radio, 1958)

Karl Popper, *The Open Society and Its Enemies* (London, 1945)

D. A. Pospelov & Ya. Fet, *Essays on the History of Computer Science in Russia* (Novosibirsk: Scientific Publication Centre of the RAS, 1998)

Paul Craig Roberts, *Alienation and the Soviet Economy* (Albuquerque: University of New Mexico Press, 2002)

Kim Stanley Robinson, *The Gold Coast* (New York: Tor, 1988)

Mark Robson and William Toscano, *Risk Assessment for Environmental Health* (San Francisco: Wiley, 2007); pp. 69–77, 'Carcinogenesis'

Eli Rubin, *Synthetic Socialism: Plastics and Dictatorship in the German Democratic Republic* (Chapel Hill NC: University of North Carolina Press, 2009)

Leonard Schapiro, ed., *The USSR and the Future: An Analysis of the New Program of the CPSU* (New York: Institute for the Study of the USSR/ Frederick A. Praeger Inc, 1963)

Theodore Shabad, *Basic Industrial Resources of the USSR* (New York: Columbia University Press, 1969)

Harry G. Shaffer, ed., *The Soviet Economy: A Collection of Western and Soviet Views* (New York: Appleton-Century-Crofts, 1963)

Teodor Shanin, ed., *Late Marx and the Russian Road: Marx and 'the peripheries of capitalism'* (London: Routledge and Kegan Paul, 1983)

Myron E. Sharpe, ed., *Planning, Profit and Incentives in the USSR* (New York: International Arts & Sciences Press, 1966)

Alex Simirenko, ed., *Soviet Sociology* (London: RKP, 1967)

Yuri Slezkine, *The Jewish Century* (Princeton NJ: Princeton University Press, 2004)

Hedrick Smith, *The Russians* (London, 1976)

R. E. F. Smith, ed., *A Russian-English Social Science Dictionary*, revised and enlarged edition (Birmingham: Institute for Advanced Research in the Humanities, 1990)

Aleksandr Solzhenitsyn, *Cancer Ward*, translated by Nicholas Bethell and David Burg (London: Bodley Head, 1968)

—, *Matryona's House and Other Stories*, translated by Michael Glenny (London: Penguin, 1975)

—, *The Gulag Archipelago 2, 1918–1956, Parts III–IV*, translated by Thomas P. Whitney (London: Collins/Harvill, 1975), pp. 410–30 [thieves]; *The Gulag Archipelago 3, 1918–1956, An Experiment in Literary Investigation V–VII*, translated by H. T. Willetts (London: Collins/Harvill, 1978), pp. 506–14 [Novocherkassk]

J. V. Stalin, *Economic Problems of Socialism in the USSR*, English edition (Moscow: Foreign Languages Publishing House, 1952)

Frederick S. Starr, *Red and Hot: The Fate of Jazz in the Soviet Union, 1917–1980* (New York: OUP, 1983)

Joseph E. Stiglitz, *Whither Socialism?* (Cambridge MA: MIT Press, 1994)

Arkady and Boris Strugatsky, *Hard to be a God*, translated by Wendayne Ackerman (New York: DAW, 1974); *Trudno Byt Bogom* (1964)

—, *Monday Begins on Saturday*, translated by Leonid Renen (New York: DAW, 1977); as *Monday Starts on Saturday*, translated by Andrew Bromfield (London: Seagull Publishing, 2005); *Ponedelnik nachinaetsya v subbotu* (1966)

—, *Roadside Picnic*, translated by Antonina W. Bouis (London: Macmillan, 1977); *Piknik na Obochine* (1972)

Pekka Sutela, *Economics and Economic Reform in the Soviet Union* (Cambridge: CUP, 1991)

Michel Tatu, *Power in the Kremlin: From Khrushchev's Decline to Collective Leadership*, trans. from the French by Helen Katel (London: Collins, 1969)

William Taubman, *Khrushchev: The Man and His Era* (New York: W. W. Norton, 2003)

Charles Taylor, *A Secular Age* (Cambridge MA: Belknap Press of Harvard University Press, 2007)

T. L. Thompson and R. Sheldon, eds, *Soviet Society and Culture: Essays in*

Honour of Vera S. Dunham (Boulder CO: Westview Press, 1988)

Colin Thubron, *In Siberia* (London: Chatto and Windus, 1999)

Gary John Tocchet, *September Thaw: Khrushchev's Visit to America, 1959*, PhD thesis, Stanford 1995

Liz Williams, *Nine Layers of Sky* (New York: Bantam Spectra, 2003)

Andrew Wilson, *Virtual Politics: Faking Democracy in the Post-Soviet World* (New Haven CT: Yale University Press, 2005)

Edmund Wilson, *To the Finland Station: A Study in the Writing and Acting of History* (New York, 1940)

Jack Womack, *Let's Put the Future Behind Us* (New York: Atlantic Monthly Press, 1996)

Alan Woods, *Bolshevism – The Road to Revolution: A History of the Bolshevik Party* (London: Well Red, 1999)

World Health Organisation, *International Programme on Chemical Safety: Environmental Health Criteria 10: Carbon Disulfide* (Geneva, 1979)

I. Velvovsky, K. Platonov, V. Ploticher and E. Shugom, *Painless Childbirth Through Psychoprophylaxis: Lectures for Obstetricians*, trans. David A. Myshne (Foreign Languages Publishing House, Moscow 1960)

E. Zaleski, *Planning Reforms in the USSR 1962–66* (Chapel Hill NC: University of North Carolina Press, 1967)

A. Zauberman, *The Mathematical Revolution in Soviet Economics* (London: Royal Institute of International Affairs/OUP, 1975)

Aleksandr Zinoviev, *The Yawning Heights*, translated by Gordon Clough (New York: Random House, 1978)

Articles

I. Anchishkin, 'The Problem of Abundance and the Transition to Communist Distribution', in Harry G. Shaffer, ed., *The Soviet Economy: A Collection of Western and Soviet Views* (New York: Appleton-Century-Crofts, 1963), pp. 133–8; originally published in *Voprosy Ekonomiki* no. 1, 1962

Djurdja Bartlett, 'The Authentic Soviet Glamour of Stalinist High Fashion', *Revista de Occidente* no. 317, November 2007

— 'Let Them Wear Beige: The Petit-Bourgeois World of Official Socialist Dress', *Fashion Theory* vol. 8 issue 2, pp. 127–64

V. Bel'chuk, 'On the Relationship Between Demand and Supply of Consumer Goods During the Period of Communist Construction', *Problems of Economics* (translated digest of articles from Soviet economic journals, International Arts & Sciences Press, NY) vol. 7 no. 3 (July 1964), pp. 3–13; originally in *Nauchnye doklady vysshei shkoly, ekonomicheskie nauki* no. 5, 1963

John D. Bell, 'Giving Birth to the New Soviet Man: Politics and Obstetrics in the USSR', *Slavic Review* vol. 40 no. 1 (Spring 1981), pp. 1–16

Bibliography

Joseph Berliner, 'Informal Organization of the Soviet Firm', *Quarterly Journal of Economics*, August 1952, pp. 342–65
—, 'Economic Reform in the USSR' in John W. Strong, ed., *The Soviet Union Under Brezhnev and Kosygin* (New York: Van Nostrand Reinhold, 1971), pp. 50–60
A Boyarskii, 'On the Application of Mathematics in Economics', *Problems of Economics* (International Arts & Sciences Press, NY) vol. 4 no. 9 (January 1962), pp. 12–24; originally in *Voprosy Ekonomiki* no. 2, 1961
Elizabeth Brainerd, 'Reassessing the Standard of Living in the Soviet Union: An Analysis Using Archival and Anthropometric Data', William Davidson Institute Working Paper no. 812 (January 2006). Available at SSRN: http://ssrn.com/abstract=906590
Stephen Broadberry and Sayantan Ghosal, 'Technology, organisation and productivity performance in services: lessons from Britain and the United States since 1870', *Structural Change and Economic Dynamics* vol. 16 issue 4 (December 2005), pp. 437–66
R. Campbell, 'Marx, Kantorovich and Novozhilov: *Stoimost'* versus Reality', *Slavic Review* 40 (October 1961), pp. 402–18
W. Paul Cockshott and Allin F. Cottrell, 'Socialist Planning After the Collapse of the Soviet Union', *Revue européene des sciences sociales* vol. 31 no. 96 (1993), pp. 167–85
—, 'Calculation, Complexity and Planning: The Socialist Calculation Debate Once Again', *Review of Political Economy* vol. 5 no. 1 (July 1993), pp. 73–112
—, 'Information and Economics: A Critique of Hayek', *Research in Political Economy* vol. 16 (1997), pp. 177–202
Beatriz Colomina, 'Information obsession: the Eameses' multiscreen architecture', *The Journal of Architecture* vol. 6 (Autumn 2001), pp. 205–23
'Star City', *Colors* 45 (August–September 2001)
N. C. Davis and S. E. Goodman, 'The Soviet Bloc's Unified System of Computers', *Computing Surveys* vol. 10 no. 2 (June 1978), pp. 93–122
Theodora R. Devereux, Jack A. Taylor and J. Carl Barrett, 'Molecular Mechanisms of Lung Cancer: Interaction of Environmental and Genetic Factors', *Chest* 1996; 109; 14–19
G. Dikhtiar, 'Soviet Trade in the Period of the Full-Scale Building of Communism', *Problems of Economics* (International Arts & Sciences Press, NY) vol. 5 no. 4 (August 1962), pp. 45–52; originally in *Kommunist* no. 7, 1962
Craig D'Ooge, '"Kazam!" Major Exhibition of the Work of American Designers Charles and Ray Eames Opens', *Library of Congress Information Bulletin*, May 1999
Michael Ellman and Volodyamir Kontorovich, 'The Collapse of the Soviet System and the Memoir Literature', *Europe–Asia Studies* vol. 49 no. 2 (1997), pp. 259–79
Edith Rogovin Frankel, 'Literary Policy in Stalin's Last Year', *Soviet Studies* vol. 28 no. 3 (July 1976), pp. 391–405

J. K. Galbraith, 'The Day Khrushchev Visited the Establishment', *Harper's Magazine* vol. 242 no. 1,449 (February 1971), pp. 72–5

Rachel Goff, 'The Role of Traditional Russian Folklore in Soviet Propaganda', *Perspectives: Student Journal of Germanic and Slavic Studies* (Brigham Young University) vol. 12 (Winter 2004). Available at: http://germslav.byu.edu/perspectives/w2004contents.html

David Granick, 'An Organizational Model of Soviet Industrial Planning' in Franklyn Z. Holzman, ed., *Readings on the Soviet Economy* (Chicago: Rand McNally, 1962)

Gregory Grossman, 'Innovation and Information in the Soviet Economy', *American Economic Review* vol. 16 no. 2 (May 1966), pp. 121–2

Mark Harrison, 'Soviet economic growth since 1928: The alternative statistics of G. I. Khanin', *Europe–Asia Studies* vol. 45 no. 1 (1993), pp. 141–67

—, 'Coercion, compliance and the collapse of the Soviet command economy', *Economic History Review* vol. 55 no. 3 (2002), pp. 397–433

—, 'Post-war Russian Economic Growth: Not a Riddle', *Europe–Asia Studies* vol. 55 no. 8 (2003), pp. 1323–9

F. A. Hayek, 'The Use of Knowledge in Society', *The American Economic Review* vol. 35 issue 4 (September 1945), pp. 519–30

Stephen S. Hecht, 'Tobacco carcinogens, their biomarkers and tobacco-induced cancer', *Nature Reviews Cancer* 3 (October 2003), pp. 733–44

Oleg Hoeffding, 'The Soviet Industrial Reorganization of 1957', in Franklyn D. Holzman, ed., *Readings on the Soviet Economy* (Chicago: Rand-McNally, 1962)

Franklyn D. Holzman, 'The Soviet Bond Hoax', *Problems of Communism* 6 no. 5 (1957), pp. 47–9

R. Judy, 'The Economists', in G. Skilling and F. Griffith, eds, *Interest Groups in Soviet Politics* (Princeton NJ: Princeton University Press, 1971)

Olga Karpushina, 'At the Intersection of Genres: Galich's Generic Montage', in *Studies in Slavic Cultures IV: Bakhtin* (Slavic Department, University of Pittsburgh, September 2003). Available at: www.pitt.edu/~slavic/sisc/SISC4/index.html

A. Kats, 'Concerning a Fallacious Concept of Economic Calculation', *Problems of Economics* (International Arts & Sciences Press, NY) vol. 3 no. 7 (November 1960), pp. 42–52; originally published in *Voprosy Ekonomiki* no. 5, 1960

Aron Katsenelinboigen, 'Application of Mathematical Methods in Economic Research', *Problems of Economics* (International Arts & Sciences Press, NY) vol. 5 no. 1 (May 1962), pp. 26–32; originally in *Vestnik Akademii Nauk SSSR* no. 9, 1961

G. I. Khanin, '1950s – The Triumph of the Soviet Economy', *Europe–Asia Studies* vol. 55 no. 8 (December 2003), pp. 1,187–1,212

A. Komin, 'Economic Substantiation of Purchase Prices of Agricultural

Products', *Problems of Economics* (translated digest of articles from Soviet economic journals, International Arts & Sciences Press, NY) vol. 5 no. 9 (January 1963), pp. 29–36; originally in *Planovoe Khosyaistvo* no. 7, 1962

V. Kossov, Yu. Finkelstein and A. Modin, 'Mathematical Methods and Electronic Computers in Economics and Planning' [report of Novosibirsk conferences, October and December 1962], *Problems of Economics* (International Arts & Sciences Press, NY) vol. 6 no. 7 (November 1963); originally in *Planovoe Khozyaistvo* no. 2, 1963

A. N. Kosygin, 'On Improving Industrial Management, Perfecting Planning, and Enhancing Economic Incentives in Industrial Production', *Problems of Economics* (International Arts & Sciences Press, NY) vol. 8 no. 6 (October 1965), pp. 3–28; originally in *Izvestiya*, 28 September 1965

N. I. Kovalev, 'Problems in Introducing Mathematics and Electronic Computers in Planning', *Problems of Economics* (International Arts & Sciences Press, NY) vol. 5 no. 4 (August 1962), pp. 53–61; originally in *Planovoe Khozyaistvo* no. 8 (1961) and *Voprosy Ekonomiki* no. 12 (1961)

—, 'Scientific Planning and a Rational System of Economic Information', *Problems of Economics* (International Arts & Sciences Press, NY) vol. 6 no. 7 (November 1963), pp. 3–17; originally in *Voprosy Ekonomiki* no. 12, 1962

Paul Krugman, 'The Myth of Asia's Miracle: A Cautionary Fable', *Foreign Affairs* vol. 73 no. 6 (November/December 1994), pp. 62–78

S. S. Kutateladze, 'The Path and Space of Kantorovich', talk at the international Kantorovich memorial conference, Euler International Mathematical Institute, St Petersburg, 8–13 January 2004

Yevgeny Kuznetsov, 'Learning in Networks: Enterprise Behaviour in the Former Soviet Union and Contemporary Russia', in Joan M. Nelson, Charles Tilley and Lee Walker, eds, *Transforming Post-Communist Political Economies* (Washington DC: National Academy Press, 1997)

Oskar Lange, 'The Computer and the Market' in C. Feinstein, ed., *Capitalism, Socialism and Economic Growth: Essays Presented to Maurice Dobb* (Cambridge: CUP, 1967), pp. 158–61

Elizabeth Lee, 'Health Care in the Soviet Union. Two. Childbirth – Soviet Style', *Nursing Times* (1984) 1–7 February; 80 (5): 44–5

Herbert S. Levine, 'The Centralized Planning of Supply in Soviet Industry', in Franklyn Z. Holzman, ed., *Readings on the Soviet Economy* (Chicago, 1962)

E. G. Liberman, 'Planning Production and Standards of Long-Term Operation', *Problems of Economics* (International Arts & Sciences Press, NY) vol. 5 no. 8 (December 1962), pp. 16–22; originally in *Voprosy Ekonomiki* no. 8 (1962)

—, 'Are We Flirting With Capitalism? Profits and "Profits"', *Problems of Economics* (International Arts & Sciences Press, NY) vol. 8 no. 4 (August 1965), pp. 36–41; originally in *Soviet Life*, July 1965

Angus Maddison, 'Measuring the Performance of a Communist Command

Economy: An Assessment of the CIA Estimates for the USSR', *Review of Income and Wealth* vol. 44 no. 3 (September 1998), pp. 307–23

Anna Malpas, 'Style for Socialists', *Moscow Times*, 27 April 2007

—, 'Suits You, Ilyich', *Moscow Times*, 14 November 2008

John McClure and Michael Urban, 'The Folklore of State Socialism', *Soviet Studies* vol. 35 no. 4 (1983), pp. 471–86

James R. Miller, 'History and Analysis of Soviet Domestic Bond Policy', *Soviet Studies* 27, no. 4 (1975), p. 601

P Mstislavskii, 'Quantitative Expression of Economic Relationships', *Problems of Economics* (International Arts & Sciences Press, NY) vol. 4 no. 9 (January 1962), pp. 3–12; originally in *Voprosy Ekonomiki* no. 2 (1961)

V. S. Nemchinov, 'Value and Price Under Socialism', *Problems of Economics* (International Arts & Sciences Press, NY) vol. 4 no. 3 (July 1961), pp. 3–17; originally in *Voprosy Ekonomiki* no. 12 (1960)

V. V. Novozhilov, 'On Choosing Between Investment Projects', translated by B. Ward, *International Economic Papers* 6 (1956), pp. 66–87

—, 'Calculation of Outlays in a Socialist Economy', *Problems of Economics* (International Arts & Sciences Press, NY) vol. 4 no. 8 (December 1961), pp. 18–28; originally in *Voprosy Ekonomiki* no. 2 (1961)

Felix J. Oinas, 'Folklore and Politics in the Soviet Union', *Slavic Review* 32 (1973), pp. 45–58

Peter Osnos, 'Childbirth, Soviet Style: A Labor in Keeping With the Party Line', *Washington Post*, 28 November 1976, pp. G13–G14

Alex Soojung-Kim Pang, 'Dome Days: Buckminster Fuller in the Cold War' in Jenny Uglow and Francis Spufford, eds, *Cultural Babbage: Technology, Time and Invention* (London: Faber and Faber, 1996), pp. 167–92

Vsevolod Pugachev, 'Voprosy optimal'nogo planirovaniia narodnogo khoziaistva s pomoshch'iu edinoi gosudarstvennoi seti vychistel'nykh tsentrov', *Voprosy Ekonomiki* no. 7 (1964), pp. 93–103

Andrew Roberts, 'Moscow Mule', *The Independent* Motoring Section, 11 October 2005, p. 7

Paul Craig Roberts, 'My Time with Soviet Economics', *The Independent Review* vol. 7 no. 2 (Fall 2002), pp. 259–64

Gertrude E. Schroeder, 'Soviet Economic Reform at an Impasse', *Problems of Communism* vol. 20 no. 4 (July–August 1971), pp. 36–46

—, 'The "Reform" of the Supply System in Soviet Industry', *Soviet Studies* vol. 24 no. 1 (July 1972), pp. 97–119

Piotr Siuda, 'The Novocherkassk Tragedy, June 1–3 1962', *Russian Labour Review* 2, 1993

Jessica Smith, 'Siberian Science City', *New World Review*, third quarter 1969, pp. 86–101

V. Sokolov, M. Nazarov and N. Kozlov, 'The Firm and the Customer', *Problems of Economics* (International Arts & Sciences Press, NY) vol. 8 no. 4 (August 1965), pp. 3–14; originally in *Ekonomicheskaya Gazeta*, 6 January 1965

Charles N. Steele, 'The Soviet Experiment: Lessons for Development' in Julian Morris, ed., *Sustainable Development: Promoting Progress or Perpetuating Poverty* (Profile Books, London 2002)

S. Stoliarov and Z. Smirnova, 'Analysis of Price Structure', *Problems of Economics* (International Arts & Sciences Press, NY) vol. 6 no. 9 (January 1964), pp. 11–21; originally in *Vestnik Statistiki* no. 1, 1963

Dora Sturman, 'Chernenko and Andropov: Ideological Perspectives', *Survey* 1 (1984), pp. 1–21

V. G. Tremi, 'The Politics of Libermanism', *Soviet Studies* 19 (1968), pp. 567–72

Unsigned article, 'Economics and Politics', *Problems of Economics* (International Arts & Sciences Press, NY) vol. 7 no. 11, March 1965; originally in *Ekonomicheskaya Gazeta*, 11 November 1964

Unsigned article, 'Results of the Work of the Chemical Fibres Industry for 1968', *Fibre Chemistry* vol. 1 no. 2 (March–April 1969), pp. 117–20; translation of *Khimicheskie Volokna* no. 2 (March–April 1969), pp. 1–3

Tatyana Zaslavskaya, 'The Novosibirsk Report', English translation by Teresa Cherfas, *Survey* 1 (1984), pp. 88–108

P. Zhelezniak, 'Scientific Conference on the Application of Mathematical Methods in Economic Studies and Planning', *Problems of Economics* (International Arts & Sciences Press, NY) vol. 3 no. 7 (November 1960), pp. 3–6; originally in *Planovoe Khozyaistvo* no. 5, 1960

Ye. Zhukovskii, 'Building the Svetlogorsk Artifical Fiber Plant', *Sovetskaya Belorussya*, 2 December 1962; translated in *USSR Economic Development, No. 58: Soviet Chemical Industry*, US Dept of Commerce Joint Publications Research Service report 18,411, 28 March 1963, pp. 17–20

News reports

Current Digest of the Soviet Press (Ann Arbor MI: Joint Committee on Slavic Studies) vol. 11 no. 30, pp. 3–4, 7–12, and vol. 11 no. 31, pp. 10–13 – press reaction to the American exhibition; vol. 13 no. 42, pp. 13–17, and vol. 13 no. 43, pp. 18–23 – readers' letters to *Kommunist* on the Party Programme; vol. 13 no. 45, p. 25 – Khrushchev's speech on the Party Programme to the XXII Congress of the CPSU

The First Man in Space. Soviet Radio and Newspaper Reports on the Flight of the Spaceship Vostok, compiled and translated by Joseph L. Ziegelbaum, Jet Propulsion Laboratory/Astronautics Information Translation 22, 1 May 1961 (JPL, Calfornia Institute of Techology) – Gagarin's first flight

Life Magazine vol. 47 no. 6 (10 August 1959), pp. 28–35 – pictures of the American exhibition

Literaturnaya Gazeta no. 27 (1969), p. 10 – trial of deputy director of pig farm

New York Times vol. 108 no. 37,072 (25 July 1959), pp. 1–4 – Khrushchev and Nixon's 'kitchen debate' at the American exhibition

Time Magazine, 12 February 1965, 'Borrowing from the Capitalists' –
  Liberman and economic reform

Websites

Banknotes
http://commons.wikipedia.org/wiki/Category:Banknotes_of_the_Soviet_
  Union,_1961

Russian cars
www.autosoviet.com

Alexander [Aleksandr] Galich
www.galichclub.narod.ru/biog.htm

The Jewish Women's Archive
http://jwa.org/encyclopedia/article/berg-raissa-lvovna

Soviet literature
www.sovlit.com

Michael Swanwick's blog
http://floggingbabel.blogspot.com/2008/02/khrushchev-isnt-he-russian-
  novelist.html [sic]

Unrealised Moscow
http://www.muar.ru/ve/2003/moscow/index_e.htm

Film and television

Adam Curtis, dir., 'The Engineers' Plot' (TV documentary), programme 1 of
  Pandora's Box, BBC TV 1992
Georgii Daniela, dir., *Ya shagayu po Moskve* ('I Walk around Moscow'), 1964
Marlen Khutsiev, dir., *Zastava Ilicha/Mne Dvadtsat' Let* ('Ilich's Gate'/'I Am
  Twenty'), 1961 released 1965
Marlen Khutsiev, dir., *Iyulskii Dozhd'* ('July Rain'), 1967
Mikhail Romm, dir., *Devyat' dnei odnogo goda* ('Nine Days in One Year'),
  1962